# Screening
# Race in
# American
# Nontheatrical
# Film

ALLYSON NADIA FIELD    MARSHA GORDON    EDITORS

Duke University Press    Durham and London    2019

Designed by Courtney Leigh Baker
Typeset in Minion Pro, Clarendon, and Din by
Westchester Publishing Services

Library of Congress Cataloging-in-Publication Data
Names: Field, Allyson Nadia, [date] editor. | Gordon,
Marsha, [date] editor. | Stewart, Jacqueline Najuma, [date]
writer of the foreword.
Title: Screening race in American nontheatrical film /
edited by Allyson Nadia Field and Marsha Gordon ;
with a foreword by Jacqueline Najuma Stewart.
Description: Durham : Duke University Press, 2019. |
Includes bibliographical references and index.
Identifiers: LCCN 2019006361 (print)
LCCN 2019012085 (ebook)
ISBN 9781478005605 (ebook)
ISBN 9781478004141 (hardcover : alk. paper)
ISBN 9781478004769 (pbk. : alk. paper)
Subjects: LCSH: Race in motion pictures. | Race awareness
in motion pictures. | African Americans in motion
pictures. | Minorities in motion pictures. | Motion pictures
in education—United States. | Ethnographic films—
United States. | Amateur films—United States.
Classification: LCC PN1995.9.R22 (ebook) | LCC
PN1995.9.R22 S374 2019 (print) | DDC 791.43/65529—dc23
LC record available at https://lccn.loc.gov/2019006361

Cover art: (*Clockwise from top left*) *Untitled* (Hayes family, 1956–62), courtesy of the Wolfson Archives at Miami Dade College; *Day of the Dead* (Charles and Ray Eames, 1957); *Easter 55 Xmas Party* (1955), courtesy of the University of Chicago/Ghian Foreman; Gee family home film, courtesy of Brian Gee and Center for Asian American Media; *The Challenge* (Claude V. Bache, 1957).

# Screening Race in American Nontheatrical Film

January 2020

Happy Birthday!

Dearest KK,
Happy Birthday!

Qinghua family
1/11/2020

WITH A FOREWORD BY **JACQUELINE NAJUMA STEWART**

*Screening Race in American Nontheatrical Film* has a page on the Duke University Press website that provides links to streaming versions of all of the digitally available films discussed in the book. The companion website is organized by chapter to better aid readers in accessing the films discussed in this collection.

https://www.dukeupress.edu/Features/Screening-Race

# Giving Voice, Taking Voice

## Nonwhite and Nontheatrical

JACQUELINE NAJUMA STEWART

When night comes, and she has had several drinks and sleeps, it is easy to take the keys. I know now where she keeps them. Then I open the door and walk into their world. It is, as I always know, made of cardboard.—JEAN RHYS, *Wide Sargasso Sea*

When novelist Jean Rhys gives voice to Bertha Mason, the "madwoman in the attic" who makes brief, mysterious, and destructive appearances in Charlotte Brontë's *Jane Eyre* (1847), she offers an intriguing model for revisionist historiography.[1] *Wide Sargasso Sea* is a postcolonial counter-bildungsroman. Rhys takes Mr. Rochester's melodramatic, marriage-proposal-busting sob story from Brontë's novel—the one about his ill-fated, secreted nuptials with Bertha during his days in Jamaica—as her starting point, and crafts an affecting account of the complex and brutal legacies of slavery and colonialism. In Rhys's hands, Bertha's Creole background becomes more than a self-evident marker of her bestial non-Englishness—as "monster," "intemperate and unchaste" with a "black and scarlet visage"—that must be locked up in Thornfield Hall's garret under the (sometimes inebriated) guard of Mrs. Poole.[2] Instead, when Bertha is at the center of the tale, we get her real name (Antoinette), and her Creole identity becomes a complex, crumbling colonial inheritance that brings a continuum of racial identities into relief, from an insurgent black Caribbean servant class to white English interlopers like Mr. Rochester scouring the edges of the British Empire for its resources, financial and human. More recently, Alice Randall attempts a similar reorienting in her 2001 novel *The Wind Done Gone*, a retelling of Margaret Mitchell's 1936 blockbuster novel *Gone with the Wind*, from the perspective of a mixed-race slave, that pushes Scarlett O'Hara (renamed "Other") and *GWTW*'s other fabled white characters to the margins of the narrative.[3]

There are instructive connections between these literary works and the revisionist work of this collection. *Screening Race in American Nontheatrical Film* turns our attention away from the subjects and subjectivities that have long occupied the center of scholarly and popular film histories, using race as the fulcrum. Editors Allyson Nadia Field and Marsha Gordon posit that attentiveness to questions of race can illuminate a range of film production, distribution, exhibition, and reception practices that have gone underexplored in our focus on narrative, feature-length fiction films made for commercial release. This volume builds upon Field's and Gordon's previous, field-expanding scholarship on sponsored and educational films, work that has contributed substantially to the growing body of scholarship on orphan films of many types (including home movies, student films, medical films, training films, and others). In bringing these essays together, they continue to identify the pivotal but understudied roles race has played not just in (so many) individual orphan films, but within the larger systems of visual, cultural, and ideological production that constitute film in all of its forms.

The type of film considered in this book, nontheatrical film, is such vast terrain that it would require tremendous labor to gauge its scope, to trace its known paths and forge new ones, to excavate its layered, sometimes buried, histories. But perhaps this work should not be described with such violent language of exploratory empiricism. In scholarly efforts to account for nontheatrical film, we can be daunted by both the sheer amount and variety of films that fall under this umbrella (much of which actually survives in material form), and the lack of archival, methodological, and pedagogical guides available to us as compared with those that have been developed for theatrical film. Thus it may be tempting to take up the language, and methods, of explorers or pioneers when approaching nontheatrical works. One of this book's most valuable lessons, however, is that nontheatrical film is a landscape that will likely never be mapped definitively.

The essays collected here suggest ways of thinking about nontheatrical film that echo Jean Rhys's delineation of the "madwoman's" backstory as one necessarily fashioned (in its plot points and oblique narrative style) by racialized histories of repression and contradiction. That is, these wonderfully detailed case studies cannot simply transfer the same research and analytical methods long used for theatrical film, and thereby annex the nontheatrical as a new, and fully knowable, scholarly settlement. Instead, by foregrounding race, the contributors to this volume evoke nontheatrical film's polyvocal and often enigmatic qualities, much as Antoinette's story opens onto a sea of evidentiary questions and interpretive possibilities that is both wide and deep.

Signal among these questions and possibilities are considerations of nontheatrical film's relationships to Hollywood and to theatrical film presentation. The term "nontheatrical" was used with clearly positive connotations by the makers and marketers of sponsored and educational films across the twentieth century. Embracing its differences from commercial, entertainment-oriented film product, this self-described nontheatrical film world did not understand itself as an entirely marginal one, particularly given the volume of work it generated and circulated, and the staggering numbers of viewers it reached in venues including schools, churches, factories, libraries, museums, world's fairs, and many, many more. Haidee Wasson makes the provocative claim that "the vast technological infrastructure and the expansive film viewing practices that have long existed outside of the idealized world of commercial movie theaters announces irrevocably that the idea of nontheatrical exhibition is so broad as to border on being meaningless."[4] Wasson flags a terminological issue that begs further debate among scholars. We know that "nontheatrical" had great utility for the individuals and industries that produced works for noncommercial spaces (although nontheatrical films were occasionally shown in theaters and were shown widely in spaces—like department stores—where other things were being sold, or for the purposes of stimulating consumption more generally). We must ask, then, how the intentional act of combining multiple film practices under the nontheatrical umbrella functioned to serve the pedagogical, ideological, and financial interests of those who embraced it as self-descriptive.

We might consider this issue in relation to the use of the term "minority" to describe, within various U.S. political and institutional contexts, a shared status among multiple identity groups of people who are not white. "Minority" obviously attempts to call attention to legacies of racial discrimination within, say, corporate or educational institutions in which people of color have been underrepresented relative to their numbers in surrounding populations. But it is also a term that connotes a minor positionality, which can produce awkward if not disempowering effects. Would a group of college students interested in chemistry, or Ultimate Frisbee, or Russian culture organize themselves as a/the Minority Student Association? Moreover, as contemporary language about U.S. racial demographics—particularly in journalistic discourse—speaks straight-facedly of our transition to a "majority minority" population, we can see the "meaninglessness" (Wasson's term again) of hard numbers in the face of discursive traditions that have for so long served to identify center and margins, to designate others, and/or to embrace one's own difference.

The way in which "minority" has become shorthand for multiple and intersecting issues of racial identification, oppression, and (potential) empowerment serves as a helpful guide for understanding how the term "nontheatrical" has functioned as a reflection on power. What the nontheatrical film community was marking then, and what we as film scholars are tracking now, is the issue of who controls the moving image as a means to shape the ways in which people see themselves and their place(s) in the world. In pointing to the places where nonwhite people and nontheatrical films have overlapped, this book displays a stunning array of moments and locations at which desires to understand racial identities, disparities, and subjectivities meet, with disparate effects.

Importantly, we learn across this book that nontheatrical film does not stand entirely in opposition to theatrical film, but rather is entangled with it and its racial ideologies on multiple levels. Despite the negation implied in the label "nontheatrical," we see much crossover of personnel (writers, directors, and actors) between nontheatrical and theatrical film industries. Not surprisingly, then, we see important similarities in form and style. Nontheatrical films on the higher-capitalized end, such as educational and sponsored films, use storytelling and visual techniques that are familiar from commercial films, such as classical narrative structures, clear character motivation and psychology, and continuity editing.

And while it has been argued that most nontheatrical film types are linked in their bid for a kind of social usefulness (i.e., edification over profit), they can nonetheless reflect the limits imposed by the dominant thinking about race within which they are produced. *The Corner* (1962), for example, directed by Northwestern University film student Robert Ford, is a sponsored documentary about the Vice Lords social club (or street gang, depending on your point of view) that features a range of moving and insightful first-person accounts of the struggles of growing up black, male, and poor on Chicago's West Side. It also features extraordinary details of the spaces and styles of black youth interaction, demonstrating a clear rapport between Ford and his film subjects.[5] *The Corner* sets up the presentation of the Vice Lords' voices with an anonymous male narrator speaking over a freeze-frame of the film's central character, Clarence Smith. The narrator tells us that what follows is "a description of their world as they see it." The same narrator comes back at the end of the film to ask, over several images of Clarence squatting alone in front of the neighborhood hot dog joint, "When time comes for them to leave the corner . . . who will have the patience to help them make the adjustment from the law of the streets to the laws of society?" This narrational bracketing seeks to establish the authenticity of the film's portraits, creating a sense of empathy for the plight of African American youth lacking adequate educational, recreational, and job opportunities. But this strategy also reveals the presence of the filmmaker as an outsider who is presenting and interpreting the film's visual and sonic information. The fact that *The Corner*'s framing narration is performed by a voice that does not use the black teen slang or the West Side Chicago accent that is so pronounced in the Vice Lords' speech raises questions about the faith or interest this film has in the ability of the film's subjects to describe "their world as they see it," not to mention the expectations and needs of the film's presumably predominantly white audiences (likely social services professionals) who view this lower-class black world from the outside.

This is, of course, an issue that emerges in the wide range of theatrical, fictional social problem films about race produced by independent filmmakers and Hollywood studios, particularly during the civil rights era. From Joseph L. Mankiewicz's *No Way Out* (1950) to Shirley Clarke's *The Cool World* (1963), we get significant representations of the tensions seething within African American communities, communicated through a range of approaches attempting to achieve psychological and/or sociological realism in their renderings of black characters and their worlds. These filmmakers are grappling with nothing less than the country's failure to uphold the tenets of democracy and the urgent need to address the still-unresolved social and psychological consequences of slavery and systematic racial oppression. When social problem films prioritize white viewers in their modes of address, they risk objectifying their nonwhite subjects and simplifying their representations of the causes of racial troubles. Like their theatrical counterparts, nontheatrical films about racial issues routinely work to explain nonwhite subjectivity to white viewers, showing nonwhite subjects responding to the indelicate but perennially fascinating question (per W. E. B. Du Bois), "How does it feel to be a problem?"[6]

This is the question Rhys takes up in her rendering of the inner life of Bertha (real name Antoinette)—elaborating her first-person voice, her memories and dreams, her sensory experiences. Activating identification and empathy is of course one of the cinema's most compelling operations, so it comes as no surprise that nontheatrical films would use many of the strategies that engrossed viewers of commercial films in movie theaters. When it comes to "minority" subjects, we can watch how films made in both

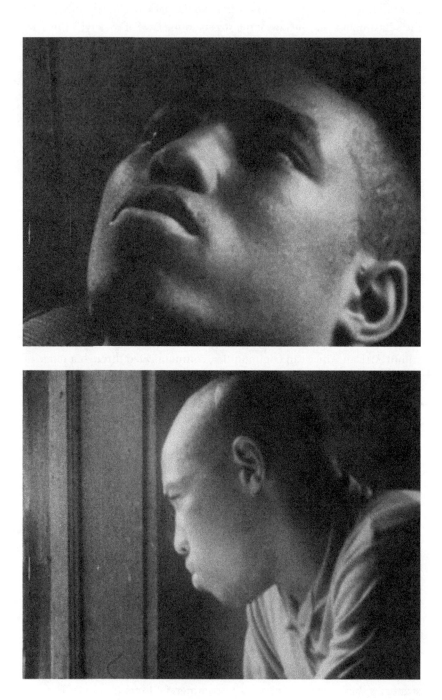

FIGURES F.1–F.3. *The Corner* (Robert Ford, 1962). Stills courtesy of Chicago Film Archives.

modes negotiate the complexities of making suppressed subjectivities visible and marginalized voices heard. If nontheatrical films aspire to open up new and useful ways to look at a range of subjects—to inform, to educate, to spur to action—how exactly do they use their nontheatrical status to do so? Close analysis is one of the most effective methods used in the studies featured in this volume, marking the importance of considering questions of film style even for films that would seem not to understand themselves primarily as art or entertainment. These moments of close reading are important not just for what they suggest about the general approaches in educational or sponsored or activist films, but also for what they say about the individual texts being read, and the nuances of the representational strategies being brought to bear on the overdetermined subject of race in American society.

Stylistic analysis is also valuable for films on the lower-capitalized end of the nontheatrical spectrum, films not produced for broad markets or even for public uses. Footage of ethnographic research, church activities, or family rituals also rewards consideration of style (e.g., camerawork, editing, performance) for what it can tell us about the goals of the filmmakers and the relations between the filmmakers, their subjects, and their audiences. Films like these may not understand themselves to be making an argument or advocating changes in thought or behavior. And yet, of course, acts of documentation are never neutral, and films of these sorts are shaped by particular notions of culture and community, normativity and difference, that we can read in the ways in which the camera is positioned and footage is organized. Close readings of nontheatrical films need not aspire to identify auteurist tendencies or nail down generic codes, though it can help us to recognize patterns across works. Attention to nontheatrical film styles can also point us to aspects that have not been thoroughly interrogated in the study of theatrical, narrative films, such as the effects of incidental, accidental, and unplanned elements within the frame, the kinds of elements that are so evident in films with lower production values and films made by nonprofessionals.

I think about these seemingly incidental elements quite a bit in my work on the South Side Home Movie Project (SSHMP) in Chicago, an archival and community engagement program I founded in 2005 (thanks to Jasmyn Castro for the shout-out in her contribution to this book). The family films archived by the SSHMP illustrate vigorous effort on the part of black families to show themselves living well, loving their families, supporting their communities, and traveling across the country and around the world. Like all home movies, this footage not only documents concrete places and historical moments, but also displays more ephemeral practices such as glances and smiles, dances and hugs, cooperative poses and skeptical disdain for the camera. Home movie mise-en-scène is replete with objects, some placed by the filmmakers and their families (e.g., home decor), many outside of their control (e.g., elements of street and other public scenes). As we seek to make this footage widely available to the many constituencies we think it would benefit (including scholars, k–12 students and teachers, artists, genealogists, community residents), we are constantly asking ourselves how best to describe the contents of home movies, given their overwhelming detail. In constructing our catalog, we have been wondering how to provide a useful guide to this long undervalued body of work.[7] Recognizing that people might search this footage for elements that extend far beyond the Library of Congress Subject Headings (lcsh) that govern cataloging practices, sshmp archivist Candace Ming has been developing a taxonomy specific to home movies that draws on the important models offered by the Center for Home Movies, the Chicago Film Archives, and the Texas Archive of the Moving Image, modified to reflect the particularities of our collection.[8]

What we are learning is that, try as we might to anticipate what people might look for in home movies, our descriptive work is most effective when it is understood as an ongoing and interactive endeavor. We conduct oral histories with the families who participate in the project, eliciting information about what we are seeing on-screen. And we invite active, vocal participation at screenings that we host across the South Side, noting viewer comments that add helpful detail to our catalog descriptions. The dialogue engendered by home movies—which were, of course, accompanied by ample conversation in living rooms and basements during family gatherings—is a boon to researchers. We at the sshmp have come to appreciate the ongoing, symbiotic relationship between the home moviemakers, subjects, and audiences (original and current), and the advantages to activating these relationships continually in our efforts to contextualize and interpret this material.

Here is a fundamental difference between theatrical and nontheatrical film: the wider spaces nontheatrical films provide for audience interaction. While lively fan cultures are certainly important aspects of theatrical film history, movie theaters—the idealized site for film exhibition—are designed for audiences to engage with the screen and not with each other. Even the orientation and fixity of movie theater seats is not conducive to conversation after a film. Proper audience decorum prohibits talking during film screenings (though laughter and screams are acceptable for certain genres). But films across the nontheatrical spectrum are designed to spark conversation, to

FIGURES F.4–F.6. *Easter 55 Xmas Party* (1955). Film held in the Jean Patton Collection, South Side Home Movie Project, University of Chicago, with gratitude to Ghian Foreman.

motivate audiences to speak. From classroom conversations sparked by educational films to postwar group discussion films on race relations described by Anna McCarthy to convivial private screenings of family films, viewers convened outside of movie theaters are invited to process aloud what they have seen, to verbalize the relationships between their lives and the worlds pictured on-screen.[9] And when we consider the invitation to speak offered by nontheatrical films in tandem with traditions of vocal film viewing among marginalized viewers of many sorts (people of color, LGBTQ audiences, young viewers), we can see a striking range of reception strategies that may not be as nonnormative as classical film theories would lead us to believe.

We might say then that nontheatrical films made by, for, and about non-white people point to radical new ways of understanding film-viewer relations and open up key spaces for film and, by extension, social critique. Even when nontheatrical films struggle with the politics of giving voice to non-white subjects, their very mode is designed to facilitate the voicings of viewers. Now that we are paying closer attention to the ways in which nontheatrical film has coexisted with theatrical film, we are gaining new perspectives on what we have for so long taken to be the medium's most meaningful and influential iterations. *Screening Race* offers compelling new views of the landscapes of film history, in which Hollywood no longer dominates from the center. We learn in these pages of the myriad ways in which nontheatrical films both represented race and stimulated active dialogue about race among its viewers. Looking from these new, previously ignored vantage points, we begin to see Hollywood's treatments of race as Antoinette saw Thornfield Hall. They appear to be "made of cardboard"—vulnerable fictions far less equipped than nontheatrical films to accommodate the potentially destabilizing active participation of the Other.

FILMOGRAPHY

All available films discussed in the foreword can be streamed through the book's web page at https://www.dukeupress.edu/Features/Screening-Race.

*Easter 55 Xmas Party* (1955), 8 min., 16mm
ACCESS: Jean Patton Collection, South Side Home Movie Project, University of Chicago.

*The Corner* (1962), 27 min., 16mm
PRODUCTION: Northwestern University Department of Radio, Television, and Film.
DIRECTOR: Robert Ford. MUSIC: Carver Blanchard, Red Brown, Dick Carlson, Jim DiPasquale, Brad Epst, Paul Matheny, Rob McEnany. ACCESS: Chicago Film Archives.

NOTES

1   Sandra M. Gilbert and Susan Gubar, *The Madwoman in the Attic: The Woman Writer and the Nineteenth-Century Literary Imagination* (New Haven, CT: Yale University Press, 1979).

2   Charlotte Brontë, *Jane Eyre* (London: Dent, 1847; New York: Dutton, 1953), 309, 306, 310. Citations refer to the Dutton edition.

3   Alice Randall, *The Wind Done Gone* (Boston: Houghton Mifflin, 2001).

4   Haidee Wasson, *Museum Movies: The Museum of Modern Art and the Birth of Art Cinema* (Berkeley: University of California Press, 2005), 36.

5   *The Corner* was preserved by Chicago Film Archives and can be viewed on their website: Robert Ford, dir., *The Corner* (1962), Robert Ford Collection, 1962–1964, F.2012-04-0005, Chicago Film Archives, http://www.chicagofilmarchives.org /collections/index.php/Detail/Object/Show/object_id/15253.

6   W. E. B. Du Bois, *The Souls of Black Folk* (Chicago: McClurg, 1903; Oxford: Oxford University Press, 2007), 7. Citations refer to the Oxford edition.

7   See South Side Home Movie Project, https://sshmpportal.uchicago.edu.

8   The Center for Home Movies, "The Center for Home Movies 2010 Digitization and Access Summit: Final Report" (January 2011), 9–23, http://www .centerforhomemovies.org/Home_Movie_Summit_Final_Report.pdf. Chicago Film Archives (founded in 2003 by Nancy Watrous) and the Texas Archive of the Moving Image (founded in 2002 by Caroline Frick) are pioneering regional film repositories documenting nontheatrical film histories.

9   Anna McCarthy, "The Politics of Wooden Acting," in *The Citizen Machine: Governing by Television in 1950s America* (New York: New Press, 2010), 83–118.

ACKNOWLEDGMENTS

Any collection of essays is only as good as its contributors, and we have had the great fortune of working with a group of top-notch, innovative, and also immensely patient scholars on this project. Throughout the process of putting this collection together, we have been impressed by our contributors' uncompromising investment in understanding how American film culture attempts to make sense of race. We thank them for their excellent scholarship, archival advocacy, and deep commitment to nontheatrical film studies.

Dino Everett, the Hugh M. Hefner Archivist of the University of Southern California, is the guardian angel of this project. He has been instrumental in identifying relevant films in USC's archives and making them available for scholarly research and exhibition during our collaborations at the Echo Park Film Center. He was also gracious enough to do so for many of the contributors to this volume as they worked on their essays. Dino's generosity and can-do spirit is unparalleled in the profession, and we are immensely grateful to have had him on our team.

Thanks as well are due to Lisa Marr and the Echo Park Film Center for hosting a series of screenings, "Race and Place in Nontheatrical Film in Los Angeles," that served, in many ways, as the genesis for this book. We would like to thank Mark Quigley at the UCLA Film and Television Archive for helping us identify and locate many of the films discussed in this book, some of which were projected at our "Race and Place" events at the Echo Park Film Center. Mark's enthusiasm for 16mm film and his astute insights have made this a stronger project.

Ashley Truehart and Aurore Spiers, doctoral students in cinema and media studies at the University of Chicago, assisted in preparing the manuscript and the companion website. Dan Morgan generously offered suggestions on the introduction and gave recommendations that greatly strengthened the collection.

Elizabeth Ault at Duke University Press has been absolutely delightful to work with. She was responsive and enthusiastic, and pushed us when we needed to be pushed. Thanks to the entire production team, especially Kate Herman, Liz Smith, and Jessica Ryan, for their careful attention to the book's many components. We are also grateful for the recommendations and feedback of the two anonymous readers. Their close attention to each chapter, as well as to the book as a whole, made this a stronger collection.

Finally, we want to thank Bob Dickson, Alan Gorg, and Trevor Greenwood, whose astounding film *Felicia* (1965) functioned as the catalyst for this project. We appreciate their work and their openness to us, as we do Felicia Bragg's, whose reaction to seeing herself as a teenager in their film so many years later continues to remind us of the lasting and affective power of moving images, theatrical and nontheatrical alike.

# Introduction

ALLYSON NADIA FIELD AND MARSHA GORDON

*Screening Race in American Nontheatrical Film* is a collection of essays investigating representations of and engagements with race in American nontheatrical films of the twentieth century. This collection builds on existing scholarship in nontheatrical film studies but broadens the field to take up the treatment of race. Tracing the contours of race in nontheatrical film is neither a trivial nor an esoteric activity; over the course of the past century, these films have been a significant way that Americans encountered ideas about race, difference, and community. In a moment when discourses about and resistance to white supremacy are at the fore, this collection takes seriously the presence of race in nontheatrical forms—even when such considerations had almost no place in the dominant theatrical universe.

Taking up a range of contexts—educational, cultural, industrial, civic, and private—this collection shows that nontheatrical films tell a unique story about race and cinema, one that has been sidelined by the outsized importance of commercial feature films in the field of cinema studies. The topics covered here provide an instructive and sometimes surprising glimpse into the ways that audiences encountered such racially engaged films: as shoppers in Wanamaker's department stores in the early 1900s, as churchgoers in Tennessee in the 1920s, as television viewers in the 1950s, as police officers in the 1960s, or as students in a filmmaking class in the 1970s. The range of cases discussed here marks a radical and exciting disruption of the Hollywood model of production and distribution. If the big screens marginalized people of color, small screens often helped to balance the scales.

This collection situates its intervention at the intersection of two important areas of scholarly inquiry. First, it contributes to scholarship that addresses the historical marginalization of films by and about people of color in film canons, classrooms, and critical inquiry. Second, the book achieves this correction by paying attention to another neglected area of scholarly attention, films produced for and exhibited in nontheatrical venues. Taken as a whole, this collection of essays enriches our understanding of the ways in which films were produced and circulated in a multiethnic culture trying to make sense of its not always welcome pluralism.

Rather than a comprehensive survey—which, given the sheer number of nontheatrical films produced in the United States, would be impossible—*Screening Race in American Nontheatrical Film* offers a selective transhistorical and comparative lens. The films under discussion in the chapters that follow are critically appraised just as they initially circulated: as components of broader multiracial and multiethnic cultural spheres. Most scholarship on race and ethnicity in American film, theatrical or otherwise, tends to isolate its topic, whether it involves African American, Asian American, Latino/a, Native American, or other subjects. This collection's refusal to adhere to that compartmentalization reflects the way that the films themselves were conceived and projected, while also acknowledging the inequities that result from racial stratification. Each chapter traces issues relating to race, identity, politics, class, and environment at various moments in American film history across student films, educational films, sponsored films, anthropological and ethnographic films, community-made and -screened films, church films, home movies, and other types of useful films that engage with American multiculturalism. This collection begins to map a subfield, reframing the study of race on film to provide a more nuanced understanding of the role it has played in American life and providing a substantial new body of knowledge across a wide historical period and from a range of conceptual and theoretical perspectives.

## American Nontheatrical Film History

Nontheatrical film had a significant presence in twentieth-century life, one that has recently received sustained attention by scholars seeking to understand American film produced beyond Hollywood's realm and reach. In *Learning with the Lights Off: Educational Film in the United States*, the editors argue that despite a history of scholarly neglect, nontheatrical films "tell us a great deal about the shape (and shaping) of the cinematic century."[1]

Similarly, in his work on "advanced" amateur filmmaking, one of the many types of noncommercial and nontheatrical film production that developed with the introduction of 16mm film in 1923, Charles Tepperman argues that such alternative practices "can provide us with crucial insight into American society's collective visual imagination during the mid-twentieth century."[2] Indeed, *Screening Race in American Nontheatrical Film* emerges from the realization that nontheatrical films vastly outnumbered their Hollywood counterparts for much of film history. As John Mercer observes, "In 1977 fewer than three hundred feature films were started by the major studios in Hollywood, but over 15,000 nontheatrical films were completed."[3] These films operated in many contexts—at schools and churches, for example—that intended to influence the thinking and behavior of their constituents. Nontheatrical films' very different and less centralized means of production, distribution, and exhibition allowed for a fascinating diversity that was never possible in the more controlled, corporate, and white-male-dominant environment of Hollywood.

Nontheatrical films were not bound by the same kinds of commercial and political parameters as their theatrical counterparts, allowing for a more expansive conceptualization of nonwhite representation, among other things. As Haidee Wasson and Charles Acland observe, "Film technologies—screens, projectors, and cameras—were long ago integrated into a surprising range of spaces and situations, shaping the aesthetics as well as the display of and engagement with motion pictures. And these places, beyond conventionally defined movie theaters, . . . [have] been a key site for the formation and reformation of cinema itself."[4] In point of fact, the history of moving images in the United States has taken place largely outside of movie theaters. Nontheatrical films reformed the nature and purpose of cinema.

Responsive to the complex realities of nontheatrical film history, this collection of essays aims to correct the imbalanced nature of the discipline of film studies up to this point in time—privileging, on the one hand, theatrical films, feature films, and Hollywood studio films; on the other, films made by and featuring white people. Not only have theatrical film studies dominated much of scholarly film history, but the exclusion of scholarship about films made by, about, or for nonwhite people fails to do justice to the richness and breadth of racial representation in American cinema. There are, of course, some significant scholarly precedents for this collection. *Screening Race in American Nontheatrical Film* grows out of a body of research that was largely inspired by the Orphan Film Symposium, founded by Dan Streible and his colleagues at the University of South Carolina in 1999. That symposium focused scholarly attention on a significant body of films that had previously been ignored, neglected, or relegated to footnotes and has inspired a recent wave of scholarship on nontheatrical film.[5]

While most scholarship of this sort tends to focus on a specific nontheatrical type—educational films, home movies, student films, documentaries, anthropological films, sponsored films, and so on—this collection deliberately unites these subcategories with the consideration of race as its organizing principle. This strategic move corrects a gap in the wider scholarship with regard to nontheatrical film and race, opening up possibilities for future work that builds on the branches of inquiry here. These chapters are united by a shared core value: prioritizing the way race was envisioned and mobilized on screens and by makers with very different agendas than their Hollywood counterparts.

Though there are some notable exceptions, by and large the body of scholarship on nontheatrical film is focused on white makers, subjects, and audiences, or addresses issues of race as secondary to other concerns, such as various sites of exhibition.[6] What *Screening Race in American Nontheatrical Film* offers is a defining focus not on film types but on racial representation, identities, and politics across an array of nontheatrical media produced in the United States, and consequently across a range of producers, subjects, audiences, genres, and periods.

*Screening Race in American Nontheatrical Film* asks readers to reconsider the ways that films were used to address, define, and grapple with race over the course of the twentieth century. Each contribution to this volume offers an alternative imagination of American film history, reframing accepted objects of study to consider how Americans produced and consumed race on screens that interacted with viewers far outside the reach of movie theaters. From department store to classroom to community center, nontheatrical films engaging with race allowed diverse audiences to experience narratives and encounter representations that they could not experience anywhere else. This collection, then, constitutes a cinematic remapping, encouraging readers to rediscover a world in which moving images were integrated in and reflective of lives that were excluded in most mainstream exhibition contexts.

The challenges of cultivating this kind of scholarly work are numerous, and the authors in this collection often reflect on these challenges, which include locating these materials (since so many nontheatrical films languish in the neglected corners of archives if they have been fortunate enough to survive deacquisition, a plight not dissimilar to that of silent film before the 1978 International Federation of Film Archives Congress in Brighton);

researching them (since relatively little is documented and preserved in terms of primary resources about the nontheatrical universe); making them accessible (since so few of the films are readily available in their native format of 16mm or on DVD, though, increasingly, more are materializing in digitized forms online); and, last but not least, winnowing down their overwhelming numbers to form a manageable body of films that illuminate certain film historical and cultural issues. Studying nontheatrical films with race as the galvanizing focus also enriches our understanding of related theatrical works, such as those made by the L.A. Rebellion group of black filmmakers (whose work included theatrical and nontheatrical films) or even, often by virtue of their contrast, the stories told in mainstream theatrical narratives coming out of the Hollywood studios.[7]

This book proceeds along a chronological arc, starting with a discussion of films produced in 1908 and ending with recent remediations of historical home movies. Each chapter focuses on the ways that nontheatrical films offer contemporary students and scholars a unique perspective on the history of race in American culture, as well as a new window through which to explore film history. To that end, we have made every effort to provide access to digital versions of the films under discussion through the book's companion website. Each chapter stakes out its own framework within film history, cultural history, and critical race studies, offering readers specific lenses through which to view the films under discussion. The volume concludes with a comprehensive aggregated bibliography of scholarship related to race and nontheatrical film.

The essays collected here explore relevant, timely, and deliberately wide-ranging areas of study, from films produced by Puerto Rican teenagers as part of activist filmmaking programs in New York City in the late 1960s, to films made for department store exhibition at the turn of the century that offer a window into Native American representational and political issues, to a film made by Charles and Ray Eames focused on a Mexican folk tradition, to a now-forgotten 1960s film about African American life produced by the National Urban League that was seen by an estimated 4.5 million viewers during its nontheatrical distribution life. Still, this volume is far from exhaustive; its gaps indicate how much of film history remains obscured, and how much of that history might be marshaled to better understand the way race has been represented, negotiated, and figured at various points in American history. One need only think about contemporary nontheatrical media—for example, cell phone images of police violence or, for that matter, police body camera footage—to connect nontheatrical film's past to present-day iterations of this legacy, and to understand why the study of such images is so urgently needed.

## Finding *Felicia*

This collection grew out of relationships and archival discoveries. In 2005, Rick Prelinger, founder of the Prelinger Archive, acquired a set of deaccessioned 16mm educational films from the Buffalo, New York, school district. Rescuing these films destined for the dumpster, Prelinger sent the lot to A/V Geeks Archives founder Skip Elsheimer, who archives, digitizes, and exhibits educational film. When Marsha Gordon began researching educational films about race for her contribution to her coedited collection *Learning with the Lights Off*, Skip screened numerous titles from his collection for her. Among them was a thirteen-minute 16mm film from 1965 titled *Felicia*, about a sixteen-year-old African American high schooler, Felicia Bragg, living in the Watts neighborhood of Los Angeles.[8]

Shot over the course of a year and finished prior to the August 1965 uprisings that would bring national attention to the area, *Felicia* depicts a world that would become well documented in the aftermath of what the media at the time routinely referred to as the "riots." Although it was made by three white UCLA film students, Alan Gorg, Bob Dickson, and Trevor Greenwood, the film relies upon Bragg's unscripted ruminations as its sole narration, offering a poetic and poignant meditation on race, class, and urban community. Its formalism and open-ended narration are more reminiscent of art filmmaking than classroom films, and its thoughtful narrator comes across as wise beyond her years. Far from the objectifying lens of the news media or the sensationalizing frame of Hollywood's portrayal of so-called ghetto life, *Felicia* presents an intimate portrait of a young girl and a neighborhood— both on the brink of change.

Made as a side project outside of the filmmakers' UCLA coursework, *Felicia* was sold to educational film distributor Bailey Film Associates (BFA) and marketed as one of a series of films titled *Minority Youth* in the late 1960s and '70s. It was under these auspices that the film came to Buffalo, and this is also how it would have reached high schoolers across the country whose schools had purchased the film and whose teachers opted to show it in their classes. When Marsha Gordon saw *Felicia* several decades later, she recognized in it an early instance of a broader trend of filmmaking in Los Angeles. Operating at the nexus of student film, documentary, educational film, and art film, *Felicia* intersects with a range of films investigating a city

FIGURE I.1. Frame enlargement of Felicia Bragg, the titular subject and narrator of
*Felicia* (1965), a 16mm documentary educational film about a young woman growing
up in the Watts neighborhood of Los Angeles.

marked by de facto segregation as well as questions of identity and belonging. In particular, it brought to mind the work of a slightly younger group of
UCLA filmmakers known as the Los Angeles School of Black Filmmakers, or
the L.A. Rebellion. *Felicia*'s echoes of Italian neorealism and investment in
filming an underdocumented Los Angeles community found a striking cor-
ollary in the work of Charles Burnett, Billy Woodberry, Alile Sharon Larkin,
and other African American filmmakers who were at UCLA in the 1970s.
Intrigued by the film's resonances with the L.A. Rebellion, Marsha shared
the film with Allyson Nadia Field, who was working on the L.A. Rebellion
project of the UCLA Film and Television Archive. Thus was born a multi-
year, multicomponent collaborative research project of which this book is
the culminating piece.

We interviewed the filmmakers and Felicia Bragg about the film's genesis,
production history, and circulation—as well as the afterlives of its makers
and subject. These encounters marked an important opportunity to create an extrafilmic record for a nontheatrical film, about which few documents and little production history typically survive. Theatrical films often

have copious extant documentation, allowing historians to make the kinds of rich, contextual arguments that are essential to scholarship that shapes the discipline. In our research on *Felicia* and other nontheatrical films, we have found that interviewing the makers and participants—whenever possible—greatly enriches our understanding of the films and the context of their production.

Our initial research into *Felicia*'s exhibition history, as well as the broader production and circulation of nontheatrical films about race, led to two further projects, one scholarly and one curatorial, both of which lay the groundwork for this volume. The scholarly component is a coauthored article that was published in *Cinema Journal* in 2016. "The Other Side of the Tracks: Nontheatrical Film History, Pre-Rebellion Watts, and *Felicia*" considers how *Felicia* is particularly suited to a discussion of the ways that urban spaces, and Watts in particular, were imagined in the 1960s. It also demonstrates how nontheatrical film can inform and reshape our understanding of film history and enrich discussions of documentary filmmaking, the role of student filmmakers, and other cinematic movements such as the L.A. Rebellion.

The curatorial component involved the broader universe of nontheatrical films about race. We collaborated on a series of 16mm film programs (in 2014, 2016, and 2017) at the Echo Park Film Center, a community-based filmmaking and screening cooperative in Los Angeles. With the assistance of archivist Dino Everett at the University of Southern California (USC), we selected films from the 1940s to the 1970s concerned with Native Americans, Mexican Americans, Asian Americans, and African Americans around the theme of race and space in Los Angeles. Out of this experience grew the realization that *Felicia* is connected to a broader set of nontheatrical films of its period that approach questions of social inequity through the lens of race.

To give *Felicia* wider attention, we successfully nominated it to the 2014 National Film Registry of the Library of Congress. The Academy Film Archive, where codirector Dickson worked until his retirement in 2018, subsequently preserved the film in 2016. Considered collectively, our research, scholarship, and archival advocacy with regard to *Felicia* aimed to underscore the intellectual stakes of the film, and its institutional preservation has enabled it to reach a wider audience. In this way, *Felicia* serves as a model for the twin aims of the book, bringing scholars and archivists together to assess and preserve nontheatrical films, and to engage in rigorous research into their significance with a special focus on race.

While Hollywood's long history of racial (mis)representation is well documented, the corresponding academic focus on mainstream theatrical films had resulted in a disproportionate presumption about which films have significance and impact. This volume challenges that framework. It is an indisputable fact that the moving image landscape is far more varied and complex than the relatively small number of films produced for theatrical release, which means that any treatment of race and cinema must extend beyond the border of theatrical work. A guiding argument of this book is that nontheatrical screens exhibited their own perspectives on race, often in striking contrast to their theatrical counterparts. From the silent era to the displacement of film by video and digital media as the prevalent production and distribution formats in the late twentieth century, moving pictures permeated all aspects of American life outside of the movie theater, ranging from industry and government to the home, classroom, and community. Alongside—and often in distinct refutation of—the fictional narratives projected by Hollywood to moviegoing audiences, nontheatrical films provided wildly different visions, showing other subjects, addressing other audiences, and asserting other perspectives. Whether it's the educational framework of the classroom film and student film, the anthropological gaze of the ethnographic film, the entrepreneurial impetus of the sponsored film, or the intimacy of the home movie, these other perspectives often inform films made for audiences outside of theatrical entertainment. How these films have engaged with the complexities of racial formations in the United States is the concern of the essays collected in this volume.

## Race and Nontheatrical Filmmaking in Los Angeles (and Beyond)

*Felicia* is far from being the only nontheatrical film set in Los Angeles to take on the topic of race. It was, in fact, part of a much wider tendency in filmmaking of the time, which we want to briefly consider here to set the stage for the contributions to this volume, which collectively assert the value of nontheatrical filmmaking's offerings on the subject of race. One of the films we included in the first "Race and Space" screening event at the Echo Park Film Center, *Akira* (David Espar, 1971), focuses on the experiences of another teenager, a relatable subject for its intended classroom audience. (Along with *Felicia*, *Akira* was marketed by BFA as part of the *Minority Youth* series in the late 1960s and '70s.) In contrast to *Felicia*, however, *Akira* is less rooted in its location, an unidentified California town. Instead, its perspective is explicitly generalizable: many aspects of Akira's circumstances are presented as relevant to teenagers, irrespective of racial identity or location. However, race and national origin are key issues, as high

FIGURE I.2. Teenager Akira Tana at prayer with his parents in the opening and closing sequences of *Akira* (1971).

school senior Akira Tana discusses his feelings of being caught in between cultures—the traditional Japanese values of his parents and the styles, activities, and interests shaping teenage life in California in the early 1970s (including rock music and marijuana). This ambivalence provided points of entry for classroom discussions concerning identity, generational conflicts, cultural differences, and what it means to be American.

Akira connects his ruminations about his life and family to broader questions of cultural identity and belonging. In one notable sequence, Akira talks about his parents' immigration to the United States in 1939–40 and their subsequent internment in relocation camps during World War II. His mother and older brothers were sent to Lompoc, while his father, a Buddhist minister seen as suspect by the U.S. government, was sent to New Mexico. Although the film slips in such undertaught aspects of American history through the prism of personal experience, it moves away from politics, concluding with Akira's high school graduation and his ruminations about his future beyond high school and college, one that promises more choices than were afforded to his parents. The final scene is a repetition of the opening sequence of Akira and his parents at prayer, suggesting that the narration is a kind of internal dialogue of a thoughtful teenager at the crossroads of his life.

As this brief discussion of *Felicia* and *Akira* demonstrates, we soon realized through this process of research, curation, and exhibition that there was a rich universe of nontheatrical films that were made specifically to engage with issues of race, and that these films had gone largely unnoticed by scholars of film history. Along with this loss as accessible objects of study, the neglect of these films has contributed to an imbalanced history of American cinema. Film historical accounts have consistently privileged the presentation of race and class in theatrical cinema, produced largely by the Hollywood studios. To demonstrate the possibilities represented by the study of nontheatrical film along the prism of race, what follows in the remainder of our introduction considers a selection of films made in Los Angeles in the post–civil rights era. Using the example of Los Angeles in this period is purposeful: Los Angeles is the locus of the film industry, a city rich in racial and ethnic diversity, as well as one with a long history of racial oppression and conflict. Nontheatrical filmic engagements with the racialized geography of Los Angeles at this time represent a rich subset of American film production, one that is emblematic of the possibilities for social engagement, critique, and resistance that nontheatrical filmmaking embodies. These films offer a map of lived experience for the inhabitants of a dynamic yet deeply segregated city.

On the big screen, 1960s Los Angeles was imagined in films like the lighthearted teen musical *Muscle Beach Party* (William Asher, 1964), starring Annette Funicello and Frankie Avalon; *The Graduate* (Mike Nichols, 1967), featuring Dustin Hoffman's breakthrough role as an affluent but lost college graduate; *They Shoot Horses, Don't They?* (Sydney Pollack, 1969), a Depression-era fable about dreams and disappointment; as well as in other mainstream films that were as fantastically and impossibly white, marginal characters of color notwithstanding. While important exceptions to the imagined whiteness of the city did coexist alongside these theatrical films—most notably *The Exiles* (1961), Kent Mackenzie's story of Native American life in the Bunker Hill neighborhood of the city—such films were few and far between, with limited reach in the culture at large.

Nonwhite Los Angeles would not gain any significant commercial theatrical presence until the 1970s, with controversial results. The first concentration of nonwhite subjects in a Los Angeles setting occurred in films such as Melvin Van Peebles's *Sweet Sweetback's Baadasssss Song* (1971), which gave its black director and star the run of the city; a slew of blaxploitation films, like the white-produced and -directed *Cleopatra Jones* (Jack Starrett, 1973), which flaunted crime, drugs, sex, and pimp culture, or the African American–directed *Dolemite* (D'Urville Martin, 1975), about a pimp on a revenge mission; comedies like *Car Wash* (Michael Schultz, 1976), about a diverse group of characters and their exploits; and the aesthetically intriguing, dignifying, but commercially marginal films of the L.A. Rebellion, such as Haile Gerima's *Bush Mama* (1975) and Charles Burnett's *Killer of Sheep* (1977).

One need only look outside the movie theater in the same time period, however, to discover a wealth of films that correct the erroneous impression of Los Angeles's whiteness. As we dug deeper into the archives, we became especially interested in a body of nontheatrical films from the 1960s and '70s concerned with Los Angeles's nonwhite populations at a time in which the city was at an especially tumultuous crossroads, much of it revolving around race, class, and segregated neighborhoods. This locus of nontheatrical filmmaking energy is partly a result of the rich film school culture of the city, with UCLA and USC populating the region with students in need of local subjects for fiction and nonfiction film projects. Many of these students would go on to work in the motion picture industry following graduation, including the nontheatrical film industry. Some continued to work on personal projects, often garnering distribution for classroom or community use. As it turns out, these filmmakers frequently turned their lenses on parts of the city that were ignored in mainstream media, motivated in no small part by an emergent culture of student activism that encouraged equitable thinking about society and social privilege in particular.

As with *Felicia* and *Akira*, the struggle for self-identity in a sometimes hostile environment is also the subject of *The Eastside Story* (Morteza Rezvani, 1974), a fiction film shot with a neorealist aesthetic. *The Eastside Story* is a poetic adaptation of Danny Santiago's short story, "The Somebody," about a Chicano teenager's identity crisis after his gang has moved away following the demolition of their East Los Angeles neighborhood. Like *Felicia*, the neighborhood is introduced through the wanderings of the main character, who walks through largely empty streets and overgrown lots. Also like *Felicia*, the camera shoots this film's protagonist through the frame of abandoned buildings, figuring his movements as confined by the environmental degradation that surrounds him.

The story is narrated by an old man sitting at a bus stop who directly addresses the spectator: "This is a big day for Bulle—today he quit school and he's going to go to work as a writer." The optimism of this statement is quickly undercut by the clarification that Bulle is going to write on fences, buildings, "on anything that comes along," with his gang name "Bulle de los Cerros." A construction company has bought the land that constituted the gang's territory, forcing them all to move away, apart from Bulle's family and a few others. Despite the entreaties of the old man and a boy's club community leader for him to straighten out, Bulle wanders the streets, desecrating a rival gang's tags. He daydreams about having "the best damn funeral in East L.A." The film ends with Bulle at an unresolved impasse, clutching the metal fence of a highway overpass. The last shot lingers in freeze-frame, like the concluding close-up of Antoine Doinel in *The 400 Blows* (François Truffaut, 1959), with the ocean replaced by the highway leading to downtown Los Angeles. The film presents a changing city in which forces like urban development and gentrification have a direct impact on the self-identity of its most vulnerable inhabitants. Like *Felicia* and *Akira*, *The Eastside Story* represents both the private and public spaces inhabited by a character whose relationship to his environment and the film's open-endedness invite various interpretations from classroom audiences.

The vulnerability of certain populations in Los Angeles is also the subject of *A Sense of Community* (Jeremy Lezin, 1976), which begins with a title card staking the film's claim to the specific place and time during which the documentary was made: "Downtown Los Angeles, 1976." The film's director, Jeremy Lezin, was a film student at USC who used a class assignment to explore the subject of "'home work,' where garments were produced at workers' homes for sub-minimum wages. It was essentially a sweat shop situation, but farmed out so the perpetrators couldn't get caught easily."[9] What he documented was a church-owned sewing operation staffed by undocumented immigrants from Mexico.

The first images of the film show Mexican men and women entering a gate, walking down exterior stairs toward the basement in which they labor, and the gate being closed behind them. The camera lingers on a man who adds a locked chain to secure the gate, accompanied by amplified sounds of the chain, the first signal that the film intends to expose inequity without employing extradiegetic commentary. The film cuts to the interior of a Catholic church basement, where workers labor at sewing machines. Lezin explains that the church was "just a few blocks from USC," where "shirts for Penny's and Woolworth were being produced in the basement." The first narrator of the film is Noe Falconi, the pastor of the church, who talks about his role as the leader of the "sewing center program." As Falconi offers his perspective on the positive impact of the program, Lezin shows him entering the compound, using a key to open the gate and then to lock it again,

FIGURES I.3–I.5. The final sequence of *The Eastside Story* (1974).

FIGURE I.6. One of several recurring shots in *A Sense of Community* (1976) of a gate that leads to the church basement being locked, either to keep workers in or to keep immigration officials out, depending upon whose version of the story you believe, the pastor's or the laborers'.

indicating the pastor's freedom in contrast to the workers locked in below. Lezin explains that Falconi

> was very proud that he provided a living for immigrants and even housed them on the premises. He showed me around, but had a very different perspective than I did on what we saw. . . . The first thing that I did was interview workers on their days off, away from the church. I learned that their reality was quite different than the one proposed by Noe. They had arrived years before, with promise that they would be trained and sent out into the real world to earn a decent living. But the truth was that they were never offered these outside opportunities. They lived and worked on the property and were chained in during the day.

The film proceeds to undermine Falconi's representation of the sewing center, weaving his narration into contradictory reports from the workers, who discuss their lack of opportunities to advance or earn minimum wage, and the threat of losing their jobs should they want to take a day off.

FIGURE 1.7. Pastor Noe Falconi preaching while the hat is passed for donations from his parishioners, many of whom work in the church sewing facility that he oversees.

By the end of the film, it is apparent that the film's title is ironic and that the church facilitated the exploitation of the most vulnerable members of the Mexican community in Los Angeles. We see Falconi, speaking from the pulpit, espousing the need for churches in poor communities to tie their existence to businesses in order for parishioners to have enough money to give back to the church. This is accompanied by a shot of the hat being passed in church, with parishioners dropping money into it. Lezin's film links race, religion, ethnicity, and immigration status to the confines of an exploitative space. While very different films, *The Eastside Story* and *A Sense of Community* depict the ways that cities trap their most vulnerable inhabitants in inescapable situations. The impasse Bulle feels at the loss of his gang is not unrelated to the church's exploitation of the undocumented laborers: Bulle clutches at the fence that demarcates zones of the city, and the garment workers are locked in the basement, unable to inhabit a free community. These films, focused on different kinds of people in different circumstances, both envision a circumscription of their subjects. This is a recurrent idea linking many nontheatrical films about race in Los Angeles, suggesting the degree to which a case study approach to analyzing such films reveals connections to larger patterns of representation, which are often—as in this case—tied to social inequities that the filmmakers sought to document, and also, perhaps, to rectify.

The pessimism these films convey with regard to their subjects' limited social and physical mobility is also shared in a film about a different Los Angeles neighborhood. *The Savages* (1967), directed by *Felicia* codirector Alan Gorg, was shot in Venice, a neighborhood on the other side of the city from Watts and where Gorg lived at the time. It focuses on the ways that so-called ghettoizing serves to reinforce segregation, conflict, and underdevelopment. Venice is now a wealthy area of the city, but at the time, it and Watts were two of the poorest neighborhoods in Los Angeles, populated largely by working poor and un- or underemployed African Americans who could not afford to live elsewhere.[10] *The Savages* proceeds as a series of fly-on-the-wall scenes with almost entirely nonsynchronous first-person dialogue set to a jazz soundtrack. Where *Felicia* is infused with both realism and a sense of hope, *The Savages* paints a much more fatalistic portrait of a community plagued by economic disenfranchisement, violence, and resignation. It also makes a strong statement about white perceptions about the so-called ghettos of Los Angeles.

*The Savages* begins with a framing device that situates the predominantly black neighborhood of Venice in relation to white spaces, imagined here as the verdant idyll of a park with a baseball field and small lake. Images of a white man napping on the grass are followed by another white man and his son throwing a football, accompanied by unsynchronized voice-over narration, implicitly from these men's points of view. One asks a series of questions: "Why shouldn't I want to strive and achieve a home in the suburbs? What's wrong with this? . . . Shall we take every person who makes more than so much money and take it away from him like he was a criminal? You want to go out directly and take half his paycheck and find some Negro down in the ghetto and say, 'Here, take half my paycheck'?" Another makes a more direct argument: "A Negro owes it to himself to try to better himself. Now he could try to learn to dress properly, to talk properly, to keep himself in a situation that will not say, 'Well, he's like a wild savage—look at him, he ought to go back to the jungle.'"[11]

The title of the film derives from this unsympathetic framing of the subject, with the derogatory perspective of white privilege articulated in tandem with images of a park backdrop that shifts to an urban setting for the rest of the film. Most of the remainder of *The Savages* is narrated—in unscripted documentary voice-over, as with *Felicia*—by Robert Castille, an African American man who often appears on-screen; the film also features, as the

FIGURE I.8. In *The Savages* (1967), the film's central narrator, Robert Castille, talks about his challenges and disappointments as he traverses his blighted neighborhood at film's end.

credits put it, the "Youth of West Venice." While Gorg's camera explores the neighborhood, Castille's unsynchronized voice-over reveals another, opposing view on race and space: "If you grew up in Venice, if you were forced to come to Venice and live, if you don't know it before you get here, you find out pretty soon that you're coming right into nothing. Some people, they don't want to live in Venice. I mean, uh, it's either Venice or Watts is the only choice you have, if the guy's even got a job, I mean, he's just barely making it, you know? That, uh, it's not the fact that he don't want to do, it's that he can't do any better."[12]

Gorg structures the opening portion of the film around this contrast in viewpoints about race and space, with voices of white privilege not just dismissing the black population of the ghetto as useless, but bemoaning the burden that their alleged savagery causes for presumably white, suburban achievers. Even this narration, however, points to a geographical disparity between suburban escape and urban confinement, which Castille essentially affirms when he describes Venice and Watts as traps. As images of Castille at home with his wife, Dorothy, appear on screen, his narration explains that

Dorothy wants to move out of Venice and that what "she doesn't like is the living conditions of the people around her."

Although this affirms the idea of Venice as a place from which to escape, the representation of the Castille family—mother, employed father, and two children—is an important refutation of the idea of unproductive so-called savagery with which the film opens. It is also an implicit rebuttal to the Moynihan Report's critique of inner-city black family life.[13] But the film also depicts a group of young, seemingly aimless African American men complaining about incarceration, racism, and the lack of options in their lives and futures. Cutting back to the Castilles at home, Robert's narration implicitly comments on the youth just pictured: "The kids that hang around on the corner up there, at one time they had high hopes. I mean hopes as high as Jackie Robinson, but their hopes were killed. And I mean, to have to live in these conditions and there's nothing you can do about it and you listen to the news and watch the T v, the reports about our great society, and you just drop down and go down farther, you lose your zest, you don't want to continue."

The film cuts back and forth between scenes of Castille, who tells his life story, and black youths at a party, dancing, smoking, and drinking. Their narration conveys a community plagued by hopelessness and futility, even paralysis, while Castille recounts a life of hardship and discrimination, recuperated only by a personal desire to obtain a better life for his family. Through this formal structure and despite his status as a white man living in a largely black community, Gorg was able to produce, as *Film Library Quarterly* observed, an "insider's view of ghetto conditions," one that goes beyond the film's frame of incomprehension and lack of compassion: "The best way to look at life in the American ghetto is to go there. For those who cannot make the trip in person, this film is a fairly good alternative."[14]

Many nontheatrical films about race and place are, in fact, urban films, puzzling through the limitations determined by geography in Los Angeles. Yet there were other models, too. *Cotton Eyed Joe*, shot by usc film student John McDonald in the fall of his senior year in 1970, is a twelve-minute hybrid film about an African American man named Joseph Wagner, who lives in a makeshift encampment near Chavez Ravine.[15] Although employing documentary aesthetics, the film is presented as an artfully composed day-in-the-life narrative, with obviously reenacted scenes that recall Ivone Margulies's theories about "the indexical value of reenactment," which lends the film an evidential quality compounded by the fact that Joe is, in this case, playing himself.[16] Unlike most other films made in this time period

FIGURE I.9. Behind the scenes during the *Cotton Eyed Joe* shoot in 1970: (*left to right*) the film's subject, Joseph Wagner; director John McDonald; Jenova Caldwell, one of the five-person crew. Photo courtesy of John McDonald.

that depicted people of color in Los Angeles, *Cotton Eyed Joe* depicts life in a nonurban setting that is outside conventional society.

*Cotton Eyed Joe* consists of brief visual interludes showing Joe at the old Cornfield Railyard and in San Pedro on the train tracks as well as walking through the city and earning money at a blood bank. However, it primarily takes place in and around Joe's encampment near Elysian Park, where it dramatizes a real-life incident involving the vandalizing of Joe's camp. This reenactment scene is the emotional centerpiece of the film. A dynamic montage of quick cuts set to percussive music shows three young boys vandalizing Joe's homesite while he's away. When Joe returns and finds the boys in his camp, a series of silent shot–reverse shots ensues. Joe stares directly into the camera, implicitly at the young boys but also at the viewer; one of the boys stares back, conveying a sense of shame for what he has done. Nina Simone's song, from which the film's title derives, enters the soundtrack as

FIGURE I.10. After his makeshift home site is vandalized, Joe puts his house back in order in *Cotton Eyed Joe* (1970).

Joe walks the rails at dusk. Simone sings a pointed question, confirming the film's interest in place: "Where do you come from?"

These train tracks signify in a very different way than they do in *Felicia*, where they are used to alert the audience that they are about to enter a section of Los Angeles that has been defined in the popular imagination by poverty and disenfranchisement, and about which they presumably have little experiential knowledge. Joe both walks and sits on the tracks, occupying them in the same way that he does the land he lives on. Joe's decision to remove himself from the city proper—he is literally a bystander as cars rush by on the freeway below him—allows the film to avoid many of the usual issues about race and space in this time period, such as police treatment. It also suggests a refusal by Joe to be circumscribed in ways seen in the other films under discussion here; think, for example, of the spatial containment at play in *The Eastside Story*, *A Sense of Community*, and *The Savages*.

In contrast to most of the socially engaged nontheatrical films of the time, which tend to highlight problems that often seem insurmountable, *Ujamii Uhuru Schule Community Freedom School* (Don Amis, 1974), a documentary film about an Afrocentric elementary school in South Central Los Angeles,

FIGURE I.11. *Ujamii Uhuru Schule Community Freedom School* (1974).

offers an uplifting solution to the implicit problem of educating disenfranchised members of the African American community in Los Angeles. Amis made the film as his first major assignment while in film school at UCLA, a Project One film shot in 8mm with nonsynchronous sound. It is also one of the few Project One films made by an L.A. Rebellion filmmaker that is documentary in approach. Amis shot the film in an observational mode over three different occasions and then edited the footage together to present a day in the life of the school. To accompany the teacher's voice-over about the mission of the school, Amis filmed students and teachers through their day as they sang songs, wrote, participated in self-defense training, played, and learned self-affirming principles derived from Swahili concepts. In editing, he peppered shots of the young students with inserts of the students' art, inspirational quotes, and portraits of black leaders that decorated the classroom—all of which made the school "a good visual" for Amis's camera.[17]

*Ujamii* represents a community mobilizing for self-transformation through the instillation of cultural affirmation in its young people. For Amis, being a member of the community that he was filming, "looking and dressing like everyone else," allowed access to the children's world without the self-consciousness

that might meet an outsider.[18] (One might think here about the tense interviews in *Black on Black*, discussed by Joshua Glick in his contribution to this
book, or even the slightly nervous shrug of *Felicia* in her brief on-camera interview sequence with the white filmmakers.) It is also distinctive for being
celebratory rather than espousing the pessimism that characterizes the other
L.A. Rebellion Project One films that focus on racism manifest through economic inequalities, drug use, sexual assault, and child abuse, or even films
like *The Savages* and *A Sense of Community*.[19] Amis's portrait of a school
nearly a decade post–Watts Uprising affirms black cultural practices and the
cross-generational instillment of self-respect that ran counter to the pernicious ideas about black inferiority that plagued inner-city public education.

As just this handful of films indicates, nontheatrical films offer ways of
looking at Los Angeles that are absent from their Hollywood counterparts. Encountering such a diverse array of films amid the vast universe of forgotten
educational, sponsored, and amateur films affirms the ways that nontheatrical (and mostly 16mm) films of this era offer a perspective absent from, yet
complementary to, the theatrical universe of the time—one that contributes to a richer understanding of film history and of the pluralistic nature of
American society. As the proliferation of educational films dealing with race
post-1965 points to, 16mm film was a key way that people encountered questions of race and were exposed to issues of social inequity. These films were
made at a pivotal moment during which sweeping changes to Watts, Venice,
Bunker Hill, and kindred neighborhoods across the nation were transpiring;
they were also distributed in the context of a national grappling with social
issues that often pivoted back to the way the nation was reckoning with race.

Los Angeles is not a unique case. Far outside of the cities in which they
were produced, 16mm films circulated widely, in schools, community centers, churches, and any other exhibition venue in possession of a 16mm
projector. A survey of educational film marketing materials of the period
indicates a need for films representing diverse populations. One of the oldest
and largest educational film producers and distributors, Encyclopaedia Britannica, published an annual catalog that is instructive in this regard. Perus-
ing their 1977–78 edition, one encounters many films seeking to engage nonwhite subjects and audiences. Such diversity was totally absent twenty years
prior, and quite rare even a decade before.[20] Just one page of the Family,
Friends, and Neighborhood section of the 1977–78 catalog advertises three
films—out of only eight on the page—exploring African American, Chinese
American, and Native American subjects: *The Blue Dashiki: Jeffrey and His*

*City Neighbors*, *Pamela Wong's Birthday for Grandma*, and *Shelley White-bird's First Powwow*.[21]

Film historians can learn many lessons from such films. With just the small sampling discussed here, we begin to see how one of the nation's major cities was organizing and defining itself along racial and economic lines, as well as where resistance to the dominant social order was bubbling up. These short films render the politics of race and space visible. Taken collectively, they convey racial and geographical boundaries through the eyes of the people who inhabited—and were often contained by—them, even when the films made about these communities were produced by outsiders to those communities. For those who were unrepresented or misrepresented in the dominant theatrical cinema, nontheatrical films often provided their only filmic record.

As film scholars continue to push the canonical boundaries of the discipline, more and more such nontheatrical, ephemeral, and orphan films will be rediscovered, and this collection of essays contributes to the necessary process of contextualization and canonization. Some of these films will rightly be recognized as major archival finds. They certainly need to be considered vital to our understanding of film history and American culture. Despite varying foci and perspectives, such films often share as their generative principle the widely held belief that "prejudice may be tempered by education," by conveying knowledge, asking questions about the social order, and encouraging empathy.[22] Acknowledging the importance of the long-standing tradition of nontheatrical films to film history not only challenges the stability and primacy of established canons, it better reflects the ways in which spectators have consumed film as well as the multimodal media environment in which motion pictures have been produced. This collection of essays marks a long-overdue moment of staking out films worth watching, studying, and discussing that existed outside of the theatrical universe and that, instead of ignoring nonwhite America, dealt squarely with issues of race and identity.

FILMOGRAPHY

All available films discussed in this chapter can be streamed through the book's web page at https://www.dukeupress.edu/Features/Screening-Race.

*Akira* (1971), 14 min., 16mm
DIRECTOR: David Espar. ACCESS: UCLA Film and Television Archive.

*Cotton Eyed Joe* (1970), 12 min., 16mm
DIRECTOR: John McDonald. WRITER: John McDonald. EDITOR: Maureen Smith.
CAMERA: John McDonald. ACCESS: USC Hugh M. Hefner Moving Image Archive.

*The Eastside Story* (1974), 17 min., 16mm
DIRECTOR: Morteza Rezvani. ACCESS: USC Hugh M. Hefner Moving Image Archive.

*Felicia* (1965), 12 min., 16mm
PRODUCTION: Stuart Roe. DIRECTORS: Bob Dickson, Alan Gorg, Trevor Greenwood.
DISTRIBUTOR: University of California Extension Media, Bailey Film Associates
(BFA). ACCESS: Academy Film Archive, USC Hugh M. Hefner Moving Image Archive,
A/V Geeks Educational Film Archive.

*The Savages* (1967), 28 min., 16mm
DIRECTOR: Alan Gorg. DISTRIBUTOR: University of California Extension Media.
CAMERA: Alan Gorg, Kit Grey, Ivan Craig, Joe Hanwright. ACCESS: UCLA Film and
Television Archive.

*A Sense of Community* (1976), 5 min., 16mm
PRODUCTION: Jeremy Lezin. DIRECTOR: Jeremy Lezin. WRITER: Jeremy Lezin.
CAMERA: Dennis Weinschenker. ACCESS: USC Hugh M. Hefner Moving Image
Archive.

*Ujamii Uhuru Schule Community Freedom School* (1974), 9 min., Super 8mm
PRODUCTION: Don Amis. DIRECTOR: Don Amis. WRITER: Don Amis.
DISTRIBUTOR: UCLA Film and Television Archive. CAMERA: Don Amis. EDITOR:
Don Amis. ACCESS: UCLA Film and Television Archive.

NOTES

1   Devin Orgeron, Marsha Orgeron, and Dan Streible, Introduction to *Learning with the Lights Off: Educational Film in the United States*, ed. Devin Orgeron, Marsha Orgeron, and Dan Streible (New York: Oxford University Press, 2012), 5.
2   Charles Tepperman, *Amateur Cinema: The Rise of North American Moviemaking, 1923–1960* (Berkeley: University of California Press, 2015), 13.
3   John Mercer, *The Informational Film* (Champaign, IL: Stipes, 1981), iii.
4   Haidee Wasson and Charles R. Acland, "Introduction: Utility and Cinema," in *Useful Cinema,* ed. Charles R. Acland and Haidee Wasson (Durham, NC: Duke University Press, 2011), 2.
5   For more on the orphan film movement and the related symposium, see Dan Streible, "Saving, Studying, and Screening: A History of the Orphan Film Symposium," in *Film Festival Yearbook 5: Archival Film Festivals*, ed. Alex Marlow-Mann (St. Andrews, U.K.: St. Andrews Film Studies, 2013), 163–76. See also Orgeron, Orgeron, and Streible, *Learning with the Lights Off*; and Acland and Wasson, *Useful Cinema*.
6   Stephen Charbonneau, *Projecting Race: Postwar America, Civil Rights and Documentary Film* (New York: Wallflower, 2016), makes the most sustained interven-

tion in the scholarship to which this volume contributes. Charbonneau focuses solely on documentaries and sponsored educational films using "documentary approaches," and his attention to style and meaning is a useful example of one way nontheatrical scholarship might employ some tools that undergird traditional film studies. Recent examples of scholarly treatments of nonwhite nontheatrical filmmaking or film representation include Allyson Nadia Field, *Uplift Cinema: The Emergence of African American Film and the Possibility of Black Modernity* (Durham, NC: Duke University Press, 2015); Cara Caddoo, *Envisioning Freedom: Cinema and the Building of Modern Black Life* (Cambridge, MA: Harvard University Press, 2014); Joseph Clark, "Double Vision: World War II, Racial Uplift, and the All-American Newsreel's Pedagogical Address," in Acland and Wasson, *Useful Cinema*, 263–88; Marsha Orgeron, "'A Decent and Orderly Society': Race Relations in Riot-Era Educational Films, 1966–1970," in Orgeron, Orgeron, and Streible, *Learning with the Lights Off*, 424–41; Heide Solbrig, "The Personal Is Political: Voice and Citizenship in Affirmative-Action Videos in the Bell System, 1970–1984," in *Films That Work: Industrial Film and the Productivity of Media*, ed. Patrick Vonderau and Vinzenz Hediger (Amsterdam: University of Amsterdam Press, 2009), 259–82. Tepperman, *Amateur Cinema*, includes a discussion of James and Eloyce Gist's religious films, the filmmaking projects of the Harmon Foundation, and the performance of African American vaudeville actor Leonard "Motorboat" Sturrup in *Mr. Motorboat's Last Stand* (John Flory, 1933).

7   For more on the L.A. Rebellion, see Allyson Nadia Field, Jan-Christopher Horak, and Jacqueline Stewart, eds., *L.A. Rebellion: Creating a New Black Cinema* (Berkeley: University of California Press, 2015).

8   The 1965 version of the film is viewable online, courtesy of Skip Elsheimer's A/V Geeks Archive, at the Internet Archive, http://archive.org/details/Felicia1965. For a more thorough account of the film and its production, see Marsha Gordon and Allyson Nadia Field, "The Other Side of the Tracks: Nontheatrical Film History, Pre-Rebellion Watts, and *Felicia*," *Cinema Journal* 55, no. 2 (February 2016): 1–24.

9   Background information on *A Sense of Community* derives from an email exchange that took place between Marsha Gordon and Jeremy Lezin in March 2016.

10  Background information about *The Savages* is taken from a series of emails between Alan Gorg and Marsha Gordon over the course of January and February 2016.

11  In an April 26, 2015, email from Alan Gorg to Marsha Gordon, Gorg explains, "Those bigoted remarks came from white teachers [at Venice High School, 'where the young guys in THE SAVAGES had to go'], but the two white men over whom their audio is played at the beginning of the film are myself and my friend, filmmaker Dan McLaughlin from UCLA, posing as if having done the voice-overs."

12  In a February 26, 2013, email to Marsha Gordon, Alan Gorg remembered that "Robert and Dorothy Castille's home address [was] at 621 San Juan in Venice, where we shot THE SAVAGES scenes with the Castille family. Bob had been working for a military weapons place down the coast south of Venice when we first met him. He was the head of the Venice Civic Improvement Union (VCIU), a primarily African-American non-profit in the Venice ghetto."

13  Daniel P. Moynihan, *The Negro Family: The Case for National Action* (Washington, DC: Office of Policy Planning and Research, U.S. Department of Labor, 1965).

14  Philip Levering, review of *The Savages*, *Film Library Quarterly* (winter 1968/69): 51.

15  Background information on *Cotton Eyed Joe* derives from email correspondence and phone calls between Marsha Gordon and John McDonald that took place in January 2017.

16  Ivone Margulies, ed., *Rites of Realism: Essays on Corporeal Cinema* (Durham, NC: Duke University Press, 2003), 220.

17  Don Amis, oral history interview by Jacqueline Stewart, November 2, 2010, L.A. Rebellion Oral History Project, UCLA Film and Television Archive.

18  Amis, oral history.

19  For a thorough discussion of the L.A. Rebellion Project One films, see Allyson Nadia Field, "Rebellious Unlearning: UCLA Project One Films (1967–1978)," in Field, Horak, and Stewart, *L.A. Rebellion*, 83–118.

20  In 1968, Helaine Dawson bemoaned the fact that "educational film producers" were just starting to make films to correct the long-standing problem of "too few with multiracial representation." Helaine Dawson, *On the Outskirts of Hope: Educating Youth from Poverty Areas* (New York: McGraw-Hill, 1968), 104. Thomas G. Smith, who started working for EB Films in the mid-1960s, recalls that change was afoot for the company in this period owing to a number of factors, including corporate concerns about being able to distribute racially pluralistic films in the southern United States. Smith recalls, "In the years before [ca. 1965] they deliberately tried to exclude African American faces from their films. One old time producer said if they were shooting a classroom full of kids, they'd frame the shot to exclude children of color. The EBF film *People along the Mississippi* (1951) was an exception and the filmmakers—Gordon Weisenborn and John Barns—had to fight to keep an episode showing an African American child playing with two white children. I don't know if sales in the South were affected by this but the scene stayed in the film. When I began making films for them, the federal government was heavily subsidizing educational materials and they mandated that films be integrated. This meant that filmmakers had to search out minorities and make sure they were cast in the film." Tom Smith to Marsha Gordon, email, May 22, 2017.

21  Encyclopaedia Britannica 1977–78 catalogue, collection of Marsha Gordon, p. 24.

22  Robert Conot, "The City's Not for Burning," in *Education and the Urban Crisis*, ed. Roger Woock (Scranton, PA: International Text Book, 1970), 51. Originally published in Robert Conot, *Rivers of Blood, Years of Darkness* (New York: Bantam, 1969).

# 1

## "A Vanishing Race"?

### The Native American Films of J. K. Dixon

CAITLIN McGRATH

On November 22, 2014, National Public Radio aired a show titled "Imagined Nations: Depictions of American Indians." Produced as an episode of WAMU's *Backstory*, the series aimed at giving "historical perspective to the events happening around us today," with this episode focusing on the controversy over the Washington, DC, NFL team's name, the Redskins.[1] The show contextualized the debate by exploring key moments, "taking a long look at how Native peoples have been represented—and misrepresented—in U.S. history." The sixth and penultimate segment of the show, titled "Cigar Store Colossus," detailed the never-completed National American Indian Memorial in New York Harbor proposed in 1913 by Rodman Wanamaker, the son of John Wanamaker, founder of the Wanamaker department stores.

*Backstory* framed Wanamaker's portrayal of Native Americans as an unequivocal misrepresentation. This viewpoint could well have been informed by a 1979 piece written by William Franz, "The Colossus of Staten Island," echoed in the segment's title.[2] Though he was not mentioned in the show, Wanamaker's public lecturer and filmmaker, J. K. (Joseph Kossuth) Dixon, produced Wanamaker's Native American films and photographs and also championed the memorial. In his discussion of Dixon, Franz exhibits a deep skepticism of his work; he describes, for instance, "bombastic introductory remarks by 'Doctor' Joseph Kossuth Dixon, head of Wanamaker's 'education department' and the leader of his earlier Indian expeditions," implying not only that Dixon was not a doctor but also that the education department was not a serious endeavor.[3]

FIGURE 1.2. Hand-modified print of proposed Indian Memorial, 1913,
New York. Mathers Museum of World Cultures, Indiana University.

Franz's assessment of Dixon has been echoed in the work of historians Russel Lawrence Barsh and Alan Trachtenberg.[4] For Barsh, Dixon was a Rasputin figure. He compares Dixon's films of Native Americans to Joseph Conrad's *Heart of Darkness* (1899), echoing Chinua Achebe's influential call to banish such representations from the canon.[5] In his analysis of the various iterations of *Hiawatha*, Trachtenberg's chapter on Dixon paints him as a charlatan; he notes the mixture of education and display, but reads Dixon's involvement with Native Americans as an "opportunity to act out his impulses as a romancer."[6]

This chapter does not deny Dixon's paternalism. The aim is rather to reveal the complexities at work in the intersection of his protoethnography, educational imperatives, Native American advocacy, and involvement in a capitalist enterprise. Dixon was working in the early days of anthropology and ethnography. To dismiss him as a salvage anthropologist because he spoke of "the vanishing race" condemns his images, and the history they contain, to a kind of oblivion.[7] His sentimentality has led to a wholesale rejection of his work, which overlooks the unusual uses of nontheatrical film within Wanamaker's display practices and is more accurately described as an instance of what Ben Singer has termed "ambimodernity": "Modernity is better understood as a heterogenous area of modern and counter-modern impulses, yielding cultural expressions that reflected both ends of the spectrum, along with, and perhaps more frequently, ambivalent or ambiguous positions in between."[8] Further, Dixon's photographs and films have not been appreciated in conjunction with his fight for the rights of Native Americans who served in World War I and his repeated attempts to get Congress to reconsider its stance on extending the benefits and privileges of U.S. citizenship to Native Americans.[9] Dixon's films—and the accompanying illustrated lectures, performances, and displays—were part of a complex system of in-house and traveling entertainment dedicated to an educative and moral goal, and were deployed in his fight for Native American enfranchisement. To tell this history without consideration of nontheatrical media as a tool for public education impoverishes any understanding of why these images were made and how they circulated.

Between 1908 and 1913, Dixon made three photographic and filmmaking expeditions to over 80 Native American communities, visiting 169 different tribes.[10] The resulting 8,000 photographs and 34,000 feet of film were edited into a series of photographic exhibitions, illustrated lectures, and plans for three films—*Hiawatha*, *The Battle of Little Big Horn*, and *The Last Great Indian Council*—with *Hiawatha* being shown extensively from 1908 through

1913.[11] Researching this massive creative output presents several challenges. Dixon's extant photographs, papers, ephemera, and film fragments are spread among three locations: Indiana University's Mathers Museum, the Historical Society of Pennsylvania (HSP), and the Smithsonian's Human Studies Film Archive (HSFA), where the remaining film fragments are housed. Many of Dixon's photographs (which include some production stills) have survived and are held at the HSFA and in the Wanamaker collection of the Mathers Museum, while paper materials, which include John and Rodman Wanamaker's correspondence, are in the HSP archives.[12] There were over seventy reels in the Wanamaker collection in the 1920s, ranging from in-house productions of short clips to accompany illustrated lectures, longer freestanding films, and commercially produced (and purchased) educational and fiction films. Susan Applegate Krouse helped process the film fragments now housed at HSFA in 1985 when they were "discovered in a basement in Red Lodge, Montana, wrapped in newspapers from 1911."[13] The length of existing footage is quite close to that of Reel 70 of the Wanamaker catalog, which is described as "cutouts, not be used but to be saved. For File Only. 1,000 feet."[14] Krouse and others at the Smithsonian determined that their footage was likely the outtakes.

These surviving archival materials suggest an evolution of Dixon's position over the course of these three expeditions, over time seeing his films and photographs as impetus and support for conveying the necessity of enfranchisement to the public and the U.S. government. Dixon's involvement with the Wanamakers began in 1907, with his employment as a photographer and lecturer for the country's wealthiest father-son department store magnates. The Wanamakers strove to provide what they described, in one of their oldest slogans, as "More Than Just a Store."[15] This "more" manifested itself in numerous ways, one of which was to serve as a hybrid news outlet and educational resource. The first two expeditions, in 1908 and 1909, seem to have been motivated by this declared desire to bring the world within reach. The final expedition, in 1913, was more focused on Native American citizenship, shortly following the groundbreaking for the ill-fated National American Indian Memorial. The collaboration between department store magnate and filmmaker/public lecturer, and the ensuing films, photographs, and public lectures, reveals an approach to visual media as an educational tool at a time when Native American culture was little understood by the general public.[16] Dixon may not have been an acknowledged part of the burgeoning field of anthropology, but he was keenly aware of visual media's ability to influence public sentiment in matters related to indigenous cultures. In order to understand his awareness of visual media's power, we must account for Dixon's work at the Wanamaker department stores and his earlier work as a lecturer for Kodak.

"A Vast Public Museum": The Wanamaker Stores'
Culture of Visual Display

In promotional literature, Wanamaker described one of his stores as "a vast public museum" and the Egyptian Hall, on the third floor where public lectures and performances took place, as "This Splendid Temple . . . devoted to the cause of Music and Education." He proclaimed the stores' higher attendance numbers (in comparison to those of other museums or art galleries) were a result of Wanamaker's egalitarian (free) admission policies.[17] Wanamaker's first store, the Grand Depot, was modeled on the architecture of the world's exhibition, and its 1876 opening was timed to coincide with that year's Centennial Exhibition in Philadelphia, for which Wanamaker served as chairman of the Board of Finance. Wanamaker strove for more than visual similarities to cultural predecessors, however. Company literature proclaimed, "To give people the things they want is not enough for the Wanamaker stores. . . . They must be a leader in taste—an educator. . . . They go a step farther . . . and present exhibitions and lectures by men of national reputation, in Science, History, Literature, Art and Music. . . . Educative exhibits of art and life and history have been part of the Wanamaker purpose from the beginning."[18] Wanamaker aspired to create a store culture of uplift and high-class entertainment: education with a touch of wonder and amusement.

But what did a store striving to be a "vast public museum" look like? After the success of the Grand Depot, Wanamaker moved to a new property just down the street, built another store next to it, joined the two, and expanded again. The final building at the corner of Juniper and Market Streets in Philadelphia represented an evolution from the single-story, radial-planned world exhibition model of the Grand Depot toward a multistory Greco-Roman museum, with an open atrium on the ground floor, classical marble columns, and themed auditoriums on the upper levels. These auditoriums, Greek Hall and Egyptian Hall, were flexible spaces that at times displayed merchandise such as ladies' fashions and grand pianos but were increasingly used as lecture halls to hold crowds of two thousand or more. Wanamaker

EGYPTIAN HALL — NEW WANAMAKER STORE — PHILADELPHIA

FIGURE 1.3. Postcard of the Egyptian Hall, Wanamaker store, Philadelphia, featuring John Philip Sousa's Military Band, 1908. Courtesy of Glenn Koch.

expanded his empire to New York City with the purchase of the former A. T. Stewart Department Store, turning it into a hybrid store-museum, with a permanent exhibition hall, Wanamaker Auditorium, with fixed seating for 1,500.[19]

The Philadelphia store's organizational structure involved what I have divided into three tiers of engagement, each reflecting a more structured and focused educational agenda. Confidence in the power of visual media as an educational tool permeated all aspects of Wanamaker's display practices, from the casual in-house displays to the public lectures to the employee school system. The first tier included large-scale displays on the lower floors that utilized the open space of the main atrium, which was known as the Grand Court. Examples included a morning concert demonstration of an early phonograph in 1907, or the celebration of John Wanamaker's birthday in 1911, when over ten thousand guests crowded into the Grand Court. On this occasion, a show of lantern slides and films celebrating his lifetime achievements were projected on an enormous screen draped over the upper balcony.[20]

Unifying this tier were slightly smaller thematic exhibits dotted throughout the store, which customers might happen upon without explicitly seeking them out. For example, the third and fourth floors contained replicas of the birthplace cottage of Robert Burns, King Edward's coronation chair and crown, a series of wax tableaux depicting the French Revolution, and a Japanese gate. These displays were often tied into celebratory days during the store's Anniversary Month of March, which had a different theme each day—Paris Day, Scottish Day, and so on.[21]

The second tier consisted of daily illustrated lectures that usually took place in the Egyptian or Greek halls. These lectures utilized lantern slides, were free and open to the public, and covered topics from architecture to zoology. They were led either by local academics from area institutions such as the University of Pennsylvania or Temple University or by famous authors or experts. Once Dixon was hired, he became the head lecturer and began incorporating films.

The third tier concerned the formal education of the store employees, which took place on the upper floors and roof of the store. The store school began by offering classes for young boys and girls who worked on the shop floor and expanded over time into the accredited University of Trade and Applied Commerce, with classes not only on topics relevant to the store's operation but also on subjects that contributed to a well-rounded arts and science degree. By 1911, over 7,500 students had passed through the Wanamaker classrooms, and a significant portion of employees received some degree of education from the twenty-four full-time teachers employed in the Wanamaker system. Film was also integral to this final tier. In a letter dated June 14, 1916, to film producer George Kleine, H. H. Kaeuper, director of education at the Philadelphia store, wrote, "We are particularly desirous of finding films that will effectively supplement classroom work in history, geography, and general school and commercial subjects."[22] Dixon was most heavily involved in the second and third tiers, focusing on the role of films and photographs in the transmission of knowledge. It was from this position as in-house lecturer and educator that Dixon traveled to capture images— both film and photographic—of Native Americans.

It is not clear who initiated the first expedition, though the Wanamakers had long expressed an interest in Native Americans, beginning with John Wanamaker's trip west for a restorative cure in his youth. As he told his biographer, "Sad was it to witness their desolation and listen to the story of their suffering wrongs—Oh! That their history could be blotted from the page of remembrance for Alas! It is a bitter reflection upon the humanity and christianity [sic] of the White Man."[23] In 1900, John Wanamaker began donating large sums of money to the University of Pennsylvania Museum to fund a series of expeditions.[24] Franz Boas was consulting with the museum at the time, and Wanamaker became interested in funding research into Native American culture, donating a "rare Indian totem" in 1901.[25] In November 1903, a display of Wanamaker's collection of Native American items was announced by the Penn Museum, and in 1905 he donated his entire private collection of over three hundred items. A subsequent, larger exhibition showcasing the bequest opened the same year.[26]

In the first two expeditions in 1908 and 1909 to the Crow Reservation in Montana, Dixon photographed and shot footage for three films. The nonfiction short *The Last Great Indian Council* attempted to gather all the most senior Indian chiefs to be photographed and filmed. The film of Custer's Last Stand, *The Battle of Little Big Horn*, was part of the popular historical reenactment genre in early cinema, functioning as a kind of newsreel by providing the public with visuals to match the accounts in print, though Dixon was dissatisfied with the footage, and it was never edited into a completed film.[27] Dixon engaged a number of Native Americans who had been at the original battle more than thirty years earlier, to provide a measure of authenticity as well as to move away from using white actors in redface, a widely employed practice.[28] For his most popular film, *Hiawatha*, a film adaptation of Longfellow's epic poem, Dixon again employed Native Americans rather than whites in makeup, a point he made sure to promote.[29] Upon Dixon's return after both the 1908 and 1909 expeditions, displays of ephemera, photographic exhibits, film screenings for schoolchildren, and a children's primer on the story of Hiawatha were produced in the Philadelphia and New York stores as tools for his form of spectacular pedagogy.[30]

Since only fragments of these films remain (in the case of *Hiawatha*, only stills), it is difficult to assess the relationship between Dixon and his actors or the quality of the films themselves. Surviving descriptions of his multimedia performances, scripts of his lectures, and outtakes and production stills, give a sense of the final product and the filmmaking process, however. All three films, though they range from documentary to reenactment to fictional film, exhibit a romanticism typical for the period, as well as moments of engagement with the Native Americans as individuals. Dixon worked with Native American photographer Richard Throssel, and he did not shy away from documenting Native Americans as modern contemporaries, as with his photo of Crow Chief Plenty Coups driving a car. Publicly, Dixon focused on representing Native American culture as under threat, but there are photographs and glimpses in the films of a more complicated truth.

FIGURE 1.4. Portrait of Hiawatha and Minnehaha from 1908 filming of *Hiawatha*, Crow Reservation, Montana. Mathers Museum of World Cultures, Indiana University.

## "The Eye Is a Great Educator": Dixon and the Pedagogical Potential of the Visual Image

In a letter discussing the screening of *Hiawatha* in the New York store's auditorium, Dixon underscores the primacy of the moving image: "I very much want people to go from that auditorium saying that they never saw such pictures as at Wanamaker's. They will forget the music, they will forget what I say, but they will never forget what they see. The eye is a great educator."[31] Dixon's emphasis on the visual was partly a result of his years working for Kodak, where his job was to draw attention to the potential of the medium.

In 1904, Dixon began working for George Eastman as a traveling lecturer with the Kodak Exhibition in Europe and in the United States, where he quickly became respected for his illustrated lectures and demonstrations of photographic equipment.[32] The Kodak Exhibition began touring the United States and Europe in 1896 with a series of prints displayed on screens set up in hotels, lecture halls, public meeting spaces, and churches. Although the traveling lecture was well established in 1904, excitement over Dixon in both testimonials and reviews indicate that this was a new phenomenon for the Kodak Exhibition. In his work for Kodak over the course of three years, Dixon performed from a script with hand-tinted lantern slides, the photographic screens, and—for the first time—films. Dixon boasted to Eastman that he had acquired films for his lectures from the new Urbanora series on personal loan from film producer Charles Urban, using the films to start and end most of his lectures.[33] Coming in 1904, at the beginning of Urban's career, this collaboration suggests a measure of Urban's belief in the Kodak Exhibition's mission of outreach and education and, more specifically, recognition of a like-minded soul in Dixon.

Much like motion picture exhibitors and lecturers Lyman Howe and Burton Holmes, and even Sagar Mitchell and James Kenyon in the U.K., verisimilitude ensured the success of his performances. The key difference between Dixon and his contemporaries was that Dixon had to answer to George Eastman. While the upside of having the sponsorship of the Eastman Kodak Company was the security of a salary and the backing of perhaps the most well-known name in photography, it came with distinct challenges. For example, churches were key venues for his traveling programs, and they often balked at the "trade idea" of promoting Kodak products though the lectures.[34] More importantly for his later work as a pedagogue at Wanamaker's, Dixon was using the technology, format, and visual tools of the illustrated lecture to sell the underlying technology—cameras, lenses, and film. As such,

Dixon's relationship to photography and film was different from that of other lecturers. Howe and Holmes used technology to lecture on a subject; Dixon was using various subjects to lecture on and market a technology. Lectures such as "The Call of the Kodak," "The Fruit of the Lens," and "The Kodak, a Moral Force" indicate Dixon's approach. The aims of the exhibition were to raise the profile of photography as an art form, while Dixon's job was to assure the audience that, through the wonders of Kodak equipment, the same images were achievable by everyone. Using technology to sell technology prepared Dixon for another balancing act: packaging education as entertainment to be consumed within a department store.

## "Too Many Prayers and Not Enough Potatoes": Dixon at Wanamaker's

In mid-1905, between his first and second seasons with Kodak, Dixon produced a small pamphlet, "Just Hatched," laying out the tenets of his most popular lectures. In it he announced, "A Great moral and educational idea has just broken its shell."[35] He repeatedly mentioned the "intellectual and moral force" of photography, an idea he included in his correspondence with George Eastman, to whom he wrote: "I love it—there is an educational and moral value to it."[36] This idea that photography and film had the power to uplift was in tune with the outlook of John Wanamaker, whose Quaker background compelled his educational philanthropy as a necessity to balance his stores' commercialism. Wanamaker did not want passive consumers. Dixon's challenge to audiences to become engaged could help further realize Wanamaker's vision of a "vast public museum" to foster "education with a touch of wonder and amusement."

On January 5, 1907, John Wanamaker wrote an offer of employment to Dixon in St. Louis, where he was touring with the Kodak Exhibition: "I duly received your letter and confirm the engagement with you at Three Hundred Dollars per month, to take up work in the Photographic Departments of our New York and Philadelphia stores, especially in conjunction with Mr. Wilson in Philadelphia."[37] Although Dixon's agreement with George Eastman required only one month's notice, Wanamaker wrote to Dixon on the same day inquiring whether he might be released sooner to the mutual benefit of Wanamaker and Eastman: "I believe Mr. Eastman's business will be greatly advanced by the new departure that we shall be the leaders of and that he will want to give us his support as much as we will want to have it."[38] The impact of Dixon's use of film at Wanamaker's was immediately felt. On

March 27, 1907, for Pennsylvania Day, films were shown in the Philadelphia Wanamaker store for the first time and, according to newspaper accounts, the audience numbered five thousand.[39]

As Dixon began lecturing in earnest, Wanamaker kept close watch, as evidenced by a letter of constructive criticism sent to Dixon a few months into his tenure, which provides insight into the experience of the lectures:

> I stood in the back row yesterday afternoon, because I could not get any closer to you, and listened to your lecture as you showed pictures of the store. The crowd was all right, the pictures were all right, and you were very stately yourself and handsome, but your voice did not carry except when you "thundered." I think the lecture was prosy. In these days people do not want thick sandwiches between the pictures, especially when they find an advertisement tagged on them. It reminds me of a friend of mine some years ago when visiting Saratoga, who had been accustomed to staying at Dr. Strong's sanitarium. I supposed of course my friend would be stopping at Dr. Strong's, but he told me he was not. I asked him why, and alluding to the family worship there every morning he said "had too many prayers and not enough potatoes." I am thinking of that in connection with your lecture. It wants more pictures and two or three epigrams between them. I hear on all sides congratulations over your work.[40]

Wanamaker wanted his patrons to become actively involved in the store's ecosystem of education and entertainment. In this instance, he asked for less talking and more images, understanding the entertainment value of using moving images as a tool for engaging visitors. These lectures were more than an afternoon at the picture show. They served as an alternative public education for large numbers of the middle-class patrons that constituted the stores' primary clientele. Audiences were unusually large compared to those of the standard fifty to one hundred people in the storefront nickelodeons of the day.[41] In his public lectures at the stores, Dixon regularly spoke to crowds of up to two thousand.[42] In addition to using the format of multimedia presentations from the Kodak Exhibition for his work at Wanamaker's, Dixon was making films in-house as well as purchasing films from Urban and Kleine.

Increasingly, Dixon's lectures melded with preexisting systems for selling modern life through all of Wanamaker's cultural and technological displays and exhibits as outlined above in the tiered system while anticipating how this form of display could generate a desire for goods that visitors did not even know they wanted. For example, commercially produced films—such as Edison's

*Paul Revere* (1907) and Porter's *The Teddy Bears* (1907)—were repurposed for the educational and consumer aims of the store, respectively; *The Teddy Bears* was included in the 1907 holiday program for Christmas shoppers.[43]

Similarly, themed celebrations of commemorative days at the stores such as Old Folks' Day, Grand Army Day, Children's Day, Paris Day, Shamrock Day, and so on were opportunities for the stores to create a festive atmosphere, to highlight related goods, and to create public edutainment with displays of wax figures, art shows, re-creations, and lantern-slide lectures. Once Dixon joined the staff, film was woven into these celebratory days, usually as part of his illustrated lectures. Compiled by Dixon, a total of forty-three completed films are listed in the only known catalog of films owned by Wanamaker's.[44] A little over half were films purchased from outside firms, including commercially produced films. The list also featured many nontheatrical subjects such as *The Paris Flood*, *Logging in Norway*, *Atlantic Sea Voyage*, *Funeral of King Edward VII*, *Life of the Bee*, *Paris Fashions*, *Perils of the Alps*, *Life in a Burma Teak-Wood Forest*, and *Royal Drive through London*.

It was into this system of educational display that the first expedition to the Crow Reservation was introduced in 1908. Instead of isolating Dixon's Native American photography and filmmaking as Trachtenberg, Barsh, and others have done, understanding these materials as part of a larger system for public education places them in a different light. In this way, the display of Native American materials within the store was not an anomaly. Rather, these lectures were equal parts history, literary adaptation, and—over time for Dixon—social justice advocacy, honed between 1908 and 1916 to provide an easily digestible message to the general public about the current conditions of Native Americans and what he perceived to be their plight.[45] This campaign ranged from lectures for the general public to messages crafted for politicians in Washington, DC, whom Dixon lobbied in the 1920s to make substantive moves toward granting the rights and privileges of U.S. citizenship to Native Americans. Dixon's efforts to raise public consciousness about the unjust treatment of Native Americans on reservations was always grounded in and reinforced by his use of films and photographs as tools for drawing out "the eye [as] a great educator."

## "In All Fairness": Dixon Advocates for Native American Citizenship

There were three large-scale attempts to gather the experiences of Native Americans in the Great War. Two were made by governmental agencies—the Office of Indian Affairs, tasked with tracking Indian assimilation, and the U.S. Army's Historical Section—looking for evidence of the "Indian as warrior" to make a case for their use as scouts. The third was made by Dixon.[46] Unlike the other two efforts, Dixon let Native Americans speak for themselves, transcribing their memories directly rather than relying on an officer to interpret their answers.[47] He also asked them questions the government did not think to ask—about their loss of livelihood, land, or property, and the emotional effects of World War I. His photographs and first-person interviews with returning servicemen, which he collected between 1917 and 1926 and intended to publish before his death in 1926, were not published until 2009. Krouse argues that Dixon was invested in the case for U.S. citizenship for Native Americans and marshaled his documentation to this end. As a result, "his records illuminate the struggle for Indian citizenship, and the confusion surrounding citizenship status for Indians, in the early decades of the twentieth century."[48] Dixon's records are the only ones from this period that represent the viewpoints of Native Americans concerning their experiences in World War I and its aftermath.[49]

This shift from recording to advocating occurred during the 1913 expedition to all 169 Native American communities in the United States. Krouse locates the shift at the dedication of the site for the National American Indian Memorial, where a number of the chiefs in attendance stated that they finally felt heard by the U.S. government. The chiefs were urged to sign the Declaration of Allegiance to demonstrate to leaders in Washington that they were not the stereotypical warring Indians and instead were keen to have enfranchisement for their communities. In fact, a number of the chiefs who came to the dedication of the memorial site helped draft the Declaration of Allegiance.[50]

After returning from the 1913 expedition, Dixon focused his efforts on further educating the public through the San Francisco Panama-Pacific International Exposition of 1915, where the Wanamakers had a pavilion in the Palace of Education, titled the Rodman Wanamaker Historical Expedition to the North American Indian. The pavilion won a Gold Prize for its contributions to the cause of Native American citizenship. Dixon's accompanying lectures, which included his photographs and films, were a resounding success. The exhibit was praised for its contributions to public education, as a contemporary newspaper report reveals: "Examination of the Indian from the realm of politics is the goal of the Wanamaker campaign. It is proposed to crystallize public sentiment into a pressure, which will lift the administration of Indian affairs out of its present politics-ridden condition and make it non-partisan, humanitarian and just. For perhaps the first time the conditions under which the Indian is forced to exist are being made public."[51]

FIGURE 1.5. Thirteenth Infantry, Co. G., *Group of Indians*, March 31, 1919, Camp Mills, Long Island, New York. Mathers Museum of World Cultures, Indiana University.

The *New York Herald* described Dixon's work during the exhibit by noting that "resolutions memorializing Congress to redress Indian wrongs were adopted unanimously."[52]

After this successful public awareness campaign at the 1915 exposition, Dixon began arguing for Native Americans to be given citizenship in exchange for military service. As Dixon described his efforts to his patron, Rodman Wanamaker, "If a man is willing to lay his life on the altar of his country, he should, in all fairness have the privilege of becoming a part of that country, sharing its privileges, possibilities and obligations."[53] In 1917 and 1918, Dixon lectured in Philadelphia, Washington, DC, and New York, arguing that Americans could not in good faith claim to be on the right side of history during the Great War without first dealing with their own injustices at home. He implored, "Is it not time to clear our own land of autocracy before we attempt to wipe autocracy from the map of Germany? Isn't our treatment of the Indian too autocratic and too despotic? Have we not interred a whole race of people—not for a period lasting during the war, but for life?"[54]

## The Afterlife of Dixon's Images

Previous considerations of John and Rodman Wanamaker have tended to dismiss the wealthy entrepreneurs as solely committed to capitalism and have posited Dixon as a racist opportunist. With this chapter, I have presented evidence for a more nuanced view that includes the Wanamaker enterprise's use of nontheatrical media for communication and education. If we see the department store only as a space of display and commerce, it is easy to construe Dixon's work as consisting of little more than superficial showmanship. But when we probe the myriad levels of educative engagement undertaken at the store, the role of film becomes more complex.

Trachtenberg echoes Franz in his dismissal of the store's educational projects: "The imprint of Rodman Wanamaker signified not only a term of ownership under the capitalist form but also a mode of display (though this was disguised under the heading of 'education') designed to bring potential customers into the store and add another facet of pleasure to Wanamaker merchandise."[55] Understood in the full context of its mission and operations, education was actually a major undertaking within the department store, and one for which film became a fundamental component starting in 1907. Education and commerce are not antithetical: the Wanamakers were successful entrepreneurs who also were committed to an educational ideal. Dixon was a savvy producer of photographs and films who was cognizant of visual media's potential to sway audiences, and along the way became an outspoken advocate for Native American enfranchisement.

In some cases, the photographs and films Dixon took are the sole surviving record of communities. As Krouse describes his efforts to document "the vanishing race," "Dixon's lasting contribution rests not in his advocacy, nor in his bombastic and argumentative prose, but in this data he collected, beginning with his photographs and ending with his documentation of Indian veterans."[56] In the brief excerpts that have survived, Native Americans look into the camera or playfully act out their roles assigned by Dixon. The images of Native Americans not statically posed or passively acting out an assigned role are records of active engagement with the process of representation. The relevance of Dixon's images to Native American communities has also been borne out over time. When Dixon's photographs were put on display at the Mathers Museum, some family members were able to identify and see images of their ancestors for the first time. Krouse herself came to the Dixon photographs and films with a general interest in North American Indians and found images of her own Oklahoma Cherokee tribe in the collection. Dean Curtis Bear Claw used some of Dixon's footage in his 1992 documentary about Crow history, *Warrior Chiefs in a New Age*, which recounted the lives of two chiefs of the reservation era, Plenty Coups and Bear Claw's grandfather Medicine Crow.

The varied educational endeavors within the New York and Philadelphia Wanamaker department stores constituted an ecosystem that relied heavily on a multimedia environment that is crucial to understanding Dixon's and the Wanamakers' engagement with Native American culture. Dixon used the term "vanishing" to galvanize public sentiment, and he strove to utilize his platform as a public lecturer to influence the U.S. government. The proposed memorial was to house a museum in its base that included all of Dixon's photographs and films as well as ephemera and artifacts gathered from his travels. However, what is remembered—and mythologized—are the ostentatious plans for the statue above the museum. World War I was the cause of the memorial's abandonment—by Dixon, the Wanamakers, and the public—but it also provided the impetus for Dixon's new approach to his educative missions, leading to the series of interviews of Native American soldiers who served a country that did not acknowledge them as citizens. Dixon's work must be understood within the context of the Wanamaker network of educational display and Dixon's own developing understanding of the inherent power of the image. That these images and films have continued to be interpreted and repurposed by later generations—Krouse and Bear Claw—speaks to their enduring relevance and to the need to bring them out of obscurity.

FILMOGRAPHY

All available films discussed in this chapter can be streamed through the book's web page at https://www.dukeupress.edu/Features/Screening-Race.

*Dixon-Wanamaker Expedition to Crow Agency* (1908), original length unknown, silent, 35mm (original)
PRODUCTION: Joseph Kossuth Dixon and Roland Dixon. DIRECTOR/WRITER/
CAMERA: Joseph Kossuth Dixon and Roland Dixon. ACCESS: Human Studies Film Archive, Smithsonian. SUMMARY: Inducted onto the Library of Congress National Film Registry in 2018, this film footage is the only known surviving film from the 1908 Rodman Wanamaker–sponsored expedition to record American Indian life in the West. Filmed by Joseph K. Dixon and his son, Roland, the film captures rare glimpses of life on Crow Agency, Crow Fair, and a re-creation of the Battle of Little Bighorn featuring four of Custer's Crow Scouts. Film was donated to the Human Studies Film Archives, National Museum of Natural History, Smithsonian Institution, and preserved by Cinema Arts in 1983.

NOTES

1 All of the information about and quotes from the show can be found at "Imagined Nations: Depictions of American Indians," *Backstory*, National Public Radio, November 22, 2014, http://backstoryradio.org/shows/imagined-nations/.

2 William C. Franz, "The Colossus of Staten Island: A Ponderous Memorial to a People Who Refused to Vanish," *American Heritage* 30, no. 3 (April/May 1979): 96–98.

3 See also Joy Porter, ed., *Place and Native American Indian History and Culture* (New York: Peter Lang, 2007); Lucy Maddox, *Citizen Indians: Native American Intellectuals, Race and Reform* (Ithaca, NY: Cornell University Press, 2005); Eric L. Buffalohead and M. Elise Marubbio, eds., *Native Americans on Film: Conversations, Teaching, and Theory* (Lexington: University Press of Kentucky, 2013); M. Elise Marubbio, *Killing the Indian Maiden: Images of Native American Women in Film* (Lexington: University Press of Kentucky, 2006); Michelle H. Raheja, *Reservation Realism: Redfacing, Visual Sovereignty, and Representations of Native Americans on Film* (Lincoln: University of Nebraska Press, 2010).

4 Alan Trachtenberg, *Shades of Hiawatha: Staging Indians, Making Americans, 1880–1930* (New York: Hill and Wang, 2004); Russel Lawrence Barsh, "An American Heart of Darkness: The 1913 Expedition for American Indian Citizenship," *Great Plains Quarterly* 13, no. 2 (spring 1993): 91–115.

5  Chinua Achebe, "An Image of Africa: Racism in Conrad's 'Heart of Darkness,'" *Massachusetts Review* 18 (1977): 18.

6  Trachtenberg, *Shades of Hiawatha*, 233. The accounts of Dixon by Trachtenberg and Barsh have been repeated by later writers and have led to an image of Wanamaker and Dixon as unredeemable. See Steven Conn, *History's Shadow: Native Americans and Historical Consciousness in the Nineteenth Century* (Chicago: University of Chicago Press, 2004); Sherry Smith, *Reimagining Indians: Native Americans through Anglo Eyes, 1880–1940* (Oxford: Oxford University Press, 2000); Peter C. Rollins and John E. O'Connor, eds., *Hollywood's Indian: The Portrayal of the Native American in Film* (Lexington: University Press of Kentucky, 2003); Edward Carter, ed., *Surveying the Record: North American Scientific Exploration to 1930* (Philadelphia: American Philosophical Society, 1999).

7  David R. M. Beck, "The Myth of the Vanishing Race," in *Edward S. Curtis and the North American Indian Project*, Northwestern University and American Memory Project (Washington, DC: Library of Congress, 2001). Dixon's own collection of photographs and essays from 1913 was titled *The Vanishing Race* (Garden City, NY: Doubleday, Page, 1913).

8  See Ben Singer, "The Ambimodernity of Early Cinema: Problems and Paradoxes in the Film-and-Modernity Discourse," in *Film 1900: Technology, Perception, Culture*, ed. Klaus Kreimeier and Annemone Ligensa (Bloomington: Indiana University Press, 2009), 38.

9  Susan Applegate Krouse, *North American Indians in the Great War* (Lincoln: University of Nebraska Press, 2007).

10  Krouse, *North American Indians*, 11.

11  See *Wanamaker Primer on the North American Indian: Hiawatha Produced in Life* (Philadelphia: John Wanamaker, 1910); and *The Vanishing Race* (Philadelphia: John Wanamaker, 1913).

12  There is only a very small snippet on the HSFA site, accessible through the book's web page at Duke University Press. Krouse wrote two earlier articles that have been referenced by Alison Griffiths, *Wondrous Difference: Cinema, Anthropology, and Turn-of-the-Century Visual Culture* (New York: Columbia University Press, 2002); and Fatimah Tobing Rony, *The Third Eye: Race, Cinema, and Ethnographic Spectacle* (Durham, NC: Duke University Press, 1996), where Dixon is mentioned briefly in the context of early anthropology and ethnography. See Susan Applegate Krouse, "Filming the Vanishing Race," in *Visual Explorations of the World: Selected Papers from the International Conference on Visual Communication*, ed. Jay Ruby and Martin Taureg (Aachen: Edition Herodot im RaderVerlag, 1987); and Susan Applegate Krouse, "Photographing the Vanishing Race," *Visual Anthropology* 3, nos. 2–3 (1990): 213–33.

13  Krouse, "Filming the Vanishing Race," 258.

14  "List of Indian Motion Picture Film for Use in Indian Lectures," Mathers Museum of World Cultures, Indiana University, Bloomington, MMUS-057-025-9.

15  See Joseph Herbert Appel, *Golden Book of the Wanamaker Stores: Jubilee Year, 1861–1911* (Philadelphia: John Wanamaker, 1911).

16 For more on the history of educational cinema, see Devin Orgeron, Marsha Orgeron, and Dan Streible, eds., *Learning with the Lights Off: Educational Film in the United States* (New York: Oxford University Press, 2012), in particular Jennifer Peterson's and Oliver Gaycken's chapters.

17 Wanamaker compared the number of annual visitors to his stores to those of the Metropolitan Museum of Art, arguing that his lack of admission price democratized the experience and gave more of the public the chance to experience art and culture. Appel, *Golden Book*, 249.

18 Appel, *Golden Book*, 238.

19 Wanamaker bought the A. T. Stewart Department Store in 1896. Appel, *Golden Book*, 292.

20 This birthday event is described in in-house records, Jubilee Night, October 28, 1911, box 48.52, HSP. The films produced in-house by Dixon are listed in the catalog of films held by Wanamaker's generated by Dixon in the 1920s and now held by the Mathers Museum, MMUS-WD folder 57.

21 For more on the history of late nineteenth- and early twentieth-century exhibition culture, see Philippe Harmon, *Expositions: Literature and Architecture in Nineteenth-Century France* (Berkeley: University of California Press, 1992).

22 H. H. Kaeuper to George Kleine, June 14, 1916, Educational Films 1916, 1920–30 folder, Container 18, George Kleine Papers, Manuscript Division, Library of Congress, Washington, DC.

23 Herbert Adams Gibbons, *John Wanamaker* (Port Washington, NY: Kennikat Press, 1926), 36.

24 Large Black Scrapbook, number 1, HSP, Philadelphia.

25 Large Black Scrapbook Series, HSP. Later, between 1914 and 1916, Rodman Wanamaker funded the work of Louis and Florence Shotridge, a husband-and-wife team, to return to Alaska to record the Tlingit language and cultural practices.

26 Large Black Scrapbook, number 1, HSP.

27 The reenactments of the Boer War (1900) perhaps were some of the earliest examples of this trend. See Kristen Whissel, "Early Cinema Encounters Empire: War Actualities, American Modernity, and Military Masculinity," and "Placing Audiences on the Scene of History: Modern Warfare and the Battle Reenactment at the Turn of the Century," in *Picturing American Modernity: Traffic, Technology, and the Silent Cinema* (Durham, NC: Duke University Press, 2008).

28 Seen most recently in the documentary *Reel Injun* (Neil Diamond, Catherine Bainbridge, and Jeremiah Hayes, 2009).

29 This was not the first film version of *Hiawatha*. Theatrical productions of *Hiawatha* were popular across the country, and three motion pictures were either finished or in production at the time. See Andy Uhrich, "'Beautiful to the Eye, Pleasing to the Ear': Educational Performance in *A Pictorial Story of Hiawatha* (1904–1908)," *Early Popular Visual Culture* 13, no. 4 (2015): 256–75.

30 Large Black Scrapbook series, box 20, Scrapbook 8.1909.3.1, HSP. According to numerous clippings and internal advertisements, *Hiawatha* was shown daily in the Egyptian Hall at this time.

31  Dixon to M. J. Chapman, April 1, 1909, MMUS-WD folder 40, page 35, Wanamaker Papers, Mathers. In the same letter he continues, "The screen must be in size 22×24 [feet]. . . . The screen is to hang on a Hartshorn roller and when it falls there should be a rod of sufficient weight at the bottom to pull this screen absolutely taut, four-square. It ought to hang as straight and taut as a pane of glass."

32  There was no contract per se. Dixon was engaged for £546 per year. In the summer of 1905, he moved back to America to tour with the Kodak Exhibition, this time on a basis of $60 per month, with one month's notice for termination. It seems it was these terms that Wanamaker was eager to break. Eastman Papers, George Eastman Museum (GEM), Rochester, NY.

33  Dixon to George Eastman, April 4, 1905, GEM.

34  Dixon to Mr. George Davison, March 15, 1905, 1, GEM.

35  J. K. Dixon, "Just Hatched," 7, MMUS-WD-022.

36  Dixon to Eastman, April 4, 1914, GEM.

37  John Wanamaker to Dixon, January 5, 1907, Letterpress folders, HSP.

38  Wanamaker to Dixon, January 5, 1907.

39  "Pennsylvania Day Thousands at Brilliant Celebration at Wanamaker's," *Philadelphia Inquirer*, March 28, 1907, 2. See also Large Black Scrapbook Series, 1909, 48–60, HSP.

40  John Wanamaker to Dixon, October 16, 1907, Letterpress folders, HSP.

41  A closer approximation to Dixon's public lectures were the lectures held at the Armour Institute in Chicago and the Pratt Institute in Brooklyn, but the Wanamaker series was free and open to the public and within a commercial establishment, setting the store's activities apart.

42  Appel, *Golden Book*, 257. The title "Dr." seems to have been purely honorary. Dixon is also at times referred to as Reverend.

43  Presumably these films (*Teddy Bears*, *The Night Before Christmas*, and *The Midnight Ride of Paul Revere*) were the Edwin S. Porter films of the same year. For more on contemporary examples of *Paul Revere* in a theatrical context, see Charles Musser, *Before the Nickelodeon: Edwin S. Porter and the Edison Manufacturing Company* (Berkeley: University of California Press, 1991), 430–31.

44  "Educational and Store Films, Positive and Negative, Where positive prints have been purchased from outside firms, words 'No Negative' will be placed, following the title of each reel." "Miscellaneous notes, lists of slides, lists of motion pictures for lectures," MMUS-WD folder 57, Mathers.

45  Some of his lecture notes survive in the Wanamaker Papers at the Mathers Museum.

46  Krouse, *North American Indians*, 5.

47  Interviews were conducted in English, but were not synopsized as the military had done. Dixon quoted the servicemen directly, in their own words.

48  Krouse, *North American Indians*, 6.

49  Many of these interviews are published in their entirety in Krouse, *North American Indians*.

50  Krouse, *North American Indians*, 10.

51  "Wanamaker's Indian Exhibit Wins Medal," Wanamaker clipping file, HSP.

52  "Wanamaker Gift Will Help Indian," *New York Herald*, October 19, 1915, HSP.

53  Dixon to Rodman Wanamaker, March 25, 1917, Wanamaker Documentation, in Krouse, *North American Indians*, 11.

54  Speaking to the Poor Richard Club in Philadelphia, quoted in Krouse, *North American Indians*, 12.

55  Trachtenberg, *Shades of Hiawatha*, 232.

56  Krouse, *North American Indians*, 7.

**2**

## "Regardless of Race, Color, or Creed"

Filming the Henry Street Settlement
Visiting Nurse Service, 1924–1933

TANYA GOLDMAN

Founded in 1893 by nurse and social reformer Lillian Wald, the Henry Street Settlement was one of many Progressive Era reform organizations developed in response to industrialization, mass immigration, and urban overcrowding. Situated in the heart of Manhattan's Lower East Side, the organization developed a wide range of service initiatives, including its pioneering Visiting Nurse Service (VNS), committed to providing health care to the urban poor "regardless of race, color, or creed."[1]

By 1923, the VNS had expanded operations from its original house on Henry Street to more than twenty offices across three of New York City's boroughs. Approximately 250 nurses traveled the city, seeing upward of fifty thousand patients in their homes per year. Staff also managed several specialized maternity centers. What made the service so indispensable was its commitment to providing care irrespective of a patient's ability to pay. As such, the settlement relied extensively on donations to sustain operations. Nearly half of its financial support came from benefactors and annual fund-raising drives; only 5 percent came from patients.[2] In addition to fund-raising, community outreach to raise awareness among the city's "needy-sick" was also a constant concern.[3] By the early 1920s, Henry Street had developed an annual schedule of promotional campaigns that utilized nearly all of the era's available media platforms. In 1924, motion pictures joined the organization's arsenal of newspaper ads, mailers, posters, leaflets, and department store window displays. A total of three films—intended to either solicit funds, educate the community, or share information with colleagues—were produced within the next decade.[4]

This chapter considers Henry Street's adoption of moving images as part of its promotional apparatus and assesses how each film depicted the organization's efforts to serve New York's diverse populace. Heeding Charles Acland and Haidee Wasson's call to interrogate the complex relations between moving images, institutions, and exhibition locales, this chapter situates each work amid the organization's broader philanthropic goals.[5] Analysis of these films demonstrates how each one's distinct intended use mediated depictions of racial and ethnic difference. What emerges is a contradictory strain of interracial and interethnic inclusion whereby Henry Street's films—in spite of the service's comparatively forward-thinking policies—still largely project their contemporary social mores.

## Lillian Wald and the Progressive Impulse

Lillian Wald's settlement is unique among its British and American peer institutions in that it was the first initiated and run by a trained nurse. Wald's influence on developing public health nursing as a viable career for young women of all racial backgrounds is broadly recognized.[6] While best remembered for her efforts to professionalize nursing and reform child labor laws, Wald also possessed a markedly forward-thinking approach to race relations for her time. As an early supporter and board member of the NAACP, she hosted one of its first meetings at Henry Street in 1909, when city ordinance still prohibited integrated meetings. Wald also publicly characterized segregation as "an invidious and subtle poison" and in her 1934 autobiography claimed that Henry Street was the first nursing organization to provide equal salaries to black and white nurses.[7]

Wald's commitment to interracial tolerance informed the organization's internal politics. For example, in 1921 Wald and the board received word from a white businessman about the poor treatment that one of his "colored secretaries" received while dining with white colleagues at a Henry Street–owned restaurant. The board chastised the establishment's proprietor, who soon resigned. Several years later, Wald stood by her decision to house a black nurse at the original settlement despite the ire of several donors.[8]

The VNS, however, did not initially court the involvement of black nurses. Rather, Henry Street's first black nurse approached Wald herself in 1906, asking for support to create an outpost to serve her own community. In her writings, Wald encouraged nurses to live within the communities they served to cultivate an "organic relationship" with patients.[9] Considering the de facto segregation of many New York neighborhoods, Wald's focus on "organic" communal connection possesses inherent segregationist implications, even if such policies were well intentioned. Indeed, maintaining the color line was organizational policy as black nurses were forbidden to visit white homes, nor were they promoted to senior positions at clinics outside their own neighborhoods. A black nurse's service to "her own people" is a consistent trope across VNS promotional materials, reflecting the era's prevailing social order.

## Helping Hands (1924)

Henry Street's decision to add moving pictures to its annual pledge drive was announced at a February 1924 campaign committee meeting. Bray Productions, an established producer of animated and sponsored films, began production in late September. The resultant thirteen-minute short, *Helping Hands* (1924), depicts a philanthropist shadowing two real Henry Street nurses on their rounds.[10]

The film opens on the lush grounds of the Pierson family estate as Alice, a white Henry Street nurse, visits her childhood friend Marion, whose father is a prosperous businessman. The three characters, all well dressed to connote their class, congregate on an outdoor patio. Marion proudly tells her father that Alice has just completed nursing school. Desiring to be "useful," Marion urges her father to help the organization. Pierson is eager to learn more about the VNS, and Alice promises to secure permission for him to accompany her in the field.

The next day, James and Marion Pierson shadow Alice on her rounds. In a long shot, the trio walks toward the steps of an apartment building. This framing provides a glimpse of the congested neighborhood sidewalk, a counterpoint to the open green space of the Pierson estate. Inside Alice tends to a sick white mother in bed. Two children dutifully sweep the apartment as Alice works and the Piersons observe. Marion compassionately places a hand on one of the children's shoulders, a gesture evoking "sympathetic knowledge," a practice advocated by settlement house pioneer Jane Addams. The group soon enters a second tenement, and the Piersons vanish from the screen as Alice dutifully treats a bedridden white girl. A worried mother hovers nearby.

After this second visit, Alice informs the group that they will take a taxi to see one of the "colored nurses." The camera cuts to a light-skinned black nurse, Miss Smith, checking her wristwatch and awaiting the trio's arrival.

FIGURE 2.1. *Helping Hands* (Bray Productions, 1924). Visiting Nurse Service of New York Collection, USC Hugh M. Hefner Moving Image Archive.

FIGURE 2.2. *Helping Hands* (Bray Productions, 1924). Visiting Nurse Service of New York Collection, USC Hugh M. Hefner Moving Image Archive.

Exiting the cab, Mr. Pierson warmly shakes her hand, commenting, "Your uniform looks like the garb of a friend." This handshake and intertitle connote a bridge of interracial relations and Pierson's progressive outlook on racial equality.

The camera cuts to the interior of another single-room apartment where two black children sit as their mother vigorously scrubs laundry on a washboard. As Miss Smith enters, the mother greets her. An intertitle follows: "Laws, Miss Henry Street, honey, Gardenia am sittin' here waitin' for you for the last hour." Since Alice's previous visits do not depict patients speaking, one must question Bray's decision to give voice to the black mother, as well as the implication that Miss Smith arrived later than expected. The intertitle's language punctuates the class divisions between these two figures of black femininity—that of the unkempt, dark-skinned, indigent mother and the uniformed, lighter-skinned nurse, a beacon of racial uplift and middle-class aspiration. This meeting invokes a precarious balance between progressive and regressive racial representation as the depiction of Miss Smith as responsible and attentive is counterbalanced by the stereotypical portrayal of the helpless, uneducated black urban poor.

Following Miss Smith into the apartment, Alice also warmly shakes the black mother's hand, echoing Mr. Pierson's greeting of Miss Smith outside. Curiously, the Piersons are not shown within the patient's home. Miss Smith administers first aid care to a wound on the young girl's leg before the camera abruptly cuts to a VNS clinic where Alice leads a class on newborn care. This lesson is shown with a series of iris transitions to condense the length of screen time. This technique also highlights the comparatively short amount of screen time given to Miss Smith, as Alice's methodical actions contrast the basic aid performed by the black nurse.

Finally, a staged shot captures a large group of nurses. The camera pans left to right, revealing roughly 45 of the service's 250 uniformed nurses. A small cluster of light-skinned African American nurses stand together at the far left of the overwhelmingly white group. The appearance of these nurses, dressed identically to their white peers, projects an image of professional parity, specialized knowledge shared across racial lines. This projection, however, is tempered by the posture of a white nurse standing immediately to the group's left, back turned to her black colleagues. While it is impossible to know the subject's intent, the resultant positioning suggests an internal ambivalence toward racial integration and equality among members of the VNS, even while publicly touting its employment of African American

FIGURE 2.3. *Helping Hands* (Bray Productions, 1924). Visiting Nurse Service of New York Collection, USC Hugh M. Hefner Moving Image Archive.

personnel. The film ends with Pierson pledging his financial support to the cause.

*Helping Hands* reflects what Constance Balides characterizes as reform publicity's tendency to blend didacticism with sociological display, an "address both to a social subject who [is] part of a social formation of reform and to a civic subject who [is] enjoined to do something about social problems based on social facts and a sympathetic understanding of the circumstances of others."[11] Additionally, in demonstrating the value of the VNS by presenting examples of its activities, *Helping Hands* enacts what Allyson Nadia Field has characterized as a "before-and-after" syntax of uplift narratives whereby an institution's transformative powers are illustrated by contrasting pre- and postservice conditions.[12] Pierson's journey through the field also echoes a subset of the industrial process film, the factory-tour or visitor film. Writing of the Volkswagen Autostadt factory films, Patrick Vonderau likens the spectator's experience to touring in a cultural sense, which "has more to do with regulated action in semiotic arrangements toward a concrete economic result. What is made productive in the cultural technique of the tour is less the factory *than the visitor him- or herself*" (emphasis added).[13] While Vonderau is speaking of automotive assembly and its effects

[56]   Tanya Goldman

on tour attendees, a similar point can be made with regard to diegetic philanthropy in *Helping Hands*. That is, through his tour, Pierson is produced as a philanthropic subject. Thus, through didacticism, sympathetic appeal, and a show-and-tell model, *Helping Hands* constitutes an attempt at philanthropic mimesis by presenting behavior that the film hopes its similarly wealthy, civic-minded addressees will replicate.

In the absence of exhibition records, campaign committee meeting minutes allow for reasonable speculation about the circumstances of the film's exhibition and its intended use to solicit donations. At the start of production, members discussed placing the film in "better-class picture theaters" during the fall canvass. Plans were also discussed to screen *Helping Hands* at a fund-raising gala dinner, on-site at VNS headquarters for visitors, and at several "parlor conferences" hosted at patrons' homes.[14] The decision to commission a new one-reel motion picture in late 1926 also indicates that the organization continued to value film as a mode to persuade and promote—though they committed only $500 to the new production, a quarter of the $2,000 spent on the earlier project. An independent producer named Frank R. Abrams was hired for the project.[15]

## *The Visiting Nurse* (1927)

Perhaps due to its lower budget, *The Visiting Nurse* dispenses with a frame narrative and proceeds like a travelogue.[16] This less structured syntax allows the film a more flexible mode of address and the leeway to speak to a broader audience. While produced specifically for Henry Street's spring 1927 fund-raising drive, extant records indicate that the film played for a dual audience: local donors and potential patients. Given its need to simultaneously speak to two difference audiences, *The Visiting Nurse*'s depiction of racial and ethnic service differs subtly from that of *Helping Hands*.

The fifteen-minute film begins with a series of intertitles informing the viewer that the VNS "answers calls from the people of all nationalities and all faiths" and is driven by "universal brotherhood." A uniformed white nurse is characterized as "a guardian of New York's homes." Amid scenes of white nurses working, an intertitle reminds the viewer that service is free of cost for those unable to pay, informative for potential patients and justifying a need for donations from wealthier viewers.[17]

*The Visiting Nurse* deviates from its focus on undifferentiated whiteness about six and a half minutes into the film. As a white nurse walks along a busy street, she is directed toward someone requiring attention. In the next

FIGURE 2.4. *The Visiting Nurse* (Frank R. Abrams, 1927). Visiting Nurse Service of New York Collection, USC Hugh M. Hefner Moving Image Archive.

shot, the nurse speaks to a woman holding a child in front of a bread shop. The storefront's signage, Panetteria Sicliana e Napolitana, signals the area's Italian populace. In the absence of an intertitle indicating locale, the Italian window text gestures to VNS outreach in Little Italy, one of Manhattan's well-known ethnic enclaves.

The nurse's interactions with the community appear natural, suggesting familiarity and acceptance. During the same sequence, she is later shown conversing with two additional mothers, and she warmly places her hand on the head of a child, echoing Marion's similar gesture in the previous film. By showing the nurse walking the neighborhood and speaking with multiple residents, the filmmaker illustrates her value to the community at large. This white nurse's specific heritage is never explicated, contrary to Henry Street's frequent efforts to explicate the value of service to "one's own kind" within the black community. Given that the organization's policies upheld segregation of services along the color line, this occurrence suggests that white skin tone—even given the cultural contingency of whiteness during this period—overrides the nuances of European ethnic distinction.

Language is similarly used to mark difference during a brief sequence in Chinatown. An intertitle sets the stage: "For Chinatown there is Miss

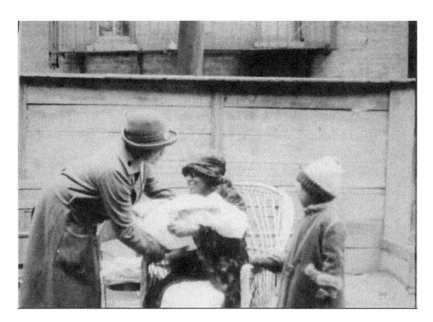

FIGURE 2.5. *The Visiting Nurse* (Frank R. Abrams, 1927). Visiting Nurse Service of New York Collection, USC Hugh M. Hefner Moving Image Archive.

Zing Ling Tai." Two establishing shots follow the nurse along streets heavily populated by Chinese-language signs. A third and final shot shows Ling Tai awkwardly posing alongside a stone-faced Asian child. Her hand is placed on the child's back. Both look directly at the camera, the nurse offering a tentative smile.

This twenty-second stretch of screen time contrasts with the Little Italy sequence that precedes it. Unlike the nurse in Little Italy who is portrayed as a beloved figure within the community, the assumption of the Chinese nurse as a welcome presence in the neighborhood is undercut by the visible unease of the child beside her. Second, Ling Tai is not shown interacting with any adults in the community, implicitly muting her appearance of professional expertise. Finally, and most pointedly, the intertitle that introduces Ling Tai is, in and of itself, an anomaly in a film where no other nurse is identified by name. In addition to strongly suggesting that Ling Tai is the only Henry Street nurse to serve her community, this singularity also renders her a token at best. Her fleeting appearance feels less about displaying VNS care than about showing her as a novelty, specimen, or emblem of inclusivity.[18]

Later, the film travels uptown to Harlem, where an intertitle informs the viewer, "24 colored nurses serve their own people." After an establishing shot of the center's exterior, a smiling employee holds the door for three entering patients. Two brief examples of care follow: the first depicting a nurse writing a doctor's referral for a patient seated beside her, the second of a blind mother passing her infant to a nurse as her older son looks on. This Harlem tour occupies about one minute of screen time.

The Harlem sequence comes immediately after a lengthy sequence capturing an infant care class led by a white nurse. Compared to the meticulous series of actions performed by the white nurse in the preceding sequence, the black labor here appears less skilled. Thus, while the aforementioned white nurse provides detailed instructions, the Harlem nurses engage in nonspecialized tasks—opening a door, sitting at a desk, and picking up an infant—and the black nurse's need to refer her patient to a doctor, rather than manage care herself, minimizes her appearance of expertise. This lesser capability is mirrored in the comparative inaction of the Harlem patients. Thus, while a white woman dutifully stands and practices her skills during the infant care class, both black mothers are seated. Though an intertitle explains that the blind mother had created a layette for her infant, the image that follows only depicts her passing the child off to a nurse. The more limited scope of activity performed by the Harlem nurses and their patients (as well as the absence of care administered by Ling Tai) creates a perception that skill is allotted unequally across racial and ethnic lines, a prevalent stereotype that contemporary black nursing professionals and educators specifically worked hard to counteract.[19]

The perception of inequality is also mirrored in the comparatively unpolished camera work that depicts the black nurses. For example, while shooting the infant care demonstration, the instructor is often centered and shown from the waist up. Subtle shifts in scale suggest multiple camera setups. In contrast, the seated black nurse and her patient are positioned in the very bottom left corner of the frame, partially clipped by its edge. Poor framing is also evident in the establishing shot of Ling Tai in Chinatown, where she is awkwardly cut across the upper chest while occupying only the very bottom of the frame.

These fleeting moments of ethnic and racial variation within the film—three minutes of total screen time in Chinatown and Harlem—can be admired for inclusivity at a time when segregation was an entrenched social norm, even in a diverse city like New York. But, just as in *Helping Hands*, these inclusive gestures are fraught with contradiction. While *The Visiting Nurse* documents black and Chinese labor within the Henry Street nurse network, their presence and presentation project a secondary, separate, and unequally skilled status.

The film closes on an image of VNS headquarters. An intertitle informs the viewer that the building was bequeathed to the organization by a long-time patron, information certainly provided to exert pressure on wealthier viewers. However, the extant version of this film contains three additional intertitles that prove the film's exhibition in less affluent local communities: the first title mentions a souvenir calendar; the next instructs viewers with health problems to visit their nearest center; and the last lists addresses of the six VNS clinics in the Bronx. That these titles are specifically tailored to the Bronx suggest that other contemporary copies (though no longer extant) contained similar neighborhood-specific information.[20] These titles confirm *The Visiting Nurse*'s use as a platform to share information with audiences it directly intended to serve. In these exhibition contexts, then, *The Visiting Nurse* offered black, Chinese, and Italian Americans the opportunity to see themselves represented on screen in unsensationalized form. Perhaps local screenings even inspired viewers to offer small-scale donations by illustrating the direct benefits of VNS service within one's own community. This dual vocality illustrates ways specific exhibition contexts frame audience reception, a point similarly demonstrated by Field in her analysis of the circulation of Hampton Institute and Tuskegee School fund-raising films in the 1910s, which reached both Northern white philanthropists and Southern black audiences.[21]

The intended double audience for the film—wealthy donors and local communities served by the VNS—is confirmed by organizational records that estimate it was shown about fifty times in the spring and fall of 1927 at headquarters and in neighborhood clubs and small movie theaters. Memos also indicate that ten- and twenty-minute speeches were tailored to precede or follow the film when it was shown to donors or neighborhood audiences.[22] The film's more flexible syntax grants it the leeway to speak to a broader, more diverse audience than *Helping Hands* and opens it up to a wider range of readings.

## The Work of the Henry Street Visiting Nurse Service in the City of New York (1933)

In 1933 a third silent film about the VNS was completed. Titled *The Work of the Henry Street Visiting Nurse Service in the City of New York*, this twenty-two-minute film was directed by Anne Marvin Goodrich, a 1926 graduate of Yale's nursing school and niece of a Henry Street board member. Contrary to the alliterative *Helping Hands*, the text-heavy, prosaic title reads like a

FIGURE 2.6. Anne Marvin Goodrich, Yale School of Nursing Class of 1926 yearbook. Yale University, Harvey Cushing/John Hay Whitney Medical Library.

professional report, and a need to foreground the service's geographic location suggests it was not designed for local audiences. Three pages of instructional commentary, highlighting specific points to bring to the attention of spectators, were prepared to accompany the film.[23] In aggregate, this suggests the film was created to exhibit at industry gatherings. Thus, designed to solicit professional attention rather than stimulate community action, Goodrich's project, with its depictions of labor, serves as a generative point of contrast to *Helping Hands* and *The Visiting Nurse*.

Since it is addressing public health practitioners, *The Work* is notably unencumbered by the demands of fund-raising and salesmanship (the film also goes unmentioned in meeting minutes, suggesting the project was made independently of Henry Street's publicity committee).[24] Its intended audience is further borne out by the matter-of-fact prose of the film's intertitles. Whereas the florid titles of 1927's *The Visiting Nurse* tout the organization's commitment to "universal brotherhood" and characterize its nurses as domestic "guardians," here titles such as "the nurses respond to calls not

[62]    Tanya Goldman

only on city streets but also to those from the outlying districts of New York" are simply functional. This change in language indicates a shift from promotional and sympathetic display to straightforward reportage that distinguishes Goodrich's film from its predecessors.[25]

*The Work* also provides greater detail and range of services than the prior Henry Street films. While the previous films featured only infant care, here Goodrich documents service to the elderly and adolescents. The film also offers a broader representation of the city's varied landscape, documenting nurses in urban Manhattan as well as in less-developed areas in Queens and the Bronx. Finally, whereas Alice and Miss Smith's *Helping Hands* home visits were quick, Goodrich focuses on step-by-step processes. Close-ups of hands unpacking medical bags demonstrate expertise using a specialized set of tools.

While this level of detail should not be confused with the rigors of a medical training film, it indicates an audience familiar with the practices and concerns of public health nursing. In light of its supplemental talking points and the absence of a soundtrack, the film was certainly conceived as a hybrid presentation intended to be accompanied by someone lecturing beside the screen. By the end of the 1930s, Goodrich had established a successful career as a health care publicity consultant with clients including the National Organization of Public Health Nursing, which had been founded in 1912 by none other than Lillian Wald.[26]

In addition to reporting on a greater breadth of nurse services, Goodrich's representation of black labor is markedly different from the VNS's previous filmed depictions of service. In a more than four-minute sequence, an African American caregiver visits a houseboat on the Harlem River. The camera spends considerable time showing the nurse's arduous journey to meet her patient. In a series of five shots, she carefully navigates a rickety walkway and wooden plank to reach her client's floating home. Once inside, she immediately starts working. A black mother passes her infant to the smiling VNS visitor. In the more than two minutes that follow, the nurse cares for the newborn. She warmly wraps the baby in a clean sheet, records its weight, and administers a shot. Close-ups focus on her hands and equipment, while the talking points document draws attention to the information she's been sharing with the mother while weighing and dressing the baby.

While still abiding by VNS policy to serve only members of her own race, this extended sequence—especially compared to the aforementioned films—celebrates the expertise and dedication of a black Henry Street nurse. Shown from a similar range across several shots that emphasize her methodical care, Goodrich visually treats her equally to her white peers. The

FIGURE 2.7. *The Work of the Henry Street Nurse in the City of New York* (Anne Marvin Goodrich, 1933). Visiting Nurse Service of New York Collection, USC Hugh M. Hefner Moving Image Archive.

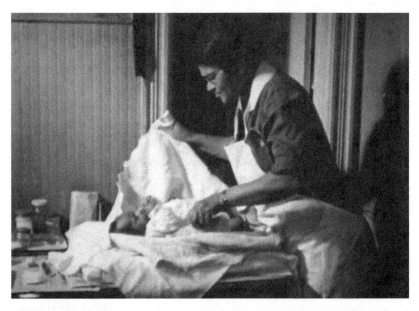

FIGURE 2.8. *The Work of the Henry Street Nurse in the City of New York* (Anne Marvin Goodrich, 1933). Visiting Nurse Service of New York Collection, USC Hugh M. Hefner Moving Image Archive.

script also foregrounds her ability to multitask by telling the lecturer to note "that nurse has been busy discussing with mother baby's diet, health habits, et cetera, during time she has been weighing and dressing baby."[27] This episode is the first time in any VNS work that a filmmaker devotes such attention to black labor. It appears that only when free from fund-raising imperatives can the organization depict the quality of African American and white nurses equally. Thus, while still showing the racial segregation of services, Goodrich's film implicitly makes an argument in line with the organization's promotional ethos: a Henry Street visiting nurse's care is meticulous "regardless of race, color, or creed."

## Conclusion

Paul Monticone observes that the "1920s remain something of a lacuna" within the field of nontheatrical film scholarship, eclipsed by a larger body of work on films from the 1910s and 1930s.[28] Attention to Henry Street's films helps address this historiographical gap by offering a case study in the ways a specific health care organization used moving images to achieve its fund-raising, promotional, and informational goals at a time when systematized welfare initiatives, the professionalization of nursing, and nontheatrical film practice were rapidly becoming institutionalized within American culture.

The visiting nurse films also illustrate the extent to which a philanthropic institution sought to promote and visualize the service of its nonwhite employees. The organization and the filmmakers working on its behalf projected a comparatively inclusionary impulse by showing both white and nonwhite nurses and patients within the same films. At the same time, these images upheld the era's prevailing segregationist social mores by presenting service divided by the color line. In these conflicting tendencies, we see how the service's desire to visually translate its policies to the screen was mediated by efforts to cater to their audiences' attitudes. Such considerations and Henry Street's films reflect the fraught nature of cinematic representation and interwoven dynamics of uplift, reform, and racial and ethnic difference in 1920s and 1930s America.

FILMOGRAPHY

All available films discussed in this chapter can be streamed through the book's web page at https://www.dukeupress.edu/Features/Screening-Race.

*Helping Hands* (1924), 13 min., silent, 35mm (original), 35mm and 16mm (extant prints)

PRODUCTION: Bray Productions, Inc. DIRECTOR/WRITER/CAMERA: Unknown. ACCESS: Hugh M. Hefner Moving Image Archive. SUMMARY: A philanthropist follows two Henry Street nurses on calls through the city and is ultimately persuaded to donate to the organization.

*Untitled/The Visiting Nurse* (1927), 15 min., silent, 35mm (original), 16mm (extant prints)
PRODUCTION: Frank R. Abrams. DIRECTOR/WRITER/CAMERA: Unknown. ACCESS: Hugh M. Hefner Moving Image Archive. SUMMARY: *The Visiting Nurse* explains the mission and scope of the organization's operations. Viewers are privy to expectant mother classes and calls to Chinatown, Little Italy, and Harlem. NOTE: A 1947 VNS inventory memo reports that elements of the film were damaged, resulting in the loss of the title slide and unspecified amounts of footage.

*The Work of the Henry Street Visiting Nurse Service in the City of New York* (1933), 21 min., silent, 35mm (original), 16mm (extant prints)
DIRECTOR/WRITER/CAMERA: Anne Marvin Goodrich. ACCESS: Hugh M. Hefner Moving Image Archive. SUMMARY: The film depicts a series of calls made by visiting nurses across Manhattan, Queens, and the Bronx. NOTE: A three-page talking points document was created to accompany the film.

RELATED FILMS

Three additional films were commissioned by the VNS before it formally split from the Henry Street Settlement in 1944. Henry Street's African American nurses were also filmed by Fox Movietone News.

*Day after Day* (1940), 14 min., partial sound, 35mm (original), 16mm (extant prints)
PRODUCTION: Dial Films, Inc. PRODUCER: Lee Dick. DIRECTOR: Fred Steward. WRITER: Sheldon Dick. CAMERA: Sheldon Dick. EDITORS: Irving Lerner, Peter Mayer. NARRATOR: Storrs Haynes. ACCESS: Hugh M. Hefner Moving Image Archive. SUMMARY: Depicts Henry Street nurses at work throughout the city, with particular emphasis on its expectant mother and infant care classes. NOTE: Only the final few minutes of soundtrack are extant. Footage was reedited into a one-and-a-half-minute fund-raising snipe that ran in city theaters in November and December 1942.

*Keep 'Em Fighting* (1942), 2 min., sound, 16mm
PRODUCTION: Unknown. DIRECTOR/WRITER/EDITOR: Unknown. NARRATION: Elizabeth Phillips. ACCESS: Hugh M. Hefner Moving Image Archive. SUMMARY: This snipe features nurse Elizabeth Phillips just back from special service with the American Red Cross in wartime Britain. The film's explicit title, patriotic music, and its direct linkage between home-front stability and overseas soldiers' morale illustrates a concerted effort on the part of Henry Street to justify its legitimacy amid mass domestic war mobilization. The short incorporates footage from *Day after Day*.

*We Carry On* (1943), 2 min., sound, 16mm
PRODUCTION: Unknown. DIRECTOR/WRITER/EDITOR: Unknown. ACCESS:
Hugh M. Hefner Moving Image Archive. SUMMARY: This fund-raising trailer—
coinciding with the Henry Street Settlement's fiftieth anniversary—demonstrates the
organization's continued efforts to use moving images to bolster their fund-raising
efforts. The film also recycles considerable footage from *Day after Day*.

*MVTN 3-885: Care and Hygiene of Colored Babies* (1929), 6 min., sound, 35mm
PRODUCTION: Fox Movietone News (Outtakes). ACCESS: University of South
Carolina's Moving Image Research Collection. SUMMARY: This sound footage depicts
black nurses demonstrating how to care for and bathe infants; similar dialogue
and actions are repeated and performed in multiple takes. This footage was never
incorporated into a Movietone newsreel.

## NOTES

In 1944, the VNS formally separated from the Henry Street Settlement House and became the Visiting Nurse Service of New York (VNSNY). Both organizations continue
to operate as separate entities today. I wish to thank John Billeci of the VNSNY for
helping me to locate these "lost" films, and Stephen E. Novak, head of Archives and
Special Collections at Columbia University's August C. Long Health Sciences Library,
for his assistance during my many visits.

1   Henry Street Settlement (HSS), *The Visiting Nurse: A New York Institution* (New
    York: Harry Powers Story, 1925). The organization's commitment to serve "re-
    gardless of race, color, or creed" is first among a list of "ten key facts" about the
    organization. Box 200, folder 19, Visiting Nurse Service of New York (VNSNY)
    Collection, Archives and Special Collections, Columbia University Health Sciences
    Library. Similar verbiage is present across promotional materials throughout the
    decade.
2   HSS, "Visiting Nurse Service Administered by Henry Street Settlement," brochure,
    1930, box 201, folder 17, VNSNY Collection. Interest from financial investments and
    fees collected from industrial organizations constitute the remaining 16 percent
    and 33 percent, respectively, of the organization's 1929 income.
3   HSS, "Report of the Visiting Nurse Service for 1923," box 206, folder 3, VNSNY
    Collection.
4   Given the well-established institutional ties between sponsored media produc-
    ers and health and reform organizations by the late 1910s, Henry Street's adoption
    of moving images in 1924 can be viewed as a belated development, particularly
    in New York, an early hub for sponsored film production. For example, Marina
    Dahlquist notes that New York City's Department of Health began holding instruc-
    tional film screenings as early as 1909. Elsewhere, Kirsten Ostherr and Miriam
    Posner have discussed early health films sponsored by the Rockefeller Foundation
    and the National Association for the Study and Prevention of Tuberculosis, respec-
    tively. Jennifer Horne and Gerry K. Veeder have also examined the work of

the Red Cross Film Bureau, active from 1916 to 1922. See Dahlquist's and Horne's essays in Marta Braun, Charles Keil, Rob King, Paul Moore, and Louis Pelletier, eds., *Beyond the Screen: Institutions, Networks and Early Publics of Early Cinema* (London: John Libbey, 2012); Ostherr's essay in Nancy Anderson and Michael R. Dietrich, eds., *The Educated Eye: Visual Culture and Pedagogy in the Life Sciences* (Hanover, NH: Dartmouth College Press, 2012); Miriam Posner's essay in Devin Orgeron, Marsha Orgeron, and Dan Streible, eds., *Learning with the Lights Off: Educational Film in the United States* (New York: Oxford University Press, 2012); and Gerry K. Veeder, "The Red Cross Bureau of Pictures, 1917–1921: World War I, the Russian Revolution and the Sultan of Turkey's Harem," *Historical Journal of Film, Radio and Television* 10, no. 1 (1990): 47–70. In her discussion of early social problem films, Constance Balides also offers an excellent overview of American Progressive Era reform publicity at industrial and civic welfare exhibitions during the 1910s in "Sociological Film, Reform Publicity, and the Secular Spectator: Social Problems in the Transitional Era," *Feminist Media Histories* 3, no. 4 (2017): 10–45.

5   Charles R. Acland and Haidee Wasson, "Introduction: Utility and Cinema," in *Useful Cinema*, ed. Charles R. Acland and Haidee Wasson (Durham, NC: Duke University Press, 2011), 13.

6   See Karen Buhler-Wilkerson, "Bringing Care to the People," *American Journal of Public Health* 83, no. 12 (December 1993): 1778–86; Marjorie N. Feld, *Lillian Wald: A Biography* (Chapel Hill: University of North Carolina Press, 2008); Susan Rita Ruel, "Lillian Wald: A Pioneer of Home Healthcare in the United States," *Home Healthcare Nurse* 32, no. 10 (November/December 2014): 597–600; and Norma G. Silverstein, "Lillian Wald at Henry Street, 1893–1895," *Advances in Nursing Science* 7, no. 2 (January 1985): 1–12.

7   This phrase was included in Wald's address to the NAACP, reprinted in Clare Coss, *Lillian D. Wald: Progressive Activist* (New York: Feminist Press at City University of New York, 1989), 71–73. Lillian D. Wald, *Windows on Henry Street* (Boston: Little, Brown, 1934), 49. In her study of race and nursing, Darlene Clark Hine characterizes Wald as a "staunch friend of black nurses," in *Black Women in White: Racial Conflict and Cooperation in the Nursing Profession, 1890–1950* (Bloomington: Indiana University Press, 1989), 101.

8   HSS, Board of Directors Meeting Minutes, March 25, 1926, and April 7, 1927, box 132, folder 38, VNSNY Collection.

9   Lillian D. Wald, *The House on Henry Street* (New York: Henry Holt, 1915), 8.

10   The title card explicitly identifies the film's two nurses as VNS employees.

11   Balides, "Sociological Film, Reform Publicity, and the Secular Spectator," 15. While Balides focuses on "sociological films," an early iteration of the social problem genre, I find this configuration equally well suited in describing the narrative strategies of Henry Street's fund-raising works, which are similarly indebted to the performative visual cultures of reform she discusses.

12   Allyson Nadia Field, *Uplift Cinema: The Emergence of African American Film and the Possibility of Modernity* (Durham, NC: Duke University Press, 2015), 16–18, 38.

13  Patrick Vonderau, "Touring as a Cultural Technique: Visitor Films and Autostadt Wolfsburg," in *Films That Work: Industrial Film and the Productivity of Media*, ed. Patrick Vonderau and Vinzenz Hediger (Amsterdam: Amsterdam University Press, 2009), 153.

14  HSS, "Publicity Program for Visiting Nurse Campaign, November 1924," box 134, folder 21, VNSNY Collection.

15  HSS, Executive Nursing Committee Meeting Minutes, March 18, 1927, box 135, folder 9, VNSNY Collection. Abrams was president and general manager of the Cameragraph Manufacturing Co. in New York until July 1917. He reemerges in the trade press in 1928–29 with brief notices identifying him as the producer of "fashion reels" for the Garment Retailers of America and a series of twenty-six "song shorts." See *Exhibitors Daily Review*, August 25, 1928, 4; and *Film Daily*, August 4, 1929, 7.

16  The surviving version of this film lacks a title card. I base its title here on text references in contemporary Henry Street memos.

17  These early scenes recycle footage from *Helping Hands*, including one of Alice's home visits. In this film, she is unnamed.

18  Ultimately, this episode is one of less than a handful of Asian representations within VNS promotional materials from this period.

19  Hine's *Black Women in White* recounts the extensive efforts of black nursing professionals and instructors to counter racial stereotypes.

20  A 1947 inventory of the VNS film collection points to the existence of reels with endings directly tailored for Manhattan and Staten Island. It also documents damage to the film's negative and the presence of footage from a board meeting (now lost). Box 29, folder 24, VNSNY Collection.

21  See Field, *Uplift Cinema*.

22  HSS, Board of Directors Meeting Minutes, April 7, 1927, and October 20, 1927, box 132, folders 44, 46, VNSNY Collection.

23  Anne (Marvin) Goodrich Waters, "Sequence of Scenes in Henry Street Movie, with Suggestions for Possible Teaching Points," and letter to Katharine Faville (director of VNS), April 1, 1938, box 183, folder 5, VNSNY Collection. Incidentally, Goodrich shares a surname with Annie Warburton Goodrich, appointed in 1917 to head the VNS and dean of Yale's nursing school during Anne Marvin Goodrich's studies. I have been unable to establish a familial connection between the two.

24  Based on my review of extant Henry Street records, it is unclear who originated the project or how it was funded.

25  This film also has the distinction of being the only one to feature footage of Wald herself, who is shown working at her desk at the very end of the film.

26  Goodrich presented moving images at a gathering of the Wisconsin State Nurses' Association in October 1934, and two of her photographs are featured in an article published by the American Nurses Association four years later. See "News," *American Journal of Nursing* 34, no. 4 (October 1934): 1023; and "For a Square Deal: For Private Duty and General Staff Nurses through Professionally

Organized Effort," *American Journal of Nursing* 38, no. 4, section 2 (April 1938). A professional brochure (circa 1937) advertises Goodrich's services as including custom-shot stills and moving images, exhibition design, and stock photographs. In addition to the Henry Street project, her filmography includes later commissions from organizations including the New York State Nurses' Association, the Children's Aid Society Housekeeper Service, and the Visiting Nurse Association of Plainfield, New Jersey, among others. Box 183, folder 5, VNSNY Collection.

27 Waters, "Sequence of Scenes in Henry Street Movie."

28 Paul Monticone, "'Useful Cinema,' of What Use? Assessing the Role of Motion Pictures in the Largest Public Relations Campaign of the 1920s," *Cinema Journal* 54, no. 4 (summer 2015): 74–99.

# 3

## "I'll See You in Church"

Local Films in African American
Communities, 1924–1962

MARTIN L. JOHNSON

Pictures aren't made in a straight line. We take a little bit of this and a little of that and then it's all looked at and selected and made into a whole. . . .

You mean you piece it together?

That's the idea, I said.

Well tell me something! she said. Isn't that just marvelous? Just like making a scrap quilt, I guess; one of those with all the colors of the rainbow in it—only more complicated. Is that it?

Just about, I said. There has to be a pattern though and we only have black and white.

Well, she said, there's Indians and some of the black is almost white and brown like me.—RALPH ELLISON, *Three Days Before the Shooting*

As the history of cinema in the United States becomes unmoored from the history of Hollywood, familiar lands become foreign countries. From new vantage points, events that were once considered to be minor or inconsequential, such as the showing of movies outside of theaters, are now cause for rethinking how cinema was experienced in the twentieth century. As small-gauge and orphan films resurface, our view of cinema history swish-pans from the few dozen movies produced in Los Angeles and New York every season to the tens of thousands, and at times hundreds of thousands, of motion pictures made every year by amateurs and professionals in the middle decades of the twentieth century. These methodological and historiographic shifts have led to many discoveries and rediscoveries of film practices that have been submerged for decades. The surfacing of a single film or collection of films appears at first as the sui generis work of pioneers and autodidacts, later as a prime example of a broad category of film practice, and finally as something ordinary that has withstood the many adversities—from chemical degradation to historical neglect—motion pictures of all types faced in the twentieth century.

Our understanding of what constitutes African American cinema has expanded as a result of these shifts. Because the classical Hollywood cinema norms that dominated the early decades of film studies resisted addressing movies made by industry outsiders, early scholarship on African American film focused on the ways in which black people were largely misrepresented in film. The rediscovery of Oscar Micheaux's films put forth another thesis, that African Americans created and supported so-called race films that constituted a countercinema to Hollywood. More recently, scholars have advanced a third argument, that African Americans put cinema to many uses, particularly those individuals and social groups who were most invested in racial uplift.[1]

In this chapter, I build on recent work on African American cinema by emphasizing films that celebrate and promote local people and places, which I call local films. Following Julia Hallam, I argue that local films are motion pictures exhibited outside the home that depict and project place, and it is this public engagement with place that distinguishes local films from adjacent genres, such as travelogues and home movies.[2] Local films were shot with the intention of public exhibition, and those who appeared in such films were often encouraged to see themselves, as well images of their community, on screen.

One of the earliest sites of nontheatrical film exhibition were religious institutions. African American churches were early adopters of motion pictures, particularly in communities where segregation ensured that many movie theaters were restricted to white audiences.[3] What follows focuses on three prominent African American religious leaders—Solomon Sir Jones in Muskogee, Oklahoma; Lonzie Odie Taylor in Memphis, Tennessee; and Bishop Richard Robert Wright in Philadelphia and South Africa—who used film to capture the lives of their congregants and document church activities, including missionary work and visits to national conventions. Although these films are now held by archives, for much of the twentieth century they were in private collections, inaccessible to and therefore unacknowledged by historians of African American or nontheatrical cinema. Shot in 16mm, a gauge that has long thought to have been the domain of a largely white, upper-class elite, particularly in the 1920s and 1930s, the films offered African Americans the opportunity to see themselves in their own communities.[4]

As Judith Weisenfeld has documented, African American religious life was of significant interest within and outside the black community in the 1920s and 1930s.[5] Anthropologists, sociologists, and commercial movie producers all created work that sought to capture experiences of African American religiosity. However, much of this work was primarily interested in the rituals and traditions of church life, not in documenting the lives of the members themselves. Within church communities, films were primarily used in three ways: to educate and inspire church members about prominent issues, to document the activities of church members and their supporters, and to allow people who attended church regularly to see themselves on screen. These case studies, then, are more than just revelations of the diversity of moving image production in African American church communities in the 1920s and 1930s. They are also an affirmation of the importance of motion pictures to African Americans, even when Hollywood had little to offer them.

## Solomon Sir Jones: The Little Baptist Giant

Solomon Sir Jones, or Dr. S. S. Jones, as he was identified most frequently in newspapers, was born in Tennessee and grew up in Memphis. In 1889, Jones volunteered to go to Oklahoma as a missionary from the American Baptist Home Missionary Society. Over the next twenty-three years, he established churches in five cities, including Muskogee, where he settled and became editor of his church's state newspaper, the *Baptist Informer*, earning the sobriquet "Little Baptist Giant" from one black newspaper.[6] By the early 1920s, Jones was one of the best-known religious leaders in Oklahoma, which was in turn a prominent center for black people in the West, and known for its all-black towns where African Americans were, for a time, able to start businesses, churches, schools, and other institutions without encountering prejudice and racist laws in effect elsewhere. In fact, it was Jones's high profile in Oklahoma, not a sudden interest in moving pictures, that likely led to his short-lived but significant foray as a filmmaker.

When Jones acquired his 16mm motion picture camera in late 1924, he was about to embark on a great adventure. A year prior, Jones had entered a contest run by the beauty products behemoth Madam C. J. Walker Manufacturing Company, which was now in the hands of Walker's daughter, A'Lelia. As Kathy Peiss has noted, African American beauty products, particularly those intended to reinforce European beauty standards such as straight hair and light skin, were critiqued by many in the black press. At the same time,

FIGURE 3.1. Flier promoting S. S. Jones farewell meeting in December 1924. Collection of the Smithsonian National Museum of African American History and Culture, gift of Naomi Long Madgett.

Now Comes Farewell Meeting!
Antioch Baptist Church, Muskogee
Friday Night, December 19th
*complimentary to*

DR. S. S. JONES

The Business Pastor,
Soul-Winner,

Leader and
Race-Builder

*He has given the people of Oklahoma and the nation 36 years of solid service. To say he has succeeded is putting it very mildly. The greatest achievement of a successful career is now crowned with a*

Trip to the Holy Land, including England, France, Switzerland, Italy, Egypt and Abyssinia

*In Palestine Dr. Jones will visit Jerusalem, Mt. of Olives, Jericho, Dead Sea, River Jordan, Bethlehem, Nazareth, Tiberias, Semakh, Haifa, and hundreds of other places in many countries*

The general public, without regard to denominational or fraternal affiliation is cordially invited. Come, hear a word and say a word. A splendid program is being arranged
Any final gift for Dr. Jones or his family will be highly appreciated

*Farewell!    Farewell!    Farewell!*

Rain or shine this is the last for a season
*Circulars and arrangements by special order of friends*

companies like that of Madam Walker were among their most loyal advertisers. Under A'Lelia Walker's leadership, the company sought to build its image among African American leaders.[7]

One of Walker's most high-profile efforts was the Trip to the Holy Land contest, apparently inspired by her own travels to Palestine. The contest was launched in early 1923, with advertisements placed in black publications nationwide. In March 1923, the *Dallas Express* ran a full-page advertisement which noted that the contest was intended to give any "Bishop, Presiding Elder, Pastor, or general office of any religious denomination" an opportunity to visit Palestine or, as it was commonly referred to in the 1920s, the Holy Land.[8] Candidate nominations were accepted until July 1, 1923, and people could vote, using coupons inserted into the packaging of Madam Walker's beauty products, until the following July. By the time the contest commenced, 358 men of the cloth—by the terms of the contest, women were

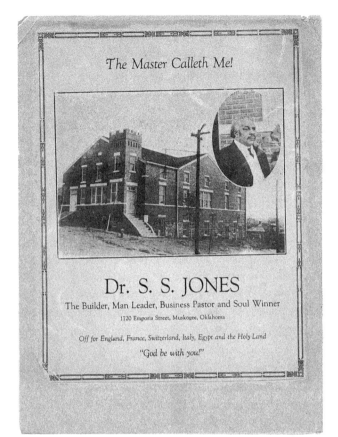

The Master Calleth Me!

Dr. S. S. JONES

The Builder, Man Leader, Business Pastor and Soul Winner

1720 Emporia Street, Muskogee, Oklahoma

*Off for England, France, Switzerland, Italy, Egypt and the Holy Land*

"God be with you!"

FIGURE 3.2. Flier advertising S. S. Jones farewell meeting in December 1924. Collection of the Smithsonian National Museum of African American History and Culture, gift of Naomi Long Madgett.

not invited to participate—had joined in the race for votes.[9] As intended, the contest quickly turned into a battle pitting regions (the mid-Atlantic, the South, the Midwest, and the West) and religions (Baptist, African Methodist Episcopal [AME], and the United Holiness church) against one another. Vote totals were regularly reported by black newspapers, and Walker's ads encouraged church organizations to lobby for their favored candidate.

Although Jones's campaign started slowly, by late 1923 he had caught up with the front-runners and was soon the only Westerner in the running. In July 1924, the contest concluded, with Jones winning third place. While he just missed winning a cash prize, he was still given a free trip to Europe and the Middle East, along with ministers from Washington, DC, Atlanta, and Cincinnati.[10] The four ministers boarded the S.S. *Paris* in January 1925 for an eight-week trip that took them through Europe—England, France, Switzerland, and Italy—before heading to Egypt and Palestine. The group also visited World War I battlefields. *The Messenger* wrote, "[The] clergy-men intend to take photographs and moving pictures of what they see on this eventful trip. These will be used in a series of lectures they will deliver upon their return."[11] The trip itself received considerable coverage in black newspapers, perhaps because Madam Walker was a prominent advertiser, with articles written before the group embarked and again on their return.

In promoting their second contest, this time offering winners a journey around the world, representatives of the Walker company noted that Jones had made good use of the films he took during the first contest: "When the Madam Walker Company announced its Trip to the Holy Land Contest, there were many skeptical people and many criticisms, but when the four contesting ministers made the trip and their pictures appeared in our col-ored weeklies and da[i]lies, embarking on the palatial Steamship Paris for this world renowned trip, crit[i]cism changed to praise. Rev. S.S. Jones of Muskogee, Oklahoma, is now covering the country giving special lectures on the countries he visited on this remarkable trip."[12] Jones gave travel lectures throughout the Midwest, where he presented a selection of the 200 photo-graphs and 60,800 motion pictures—he presumably counted every frame—he took in his travels.[13] A flyer from mid-April 1925, just a month after Jones returned from his trip, promised audiences in St. Louis "A Burning Message for All which cost thousands of dollars and almost life itself to get!"[14] In late May, he screened his travel pictures at Langston University in Oklahoma. While there, he also filmed the university's graduation ceremony, and soon after began making his local films on a regular basis, shooting eleven more reels of film in the remainder of the year.[15]

When the Solomon Sir Jones collection was acquired by Yale University in 2009, it was lauded as a rare, early collection of African American local films, mostly produced in small towns in Oklahoma.[16] But the twenty-nine-reel collection contains four reels of film that were taken during Jones's trip to Europe and the Middle East, and another eight reels that feature footage taken in other states. In addition to the Holy Land pictures, several other reels appear to have been edited for exhibition, including two that incorpo-rate footage from a commercial 16mm production, Bell and Howell's Ad-venture Series, and others that seek to draw relationships between similar events. For example, in one reel, Jones films a photograph of the devastation caused by the 1921 Tulsa race riot, in which whites burned thirty-five city blocks of the prosperous Greenwood District, while a moving image depicts the neighborhood several years later.

FIGURE 3.3. Flier promoting sermon and film screening by S. S. Jones at the Union Memorial Church in St. Louis, Missouri, 1925. Madam C. J. Walker Collection, Indiana Historical Society.

Instead of using title cards, Jones filmed a bulletin board with push-pin letters, which he changed to identify people and places and, in many cases, also date when footage was taken. The first films in the collection appear to be from December 1924, when Jones films himself and his church in Muskogee. The Holy Land images are undated, perhaps because Jones knew that he wanted to screen them over a number of years. The presence of the two Bell and Howell films in the collection, in addition to the fact that Jones began shooting in late 1924, before Kodak had a spring-wound automatic camera, suggests that Jones used Bell and Howell's Filmo camera, introduced in 1923.

Aside from his films in his church communities, Muskogee and Okmulgee, Jones seemed primarily interested in organizational activities—Baptist conventions, business meetings, and the like—or events, such as church construction, that would draw broad interest. For example, when Jones visited Boley, Oklahoma, to film a drill performance by the Camp Fire Girls and Military Boys, one paper noted that he "was present with the great addition to the race[']s progress his moving picture machine."[17] The camera's role was not merely recording events for the benefit of those who participated in them. Rather, the events he filmed were intended to be public, shown by Jones to other audiences.

It's not clear why Jones stopped making moving pictures in 1928, as he continued to tour with Holy Land movies until at least 1929, and possibly longer.[18] In March 1929, he went to St. Mary's Baptist Church in Wichita, Kansas, to show what the *Negro Star* called the "most interesting Biblical pictures that have ever been in the city of Wichita," part of a tour in Kansas that also included a stop in Topeka.[19] He continued to officiate funerals in the early 1930s and died in 1936, at the age of sixty-seven. Although Jones was an active filmmaker and exhibitor for just four years, in this period he managed to use motion pictures to enhance his reputation as a nationally prominent religious leader and businessman.

## Taylor-Made Motion Pictures

While Jones was an active filmmaker and exhibitor for just a few years, the Reverend L. O. Taylor built his career as a minister and a photographer-filmmaker in tandem. In 1931, he became pastor of the Olivet Baptist church, a new institution in Memphis's Orange Mound community, a suburban neighborhood established in the 1890s by African Americans.[20] According to a history of Orange Mound, in 1937 Taylor led an expansion of the church, including adding an auditorium, and remained pastor until 1956.[21] Although Taylor's photography, and later filmmaking, was initially separate from his church activities, he quickly integrated movies into a repertoire of creative expression—poems, essays, and sound recordings—that marked his unique place in the Memphis community.[22]

In 1977, Taylor's films and photographs were donated by his widow to the Center for Southern Folklore in Memphis.[23] In 1989, the experimental filmmaker Lynne Sachs, a Memphis native, made a documentary on Taylor titled *Sermons and Sacred Pictures*, long before historians were interested in nontheatrical film. More recently, a selection of Taylor's films have been digitized and placed online, but only on a commercial stock footage site.[24] Although an experimental documentary and a stock footage site appear at first not to have much in common, both are as interested in using Taylor's films in service of other narratives as they are in the films themselves.

For example, in *Sermons and Sacred Pictures*, Sachs uses Taylor's footage and sound recordings, interviews with his former parishioners, and her own footage of a screening of Taylor's films to re-create Taylor's role in the Memphis black community in the mid-twentieth century. Footage taken from a train, for example, is set against the audio from an interview in which someone recounts the experience of African Americans riding trains in the segregation era. While many documentaries pair primary source documents with newly recorded witness testimony, the fact that Sachs's subject is a filmmaker means that such a tactic effectively undermines an assessment of Taylor's own film practice. These early sections of the documentary, which set out to re-create the atmosphere of African American life in Memphis in the 1930s and 1940s, treat Taylor's practice as an archival one, which gains meaning only when the filmmaker situates it within contexts, such as the civil rights movement. Historic Films, the stock footage site where Taylor's films can now be viewed, repeats this logic, making these films no different than home movies or newsreels.

Rather than evaluating Taylor's films on their own merits, Sachs implicitly argues that Taylor's filmmaking activities are best understood as performance. Interviews with people who appeared in, and saw, Taylor's films in *Sermons* serve to emphasize the insularity of his productions, as if they were made only for an audience who expected to see themselves on screen. Early in the film, Sachs even reproduces the exhibition experience of Taylor's film, filming an audience in a nontheatrical space watching Taylor's films, with both the 16mm projector and the screen visible in the frame, and audio of a murmuring crowd on the soundtrack, as if people were responding to seeing friends on screen. As one unidentified interview subject says of Taylor, "he would take pictures, and edit them together, and make a presentation out of them." By emphasizing the experiential qualities of Taylor's films, Sachs's documentary embeds them within communities of viewers, who in turn saw them through their own limited perspectives on Taylor's entire body of work.

Although the website Historic Films is intended to be used by documentary producers in need of footage, its collection of Taylor's films retains the original organization of the films, so it is possible to view them as completed reels rather than just fragments. Taylor modeled his film practice on contemporary documentary practices, particularly the newsreel. In one of the title cards he made for his films, he suggests that a "Taylor Made Picture" is "bringing you news and historical records," revealing an intention to keep these films after they were shown to local audiences.

In fact, from the extant films it is clear that Taylor saw his role as a recorder of the African American experience. Title cards such as "The Negro in Business" and "The Negro in Church Life" encouraged audiences to think of the films, even when they were of their own community, as representative of much broader experiences. For example, a 1940 *Church Life* installment includes a scene depicting a river baptism with a striking intimacy. The opening shot of the film is framed to include the baptisms in the lower right of the screen and the crowd of onlookers on the riverbank in the top half of the frame. In this way, the film both witnesses the baptism and depicts others who witnessed it. This shot is followed by several shots of the congregation and finally a close-up of one of the baptisms. While the people in the shot are aware of the camera's presence, this is not a performance for the camera, but rather documentation of an ordinary event. In this way, Taylor's work echoes that of contemporary black filmmakers such as Spencer Williams, whose documentary style filming of a baptism scene in *The Blood of Jesus* (1941) serves to bring legitimacy and reverence to African American religious practices.

If Jones demonstrated the usefulness of motion pictures in church work, Taylor showed that it was possible to build an enterprise of local film production. Rather than just using scenes of local people to get them to see themselves in the movies, Taylor sought to make the experiences that marked their daily lives significant, and integrated them with other news events, such as a 1939 stop by the black gospel radio performers Wings Over Jordan, to accentuate the significance of his practice. Taylor's films of the meeting of the National Baptist Convention were also popular, though it is unclear whether these films were intended to be shown at the conventions themselves or to church members back home who wanted to see what went on in the meetings of the oldest, and one of the largest, African American organizations in the United States. Taylor continued making pictures throughout the 1940s and 1950s, creating along the way a cinematic record of the African American experience in Memphis.

## Film as Missionary Work: Bishop Richard Robert Wright in Philadelphia

Religious leaders often used their films to connect people living in different places. For example, Jones's travel films were shown alongside his local films of towns and church communities throughout the Midwest. Taylor, on the other hand, only screened movies in Memphis, but he often filmed people and places far from the banks of the Mississippi, presumably to be shown back home. Bishop Richard Robert Wright Jr. was also tied to local church communities in Philadelphia, but rather than train his camera on church members at home, he produced films during his time as a missionary in South Africa. While these films may have been screened in the places where they were made, such as the AME's mission projects in South Africa, they appear to have been primarily produced for exhibition back in the United States, occasionally to audiences who would recognize their friends and neighbors who were doing service work overseas.

Although Wright was born and educated in Georgia, as a young adult he migrated to Philadelphia, where he earned a PhD in sociology at the University of Pennsylvania. He very quickly became involved in Progressive politics and, particularly, the Social Gospel movement, with a focus on the challenges faced by black southern migrants in the north. In 1909, he was appointed editor of the AME's newspaper, the *Christian Recorder*, a position he held until 1928, when he became a pastor. In 1932, he was appointed president of Wilberforce University in Ohio, which was affiliated with the AME church. In 1936, he was elected bishop of the AME church and, in keeping with standard practice, was sent on an overseas mission for his first four-year term, arriving in Capetown on November 30 of that year.

In his autobiography, Wright does not mention his filmmaking during this period, but in scrapbooks he kept of his time in South Africa he includes a receipt for the purchase of a hundred-foot roll of Kodak film, dated October 11, 1937.[25] Like Jones, Wright became a filmmaker later in life, shooting his first film at the age of fifty-nine. In his papers, which were donated to Temple University by Wright's daughter, Ruth Wright Hayre, there are five 16mm reels, one of which is an edited film, including intertitles, of Wright's missionary work in South Africa. In February 1938, Wright returned to the United States after a serious medical issue and sought treatment at the Flint-Goodridge hospital in New Orleans.[26]

In March 1938, Wright screened his motion pictures in New Orleans, most likely to a church audience.[27] While in the city, he also sat for a portrait by Arthur P. Bedou, a studio photographer who was best known for his work with Booker T. Washington. In a letter, Bedou calls Wright's movies "bea[u]tiful," expressing hopes that "when you . . . return . . . you will bring a new set."[28] While it is not clear which films were screened by Wright, two reels in the collection were made during this period and were likely to have been seen in the Crescent City that spring. While in the United States, Wright also screened

FIGURE 3.4. Receipt
from Bishop Richard
Robert Wright's pur-
chase of 16mm film
in 1937 in Cape Town,
South Africa. Cour-
tesy of Ruth Wright
Hayre Collection,
Charles L. Block-
son Afro-American
Collection, Temple
University Libraries.

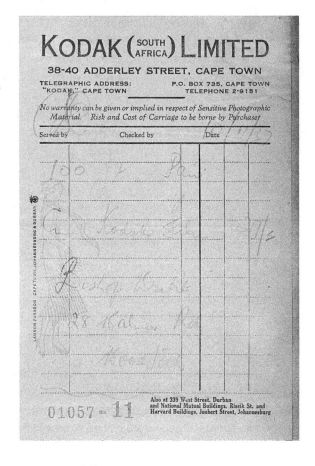

films in St. Louis, Kansas City, and other cities, most likely in AME churches rather than movie theaters.[29]

The reel opens with an intertitle: "Bishop Wright presents some views of his travels with Mrs. Wright in South Africa during 1936, 1937 and 1938 in connection with his supervision of the Fifteenth Episcopal District of the African Methodist Episcopal Church." By placing his travels within his evangelical work, Wright allows for the picture to be read either as depictions of a distant place or as records of works that were likely funded by church members in the U.S.

The early scenes in the film are arranged in chronological order, starting with shots of the countryside followed by those of a train. The next intertitle reads, "First New Year's Day in South Africa: 'Coons.'" As the following shots confirm, the footage is of Cape Town's annual Kaapse Klopse, or "Coons," minstrel festival, celebrated by South Africa's Cape Coloureds. The South

African appropriation of the slur "coons" was startling enough to Wright for him to report its usage to newspapers in the United States.[30] Subsequent shots depict other important geographical and cultural sites for Wright's audience of U.S.-based church members, including tourist attractions and church gatherings. While this footage could be read as part of a travelogue, like Jones's films of his travels in Europe and the Middle East, the fact that Wright was screening these films to AME church members, many of whom likely lent financial support to the South Africa mission or, in some cases, knew people who were doing missionary work there, made them more intimate affairs than they appear to be.

One particularly important scene comes midway through the reel, introduced by a title card that reads "Wilberforce Institute, 1000 miles north of Capetown." The institute was established by the AME church in 1908 and received almost all of its funding from AME churches in the United States. The opening shot is a 360-degree pan of a flat, barren landscape pocked with brick and stone buildings. In a subsequent shot, which appears to be slow-cranked in order to produce the illusion of frenetic activity, people clear land for the presumed construction of additional buildings. In the next shot, some of the same individuals are lined up, carrying out what appear to be military exercises. As with much of Wright's footage, these scenes can be read both as signs of progress and a demonstration of the needs of a distant community, linked by AME's ongoing relationship with South Africa.

In December 1938, Wright and a small entourage traveled to Swaziland, where he was to meet King Sobhuza II, the country's monarch, a trip that had been planned for almost two years.[31] While he does not appear to have documented this visit with his camera, in his memoirs he recalls that one of his traveling companions, Lucy Hughes, then president of the AME's Women's Home and Foreign Missionary Society, brought a camera along: "He [King Sobhuza II] came out of his office and welcomed us: my wife, Dr. and Mrs. White, Mrs. Hughes, and about a half dozen others in our party. Mrs. Hughes lifted her camera to take a motion picture of the group with the kraal in the background. As soon as she had finished her picture, King Sobhuza II raised his hand and said, 'Excuse me,' entered his office and returned with his own motion picture camera. He took views of us, one of which included me taking a picture of the king and his kraal."[32] Unlike those of Taylor and Jones, the movies were not an essential tool in Wright's ministry, and later footage, taken in Haiti, St. Thomas, and the Virgin Islands, among other places, does not appear to have been prepared for widespread exhibition. At the same time, in this anecdote Wright reveals a world in

Wilberforce Institute,
1000 miles north
of Capetown

FIGURES 3.5–3.7. Frame enlargements from Bishop Richard Robert Wright's films of South Africa, 1937–38. The Wilberforce Institute, in South Africa, was established by the U.S.-based African Methodist Episcopal church in 1908. Courtesy of the Charles L. Blockson Afro-American Collection, Temple University Libraries.

which the movies were commonplace, at least among a certain social stratum, and carried with them a democratic potential. In fact, Wright's father, Major Richard R. Wright, made his own movie debut a few years later, encouraging African Americans to support World War II in Jack Goldberg's 1943 film *We've Come a Long, Long Way.*[33]

## Archives and the Local Film

In Ralph Ellison's unfinished second novel, published in its fullest form in 2010 as *Three Days Before the Shooting*, he depicts a character named Mister Movie-Man, one of a trio of itinerant filmmakers who seek to take advantage of gullible movie-struck individuals in small towns in the South. Although it is unlikely that Ellison, who grew up in Oklahoma City, encountered S. S. Jones as a young man, Ellison's creation of this character—one of the few itinerant filmmakers depicted in fiction—seems to be based on an experience from his youth, when such flim-flam men were commonplace. In fact, in the 2002 documentary *Ralph Ellison: An American Journey*, Jones's footage is used to connote the experience of growing up in Oklahoma.

The scenes in Ellison's unfinished novel suggest a world of African American film production that is only now coming into fuller view, even though Ellison's manuscript, like the reels discussed in this essay, have been known to researchers for many years. In fact, this rhetoric of loss haunts many discussions of films made by African Americans, even when the films themselves were not lost. The local films discussed in this chapter were not for contemporary audiences alone. Rather, filmmakers took care to document these places, recording and identifying them for future generations. For example, all three filmmakers used title cards to identify the date and place of each shot, even though most itinerant filmmakers seldom took the trouble of doing so. If we place too much emphasis on their lost status, we risk losing a sense of why they were made in the first place. By resisting the urge to read these films as merely artifacts, we may open up larger questions about the African American experience of cinema in the early decades of the twentieth century.

For example, the rediscovery in 2009 of the Solomon Sir Jones films, which were acquired by Yale's Beinecke Rare Book and Manuscript Library, has been discussed as a significant find, with Currie Ballard, who purchased the films and brought them to auction in New York, giving interviews on his role in making the collection more widely known. However, as early as 1998, the writer and historian Ann Eskridge claimed that she discovered the films and exhibited them at the Henry Ford Museum in Detroit, and even incorporated them into a documentary, *Echoes across the Prairie: The Vanishing Black West*, that she made that year.[34] In fact, there were two collections of Jones's films. The larger collection, which was acquired by Ballard, contains films made for public exhibition. But Jones's home movies were given to a family friend, Clarence Long, whose sister, Naomi Long Madgett, is a prominent African American poet and publisher. In her 2006 autobiography, Madgett wrote about her early encounters with Jones, noting that he "had the vision to know that black life in Oklahoma, including the all-black towns, was important to record."[35] While these films were not in an archive until recently, they were visible enough to be mined as archival footage for other projects. In 2011, Madgett donated nine 400-foot reels shot by Jones to the National Museum of African American Culture and History, which digitized them in 2015.[36]

Likewise, L. O. Taylor's films have been known to researchers for some time, but they have not been the subject of scholarship, a situation that might change with their recent digitization. When Sachs's documentary was released in 1989, there were comparatively few published studies of nontheatrical or small-gauge film, which made the Taylor collection appear to be more of an outlier than has later turned out to be the case. Finally, although the Wright collection is smaller, his films of South Africa are not mentioned in histories of the AME church, even though they provide valuable insight into the cultural and social exchange between these church communities in the United States and South Africa in the 1930s. The visibility of African American experiences in these three collections is masked by an invisibility of the films themselves, which is itself a consequence of how these films are archived and described. While films in all three of these collections could be described merely as home movies, the fact that they were exhibited in public settings makes them more than private documentation of the past. Rather, these films can be seen as akin to work of other African American filmmakers, from George Broome to William Foster, who sought to use the cinema as a tool of racial uplift.[37]

In this chapter, I have discussed the work of three ministers who filmed church communities, and made films for these communities, in the first half of the twentieth century. While there is a strong temptation, guided by the valuation placed on the rare, the unique, and the aesthetically significant, to read such films as exemplary, I think the opposite reading, as commonplace and ordinary, is more warranted. By claiming that films like those I have discussed in this chapter were a common mode of African American motion picture production in the 1920s and 1930s, debates about the propriety of either negative stereotypes perpetuated in Hollywood films, or the countercinema of Oscar Micheaux and Spencer Williams, become less important than the fact that many African Americans were able to see moving images of themselves in institutions that they created and sustained.

To put my argument in more expansive terms, the median film in 1935, in terms of what was produced, and perhaps also what was seen, was not a B Western, but a home movie, an educational film, or a local film, like those made by the three filmmakers discussed in this chapter. By situating these films in their own time, as images that sought to capture, share, and archive African American places and people, it becomes possible to see them for what they were—local films of black life, made by individuals who were determined to document experiences that no one else would.

## FILMOGRAPHY

All available films discussed in this chapter can be streamed through the book's web page at https://www.dukeupress.edu/Features/Screening-Race.

Solomon Sir Jones, 1924–28. Beinecke Rare Book and Manuscript Library, Yale University. Twenty-nine reels of black-and-white 16mm film.

Rev. S. S. Jones Home Movies. Collection of the Smithsonian National Museum of African American History and Culture, Washington, DC. Gift of Naomi Long Madgett. Nine reels of black-and-white 16mm film.

Reverend L. O. Taylor Collection, 1936–54. Center for Southern Folklore, Memphis, Tennessee. Black-and-white and color 16mm film.

Ruth Wright Hayre Collection. Charles L. Blockson Afro-American Collection, Temple University. Five reels of black-and-white and color 16mm film.

## NOTES

1  While there is not space to review even a small portion of the relevant literature, key texts include Donald Bogle, *Toms, Coons, Mulattoes, Mammies, and Bucks: An Interpretive History of Blacks in American Films* (New York: Viking, 1973), now in its fifth edition; Pearl Bowser, Jane Gaines, and Charles Musser, *Oscar Micheaux and His Circle: African-American Filmmaking and Race Cinema of the Silent Era* (Bloomington: Indiana University Press, 2001), which has been reprinted. The third generation of scholarship begins with Jacqueline Najuma Stewart, *Migrating to the Movies: Cinema and Black Urban Modernity* (Berkeley: University of California Press, 2005); and continues with Cara Caddoo, *Envisioning Freedom: Cinema and the Building of Modern Black Life* (Cambridge, MA: Harvard University Press, 2014); and Allyson Nadia Field, *Uplift Cinema: The Emergence of African American Film and the Possibility of Black Modernity* (Durham, NC: Duke University Press, 2015).

2   Julia Hallam, "Film, Space and Place: Researching a City in Film," *New Review of Film and Television Studies* 8, no. 3 (2010): 277–96. For more on local films, see Martin L. Johnson, *Main Street Movies: A History of Local Film in the United States* (Bloomington: Indiana University Press, 2018).

3   See Caddoo, *Envisioning Freedom*, which discusses the use of films in African American churches before 1920.

4   For example, see Charles Tepperman, *Amateur Cinema: The Rise of North American Moviemaking, 1923–1960* (Berkeley: University of California Press, 2014), 37. While Tepperman does mention Eloyce Gist, whose 16mm films made in the late 1920s and early 1930s are well known, in a footnote, his reliance on the amateur trade press leads him to exclude accounts of African American film-making. Archivist Jasmyn Castro has established the African American Home Movie Archive (http://aahma.org), which includes a database of films produced by African American families, held by archives throughout the United States. See chapter 18 in this volume.

5   Judith Weisenfeld, *Hollywood Be Thy Name: African American Religion in American Film, 1929–1949* (Berkeley: University of California Press, 2007).

6   "Muskogee and Okmulgee Contend for Rev. Jones," *Tulsa Star*, March 27, 1920, 5.

7   Kathy Peiss, *Hope in a Jar: The Making of America's Beauty Culture* (Philadelphia: University of Pennsylvania Press, 2011), 209–10.

8   Advertisement, *Dallas Express*, March 31, 1923, 1.

9   "Bishop Fountain Leads in Mme. Walker's Holy Land Contest," *Dallas Express*, October 13, 1923, 1.

10  Advertisement, *Pittsburgh Courier*, August 2, 1924, 8.

11  "Industry and Business," *The Messenger*, February 1925, 112.

12  "Capetown to Be Visited by Walker Tourists on Trip around the World," *Pittsburgh Courier*, June 5, 1926, 7.

13  "Dr. S.S. Jones at Antioch Baptist," *Decatur Review*, July 22, 1927, 28.

14  Flyer, Madam C. J. Walker Papers, box 12, folder 22: Around the World and Holy Land contests, 1920s, Indiana Historical Society.

15  "Langston, Okla.," *Topeka Plaindealer*, May 29, 1925, 2.

16  See Eve M. Kahn, "Tracking the Progress of Some Special Items over the Past Year," *New York Times*, December 17, 2009, C33.

17  "Boley News," *Topeka Plaindealer*, September 18, 1925, 2.

18  The Smithsonian has acquired Jones's home movies, which were made between 1925 and 1931.

19  "St. Mary Bapt. Church," *Negro Star* (Wichita, Kansas), March 22, 1929, 3. See also "Topeka News Notes," *Negro Star*, April 12, 1929, 3.

20  Jones filmed several businesses in the Orange Mound community in 1926, though it's unclear whether he encountered Taylor during this period.

21  Carroll Van West and Laura Nickas, "Lonzie Odie (L. O.) Taylor and Taylor-Made Pictures (c. 1889)," *Tennessee Encyclopedia of History and Culture*, March 1, 2018, http://tennesseeencyclopedia.net/entry.php?rec=1674. For more on the church's history see Charles Williams, *African American Life and Culture in Orange*

*Mound: Case Study of a Black Community in Memphis, Tennessee, 1890–1980* (Lanham, MD: Lexington, 2013), 70–72.

22  Miriam DeCosta-Willis, *Notable Black Memphians* (Amherst, NY: Cambria, 2008), 300.

23  Andria Lisle, "Black and White: Three Photo Exhibits Bring the Long-Hidden World of Segregated Memphis to Life," *Memphis Flyer*, February 17, 2006.

24  In 2007, the Center for Southern Folklore received a $210,951 matching grant from the National Endowment for the Humanities to archive and preserve Taylor's photographs, film, and vinyl records. This preservation work has been completed, but due to staffing and space limitations the collection is not yet fully accessible to researchers. Digitized and watermarked copies of some of the films can be viewed on the stock footage site Historic Films (http://www.historicfilms .com).

25  Richard Robert Wright, "Receipt from Kodak, film, Oct 1937," in Scrapbooks, box 1, MS009, series II: Publications, Ruth Wright Hayre Collection, Charles L. Block-son Afro-American Collection, Temple University.

26  Richard Robert Wright, *87 Years behind the Black Curtain: An Autobiography* (Philadelphia: Rare Book Company, 1965), 244.

27  Arthur Bedou to Bishop R. R. Wright, March 19, 1938, Ruth Wright Hayre Collection. In a history of the National Urban League, Donald E. DeVore notes that Wright appeared at an organizing meeting for the league at St. Mark Fourth Baptist Church on March 6, 1938. See Donald E. DeVore, *Defying Jim Crow: African American Community Development and the Struggle for Racial Equality in New Orleans, 1900–1960* (Baton Rouge: Louisiana State University Press, 2015), 117.

28  Bedou to Wright, March 19, 1938.

29  Clippings, March 25, 1938, Ruth Wright Hayre Collection. Isabel M. Thompson, "Covering the Kansas Cities," *Pittsburgh Courier*, April 6, 1938, 22. According to the *Courier*, Wright also made stops in Washington, DC, Atlanta, Montgomery, Chicago, and Philadelphia and at Wilberforce University in Ohio, though it's not clear whether he screened his motion pictures in each city. See "Bishop Wright, Wife Return from Field," *Pittsburgh Courier*, April 30, 1938, 19. He also screened movies in York, Pennsylvania. See "Bishop Wright Will Speak to Yorkers," *Gazette and Daily*, June 24, 1939, 5. In York, Wright screened his films at an AME church, and it is likely that AME churches hosted his screenings in other communities.

30  "South Africans Call Selves 'Coons,'" *New York Age*, February 13, 1937, 2. In the article, Wright compares the festival to the Mummers Parade in Philadelphia, and Mardi Gras in New Orleans.

31  "Bishop Wright and Wife Welcomed at South Africa Post," *The Gazette* (Xenia, Ohio), December 21, 1936, 6. See also "Bishop Wright Commended by African King," *Pittsburgh Courier*, December 24, 1938, 19.

32  Wright, *87 Years behind the Black Curtain*, 250.

33  Weisenfeld, *Hollywood Be Thy Name*, 190.

34  Laraye Brown, "Exhibitions Focusing on Black History," *Toledo Blade*, February 15, 1998, G8.

35   Naomi Long Madgett, *Pilgrim Journey* (Detroit: Lotus, 2006), 16.

36   These films are now available on DVD: Richard Norman, Richard Maurice, Spencer Williams, and Oscar Micheaux, dirs., *Pioneers of African-American Cinema* (Kino Lorber, 2015).

37   For example, see Field's discussion of William Foster's "Smile" films made during World War I so African American soldiers stationed overseas could see their loved ones back home: Allyson Nadia Field, "The Ambitions of William Foster: Entrepreneurial Filmmaking at the Limits of Uplift Cinema," in *Early Race Filmmaking in America*, ed. Barbara Tepa Lupack (New York: Routledge, 2016), 62–65.

# 4

## The Politics of Vanishing Celluloid

*Fort Rupert* (1951) and the Kwakwa̱ka̱'wakw
in American Ethnographic Film

COLIN WILLIAMSON

American anthropological filmmaker Robert Gardner is widely known for beginning his career in 1951 with two films: *Blunden Harbour* and *Dances of the Kwakiutl*.[1] Both films focus on First Nations people in British Columbia known collectively as the Kwakwa̱ka̱'wakw.[2] Additionally, both films are usually discussed in the context of the emergence of ethnographic filmmaking as a serious anthropological practice in the United States during the 1950s. Around 1951, Gardner's Seattle-based production company, Orbit Films, was also associated with a mysterious third project undertaken by American avant-garde artists Sidney Peterson and Hy Hirsh. The group collected footage of Kwakwa̱ka̱'wakw ceremonial practices that were assumed to be either lost or fading. The assumption has roots in a late nineteenth-century project known as salvage anthropology, which was concerned with studying and reconstructing native cultures before they vanished with the spread of white civilization.[3] Some of the footage from the encounter between the Kwakwa̱ka̱'wakw and the filmmakers was edited into a 16mm color film that combined performances of traditional songs, dances, and rituals with images of contemporary life in a coastal community on Vancouver Island known as Fort Rupert (Tsa̱xis). The film, *Fort Rupert*, was an experiment in exploring the relationship between cultural preservation, visual ethnography, and art.

Little is known about the circulation and reception of *Fort Rupert*, and almost nothing has been written about its place in the history of American nontheatrical film, because shortly after the film was made it seems to have vanished. In his book on American ethnographic film, film scholar Scott MacDonald notes that Gardner and Peterson worked together around 1950 on a feature film project about the Kwakwaka'wakw but that, while they "did do some shooting on Vancouver Island, nothing came of their work."[4] Gardner does not mention *Fort Rupert* in any of his own writings on this early period, and scholarship on Gardner's work is notably silent on the film.[5] Because *Blunden* and *Dances* are frequently mentioned as formative experiments in Gardner's development as an ethnographic filmmaker, it is difficult to imagine that he was not involved in *Fort Rupert*, especially given the timing and the shared subject matter across all three films. Nevertheless, the extent of Gardner's involvement in *Fort Rupert* remains unclear, and the rest of the film's history is still coming into focus.

Many nonfiction films have met similar fates, but *Fort Rupert* is particularly noteworthy because of the interwoven histories to which it belongs. The Kwakwaka'wakw have intersected directly and indirectly with a range of aspects of American visual culture, from the use of photography in nineteenth-century ethnology to Jim Jarmusch's postmodern neo-Western *Dead Man* (1995).[6] In the late 1800s, the Kwakwaka'wakw, like many Native North American groups, performed at world's fairs, collaborated with anthropologists, and were romanticized in photography and visited by tourists on the premise that they were the living traces of an old, "primitive" way of life that was rapidly disappearing with the expansion of a new, industrialized one. With the emergence of the cinema, the Kwakwaka'wakw became paradoxically an enduring part of a long history of image making, much of which is relatively uncharted and largely misunderstood.

The image of the Kwakwaka'wakw as a vanishing race is misleading, to say the least. The Kwakwaka'wakw were (and are) extremely active in preserving and representing their cultures. In 1893, for example, George Hunt, a native of Fort Rupert, collaborated with the German American anthropologist Franz Boas to bring indigenous representatives from British Columbia to Chicago, where they performed traditional ways of life in an exhibit at the World's Columbian Exposition. While the performance was received by fairgoers as a spectacular display of a vanishing culture, it was also an assertion of cultural identity. Under severe restrictions by the Canadian government, which outlawed many traditional Native practices, the Kwakwaka'wakw navigated the pressures of colonialism partly by performing their culture for non-Native audiences. The historian Paige Raibmon explains, "Survival under colonialism required compromises, but these compromises were not necessarily symptoms of decline and could be signs of resiliency."[7]

The Kwakwa̱ka̱'wakw collaborated similarly with anthropologists and filmmakers throughout much of the twentieth century. With the assistance of George Hunt, people from Fort Rupert, Alert Bay, and other communities on and around Vancouver Island worked with the American photographer and filmmaker Edward S. Curtis to make *In the Land of the Head Hunters* (1914), a commercial melodrama set in a premodern past.[8] The Kwakwa̱ka̱'wakw also made films with Canadian newsreel companies and museums, the American Museum of Natural History, and anthropologists and filmmakers like Boas, Gardner, and Samuel Barrett.[9] Under the aegis of the U'mista Cultural Society in Alert Bay, the Kwakwa̱ka̱'wakw have been producing documentaries about their own culture and history since at least the 1970s, including *Potlatch . . . a Strict Law Bids Us Dance* (Dennis Wheeler, 1975) and *Box of Treasures* (Chuck Olin, 1983). Beyond research done by anthropologists and art historians like Ira Jacknis, Rosalind Morris, and Kathryn Bunn-Marcuse, the nontheatrical films from the period before the 1970s have received scant scholarly attention.[10] What remains of the films themselves tends to be fragmentary and unidentified, neglected and marginalized, and always on the verge of disappearing if not already vanished.

This essay offers a close analysis of *Fort Rupert* as one such case of vanishing celluloid that, after decades of obscurity, has resurfaced. In 2010, the Library of Congress received a 16mm copy of *Fort Rupert* when it acquired archivist and historian J. Fred MacDonald's vast collection of films and related materials. Precisely when MacDonald acquired a copy of *Fort Rupert* is unclear, as is the provenance of the print. The film is identified in MacDonald's catalog and in the film's brief credits as being produced by Orbit Films, the company that Gardner headed in the early 1950s. In 2011, a digital copy of *Fort Rupert* became widely available as part of the University of Arizona's American Indian Film Gallery project, an online collection of over 450 of MacDonald's films.

Although recovering *Fort Rupert* from the margins of film and cultural history is important in and of itself, the film sheds new light on a range of subjects from race difference and representations of Native North American peoples in nontheatrical film to the convergence of visual anthropology and the avant-garde in postwar American cinema culture. The film also offers a way into thinking about the political and cultural relevance of studying and preserving ethnographic films, particularly now that digital technologies have dramatically transformed archival practices and allowed for unprecedented access to the domain of nontheatrical film.

The goals of this chapter are preliminary: to begin placing a once-lost film in its historical context and to assess its role as an important piece of

Kwakwaka'wakw cultural heritage. My focus is on the politics of the film's aesthetic and its connection to mid-twentieth-century American ethnographic filmmaking and the avant-garde. While examining what brought the film into existence in the 1950s, I also consider the significance of its reemergence and circulation in our contemporary moment. Admittedly, a great deal of work remains to be done in collaboration with the Kwakwaka'wakw to identify the participants in *Fort Rupert* and to establish indigenous perspectives on the film. Although such work is beyond the scope of this essay, what follows is an initial step in making *Fort Rupert* part of that important conversation.

Broadly, then, *Fort Rupert* offers a way into thinking about the many afterlives of nontheatrical films and the kinds of opportunities they create for studying race and ethnicity in the cinema. As an emblem of the coiled relationship between power, race, and representation that continues to shape and reshape the history of Native peoples in the cinema, *Fort Rupert* helps us understand the crucial role that nontheatrical films play in efforts to promote the visibility, preservation, and understanding of Native cultures. The rediscovery of *Fort Rupert* thus compels us to see how the field of race and nontheatrical film is intimately tied to issues of access and circulation that demand careful consideration. As more historically marginalized films are discovered in archives and personal collections, it becomes increasingly imperative to foster collaborations between archivists, scholars, and the public that are geared toward making such films not only visible and widely available but also useful in innovative ways.

## Without History: *Fort Rupert* in Context

The people depicted in an "ethnographic film" are meant to be seen as exotic . . . as people without history, without writing, without civilization, without technology.
—FATIMAH TOBING RONY, *The Third Eye*

In many ways, *Fort Rupert* is a film without a history. It was released in 1951 by Orbit Films and was one of three 16mm ethnographic films that the production company promoted that year as part of its Northwest Indians series. The series included the ten-minute color film, *Dances of the Kwakiutl*, and *Blunden Harbour*, a twenty-minute black-and-white film about tradition and heritage in contemporary Kwakwaka'wakw life. Beyond a brief summary and a listing for purchase and rental in the autumn catalog published by Orbit's distributor, Dimensions Inc., there are very few traces of *Fort Rupert* in the historical record.[11] Of the three films released in 1951, only

*Dances* and *Blunden* seem to have received immediate critical attention. It is unclear whether *Fort Rupert* was simply overlooked or unpopular, or did not circulate widely in the 1950s.

The production of *Fort Rupert* is also a bit of a mystery. Shot in color, the film runs around fifteen minutes and includes a soundtrack and a credit sequence that names the American experimental filmmaker Hy Hirsh as the cinematographer and Morris Dowd as the sound recordist. (Dowd also worked on *Dances* and *Blunden*, which use some of the same song recordings that make up *Fort Rupert*'s soundtrack.) Although Orbit Films is listed in the credits, no other names, including those that would help with identifying members of the Kwakwa̱ka̱'wakw community who collaborated on the film, appear anywhere in *Fort Rupert*.[12] To complicate the identification of the film's makers, Ira Jacknis speculates convincingly that the film was made by the avant-garde filmmaker and then vice president of Orbit, Sidney Peterson, who reportedly traveled to Fort Rupert to conduct research for a feature-length fiction film that he and Gardner were planning to make about the Kwakwa̱ka̱'wakw.[13]

*Fort Rupert* has a distinct sketch-like quality that makes it feel as fragmentary as its history. Following the credit sequence are several shots of a totem pole intercut with a group of Kwakwa̱ka̱'wakw paddling a large canoe to Fort Rupert's shore, where the boat is greeted by what seem to be the hosts of a potlatch ceremony (figure 4.1).[14] The soundtrack consists of a Kwagiulth song overlaid with voice-over in English that introduces Fort Rupert in the 1950s as a place where, an unidentified male narrator explains, what remains of long-standing folk traditions is giving way to Westernization. The introductory narration is brief and followed by a survey of the coastal community consisting of exterior shots of children playing and adults conducting daily activities. This sequence is accompanied by another traditional song that bridges a transition to the interior of a Big House where ceremonial dances are held. The majority of the film revolves around the ceremony, which includes a Hamat́sa performance, a sacred cannibal dance that has been an enduring point of fascination for anthropologists, tourists, and filmmakers alike since the late nineteenth century. Because *Fort Rupert* represents only excerpts from several much longer dances, each of which would traditionally have its own song, the editing of the song and dance sequence as it appears in the film is quite misleading.[15]

For audiences who might be unfamiliar with the Kwakwa̱ka̱'wakw, the ethnographic meaning of the images and sounds in *Fort Rupert* is ambiguous, if not utterly elusive. The narration in the beginning of the film runs just around a minute. The remainder of the footage exists as pure spectacle without explanation or interpretation by the narrator. In this regard, *Fort*

FIGURE 4.1. *Top:* Totem pole in Fort Rupert (Tsax̱is) on Vancouver Island. *Bottom:* Arrival of the canoe on the shore of Fort Rupert (Tsax̱is) on Vancouver Island. Frame enlargements from *Fort Rupert* (1951).

*Rupert* closely resembles *Dances* and *Blunden*, which also offer minimal narration to orient audiences to their subjects. The author of a 1952 review criticized both of these other films as insufficient ethnographic documents by claiming that the narration "speaks in meaningless, pompous phrases, with hardly a perceptive motive or idea coming across to the audience. In a similar fashion the footage is edited in such a way that it is impossible to tell what is happening, has happened, or will happen."[16] Rosalind Morris and Kathryn Bunn-Marcuse have similarly criticized *Blunden* for not adequately historicizing the Kwakwa̱ka̱'wakw.[17]

The problem of history in *Fort Rupert* is clearest when we consider the film's indebtedness to the racialized ideology of salvage anthropology. As the film opens, the narrator celebrates the richness and vitality of Kwakwa̱ka̱'wakw heritage as being unparalleled in the history of Native North American peoples. He then goes on to remark, "Where totem poles now signify the security of a remote glory, telephone poles have not yet appeared to link them with the society of which they are inescapably becoming a part. . . . The majority is moving toward complete Westernization and within a few years all may have abandoned the few still existing traces of a previous culture." As an introduction to what follows, the narration traps the inhabitants of Fort Rupert between tradition and modernity, primitive and civilized, vital and vanishing in such a way that the people performing their culture do so primarily through a discourse of lack and absence created by the filmmakers that does not reflect the fact that traditional Kwakwa̱ka̱'wakw cultural practices were (and are) alive and well. The film's somewhat mournful and misleading conceit is thus that it is itself a record of the traces of a culture that will inevitably be relinquished to the past.[18]

*Fort Rupert* is fixated on making visible the "traces of a previous culture" by pairing the old and the new. In the opening sequence, shots of totem poles and other carvings are intercut with shots of everyday life in the coastal community of Fort Rupert (figures 4.2 and 4.3). Some men, women, and children in the film appear in contemporary dress while others are wearing traditional regalia over contemporary clothing (figure 4.4). In this regard, *Fort Rupert* resembles Franz Boas's ethnographic research films. In 1930–31, Boas produced a small collection of 16mm films and sound recordings at Fort Rupert as part of a larger, ongoing study of Kwagiulth song and dance traditions. In Boas's work the Kwagiulth appear similarly dressed, as in the image of Mary Hunt Johnson performing in an excerpt titled "Woman's Cannibal Dance" (figure 4.5). These kinds of images in *Fort Rupert* gesture powerfully to the cultural and economic realities of colonization, acculturation, and

FIGURE 4.2. *Top:* A young boy playing by the shore. *Bottom:* A traditional carving. Frame enlargements from *Fort Rupert* (1951).

FIGURE 4.3. Houses in Fort Rupert (Tsax̱is) on Vancouver Island. Frame enlargement from *Fort Rupert* (1951).

FIGURE 4.4. Kwagiulth in traditional regalia and contemporary clothing. Frame enlargement from *Fort Rupert* (1951).

FIGURE 4.5. Mary Hunt Johnson performing in Franz Boas's "Woman's Cannibal Dance." Frame enlargement from *The Kwakiutl of British Columbia* (1930, 1973). Courtesy of the Burke Museum of Natural History and Culture, catalog number L-5069, L-5070.

marginalization, but ultimately the film ignores these realities as such. The opening sequence seems to be designed primarily to stage a contrast with the vibrant ceremonial dance sequence that follows. The broad implication by the filmmakers is that the richness of Kwakwa̲ka̲'wakw past is all that remains of the people being documented; that the Kwakwa̲ka̲'wakw only exist as traces of "a remote glory."

From this perspective, *Fort Rupert* significantly deepens and complicates how we see Orbit Films and the landscape of postwar American ethnographic filmmaking. Morris states that "in the 1950s and 1960s, the salvage ethos was virtually hegemonic," with the exception of Gardner's film *Blunden*, which "seems to defy all the conventions of the period" by celebrating the endurance of traditional Kwakwa̲ka̲'wakw cultural practices.[19] While *Blunden* does not present Native peoples in the same liminal state as *Fort Rupert* does, it is important that both films, along with *Dances*, were framed in the Orbit catalog as salvage projects. The Northwest Indians series was promoted with the following: "Whatever the future of these people, their past has

an established eminence, a part of which has been filmed among a generation whose memory of their own heritage is failing fast."[20] Although it is beyond the scope of this essay, *Fort Rupert* invites a reevaluation of *Blunden* and
*Dances* as parts of a triptych that was premised on preserving a past or passing
way of life for American audiences. The premise has roots in early American
ethnographic and travelogue films, like those of Lyman Howe, whose selling
point for films about indigenous peoples was "See Them Now or Never."[21]

   With its minimal narration and salvage ethos, *Fort Rupert* is potentially
unreadable, especially for popular audiences, and even more so for American audiences who might be entirely unfamiliar with First Nations people,
the British Columbia region, or Canadian politics. Perhaps the film's ambiguity stems from the fact that the footage in *Fort Rupert* was not originally
meant to be made into an ethnographic film. Or perhaps it was meant to
be accompanied by a live lecture, as many nontheatrical films were and are.
While these explanations are quite likely, the film's ambiguity is probably
more directly a result of the affiliations between Peterson, Orbit Films, and
the American avant-garde.

## The American Avant-Garde Connection

The precise relationship of the avant-garde cinema to American commercial film
is one of radical otherness. —P. ADAMS SITNEY, *Visionary Film*

It is revealing that *Fort Rupert* was not made by anthropologists. Gardner
and Peterson founded Orbit Films in 1949 as an endeavor to explore their
shared interests in nonfiction and avant-garde filmmaking. In 1951, Gardner explained that the production company was invested in the relevance
of documentary filmmaking to opening up the kinds of deep engagements
with the world that are typically afforded by art.[22] It is also commonly known
that Gardner's early ethnographic film career was influenced by experimental and poetically oriented filmmakers like Maya Deren, Basil Wright, and
Dziga Vertov. Additionally, Orbit Films had strong connections to the Seattle and San Francisco art scenes and, especially through Peterson, to artists,
photographers, and filmmakers like William Heick, Stan Brakhage, Harry
Smith, and Hy Hirsh. Filmmaker and anthropologist Kathryn Ramey has
described Gardner's work with this in mind as a mode of "nonfiction poetic
cinema made in an ethnographic context."[23]

   *Fort Rupert*'s elusive aesthetic stems no doubt from these affinities between Orbit Films and the avant-garde. A San Francisco–based experimental

filmmaker, Peterson was heavily influenced by surrealists of the 1920s and '30s like Salvador Dalí and Luis Buñuel who, along with Georges Bataille, were similarly drawn to spectacles of the "primitive" and the "exotic" in anthropology's visual culture. Buñuel's highly satirical and political experimental ethnographic film *Land without Bread* (1933) is an important point of reference in this regard. Hy Hirsh, the cinematographer on *Fort Rupert*, is known for his collaborations with Peterson and Harry Smith. Smith established himself in the American avant-garde by merging his experimental art practices with his interests in anthropology and the study of Native American cultures.[24] Hirsh's work in the 1940s and 1950s tended toward abstraction and the experimental combination of music and imagery. It is thus not surprising that the majority of the footage in *Fort Rupert* focuses on song and dance practices, especially when we consider that, in 1947, Hirsh and Peterson made *Horror Dream*, an experimental dance film with a score by John Cage. It is also not coincidental that in 1951 Dimensions Inc. distributed *Fort Rupert* alongside Deren's experimental films from the mid- to late 1940s.

The avant-garde connection makes it clear that *Fort Rupert* was motivated by an aesthetic fascination with Kwakwaka'wakw arts and culture. At the time that the film was made, the American avant-garde was particularly drawn to indigenous arts of the Pacific Northwest.[25] The catalog description for Orbit's Northwest Indians series reflects this broader trend when it states, "The expressiveness of their [Kwakwaka'wakw] older art forms have influenced many contemporary painters, sculptors, and dancers. Although this art has not reached the level of popularity now enjoyed by African Negro art, there is the strong possibility that it someday will."[26] *Fort Rupert* appears to have been conceived as a kind of experiment at the interstices of art and anthropology meant, perhaps, to bring ethnography and Kwakwaka'wakw art to bear on the American avant-garde.

Peterson, Hirsh, and Gardner may in fact have seen British Columbia as an opportunity to connect with and be influenced by anthropology and indigenous art on the Northwest Coast. However, with its ambiguous ethnographic meaning, *Fort Rupert* reads strongly like a record of turning the Kwakwaka'wakw into art objects that were meant themselves to be consumed aesthetically in the same way that tourists might collect and share views of their travels. Peterson confirmed the influence of this touristic ethos in his account of working with the Kwakwaka'wakw around the time that *Fort Rupert* was made. In addition to noting that he was inspired by American anthropological work on the Kwakwaka'wakw by Boas and Ruth Benedict, Peterson remarked that one of the attractions of filming in the Pacific

Northwest was that it offered an incredible opportunity to capture authentic Native life.[27] "You could leap in almost any direction and find—Indians. We wanted to make a film about Natives. Not cowboys. Just Aborigines. Maybe there was something in the air. It was 1950, the year of *Broken Arrow*, hailed as 'the first Western since the silent days to sympathize with the Indians.' We were not, however, thinking of a Western."[28] It is not a coincidence that Peterson invokes the Western as a point of reference for his ethnographic film work with Gardner and Orbit Films. The postwar Western emerged as an emblem of a tourist culture that was increasingly turning to the photographic and filmic consumption, commodification, and aestheticization of the North American West, particularly of what remained in the 1950s of a "savage" landscape populated by "Indians."[29] While Peterson may not have set out to make a Western, *Fort Rupert* was undeniably conceived with a desire to embark on a kind of Western adventure, a desire that was filtered through the lens of his identity as an experimental filmmaker.

If, as P. Adams Sitney put it, the American avant-garde cinema was Hollywood's "other," haunting the margins of American cinema culture, then we might be inclined to see *Fort Rupert* as the product of a strong affinity between the avant-garde and the Kwakwa̱ka̱'wakw, another emblem of radical otherness in the twentieth century. And we would not be mistaken, but the affinity is fraught with the racist and colonialist ideologies that shaped *Fort Rupert* as an ethnographic salvage project. What's more, for Peterson and his colleagues at Orbit Films, the commitment to salvaging Kwakwa̱ka̱'wakw art and culture was tenuous and fleeting at best. Reflecting on the completion of what would become *Fort Rupert* and *Blunden*, Peterson explained, "for the moment, we were cured of Indians" and moved on to other projects.[30] Like the Kwakwa̱ka̱'wakw in Peterson's scenario, *Fort Rupert* would just as soon be abandoned to the margins of film history.

## Salvaging *Fort Rupert*

We are not reviving or reinventing our culture. —WILLIAM WASDEN JR. (WA̱X̱A̱WIDI), "'What the Creator Gave to Us'"

In a curious way, the fate of *Fort Rupert* initially mirrored the fate that the filmmakers *imagined* for the people they were documenting. A film about a supposedly vanishing race, *Fort Rupert* seems to have vanished early on. Unlike the two other films released in Orbit's Northwest Indians series, *Fort Rupert* was never claimed by its makers, nor does it seem to have ever been given to the people of Fort Rupert and surrounding communities who participated in making it. While Peterson is most likely *Fort Rupert*'s director, the film remains an orphan.[31] The politics of *Fort Rupert*'s marginalization are particularly acute when we consider that salvaging the film is not simply an act of returning it to the history of American nontheatrical film but of giving visibility to an integral part of Kwakwa̲ka̲'wakw history.

However neglected it may be, *Fort Rupert* is part of a rich history of loss and rediscovery that is still unfolding. Take, for example, the case of Curtis's *Head Hunters*.[32] Like *Fort Rupert*, *Head Hunters* disappeared after its release in 1914 only to be discovered decades later by Bill Holm, an American art historian, and George Quimby, a curator at the Field Museum in Chicago. In the 1970s, Holm and Quimby worked with the Kwakwa̲ka̲'wakw to turn fragments of *Head Hunters* into a film called *In the Land of the War Canoes*, which was released in 1973 by the University of Washington Press and subsequently distributed by Milestone Films. More recently, Brad Evans and Aaron Glass undertook a project to reconstruct Curtis's original version using additional footage that was newly discovered at the University of California, Los Angeles, Film and Television Archive. In 2014, this project was released in collaboration with the U'mista Cultural Society and representatives from the Kwakwa̲ka̲'wakw community who are working to show that conventional readings of *Head Hunters* as a straightforward colonialist film obscure the important process of intercultural exchange through which the Kwakwa̲ka̲'wakw performed and preserved their own cultural identity in the early twentieth century.[33]

Likewise, Kathryn Bunn-Marcuse and her colleagues in the community of Fort Rupert are working on an archival project that involves the little-known ethnographic research films about Kwagiulth song and dance traditions that Boas recorded in 1930–31, which are now housed at the Burke Museum of Natural History and Culture in Seattle. Boas was a major force in challenging the racial hierarchies that were being solidified, especially in the United States but also globally, in the early twentieth century. His collaboration with the Kwagiulth spanned decades and was largely premised on his commitment to rethinking race in anthropology. Because Boas's footage functioned as ethnographic research, it did not circulate publicly and was largely unknown until the 1970s, when Bill Holm edited the original materials into a film titled *The Kwakiutl of British Columbia*. The footage has been digitized and is being made accessible by the Burke Museum and the University of Washington Press.[34] Descendants of the people with whom Boas worked in the early 1930s are using the footage to educate younger generations about cultural identities and practices that have long been threatened by the pressures of colonization and Westernization.

Although the Orbit Films group was most likely unfamiliar with Curtis's film and Boas's footage, it is striking how much *Fort Rupert* shares with the histories of those projects. Peterson recalls that his trip to Fort Rupert originated with a request by a family in Vancouver to host a potlatch because, in 1950, such ceremonies were still outlawed by the Canadian government and, as Peterson put it, "what better way to have it than under the guise of making a movie."[35] The request most likely came from a woman named Ellen Neel, and the film project they undertook unfolded as a collaboration arranged by Neel's family, Mungo Martin, and the communities at Fort Rupert and Blunden Harbour.[36] If this is the case, and if some of the footage Peterson and Hirsh shot on this visit became *Fort Rupert*, then the film's promotion by Orbit as a salvage project needs to be seen as an act of covering over the agency of the Kwakwa̱ka̱'wakw participants, intentionally or otherwise. What the narrator calls "traces of a previous culture" are less signs of vanishing than "signs of resiliency," to borrow Paige Raibmon's words.

Like Curtis's and Boas's films, *Fort Rupert* is both a sign of resiliency and a resilient film. After decades of obscurity, a rough digital copy of the film appeared in the online collections of the American Indian Film Gallery (AIFG).[37] The AIFG copy, which credits Hy Hirsh and Morris Dowd without naming Peterson or Gardner, was made from a 16mm print of the film still held in the J. Fred MacDonald collection, which was purchased by the Library of Congress in 2010. For unknown reasons, the archival print of *Fort Rupert* at the Library of Congress is now missing the opening credits and part of the first sequence. A new high-resolution scan of this copy is being made publicly available in the hopes that better-quality images might help with future research.

In addition to having their own politics, films like *Fort Rupert* are animated significantly by the politics of their loss and rediscovery. The history of early to mid-twentieth-century ethnographic films is characterized by a powerful doubling: these are predominantly marginalized films about marginalized peoples. Indeed, the same could be said about many nontheatrical films, especially those explored in this book. Archival discoveries that shed light on the margins thus demand that we take great care to understand the discourses of race and ethnicity that are inscribed in such films, and to recognize the importance of promoting access to them, as the recent projects involving Curtis's and Boas's films have done. (Similar work is also being done with the ethnographic films produced as part of an experimental collaboration in 1966 between Navajo students and Sol Worth and his colleagues.)[38] The success of these particular projects is due in large part to ongoing efforts to develop large-scale collaborations between the Kwakwa̱ka̱'wakw, archivists, and scholars. The history of nontheatrical film is filled with opportunities to bring similar efforts to bear on individual films like *Fort Rupert* that continue to resurface.

These efforts are important because many nontheatrical films about Native North American peoples were conceived throughout the twentieth century as evidence of race difference and records of dying cultures, but they also have incredibly rich afterlives. In cases like *Fort Rupert*, the significance of these films is in how they reaffirm what Brad Evans and Aaron Glass call the "tenacity of cultural heritage" by challenging the assumptions and misperceptions perpetuated by salvage anthropology, which tends to obscure the active role that Native peoples, like the Kwakwa̱ka̱'wakw, took in preserving their heritage by performing in front of the camera.[39] The value of this idea is not limited to the historical context of an individual film. In her analysis of *Head Hunters* and Robert Flaherty's *Nanook of the North* (1922), film scholar Catherine Russell states, "While the salvage paradigm is an ethnographic allegory of colonialism, it may also preserve a utopian form of memory of some historic value to native communities."[40]

This analysis of *Fort Rupert* serves as an argument for (re)writing film history at the margins, for making a lost film visible as part of a conversation about the complex role of race and ethnicity in relation to nontheatrical film, and the need for considering how to promote access to marginalized films in ways that extend beyond the scholarly community. By bringing films like *Fort Rupert* into the spotlight, we can begin to engage meaningfully with the politics of marginalization and create new opportunities for not only understanding the historical value of nontheatrical films but also discovering new and unexpected values in archival materials. The project of determining the specific value of *Fort Rupert* to the community it represents ultimately belongs to the Kwakwa̱ka̱'wakw, and this is a project that is and will be ongoing.

FILMOGRAPHY

All available films discussed in this chapter can be streamed through the book's web page at https://www.dukeupress.edu/Features/Screening-Race.

*Blunden Harbour* (1951), 21 min., 16mm
PRODUCTION: Orbit Films. DISTRIBUTOR: Dimensions Inc. DIRECTOR: Robert Gardner. CAMERA: William Heick. EDITOR: William Heick. ACCESS: Film print

in the Robert Gardner Collection, Harvard Film Archive, Harvard University, Cambridge, MA.

*Dances of the Kwakiutl* (1951), 8.5 min., 16mm
PRODUCTION: Orbit Films. DISTRIBUTOR: Dimensions Inc. DIRECTOR: Robert Gardner. CAMERA: William Heick. EDITOR: William Heick. ACCESS: Film print in the Robert Gardner Collection, Harvard Film Archive, Harvard University, Cambridge, MA.

*Fort Rupert* (1951), 15 min., 16mm
PRODUCTION: Orbit Films. DISTRIBUTOR: Dimensions Inc. CAMERA: Hy Hirsh. ACCESS: Film print in the J. Fred MacDonald Collection, Library of Congress, American Indian Film Gallery. NOTE: Alternate titles, *Potlatch* and *Hamatsa*.

*In the Land of the Head Hunters* (1914), 66 min., 35mm
PRODUCTION: World Film Corporation. DIRECTOR: Edward S. Curtis. CAMERA: Edmund Schwinke. ACCESS: *In the Land of the Head Hunters* DVD (2014), distributed by Milestone Films. NOTE: This DVD is the outcome of a restoration project and was produced by Aaron Glass, Brad Evans, Andrea Sanborn, Milestone Films, the UCLA Film and Television Archive, the Field Museum of Natural History, and the U'Mista Cultural Society.

*The Kwakiutl of British Columbia* (1930, 1973), 50 min., 16mm
DIRECTOR: Franz Boas. CAMERA: Franz Boas. EDITOR: Bill Holm (see note). ACCESS: Film print at the Bill Holm Center for the Study of Northwest Coast Art, Burke Museum, Seattle, WA. NOTE: Bill Holm edited Boas's footage into a film in 1973. The edited film was accompanied by an extensive set of notes compiled by Holm and published by the University of Washington Press. The Burke Museum is producing a DVD version of Boas's footage and related materials in collaboration with the University of Washington Press.

## NOTES

I would first like to extend my gratitude to Sherri Labour, Lands and Resource Coordinator, Kwakiutl First Nation, and Juanita Johnston, Collections Manager, U'mista Cultural Centre, for opening a line of communication with me about *Fort Rupert* and the possibility of a collaboration, which was still developing when this book was published. I would also very sincerely like to thank Allyson Nadia Field, Marsha Gordon, Kathryn Bunn-Marcuse at the Bill Holm Center for the Study of Northwest Coast Art, Burke Museum, and Ira Jacknis at the Phoebe A. Hearst Museum of Anthropology, University of California, Berkeley, for their incredibly thoughtful and comprehensive feedback on early drafts of this essay. Finally, I would like to thank Judy Hoffman, Mike Mashon at the Library of Congress Packard Campus for Audio Visual Conservation, Jennifer Jenkins at the American Indian Film Gallery, the staff at the American Philosophical Society, and the staff at the Autry Museum of the American West for their assistance with my research.

1   Both *Dances of the Kwakiutl* and *Blunden Harbour* are available in a variety of formats. Documentary Educational Resources has published DVDs of both films, and 16mm versions can be found in the Robert Gardner Collection, Harvard Film Archive, Harvard University, Cambridge, MA.

2   *Dances of the Kwakiutl* and *Blunden Harbour* focus on two different villages on Vancouver Island: Tsax̱is and Ba'as, respectively. Kwakwa̱ka'wakw is a collective name preferred by First Nations people to describe Kwakwala-speaking communities on the northern part of Vancouver Island and surrounding areas. "Kwakiutl" is commonly and inaccurately used in its stead and, therefore, is not used here.

3   In 1951, the Kwakwa̱ka'wakw and other First Nations people were subject to a range of cultural, religious, and economic restrictions imposed by Canada's Indian Act, which banned traditional ceremonies like the potlatch between 1885 and 1951.

4   Scott MacDonald, *American Ethnographic Film and Personal Documentary: The Cambridge Turn* (Berkeley: University of California Press, 2013), 63.

5   This is also the case with an invaluable book edited by Rebecca Meyers, William Rothman, and Charles Warren, *Looking with Robert Gardner* (Albany: State University of New York Press, 2016).

6   Several scenes in *Dead Man* were inspired by Kwakwa̱ka'wakw culture, but these were in fact filmed in a Makah village in northwestern Washington. Jarmusch and critics mistakenly referred to the village depicted in the film as a "Kwakiutl" village at the time of the film's release. See Jonathan Rosenbaum, "A Gun Up Your Ass: An Interview with Jim Jarmusch," *Cineaste* 22, no. 2 (1996): 20–22.

7   Paige Raibmon, *Authentic Indians: Episodes of Encounter from the Late-Nineteenth-Century Northwest Coast* (Durham, NC: Duke University Press, 2005), 64.

8   See Bill Holm and George Quimby, *In the Land of the War Canoes: A Pioneer Cinematographer in the Pacific Northwest* (Seattle: University of Washington Press, 1980); and Brad Evans and Aaron Glass, eds., *Return to the Land of the Head Hunters: Edward S. Curtis, the Kwakwa̱ka'wakw, and the Making of Modern Cinema* (Seattle: University of Washington Press, 2014).

9   Ira Jacknis, "Visualizing Kwakwa̱ka'wakw Tradition: The Films of William Heick, 1951–63," *BC Studies*, nos. 125/126 (spring/summer 2000): 102–5.

10  Rosalind Morris, *New Worlds from Fragments: Film, Ethnography, and the Representation of Northwest Coast Cultures* (Boulder, CO: Westview, 1994); and Kathryn Bunn-Marcuse, "The Kwakwa̱ka'wakw on Film," in *Walking a Tightrope: Aboriginal People and Their Representations*, ed. Ute Lischke and David T. McNab (Ontario: Wilfrid Laurier University Press, 2005), 305–33.

11  The catalog was published in autumn 1951. A copy of this catalog can be found in the collections of the Autry Museum of the American West in Los Angeles. All future references are listed as "Orbit Films Catalog."

12  On the ambiguity of Gardner's productions, see Jacknis, "Visualizing Kwakwa̱ka'wakw Tradition," 110–11.

13  The unfinished fiction film project was titled *Souvenir of a Murder*. When Jacknis wrote his essay, he had not seen the extant copy of *Fort Rupert* but noted that *Fort Rupert* was also probably listed under the title *Hamat̓sa*. See Jacknis, "Visualizing

Kwakwaka'wakw Tradition," 109–13. A listing for *Hamat̓sa* is available in "Orbit Films—General Information," March 15, 1951, 10, a copy of which Jacknis has in his personal possession and which he generously shared with me. More context for *Souvenir of a Murder* will appear in a book in progress, edited by Ira Jacknis and Hannah Wild, on the still photographs by Robert Gardner and his colleagues of the Kwakwaka'wakw communities of Fort Rupert, Blunden Harbour, and Alert Bay, BC, 1950–51.

14  It is unclear whether the potlatch is ceremonial or a demonstration for the filmmakers, but an account by filmmaker Sidney Peterson suggests that it might be somewhere in between. See Sidney Peterson, *Dark of the Screen* (New York: Anthology Film Archives and New York University Press, 1980), 111–12.

15  Special thanks to Kathryn Bunn-Marcuse for bringing this to my attention.

16  Cecile Starr, "The Film Forum," *Saturday Review*, April 26, 1952, 36.

17  Morris, *New Worlds from Fragments*, 107; Bunn-Marcuse, "The Kwakwaka'wakw on Film," 318.

18  The inventory caption for *Fort Rupert* in the J. Fred MacDonald Collection at the Library of Congress echoes this: "*Fort Rupert*: 1951 color film re: Kwakiutl Indians of British Columbia, Canada—theirs is a civilization in decline as assimilation has almost obliterated native culture."

19  Morris, *New Worlds from Fragments*, 102.

20  "Orbit Films Catalog."

21  For an excellent discussion of Howe and his contemporary, Burton Holmes, see Alison Griffiths, *Wondrous Difference: Cinema, Anthropology, and Turn-of-the-Century Visual Culture* (New York: Columbia University Press, 2002), 213.

22  "Orbit Films Catalog."

23  Kathryn Ramey, "Ethno-Cine-Poet: Robert Gardner and Experimental Film," in *Looking with Robert Gardner*, ed. Rebecca Meyers, William Rothman, and Charles Warren (Albany: State University of New York Press, 2016), 93–94.

24  In the early 1940s, Smith also intersected with Bill Holm, who became deeply involved with documenting and preserving Kwakwaka'wakw arts and culture, a commitment he maintains today.

25  See, for example, Jackson Rushing, *Native American Art and the New York Avant-Garde: A History of Cultural Primitivism* (Austin: University of Texas Press, 1995).

26  "Orbit Films Catalog."

27  Peterson and Gardner were particularly drawn to Ruth Benedict's book *Patterns of Culture* (New York: Houghton Mifflin, 1934).

28  Peterson, *Dark of the Screen*, 109–10.

29  For more on American tourism and the postwar Western, see Matt Hauske, "Cowboy Modernity: Contexts of the Hollywood Western, 1946–1964" (PhD diss., University of Chicago, 2015). See also Griffiths, *Wondrous Difference*, 246.

30  Peterson, *Dark of the Screen*, 123.

31  Dan Streible's work on orphan films—including the indispensable Orphan Film Symposium—has brought scholars, archivists, and the public together to study marginalized, neglected, and obscured films. For an overview, see Dan Streible,

"The Role of Orphan Films in the 21st Century Archive," *Cinema Journal* 46, no. 3 (spring 2007): 124–28.

32   See Rony, *The Third Eye*, 77–98; Morris, *New Worlds from Fragments*, 39–77; and Catherine Russell, *Experimental Ethnography: The Work of Film in the Age of Video* (Durham, NC: Duke University Press, 1999), 98–115.

33   Aaron Glass and Brad Evans, introduction to Evans and Glass, *Return to the Land of the Head Hunters*, 8.

34   Preliminary information can be found in Madison Heslop, "Creating a Digital Book of Franz Boas' 1930 Kwakwaka'wakw Films," Burke Museum, August 29, 2018, https://www.burkemuseum.org/blog/creating-digital-book-franz-boas-1930 -kwakwakawakw-films; and Burke Museum, "Northwest Native Art: ArtTalk Symposium Session 1," YouTube, June 25, 2015, https://www.youtube.com/watch?v =w7HYZoPJ6hc.

35   Peterson, *Dark of the Screen*, 111–12.

36   Jacknis, "Visualizing Kwakwaka̲'wakw Tradition," 108–9.

37   *Fort Rupert* (1951), American Indian Film Gallery, http://aifg.arizona.edu/film /fort-rupert.

38   The films produced as part of this collaboration in 1966 have recently been revived in a large-scale collaborative archival project known as Navajo Film Themselves, sponsored by the University of Pennsylvania Museum of Archaeology and Anthropology, http://www.penn.museum/sites/navajofilmthemselves/.

39   Brad Evans and Aaron Glass, preface to Evans and Glass, *Return to the Land of the Head Hunters*, xxi.

40   Russell, *Experimental Ethnography*, 113.

# 5

## Red Star/Black Star

### The Early Career of Film Editor Hortense "Tee" Beveridge, 1948–1968

WALTER FORSBERG

This story begins with trims: short strips of film, most less than a few feet long. Often destined for the trash heap, these dormant celluloid scrolls are among cinema's most marginal of artifactual ephemera: unused orphan pieces that fail to make the final cut. This story's trims arrived at the Smithsonian Institution's National Museum of African American History and Culture (NMAAHC) in 2012 in a film can labeled "Unidentified Hortense Beveridge." In the initial stages of archival processing, that rusty can, its label, and the trims it contained stood out as mysterious and indeterminate—the type of materials that excite NMAAHC film conservators. While their donor, the film scholar, historian, and cinéaste Pearl Bowser, had amassed a prodigiously expansive collection containing hundreds of early race films and newsreels, audiotape oral histories with progenitors of African American cinema, documentary television newsclips from the 1960s, and diasporic African cinema of the 1980s and '90s, alongside a wealth of paper documentation, the "Unidentified Hortense Beveridge" trims would prove to be among the museum's most unique and radical moving image collections. They contained footage of some of the most controversial progressive and communist African American figures of the mid-twentieth century, convening at the height of the McCarthy-era red scare to articulate a radical political platform in direct opposition to the superexploitation of black working-class women, triply oppressed by virtue of their race, sex, and class. Yet these trims were merely the first among a body of other works, pieces of an "Unidentified Hortense Beveridge" puzzle.

This chapter unspools the story of these nonfiction films' creator and collector, Hortense "Tee" Beveridge (née Sie, 1923–93), examining the early phases of her remarkable career as a pioneering African American film editor and committed community activist filmmaker. Beveridge's biography and early filmmaking demonstrate how African American progressive and community-based nontheatrical activist films could be made despite segregation in the filmmaking industry and the anticommunist paranoia of the midcentury United States. Beveridge's oeuvre of edited and produced films provides a link between 1930s and '40s labor documentary and subsequent traditions of African American nonfiction filmmaking in the early civil rights era, and this chapter situates her work in the context of the underexamined realm of leftist, postwar, pre-vérité documentary film. As a black woman filmmaker, Beveridge's career trajectory gives practical evidence of how the segregation of the film industry in New York was initially broken along lines of gender and race.

## Methodologically Constellating Hortense Beveridge

Who was Hortense Beveridge and how might we decipher her connection to these films, beyond her name's appearance on a film can label? Beveridge is largely absent from film scholarship, and her known filmography consists of a paltry conglomeration of credits on the Internet Movie Database (https://www.imdb.com). Some biographical information is available about Beveridge in *Domestic Diversity and Other Subversive Activities*, a 2009 memoir by her husband, Lowell "Pete" Beveridge.[1] This enchanting book chronicles the struggle of the couple's midcentury interracial marriage and is an indispensable resource despite its focus on matters of marriage, life, and love rather than filmmaking. Tee Beveridge died in 1993 and cannot fill in gaps, elucidate incongruities, detail production histories, or articulate her experiences as a female African American progressive filmmaker. That many of the films in Pearl Bowser Collection cans labeled "H. Beveridge" are outtake fragments, often unfinished raw footage without credits, and of a political orientation then subject to government surveillance, means that they do not appear in educational film catalogs (often a fruitful resource in tracing histories of nontheatrical film). For these reasons, it is a challenge to splice together the details of her life and work.

Monica Dall'Asta and Jane M. Gaines's prologue to the 2015 anthology *Doing Women's Film History* positions historical objects—specifically, motion picture film prints—as momentously important "material remnants of the past," displaced in time, which they advocate be employed to evoke necessarily incomplete "constellations" to sketch a "historical montage," an "image of the past."[2] Facing "an immeasurable void that is all that went unrecorded, an oblivion from which we painstakingly draw every piece of evidence," the authors' historiographic constellation approach to unwritten histories of women filmmakers uses filmic artifacts to evoke a phantasmic image of a figure whose complete picture cannot be fully reconstructed.[3]

Following Dall'Asta and Gaines's recuperation of early Italian cinema director Elvira Giallanella, I constellate Beveridge and the surviving prints and fragments of films she made, coproduced, and collected around the contemporaneous production and cultural atmospheres she operated in. This approach is necessarily incomplete—even phantasmic—yet it will hopefully spur further research into her career and the careers of other yet-unrecognized African American nonfiction filmmakers of the same era. Thanks to previous oral histories with Pete Beveridge conducted by Pearl Bowser in 1995 and by the Brooklyn Public Library in 2012, along with additional conversations between Pete Beveridge and myself in 2015, we know about some of the coworkers and community acquaintances with whom Tee Beveridge collaborated. The archives of the New York editing union Local 771 help situate Beveridge's career in the professional New York televisual film industry of the 1950s. These sources elucidate her importance within leftist nontheatrical filmmakers and productions of the 1950s and '60s and, more broadly, enable the location of Beveridge and her work as part of the ongoing effort to build and exhibit a national film collection of the African American experience at the Smithsonian's new museum on the National Mall, amid an expansive constellation of other women workers in black film culture.

Tee (1923–1993)

Hortense "Tee" Sie was born on October 3, 1923, in New York City's Harlem neighborhood and grew up across several boroughs in households where her mother, Rachel, was employed as a domestic worker.[4] Rachel Sie was part of the first Great Migration, moving to New York from Virginia and her native Maryland in the early 1920s.[5] In 1924, Rachel Sie (née Hall) married Liberian-born Thorgues Sie, twenty-two years her senior, who had come

FIGURE 5.1. Hortense Sie (holding headset to ear) at the 1949 International Union of Students Congress. Courtesy of Lowell P. Beveridge.

to Baltimore in his thirties to study at what is now Morgan State University. Together, they had two children—Beveridge and her younger brother, Thorgues Jr., born in 1942—but their relationship dissipated when Thorgues returned to Liberia in 1947. Beveridge attended Erasmus Hall High School in Brooklyn's Flatbush neighborhood, and later George Washington Irving High School in Manhattan—both among the best public schools in the city.[6] Beveridge was then admitted to Hunter College around 1947 and majored in social work. While Beveridge's relationship with her often-absent father was "ambivalent," Thorgues Sie seems to have planted some seed of political activism in Beveridge through his instillation of appreciation for the family's African heritage.[7] Pete Beveridge recalls that thanks to Thorgues, as one of a small number of Liberians living in New York in the 1920s and '30s, the Sie household occasionally served as a meeting place for Liberian expatriates and other students from Africa studying in the U.S.—among them the future founder of the Ghanaian state, Kwame Nkrumah.

At Hunter College, Beveridge became involved in leftist political and student social justice organizations, including the Communist Party and the National Association for the Advancement of Colored People (NAACP). Her involvements were significant enough to earn her mention in the City College of New York student newspaper as a progressive leader, and she attended the congress of the International Union of Students (IUS) in Sofia, Bulgaria, in September 1949 as the executive secretary for the Committee for International Student Cooperation—a student-based distributor for IUS information, believed by the House Un-American Activities Committee to be a communist front.[8] Beveridge spent the fall of 1949 in Europe, visiting Hungary, Bulgaria, and the Soviet Union, before returning to school and her job at the communist Worker's Book Store, located at 35 East Twelfth Street in Manhattan's bookseller's row district.[9] Beveridge's job at the bookstore brought her into contact with a wide spectrum of progressive-minded customers—a group, Pete Beveridge explains, that appealed to her: "At college Tee was attracted to the Communist Party, the only political organization at that time which recognized and campaigned against the triple exploitation of black working class women. In the college cafeteria each special interest group had its own table and the CP table was the only one where black and white students sat together. Tee liked that. She joined the party and became active in the Labor Youth League and other radical student political organizations."[10]

## Cinematic Agitation, Training, and the Committee for the Negro in the Arts

Some undocumented experience during Beveridge's 1949 European trip appears to have inspired her to explore filmmaking as a way of channeling her political activism. According to Pete Beveridge, "When she came back to New York, that's when she started developing her interest in film, and became involved with the CNA. They made it possible for her to get into school, and to get her first job in the business."[11] Founded in 1947, the Committee for the Negro in the Arts (CNA) aimed "for full participation of the Negro people in the cultural life of the United States."[12] Painter and former CNA chairman Ernest Crichlow recalls the organization endeavoring "to do something about our image and get Negroes jobs in the various fields," and the CNA was one of several professional associations organized by African American talent and liberal whites to create professional opportunities for aspiring African Americans looking to work in the moving image and performing arts.[13] Prominent CNA sponsors like Harry Belafonte, Aaron Copeland, Jacob Lawrence, Canada Lee, Dorothy Parker, Sidney Poitier, and Paul Robeson abetted mentorship for participants through their personal and professional connections.[14] Two critical outcomes of Beveridge's involvement as a mentee through the CNA were her formalized film education and her acquaintance with fellow female film editors like Peggy Lawson (with whom she would go on to collaborate over the course of many years) and other leftist documentarians of the pre–World War II era.[15]

Beveridge's film training sponsorship by CNA members Lawson and her partner Leo Hurwitz provides critical evidence of a link between 1930s and '40s labor documentary traditions and subsequent practices of African American nonfiction filmmaking in the early civil rights era. Beginning in 1946, Hurwitz taught filmmaking at the New Institute for Film and Television (NIFT) in Brooklyn along with other labor documentarians like Sidney Meyers, Irving Lerner, and Paul Strand.[16] The *Brooklyn Eagle* described NIFT as a "new cinematic arts school at 29 Flatbush Ave."[17] Promoted as a GI-bill-qualifying educational program, by 1949 NIFT had 160 students and was about to expand its nighttime curriculum offerings to the daytime hours.[18] Photos from the *Brooklyn Eagle* show that NIFT was a racially integrated organization, and African American filmmaker William Greaves took courses at NIFT in 1950 before moving to Montreal to work in documentary production at the National Film Board of Canada.[19] Heavily redacted FBI reports indicate that NIFT and its president Donald Winclair were surveilled due to the political ties of several NIFT faculty members.[20]

With CNA support, according to Pete Beveridge, Tee Beveridge attended two semesters of night school film classes at New York University around 1951, yet two film fragments in the Pearl Bowser Collection suggest that Beveridge either also attended NIFT or received 16mm NIFT editing practice films directly from Hurwitz or Lawson.[21] The first fragment is a filmstrip labeled "Editing Exercises," and the second is a spool labeled "Moxon's Master." The two black-and-white films are silent and somewhat mundane. The presence of a clock in the frame and multiple splices suggest that students may have been given a reel of stock footage and assigned to edit the footage in order to visually tell a diegetic story. Both bear handwritten print-through labeling on laboratory leader that reads "New Institute for Films."

Beveridge's training and personal connections to Hurwitz, Lawson, and Strand through NIFT situate her in the often-obfuscated post–World War II, pre-vérité documentary filmmaking field. In his ambitious polemic "Carl Marzani and Union Films: Making Left-Wing Documentaries during the Cold War, 1946–53," Charles Musser examines this era of leftist documentary. Using Marzani and Union Films as its exemplars, he interrogates the historical realities of an active ecosystem of postwar, pre-vérité documentary that runs counter to prevailing documentary film scholarship.[22] Musser states that Union Films productions "continued to be marginalized because they did not easily fit within a documentary teleology that culminated in the achievement of cinéma vérité in the 1960s."[23] He convincingly demonstrates that left-wing political documentary did not terminate with Leo Hurwitz and Paul Strand's *Native Land* (1942) or Hurwitz's own *Strange Victory* (1948), but instead flourished through the 1950s.

Given Beveridge's personal ties to many of the same filmmakers, echoing Musser, I frame Beveridge's filmic output between 1949 and the 1960s as yet another important oeuvre of postwar documentary filmmaking history overlooked by film historians. The imbrication of Beveridge in this milieu of postwar left-wing political documentary filmmaking by figures like Hurwitz and Marzani is further evidenced by the presence of three Union Films–produced Progressive Party campaign film prints included in the Pearl Bowser Collection that were likely originally collected and used by Beveridge: *A People's Convention* (1948) and two titles for which Musser was unable to locate surviving copies at the time of the publication of his article, *The Case of the Fishermen* (1947) and *Count Us In* (1948).[24] Beveridge's film work demonstrates that, as Musser concludes regarding postwar documentary, "the left did not self-destruct but . . . generated significant quantities of accomplished documentary work."[25]

Unlike Marzani, however, part of Beveridge's significance lies in the rarity of her position as an African American female filmmaker during a period for which scholarship has uncovered so few others. Documentarian William Alexander, mentored by Mary McLeod Bethune at the National Youth Administration agency prior to American involvement in World War II, is one exceptional example of an African American who also made socially conscious documentary films in this era.[26] However, working for the federal government's Office of War Information to create propaganda films—most notably the *All-American News* newsreels, circa 1944–45, which aimed to positively depict African Americans and their roles in supporting the war effort—Alexander's contributions were less politically leftist or subversive than Beveridge's. The conclusions of the 1967 National Advisory Commission on Civil Disorders (known as the Kerner Commission) would directly inspire broader opportunities for African Americans already working in nonfiction film—figures like Beveridge's fellow NIFT alumnus William Greaves, who expatriated to Canada for a decade to make documentaries during the 1950s.[27] However, at the time of Beveridge's first forays into filmmaking, the Kerner Commission–inspired opportunities to spur black documentary television production such as WNET's *Black Journal* and ABC's *Like It Is* were still over a decade away for filmmakers such as Gil Noble, Charles Hobson,

St. Clair Bourne, Kent Garrett, Tony Brown, Stan Lathan, and Madeline Anderson. In this context, Beveridge can be seen as a progenerating figure in a new line of documentary—progressive and socially conscious nonfiction films created by African Americans.

## The Council on African Affairs and *South Africa Uncensored* (1952)

Beveridge's political activism in the late 1940s led her to join the Council on African Affairs (CAA)—an outgrowth of the International Committee on African Affairs, cofounded in 1937 by Max Yergan and Paul Robeson—where she merged her political activities with her nascent filmmaking skills. Robeson served as the CAA's chairman for the majority of its eighteen-year existence, and it was, according to Robeson biographer Martin Duberman, "the one organizational interest among many with which he was identified that was closest to his heart."[28] Major progressive figures of the black left were dedicated CAA proponents during its existence, including W. E. B. Du Bois, Eslanda Robeson, Charlotta Bass, Louise Thompson Patterson, and W. Alphaeus Hunton. The CAA, or simply "the Council," was "a unique voice calling for decolonization of Africa and, in particular, solidarity with the anti-apartheid movement."[29] Its initial purpose was as an informational clearinghouse for "accurate information so that the American people might play their proper part in the struggle for African Freedom."[30] In 1943, W. Alphaeus Hunton left his position in the English Department at Howard University in Washington, DC, to join the Council as its educational director.[31] Hunton transformed the Council in the next decade from an information provider to a mass organization, until it was charged with subversion under the McCarren Act in 1953 and disbanded in 1955.

The Council provided Beveridge with the opportunity to edit her first known complete film, *South Africa Uncensored*, a twenty-two-minute polemic against apartheid that was distributed by the Council and finished sometime in 1951. The film was used at events for several years, and on at least one occasion it accompanied a speech by Eslanda Robeson.[32] Production of the film by the Council is not mentioned in Hunton's personal papers, or in the Council's surviving financial records; however, a CIA internal memorandum from 1954, seeking to procure a copy of the film for surveillance purposes, cites the Council as the film's distributor.[33] The only known extant copy of the film was preserved in 2016 by film conservators at NMAAHC.

*South Africa Uncensored* is a raw and gritty piece of black-and-white agitprop, full of firsthand testimonial footage of the appalling conditions

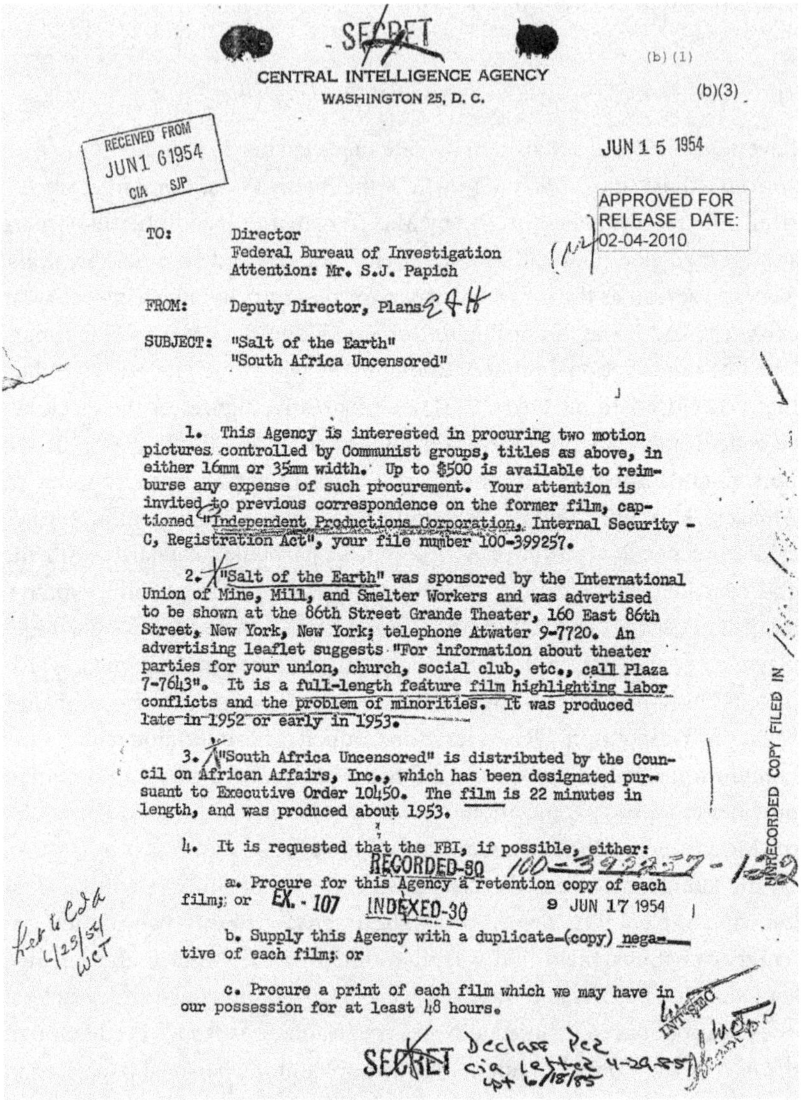

CENTRAL INTELLIGENCE AGENCY
WASHINGTON 25, D. C.

RECEIVED FROM
JUN1 6 1954
CIA    SJP

JUN 1 5 1954

APPROVED FOR
RELEASE DATE:
02-04-2010

TO:       Director
          Federal Bureau of Investigation
          Attention: Mr. S.J. Papich

FROM:     Deputy Director, Plans

SUBJECT:  "Salt of the Earth"
          "South Africa Uncensored"

1. This Agency is interested in procuring two motion pictures controlled by Communist groups, titles as above, in either 16mm or 35mm width. Up to $500 is available to reimburse any expense of such procurement. Your attention is invited to previous correspondence on the former film, captioned "Independent Productions Corporation, Internal Security - C, Registration Act", your file number 100-399257.

2. "Salt of the Earth" was sponsored by the International Union of Mine, Mill, and Smelter Workers and was advertised to be shown at the 86th Street Grande Theater, 160 East 86th Street, New York, New York; telephone Atwater 9-7720. An advertising leaflet suggests "For information about theater parties for your union, church, social club, etc., call Plaza 7-7643". It is a full-length feature film highlighting labor conflicts and the problem of minorities. It was produced late in 1952 or early in 1953.

3. "South Africa Uncensored" is distributed by the Council on African Affairs, Inc., which has been designated pursuant to Executive Order 10450. The film is 22 minutes in length, and was produced about 1953.

4. It is requested that the FBI, if possible, either:
RECORDED-50   100-3 9 2 2 5 7 - 1 5 2
     a. Procure for this Agency a retention copy of each
films; or   EX.-107   INDEXED-30     9 JUN 17 1954

     b. Supply this Agency with a duplicate (copy) negative of each film; or

     c. Procure a print of each film which we may have in our possession for at least 48 hours.

SECRET

FIGURE 5.2. Central Intelligence Agency solicitation authorization for film copy of *South Africa Uncensored* pursuant to Executive Order 10450.

FIGURE 5.3. Frame enlargement from *South Africa Uncensored*. Collection of the National Museum of African American History and Culture, gift of Pearl Bowser. Object ID# 2012.79.1.4.1a. Courtesy of the Estate of Hortense Tee Beveridge.

endured by black South Africans under apartheid. The film portrays the filth in black shantytowns lacking proper sewage systems, the country's segregated public spaces, and the vile white leisure spectacle of enjoying forced fisticuffs between black workers. Pete Beveridge recalls the film as "a putting together of news clips and films that have been smuggled out of South Africa."[34] The film's visual aesthetics reflect the source footage's clandestine and illicit provenance; much of the footage is high contrast and has a duplicated and generationally depreciated quality, occasionally out of register and causing a frame line to appear on-screen. The film's ending juxtaposes images of discrimination and police violence in Harlem as a rhetorical mirror for its intended U.S. audience. *South Africa Uncensored* lacks on-screen credits but is clearly narrated by Council chairman Robeson, whose elocution lends a reasoned gravitas to its message. In parallel with Musser's claims regarding Union Films' 1948 Henry Wallace presidential campaign films, *South Africa Uncensored* reveals Robeson's "continuation of his film career by other means and for different purposes," abetting progressive political filmmaking in a period when blacklisting embargoed his screen acting and singing career.[35]

If *South Africa Uncensored* played a propagandistic role in raising awareness and sparking outcry for an important leftist cause of the midcentury, it did so among the company of other kinds of nontheatrical "useful cinema" for progressive and educational causes in a very practical way.[36] Still a rich genre, ripe for historical inquiry, in the first seven years after 1945 it is estimated that over 25,000 nonfiction 16mm films were produced in the United States.[37] Like the Union Films made for Wallace, or Henri Cartier-Bresson's *With the Abraham Lincoln Brigade in Spain* (1937) promoting antifascists during the Spanish Civil War, films like *South Africa Uncensored* were screened at lectures, gatherings, and parties to raise money for the cause. (It was at one such gathering in Harlem—a fund-raising party sponsored by the Council, held at Beveridge's apartment at 69 East 125th Street in December 1952, and with Robeson in attendance—where Pete and Tee Beveridge first met.)[38] The Wallace campaign film catalog-pamphlet, *Films for '48: A Guide to Progressive Films and Their Use*, conceives of such films as "necessary vitamins to discussions at union and political meetings," capable of "plumping" attendance and intensifying the effectiveness of messages.[39]

Considering *South Africa Uncensored* and other film footage in Beveridge's archives as necessary vitamins to animate and illustrate political discussion and social justice provides insight into how some of these films were likely screened as illustrative tools within the broader agenda of a meeting or event. One example is Beveridge's silent, 16mm, four-minute footage of an April 1949 Harlem Trade Union Council (HTUC) meeting (called *[Harlem Trade Union Council Convention, 1949]* by NMAAHC), which may have been used to illustrate an accompanying speech at a subsequent union meeting.[40] The footage depicts a hall meeting and what is believed to be the election of sailor and labor organizer Ferdinand Smith to head the newly formed HTUC. Labor organizer Ewart Guinier also appears onstage at the meeting, a year before he became vice president of the National Negro Labor Council. The fact that the silent HTUC footage contains film-within-a-film footage of the seated HTUC audience watching a 16mm film projection of protestors wearing "Free Willie McGee" T-shirts supports the idea of film as necessary vitamins by demonstrating that 16mm documentary films were indeed shown at labor meetings.

Viewed through the conceptual lens of necessary vitamins, I want to refocus this chronicle of Beveridge's political documentary films on the

FIGURE 5.4. Frame enlargement from *[Harlem Trade Union Council, April 1949]*, featuring a screening of 16mm "necessary vitamins." Object ID# 2012.79.1.53.1a. Courtesy of the Estate of Hortense Tee Beveridge.

"Unidentified Hortense Beveridge" trims with which this chapter began. These fragments reveal a poetic resonance between their artifactual marginality as trims and the historical figures that appear in many of them. Raw footage ultimately identified as documenting the Eastern Seaboard Conference of the Sojourners for Truth and Justice, held at the Harlem YMCA on March 23, 1952, chronicles the major radical and communist African American women activists of the era, including Claudia Jones, a heroic and persecuted African American progressive who, as a leading theoretician of the midcentury Communist Party of the USA, articulated the unique "superexploitation" of black working-class women, triply oppressed by virtue of their race, sex, and class; Louise Thompson Patterson, *engagée* of the Harlem Renaissance and close associate of Langston Hughes, with whom she cofounded the Harlem Suitcase Theatre while working as a leading Marxist activist in Harlem; Ella Baker, a legendary organizer whose involvement spanned the 1930s NAACP to the 1960s Student Nonviolent Coordinating Committee; and Charlotta Bass, educator, civil rights advocate, publisher of the *California Eagle* newspaper (from 1912 until 1951), and vice presidential candidate for the Progressive Party

FIGURE 5.5. Louise Thompson Patterson, Sojourner for Truth and Justice. Object ID# 2012.79.1.4.1a. Courtesy of the Estate of Hortense Tee Beveridge.

in 1952. According to historian Erik McDuffie, "no organization was more important to black feminism than the Sojourners for Truth and Justice," which was founded in 1951 by veteran radical Louise Thompson Patterson and young thespian and poet Beulah Richardson.[41] Little other moving image footage of many of these political figures exists, and the silent cinematic specters of such McCarthy-era pariahs seem illicit while simultaneously redemptive as parts of the Smithsonian's national collections, unspooling on a film inspection bench in the shadow of the Washington Monument.

The footage focuses on a table of speakers seated onstage. Actor and organizer Paul Robeson is seated at the far left of the table. Stage left of Robeson are educator and Communist Party leader Dr. Doxey Wilkerson and his wife, Yolanda, along with CAA educational director Alphaeus Hunton, whose activist-wife Dorothy is seen as the footage's first speaker. Activist Claudia Jones is in the foreground, seated at the far right of the onstage table, and Louise Thompson Patterson can be seen in close-up wearing a Sojourners for Truth and Justice ribbon, halfway through the footage. Charlotta Bass can be seen speaking to great applause, and the second-to-last speaker in the footage is playwright Alice Childress.

FIGURE 5.6. Tee Beveridge protesting outside South African Embassy, New York (circa 1963). Courtesy of Lowell P. Beveridge.

The Eastern Seaboard Conference in March 1952 was the group's second (and last) major gathering after its inaugural Washington, DC, convention in fall 1951, and it saw the Sojourners coalesce around their organizational tenets of speaking out about South African apartheid and of fighting against the triple oppression facing working-class black women.[42] By the end of 1952, the group succumbed to the strict anticommunist policy espoused by the NAACP and ceased operations.[43] The conference's timing, its participants, and the Sojourners' activism vis-à-vis South African apartheid make it probable that the Sojourners screened the recently completed *South Africa Uncensored* at this meeting. Other footage among these trims depicts people leaving the double doors of the Lenox Avenue Club Baron—site of several CNA-sponsored plays staged by the People's Showcase Theater in 1951 and 1952—and three minutes of silent black-and-white footage of Paul Robeson dressed as Santa Claus at a Christmas party for the American Labor Party, circa 1950–52, about which less is known.[44]

## Union Woman All the Way: TV Commercials by Day, Subversive Documentary by Night in the 1950s

*South Africa Uncensored* is Beveridge's earliest-known film editing credit, and the film was produced early in her trade education. Archives of the International Alliance of Theatrical Stage Employees (IATSE) Local 771 for Motion Picture Film Editors document Beveridge's membership application to the union on November 25, 1952.[45] Over the course of the next seven years, Beveridge worked her way up through the ranks of the union, initially working for television film advertising production houses run by animators like Shamus Culhane, Dave Hilberman, and William Pomerance. On June 17, 1953, Beveridge became a full-fledged member of Local 771—the first African American woman admitted to what fellow African American female editor and eventual Local 771 member Madeline Anderson described as a "father-son union."[46]

This period marked the zenith of a villainous inquisition by the House Un-American Activities Committee and the FBI, which scrutinized the animation trade as a suspected locus for communist organizers and mind-control operatives.[47] If Beveridge's initial film training was facilitated by politically leftist filmmakers through the CNA, she came to cut her teeth as an editor in a milieu where the same kinds of people became her professional coworkers in commercial production environments. The lack of on-screen credits in television commercials afforded authorial anonymity (and, thus, paying gigs) to then-blacklisted leftist filmmakers like Hurwitz, Lawson, and John and Faith Hubley—the latter of which "had a major impact" on Beveridge as mentors, according to Pete Beveridge. Yet the lack of screen credits also makes it difficult to discern exactly which productions Beveridge worked on.[48] The surge in demand for film labor in early 1950s nontheatrical film and television likely abetted Beveridge's Local 771 membership and fueled her career opportunities; one history of the New York IATSE describes the 1950s as "the renaissance of the film industry in New York," with high-quantity television production serving "like a massive shot of adrenaline."[49]

On January 1, 1954, Beveridge gained promotion to the union rank of assistant editor at Tempo Productions, and by December 1957 she had begun a "trial period for Editorship" at MPO Television Films, graduating to full editor in March 1958.[50] A 1957 *Billboard* advertisement for MPO lists both

FIGURE 5.7. Portrait of editor Hortense Sie (circa 1950s). Courtesy of Lowell P. Beveridge.

Beveridge—still credited with her maiden name, "Hortense Sie"—and Walter Hess among its staff, and the two would later work together on short documentaries on the making of Hollywood dramatic feature films while at the Professional Films company in the 1970s. Walter Hess corroborated to me the fact that MPO made a point of hiring leftists, blacks, and the blacklisted:

> I was part of that leftist group. MPO employed a great number of what you would call leftists, as did several other companies that did similar work. Hortense and I were companions, working next to each other in the cutting room. There was only one other African American editor that I can think of at that time. . . . They were incredibly rare. Tee had a very fine reputation as an editor, especially among that group of leftists. As far as I was concerned, Tee was very reserved. She was not "Hail fellow, well met." She was her own person, and I think the fact that she was black and a woman made her careful about what she might say or do.[51]

Produced for the Hamilton Watch Company, the sponsored film *Ages of Time* (1959) survives in the Pearl Bowser Collection as representative of the commercial union work Beveridge made during daytime hours. A corporate promo in the guise of a sixteen-minute educational film on the history of timekeeping, *Ages of Time* was typical of the kinds of educational-cum-entrepreneurial work Tee edited while at MPO.

In the mid- to late 1950s, while editing corporate-sponsored films by day, Beveridge used her edit suite and her Brooklyn home as an after-hours atelier and refuge for those in need. By 1954, the Beveridges had relocated from Harlem to Crown Heights, Brooklyn, and the various brownstones they came to own over the next twenty years became "open to people who needed a meal, a place to sleep, or a meeting place."[52] In Brooklyn, Communist Party officials requested that they go underground to serve the party "in ways that people who were publicly identified as Communists could not."[53] As they did so, their home became a regular meeting place and way station for a spectrum of New York progressives, among them students from West Africa, civil rights activists on leave from Freedom Summer, South African refugees and members of the African National Congress, and various diplomats from African missions to the United Nations. Beveridge used the comfortable salary afforded by her union editor rank (nearly $30,000 a year by the early 1960s, according to Pete Beveridge), along with her access to professional editing facilities, to help out aspiring and emergent independent filmmakers.[54] Nigerian Francis Oladele was one such independent filmmaker that Beveridge helped by facilitating access to equipment and industry contacts, and she served on the advisory board for his Calpenny-Nigeria Films company. In addition to serving as editor for Amiri Baraka on his 1968 documentary *The New-Ark*, she also mentored St. Clair Bourne, Kathleen Collins, and John Killens at various early stages of their careers.[55]

Two groups of film artifacts that survive in the Pearl Bowser Collection represent Beveridge's underground cinematic labor from the mid-1950s to the mid-1960s, each providing a strong linkage to the kinds of independent African American documentary to emerge by the end of the 1960s. The first, *Hands of Inge*, is a short ten-minute black-and-white documentary about the sculptor and photographer Inge Hardison. Narrated by Ossie Davis, with Eric Dolphy playing clarinet on the soundtrack, the film was produced by African American cinematographer (and fellow IATSE member) John Fletcher and was an important personal project for Beveridge.[56] Completed around 1962, the film is most significant as a cinematic document of African American self-presentation that anticipates the arts and culture documentary segments produced for black television news programs like *Black Journal* and *Like It Is* in the late 1960s.

FIGURE 5.8. Editing *Honeybaby, Honeybaby* in Beirut (circa 1974). Courtesy of Lowell P. Beveridge.

The second group of film artifacts, called by NMAAHC *[NAACP Brooklyn Rally (May 19, 1959)]* and *[Bedford-Stuyvesant Youth in Action]*, relate to Reverend Milton A. Galamison—pastor of the Siloam Baptist Church in Brooklyn's Bedford-Stuyvesant neighborhood, which became a site for community organizing. Both sets of film fragments illustrate Beveridge's instrumental role in making African American self-presentation and documentary film central to Galamison's civil rights and community organizing efforts—the eleven-minute *[NAACP Brooklyn Rally (May 19, 1959)]* as a document of protest against police brutality and the NYPD's murder of African American Al Garrett, and the two-hour *[Bedford-Stuyvesant Youth in Action]* footage, the result of Beveridge's 1966–67 youth filmmaking educational workshops with the community group Bedford-Stuyvesant Youth in Action.

## Conclusion

Hortense "Tee" Beveridge's film career and oeuvre are important evidence for the field of early African American nonfiction filmmaking. Earlier black nonfiction self-presentation films certainly exist, such as the uplift films of the 1910s, amateur home movie films shot by Reverend Solomon Sir Jones in 1920s Oklahoma, and the fieldwork films of Zora Neale Hurston from the late 1920s to 1940. Yet works edited, made, and collected by Beveridge are distinguished by their imbrication in, and demonstration of, African Americans and women in professional film production. Beveridge's parallel output of commercial nonfiction sponsored films and underground progressive political documentary work heralds the advent of a particular racially integrated exposure for African American–authored cinema. A precursor to a pantheon of politically engaged black documentarians over a decade later, Beveridge is a critical yet heretofore unexamined link to the lineage of leftist documentary practices and directors of the 1930s, and a firsthand example of racial integration of the film industry and the American workplace. Indeed, African American documentarians did not simply appear after the integrationist recommendations of the 1968 Kerner Commission's demographic study of the state of the film and television industry.[57] Instead, figures like Beveridge, Madeline Anderson, and others working in nondirectorial cinema technician roles in the 1950s and early 1960s leveraged their perspective, influence, talent, on-the-job experience, and resources to help mentor and make the way for independent nonfiction makers of the later 1960s and '70s. Beveridge's oeuvre also demonstrates that important filmmaking need not always yield a produced, finished product, and that documentary fragments, raw footage, and filmic necessary vitamins held their own distinct value within the organizing efforts of broader social movements.

KNOWN FILMOGRAPHY OF HORTENSE "TEE" BEVERIDGE
Unless otherwise indicated, these titles are available from the National Museum of African American History and Culture's Pearl Bowser Collection. All available films discussed in this chapter can also be streamed through the book's web page at https://www.dukeupress.edu/Features/Screening-Race.

[Harlem Trade Union Council Convention, 1949], 4 min., 16mm
PRODUCTION: Unidentified.

Moxon's Master and Editing Exercises (ca. 1950), 3 min., 16mm
EDITOR: Hortense Sie.

*[Santa Paul Robeson]* (ca. 1951), 2 min., 16mm
PRODUCTION: Unidentified.

*[Sojourners for Truth and Justice, 1952]* (ca. 1952), 8 min., 16mm
PRODUCTION: Unidentified.

*South Africa Uncensored* (1952), 22 min., 16mm
EDITOR: Hortense Sie. DISTRIBUTOR: Council on African Affairs.

*Ages of Time* (1959), 16 min., 16mm
PRODUCER: Victor D. Solow. DIRECTORS: Lew Jacobs, Lloyd Ritter. WRITERS:
Tome McGrath, Lloyd Ritter. EDITOR: Hortense Sie. NARRATOR: Burgess
Meredith.

*[NAACP Brooklyn Rally (May 19, 1959)]*, 11 min., 16mm
PRODUCTION: Andover Productions. CAMERA: John W. Fletcher Jr.

*Hands of Inge* (ca. 1962), 10 min., 16mm
DIRECTOR/CAMERA: John W. Fletcher Jr. EDITOR: Hortense Beveridge. NARRATOR:
Ossie Davis.

*[Bedford-Stuyvesant Youth in Action]* (ca. 1966), 100 min., 16mm
PRODUCTION: Bedford-Stuyvesant Youth in Action. DIRECTOR/EDITOR: Hortense
Beveridge.

*"BULLITT": Steve McQueen's Commitment to Reality* (1968), 10 min., 16mm
PRODUCTION: Professional Films. DIRECTOR: Ronald Saland. WRITER: Jay Anson.
EDITORS: Howard Kuperman, Hortense Beveridge.

*Jeanette Rankin Brigade* (1968), 8 min., 16mm
PRODUCTION: The Newsreel. DIRECTORS/EDITORS: Hortense Beveridge, Ellen
Hirst, Pat Johnson, Peggy Lawson, Karen Mitnick, Lynn Phillips, Gene Searchinger.
ACCESS: Third World Newsreel.

*The Moviemakers* (1968), 7 min., 16mm
PRODUCTION: Unidentified. NOTE: A short documentary featurette on the making of
*The Green Berets*.

*The New-Ark* (1968), 25 min., 16mm
DIRECTOR/WRITER: LeRoi Jones. ASSOCIATE DIRECTOR: Larry Neal. DIRECTOR OF
CAMERA: James E. Hinton. SOUND: Edward Spriggs. EDITOR: Hortense Beveridge.
ACCESS: James E. Hinton Collection, Harvard Film Archive.

*Vienna: The Years Remembered* (1968), 9 min., 16mm
PRODUCTION: Professional Films for Metro-Goldwyn Mayer. WRITER: Jay Anson.
CAMERA: Vincent Corcoran. EDITOR: Hortense Beveridge.

*The World Premiere of "Finian's Rainbow"* (1968), 26 min., 16mm
PRODUCTION: Professional Films. EDITOR: Hortense Beveridge.

*On Location with "The Owl and the Pussycat"* (1970), 6 min., 16mm
PRODUCTION: Professional Films for Columbia Pictures. PRODUCERS/DIRECTORS: Elliot Geisinger, Ronald Saland. WRITER: Jay Anson. CAMERA: Marcel Broekman. EDITOR: Hortense Beveridge.

*The Legend of Nigger Charley* (1972), 98 min., 35mm
PRODUCER: Larry Spangler. DIRECTOR: Martin Goldman. CAMERA: Peter Eco. EDITOR: Howard Kuperman. ASSISTANT EDITOR: Hortense Beveridge.

*Martin Scorsese: Back on the Block* (1973), 7 min., 16mm
PRODUCTION: Robbins Nest Productions/Professional Films. PRODUCER: Ronald Saland. DIRECTOR: Elliot Geisinger. WRITER: Jay Anson. CAMERA: Marcel Broekman. EDITOR: Hortense Beveridge. TITLES AND OPTICALS: Cinopticals, Inc.

*Honeybaby, Honeybaby* (1974), 89 min., 35mm
DIRECTOR: Michael Schultz. EDITOR: Hortense Beveridge.

*Promises to Keep* (1974), 19 min., 16mm
PRODUCTION: Professional Films. PRODUCER: Ronald Saland. DIRECTOR: Elliot Geisinger. WRITER: Jay Anson. EDITOR: Hortense Beveridge.

*Eastwood in Action* (1976), 7 min., 16mm
PRODUCTION: Professional Films/Robbins Nest Productions. PRODUCERS/DIRECTORS: Ronald Saland, Elliot Geisinger. WRITER: Jay Anson. CAMERA: Marcel Broekman. EDITOR: Hortense Beveridge.

*Redd Foxx Becomes a Movie Star* (1976), 8 min., 16mm
PRODUCTION: Robbins Nest Productions/Professional Films. DIRECTOR: Elliot Geisinger. EDITOR: Hortense Beveridge.

*Natural Enemies* (1979), 100 min., 35mm
PRODUCER: John E. Quill. DIRECTOR/EDITOR: Jeff Kanew. ASSISTANT EDITOR: Hortense Beveridge.

*Happy Birthday, Gemini* (1980), 111 min., 35mm
PRODUCTION: Magno Sound, Inc. DIRECTOR: Richard Brenner. EDITOR: Stepham Fanfara. COEDITOR: Hortense Beveridge.

*"Fundi": The Story of Ella Baker* (1981), 63 min., 35mm
DIRECTOR/PRODUCER: Joanne Grant. EDITOR: Hortense Beveridge. ACCESS: Icarus Films.

NOTES
1  Lowell P. Beveridge, *Domestic Diversity and Other Subversive Activities* (Minneapolis: Mill City, 2010).
2  Monica Dall'Asta and Jane M. Gaines, "Past Meets Present in Feminist Film History," in *Doing Women's Film History: Reframing Cinemas, Past and Future*, ed. Christine Gledhill and Julia Knight (Champaign: University of Illinois Press, 2015), 18.

3 Dall'Asta and Gaines, "Past Meets Present," 18, 21.

4 Lowell P. Beveridge, "Biographical Notes on Hortense 'Tee' Beveridge, October 3, 1923–December 8, 1993," email to author.

5 Beveridge, "Biographical Notes." In conversation, Lowell P. Beveridge kindly provided biographical background on Tee Beveridge's parents.

6 Lowell P. Beveridge, interview by Sady Sullivan, May 23, 2012, Crossing Borders, Bridging Generations project, 2011.019.032, https://oralhistory.brooklynhistory .org/interviews/beveridge-pete-20120523/.

7 Beveridge, "Biographical Notes."

8 *The Observer Post: An Undergraduate Newspaper of the CCNY* 6, no. 8 (November 7, 1949), 1; U.S. House of Representatives Committee on Un-American Activities, *Report on the Communist Peace Offensive: A Campaign to Disarm and Defeat the United States* (April 1, 1951; reprint, London: Forgotten Books, 2013), 78–79; J. Angus Johnson, "The United States National Student Association: Democracy, Activism, and the Idea of the Student, 1947–1978" (PhD diss., CUNY, 2009); U.S. House of Representatives Committee on Un-American Activities, *Guide to Subversive Organizations and Publications (and Appendixes): Revised and Published December 1, 1961 to Supersede Guide Published on January 2, 1957 (Including Index)* (Washington, DC: U.S. Government Printing Office, 1962), 50.

9 Beveridge, *Domestic Diversity and Other Subversive Activities*, 107.

10 Beveridge, "Biographical Notes."

11 Lowell P. Beveridge, oral history interview by Pearl Bowser, 1995, collection of the Smithsonian National Museum of African American History and Culture, gift of Pearl Bowser, Object ID# 2012.79.PB.AC.002.30.

12 Committee for the Negro in the Arts, "You've Taken My Blues and Gone . . . ," undated brochure provided to author by Lowell P. Beveridge.

13 Ernest Crichlow (1914–2005), oral history interview, July 20, 1968, Smithsonian Archives of American Art, http://www.aaa.si.edu/collections/interviews/oral -history-interview-ernest-crichlow-11459.

14 Letter from Committee for the Negro in the Arts to W. E. B. Du Bois, June 7, 1951, Credo, University of Massachusetts Amherst, http://credo.library.umass .edu/view/pageturn/mums312-b131-i455/#page/1/mode/1up; Circular letter from Committee for the Negro in the Arts, June 17, 1949, Credo, University of Massachusetts Amherst, http://credo.library.umass.edu/view/pageturn/mums312 -b128-i052/#page/1/mode/1up.

15 Beveridge, interview by Pearl Bowser. Peggy Lawson was the daughter of John Howard Lawson (screenwriter, cultural manager of the Community Party USA, and one of the Hollywood Ten), and a collaborator and wife of leftist documentarian filmmaker Leo Hurwitz.

16 David Platt, "Brooklyn Has a New Film School," *Daily Worker* (New York), October 12, 1946.

17 *Brooklyn Daily Eagle*, January 15, 1947, 7.

18 Jane Corby, "Ex-GIs Focus Camera's Eye on Boro as Nation's Film and Television Center," *Brooklyn Daily Eagle*, April 10, 1949, 27.

19  Corby, "Ex-GIs Focus Camera's Eye," 27; Brenna Sanchez, "Greaves, William 1926–," *Contemporary Black Biography* (Thomson Gale, 2005), Encyclopedia.com, https://www.encyclopedia.com/education/news-wires-white-papers-and-books/greaves-william-1926.

20  Federal Bureau of Investigation, "Stanley Levison, part 5 of 14," file number 100-392452, https://vault.fbi.gov/Stanley%20Levison/Stanley%20Levison%20Part%2005%200f%20109.

21  The edge codes of these films predate Pearl Bowser's film career; as such, they likely belonged to Beveridge.

22  Charles Musser, "Carl Marzani and Union Films: Making Left-Wing Documentaries during the Cold War, 1946–53," *The Moving Image: The Journal of the Association of Moving Image Archivists* 9, no. 1 (spring 2009): 104–60.

23  Musser, "Carl Marzani and Union Films," 121.

24  Like some of the other film materials that this research attributes to Tee Beveridge, these titles all predate Pearl Bowser's career in film, yet were donated to Bowser by Pete Beveridge upon Tee's passing in 1993. While its screen title card irrefutably identifies it as *Count Us In*, Musser's article claims that this film was also known by the titles *Young People's Convention* and *The Young People Meet*.

25  Musser, "Carl Marzani and Union Films," 150.

26  Spencer Moon, *Reel Black Talk: A Sourcebook of 50 American Filmmakers* (London: Greenwood, 1997), 3.

27  Gil Noble, *Black Is the Color of My TV Tube* (Seacaucus, NJ: Lyle Stuart, 1981), 26–27.

28  Martin Bauml Duberman, *Paul Robeson* (New York: Alfred A. Knopf, 1988), 257–58.

29  Gerald Horne, "Looking Forward/Looking Backward: The Black Constituency for Africa Past and Present," *Black Scholar* 29, no. 1 (spring 1999): 30–33.

30  Duberman, *Paul Robeson*, 257.

31  Johanna Selles, "The Hunton Family: A Narrative of Faith through Generations," n.d., 9, Religious Education Association, accessed April 16, 2016, http://old.religiouseducation.net/member/06_rea_papers/Selles_Johanna.pdf.

32  "Mrs. Robeson to Speak in Boston," *Afro-American*, May 5, 1951, 8; "South African Movie Listed at John Wesley," *Courier*, March 14, 1953, 7.

33  Deputy Director, Central Intelligence Agency, to Director, Federal Bureau of Investigation, June 15, 1954, http://www.foia.cia.gov/sites/default/files/document_conversions/89801/DOC_0005497962.pdf.

34  Beveridge, interview by Pearl Bowser.

35  Musser, "Carl Marzani and Union Films," 144–45.

36  Because "useful cinema" is such a wonderful term, I invoke the idea of it as a conceptual lens to view disparate works in educational, nontheatrical, and orphan realms, as set forth in Charles R. Acland and Haidee Wasson, eds., *Useful Cinema* (Durham, NC: Duke University Press, 2011).

37  Paul A. Wagner, "What's Past Is Prologue," in *Sixty Years of 16mm Film 1923–1983* (Evanston, IL: Film Council of America, 1954), 12.

38  Beveridge, *Domestic Diversity and Other Subversive Activities*.

39  Film Division of the National Council of Arts, Sciences and Professions, *Films for '48: A Guide to Progressive Films and Their Use* (New York: National Wallace for President Committee, 1948), 3.

40  "Elect Smith Head of New Union Group," *New York Amsterdam News*, April 9, 1949, 22.

41  Erik McDuffie, *Sojourning for Freedom: Black Women, American Communism, and the Making of Black Left Feminism* (Durham, NC: Duke University Press, 2011), 173, 160.

42  McDuffie, *Sojourning for Freedom*, 178.

43  McDuffie, *Sojourning for Freedom*, 182.

44  Miles M. Jefferson, "The Negro on Broadway 1951–52—Another Transparent Season," *Phylon (1940–1956)* 13, no. 3 (3rd Qtr., 1952): 199–208.

45  Research on Beveridge's membership in Local 771 is enormously indebted to IATSE Local 700 office manager Sandy Fong-Ging, who provided access to the member file on Hortense Sie from which the majority of the dates of employment and employer details derive.

46  Moon, *Reel Black Talk*, 9.

47  Karl F. Cohen, *Forbidden Animation: Censored Cartoons and Blacklisted Animators in America* (London: McFarland, 1997), 171.

48  Beveridge, interview by Pearl Bowser.

49  What is now termed the Motion Picture Editors Guild as a part of the national IATSE Local 700 was, at the time, known as the Editors Union and had its own New York Local 771 chapter. "About Local 52," accessed February 6, 2019, https://www.iatselocal52.org/?zone=view_page.cfm&page=About2ous.

50  Archival records of the IATSE Local 700 include a letter to Local 771 from MPO's Jerry Kleppel, dated March 27, 1958, stating, "This is to inform you that Hortense Sie is now receiving an Editor's salary."

51  Walter Hess, phone interview with the author, April 21, 2016. Information about MPO from Robert McG. Thomas Jr., "Marvin Rothenberg, 79, Dies; Director of Legendary TV Ads," *New York Times*, October 2, 1997.

52  Beveridge, "Biographical Notes."

53  Beveridge, *Domestic Diversity and Other Subversive Activities*, 276.

54  Beveridge, interview by Pearl Bowser.

55  Beveridge, interview by Pearl Bowser.

56  Beveridge, interview by Pearl Bowser.

57  The National Advisory Commission on Civil Disorders, known as the Kerner Commission, was an eleven-member presidential commission established by Lyndon B. Johnson and chaired by Illinois governor Otto Kerner Jr. to investigate the causes of urban unrest and to provide recommendations. Otto Kerner and David Ginsburg, *Report of the National Advisory Commission on Civil Disorders* (New York: Bantam, 1968).

## 6

## Charles and Ray Eames's *Day of the Dead* (1957)

Mexican Folk Art, Educational Film,
and Chicana/o Art

COLIN GUNCKEL

In the last forty years, Día de los Muertos (Day of the Dead) celebrations have spread across the United States. Originating in Mexico as regionally specific combinations of indigenous and Catholic traditions, Day of the Dead is celebrated on November 1 and 2 each year and typically involves leaving offerings for the departed, through the creation of altars in homes or cemeteries.[1] Whether you are familiar with the celebration and its history or not, you have undoubtedly been exposed to a folk art–based aesthetic that circulates through an ever-expanding range of products: feature films like *Book of Life* (Jorge R. Gutiérrez, 2014); accessories like key chains, purses, and smartphone cases; costumes in Halloween stores; and even the labels of commemorative Corona beer cans or the Cerveza de los Muertos craft beer line. The widespread proliferation of this imagery in the last decade or so has sparked debate over the terms on which the holiday has traveled across the border from Mexico into the United States, and beyond. How, for instance, might one draw the line between appreciation and appropriation with regard to Day of the Dead? What are the authentic elements of this holiday and, by extension, the boundaries that allow us to map the territory of its crass exploitation? As was the case when Disney attempted to trademark the phrase "Day of the Dead" in 2013 for a forthcoming animated feature film, many of these conversations and debates have happened through cinema's relationship with the holiday.[2]

FIGURE 6.1. Title card for *Day of the Dead* (1957).

Instead of attempting to resolve these dilemmas, this essay aspires to muddy the waters even further. My decision to do so through a case study of a short, nontheatrical film produced in the United States, Charles and Ray Eames's *Day of the Dead* (1957), is motivated by the unique, pivotal status of the film and, more specifically, what its contexts of production and reception reveal about the holiday's transnational origins. It also provides a vantage point from which to appreciate how cinema has both registered and participated in the ongoing cultural exchanges between the United States and Mexico that have shaped the holiday.

Funded by the International Museum of Folk Art in Santa Fe, New Mexico, for a budget of around $12,000, the fifteen-minute film documents the practices of Day of the Dead in an anonymous Mexican village. The film focuses on the process of celebrating the holiday by tracing the cycle of folk art and decorations central to it. The first section depicts the creation of various handicrafts, from sugar and ceramic skulls to decorative dioramas and pan de muerto (bread baked specifically for placing on memorial altars). The following section consists of images of the local marketplace, accompanied by mariachi music and ambient sound, where villagers purchase these items. Although the film is composed almost entirely of still photos, during this section the filmmakers include moving images of toys and other objects. The final part of the film demonstrates how these objects are integrated into altars or *ofrendas* (offerings) in homes and in celebrations at cemeteries. Throughout, a male narrator (Edgar Kauffman Jr.) provides descriptive information about each stage of the process, while a female narrator (Esperanza Morales, uncredited), offers first-person insight into local beliefs and practices in heavily accented English. While the explicit focus of the film is on the folk objects themselves, those creating, purchasing, and using them are visibly indigenous. *Day of the Dead* thus chronicles an internal circuit of production and consumption of folk art, implicitly positing these practices and beliefs as both inherently indigenous and untouched by any forces outside this archetypical village.

Aside from the notoriety of its directors—two of the most influential designers of the mid-twentieth century—and the novelty of its subject matter, since Day of the Dead was a relatively unknown phenomenon in the United States at that point, the film might on the surface seem a rather unremarkable example of an educational film about an exotic location and its cultural practices. One could easily imagine a critique of this and other U.S.-produced educational or nontheatrical films about Latin America as the very embodiment of an othering or exoticist tourist gaze. As Jacqueline Avila has noted in the case of the World War II–era documentaries produced by the Office of the Coordinator of Inter-American Affairs, for instance, the agency consulted with the Mexican Department of Tourism to select music that would appeal specifically to U.S. viewers, while narration often provided these audiences with a guided tour through exotic and unfamiliar landscapes.[3] Indeed, *Day of the Dead* in many ways exemplifies the convergence of tourist appeal and ethnographic tendencies of U.S.-based cultural production about Mexico and Latin America during the mid-twentieth century.[4]

The film reproduces a familiar logic that associates Day of the Dead with timelessness, tradition, the folkloric, and, by implication, Mexico's indigenous population. In its desire to convey authenticity, however, the film also paradoxically disavows its own remediation of folk art through modern technology, and the imbrication of the supposedly separate spheres of the traditional and modern in this context. The Eames film, in fact, demonstrates the utter impossibility of extricating traditional and folkloric cultural productions from their travels through modern art and popular culture, and the difficulty of making clear, steadfast, or meaningful distinctions between these categories.

FIGURE 6.2. Clay *calavera* figures at the village marketplace in *Day of the Dead* (1957).

FIGURE 6.3. A woman paints a clay tree of life sculpture in *Day of the Dead* (1957).

FIGURE 6.4. A group of moving *calavera* figures in *Day of the Dead* (1957).

FIGURE 6.5. A child plays with a handmade toy in the motion sequence of *Day of the Dead* (1957).

FIGURE 6.6. A family arranges items on their home altar (*ofrenda*) in *Day of the Dead* (1957).

FIGURE 6.7. A shot of a home altar or *ofrenda* that includes items shown during the marketplace sequence of *Day of the Dead* (1957).

Examining the travels of *Day of the Dead* beyond its initial production offers yet another perspective on this dynamic. The Eameses frame the celebration of Día de los Muertos as, in the words of the film's narration, a "strong, consistent thread" of traditional practice; the circulation and reception of the film allowed these elements to be interpreted and adapted beyond this frame, further complicating the boundaries between authenticity and commodification. The Eames film draws from and participates in a long history of transnational exchange, while the representational divides it implicitly establishes between modernity and tradition, familiar and exotic, or Mexico and the U.S. are complicated by the nature of its reception by various audiences. Perhaps most notably, the film's availability and visual impact greatly influenced the embrace of the holiday by Chicana/o artists in the 1970s. This case study thus demonstrates that however one conceives of the category of nontheatrical film—as a set of generic conventions, production practices, circuits of distribution, specific modes of reception, or "a disposition, an outlook, an approach toward a medium"—understanding the representational politics of any particular film is enhanced and complicated by integrating these multiple factors into its historical analysis.[5]

*Day of the Dead* points to an ongoing history of intercultural exchange, uneven though it may have been, one in which Chicana/o artists and filmmakers of the 1960s and 1970s also participated and intervened. What many regard as the earliest and most influential Chicano-movement films—*I Am Joaquín* (Luis Valdez, 1969), *I Am Chicano* (*Yo soy Chicano*, Jesús Salvador Treviño, 1972), *Chicana* (Sylvia Morales, 1979), and *Agueda Martínez: Our People, Our Country* (Esperanza Vasquez, 1977)—not only circulated through educational film circuits but can also be considered nontheatrical films about Mexico and its art. While this unacknowledged lineage places these films in a new light, they also drew on a familiar repertoire of Mexican art and cultural production, unwittingly reproducing some of the essentializing impulses of earlier documentaries about Mexico. *Day of the Dead* thus serves as a point of departure from which to reconsider representational politics and Latina/o cultural production beyond the frame of mainstream cinema or television. If my analysis of *Day of the Dead* proposes that cinema was ultimately central to disseminating the practices and aesthetics of this holiday, the trajectory of the film also demonstrates that nontheatrical films constitute a rich yet overlooked mode of cultural production that generated influential representations of Mexico and its culture.

While known primarily as visual artists and designers, the husband-and-wife team of Charles and Ray Eames were also prolific producers of cinema, making over one hundred films between 1950 and the late 1970s. Rather than placing *Day of the Dead* within the context of their broader careers and artistic output, however, this chapter contextualizes the film within prolific cultural exchanges between the U.S. and Mexico in the mid-twentieth century. Folk art and tourism were central to this dynamic, and the Eameses were undoubtedly tapping into a long-standing interest in and market for Mexican folk art. It is these very circumstances, however, that allow for a reading of the film that undermines unidirectional notions of cultural flow and implicitly undoes conceptions of authenticity often central to the consumption and appreciation of folk art. Despite its structural insistence on folk art as an exclusively internal cultural practice, the film is one example of the circular feedback loop between Mexican folk art producers and consumers in the U.S. Historically speaking, this kind of exchange has often been paradoxically disavowed or obscured in order to reproduce static conceptions of folk art tied to timelessness and authenticity.

According to Pat Kirkham, the Eameses' cinematic output typically resided at the intersection of two interrelated phenomena: postwar experimental film culture and the concurrent explosion in the production of films sponsored by businesses, government agencies, or institutions.[6] The production of *Day of the Dead* was also coincident with the postwar popularity of educational film and the institutions, publications, and distribution mechanisms that participated in their burgeoning respectability and their value in the classroom.[7] As Katerina Loukopoulou has also pointed out, by the 1950s, "film on art" had become an identifiable genre of nontheatrical film that "developed in tandem with changing attitudes about the place of visual arts in education, culture, and society," a phenomenon that remediated the visual arts and extended arts education and appreciation beyond the walls of the museum.[8] Haidee Wasson further demonstrates that the mobilization of cinema by various museums was widespread beginning in the 1920s, although its uses varied according to specific institutional logics and mandates as they sought to engage "evolving public expectations of engagement that were being transformed by popular leisure and other modes of visual culture."[9] In fact, by the time it agreed to distribute *Day of the Dead* in 1957, Film Images, Inc. was already handling films produced by a number of arts institutions, including the Detroit Institute of Arts and the Philadelphia Museum of Art.[10]

FIGURE 6.8. Title credits for *Day of the Dead* (1957).

The funding of *Day of the Dead* by the International Museum of Folk Art fulfilled both an institutional mandate to educate audiences about Mexican folk art and indirectly advertised their substantial collection in this area. Designer and folk art collector Alexander Girard, who like the Eameses had designed for the Herman Miller Furniture Company, was an integral part of the film's production and contributed to it a number of still photographs and materials.[11] He and his wife Susan donated over 100,000 pieces of folk art from around the world to the Museum of Folk Art, constituting the vast majority of the institution's collection in this area. The production of the film emerged as the product of a mutual interest in Mexican folk art on the part of Girard and the Eameses, and of the museum's first foray into the educational and promotional potential of film production. In her review of *Day of the Dead*, modernist photographer Laura Gilpin, who also introduced its first screening at the Museum of Folk Art, extolled the value of such educational art films by explaining that they "preserve disappearing customs, and are the means of presenting material to the greatest possible audience."[12]

By the time *Day of the Dead* was produced in 1957, there was nothing particularly novel about the U.S. interest in Mexican art and culture. As

Helen Delpar has pointed out, the decades following the Mexican Revolution (1910–20) witnessed an "enormous vogue for things Mexican," a trend that included tourism, intellectual exchange, the rise of the Mayan revival style of architecture, a general interest in Mexican art, and the popularity of Mexican music.[13] Charles Eames himself had participated in this trend: he traveled around Mexico for nine months in 1933 to escape the Depression, selling paintings along the way and beginning his collection of Mexican folk art and toys.[14] More than acting as mere consumers of folk art objects, such individuals from the U.S. and Europe were key to fostering their appreciation as expressions of national culture in the postrevolutionary era. As Rick A. López has documented, a substantial number of non-Mexican individuals were, perhaps paradoxically, central to the formulation of a notion of *mexicanidad* (Mexicanness) and cultural nationalism that postulated the rural and indigenous as authentic embodiments of the nation.[15] The pioneering periodical that both reflected and stimulated U.S. interest in folk art was *Mexican Folkways* (1925–37), edited by U.S.-born Frances Toor in collaboration with muralist Diego Rivera as art editor. The bilingual magazine was sponsored by Mexico's Secretaría de Educación Pública (Secretary of Public Education) and covered art, archaeology, and music, featuring contributions from notable artists and intellectuals. *Folkways*, in addition to Robert Redfield's ethnographic writing on the town of Tepoztlán, may have also facilitated the first glimpses for interested U.S. readers of the Mexican ceremonies and celebrations related to death and Day of the Dead as early as 1930.[16]

If these were the channels through which the holiday and its artistic manifestations began to circulate across the border, this phenomenon accelerated substantially after World War II. In 1947, Toor published the encyclopedic *Treasury of Mexican Folkways*, which included drawings by artist Carlos Mérida and a chapter on the Day of the Dead. This book was reprinted multiple times throughout the 1950s and 1960s and was part of a resurgence of transnationally oriented publications and venues that promoted and made visible Mexican cultural production.[17] From 1948 to 1952, for instance, Mexico's Secretaría de Educación Pública published *México en el Arte* (Mexico in Art), a magazine very much in keeping with its predecessor *Folkways*. One issue was dedicated entirely to the artistic manifestations of Day of the Dead, including a cover portrait by Alfredo Zalce of printmaker José Guadalupe Posada surrounded by the *calaveras* (skeletons) that were a staple of his printmaking.[18] There was also an explosion of publishing on both sides of the border directed at a multinational audience and focusing on Mexican folk art and culture.[19] There were exhibitions of Mexican folk art in the

United States during this period that included works produced for Day of the Dead, and perhaps the first thesis written in the United States about the artistic production associated with Day of the Dead, which was authored in 1956.[20]

The Eameses' *Day of the Dead* was among a number of nontheatrical films produced about indigenous Mexico, preconquest civilizations, or folk art during this particular moment of intercultural exchange and tourism. These included *The Aztecs* (Coronet Films, 1955), *Doña Rosa: Potter of Coyotepec* (Orville Goldner, 1959), *Maya Are People* (Les Mitchel, 1951), *Fisher Folk of Lake Pátzcuaro* (Ralph Adams, 1951), *Pottery Workers of Oaxaca* (Ralph Adams, 1952), *Mexican Village Life* (Willard Hahn, 1958), and *Heritage from Tula* (Joseph Ehrhard and Mel Fowler, 1960), to name just a few. These films, almost without exception, focus on indigenous Mexico as the epicenter of cultural authenticity and the locus of Mexican identity. Variations of this concept were central to the official formulations of national identity and history in the postrevolutionary era, while simultaneously doubling as a strategy to attract tourists with the promise of a scenic, exotic, rural, indigenous, and authentic Mexico. Folk art and its dissemination—both physically and as mediated images—were central to this effort.

What is important to note about the role of nontheatrical films about Mexico and their circulation in the United States, however, is that they did more than simply document folk art or educate English-speaking audiences about it. Contrary to the hermetic circuit of production and consumption portrayed in *Day of the Dead*, U.S.-based patrons and collectors actively shaped the market for such items, at times dictating or guiding the kind of work produced. As Regina Marchi points out, not only did the Mexican government's active promotion of folk art revive certain artistic traditions, but "entirely new crafts were invented to please tourist desires for 'Indian' artifacts, and marketed as 'timeless' Mexican customs," some of them related to Day of the Dead.[21] In his analysis of Mexican folk art in which he productively dismantles familiar dichotomies between modernization and supposedly static, traditional, and premodern cultures, Néstor García Canclini argues that cultural production regarded as folk art has actually flourished through its encounters with modernity, tourism, and culture industries.[22] Attending to the transcultural networks and exchanges sustained by its producers undermines monolithic, romanticized conceptions of indigenous peoples embraced by the Mexican state in both its formulation of nationalism and its promotion of folk art. It is this very set of industrial forces and contexts in which *Day of the Dead* originally operated, while it simultaneously

FIGURE 6.9. Sugar skulls on display in a Mexican market in *Day of the Dead* (1957).

(and perhaps unintentionally) functioned as an agent and facilitator of these transnational dynamics.

The Eames film, by claiming that "the people that produce [folk art] are the same as the people that will buy and use it," not only denies the transnational underpinnings of the folk art market by 1957, but it also disavows the role of the filmmakers and their sponsors in this economy. More than simply documenting or (in the words of Laura Gilpin) "preserving" a supposedly timeless celebration and its accouterments, the Eameses and their cohorts had a hand in shaping them as contemporary, intercultural practices. This is not to overstate the influence of Charles and Ray Eames, nor to suggest that they or U.S.-based patrons and intellectuals deserve credit for the development of Day of the Dead. Rather, it is to suggest that such cultural texts complicate the way that we understand transnational cultural flows. Accounting for these flows impacts the way we historicize Day of the Dead, and how this dimension of the holiday's history prompts us to rethink the cultural or national boundaries that frequently dictate how we discuss art or cinema. This dynamic becomes even more apparent once we move from the context of the film's production to its distribution and reception.

Both the subject matter of the film and the reputation of its directors shaped the contexts in which it was exhibited in the decade or so after its production. Within and beyond the United States, it was shown at film festivals, at arts festivals, at a book fair, as a short film preceding a feature in an art house program, as one film in a showcase of Eames films, or as part of museum programming that focused on Mexican art.[23] The potential meanings and uses of *Day of the Dead* are inextricable from the travels of a film whose short running time and widespread availability allowed it a degree of malleability not immediately apparent within the text itself. In this sense, by expanding on García Canclini's observations, we might make a distinction between the representational politics of the cinematic text—which seem to reproduce an essentializing vision of rural, indigenous Mexico—and other representational potentials enabled by its promiscuous distribution through various contexts.

In fact, this short, fifteen-minute film had a significant yet unacknowledged impact on the way that the holiday is celebrated on this side of the border. In particular, it served as an important resource for California-based Chicana/o artists in the early 1970s who adopted Day of the Dead as part of their community-based artistic practice. Most scholars have attributed the emergence of Day of the Dead in the United States to cultural centers on the West Coast: Self Help Graphics and Art in East Los Angeles and Galería de la Raza in San Francisco.[24] According to scholar and curator Tere Romo, the celebration in these contexts was tied to the formulation of Chicana/o identity, in which "artists became part of a cultural reclamation process to reintroduce Mexican art and history, revitalize popular artistic expressions, and support community cultural activities."[25] While both cities can now take for granted the long-standing celebrations these centers established, the artists that pioneered these practices in the early 1970s faced a formidable challenge: the nearly complete lack of resources and research available about the celebration. As Self Help artist Linda Vallejo has explained, "There was no Internet at this time, so we were going to libraries and going through catalogs and literally could find nothing. We couldn't find anything in the United States, published in English, about Day of the Dead."[26] One of the key exceptions to this lack of resources was the Eames film, which had been discovered by Self Help's cofounder and director, Sister Karen Boccalero.

While relying on the film to get a sense of the aesthetics and artwork that accompanied the celebration, which could also then be integrated into art education lessons, Self Help artists went beyond simply emulating the cultural production that appears in the film. By the mid-1970s, the festivities included altar building, a parade, theatrical productions, musical performances, and an art exhibition. All of these departed in significant ways from more traditional manifestations represented in the Eames film to instead allow artists to creatively interpret the celebration and its significance. In other words, by the end of the 1970s, Day of the Dead was not only a staple of the Chicano cultural calendar; it had been adapted and reworked as an avenue for uniquely Chicana/o cultural production. In turn, their transformation of the holiday into a public celebration fundamentally influenced the way it is now practiced across the country.

This brief history demonstrates the unintended audiences and impacts that a nontheatrical film may have as it circulates through institutions and collections over time. In fact, the history of the Day of the Dead between the United States and Mexico could be written as a series of labyrinthine transactions occurring through moving image media and other cultural products. In 2015, for instance, Mexico City decided to hold the city's first-ever Day of the Dead parade, an event initially staged and popularized exclusively for the shooting of the James Bond installment *Spectre* (Sam Mendes, 2015). In other words, a midcentury film about Mexican folk art was an important inspiration for a Chicana/o celebration that transformed the event into a public parade, a practice that would then become, through a popular blockbuster, part of Mexico's own celebration of Day of the Dead. As Regina M. Marchi has argued, a transnational analysis of the holiday readily complicates "unidirectional cultural flows": "This is a case of 'third world' practices being reconfigured by a politically marginalized population in the 'first world' in ways that have not only influenced mainstream U.S. culture, but have recirculated to Mexico, influencing artistic and political expressions of the holiday there," with much of this recirculation occurring through moving image media.[27]

But the example of *Day of the Dead* also demonstrates how social movements could creatively adapt, apply, and rethink such films in the process of establishing new practices, formulating new conceptions of identity, and engaging in battles over media representation. In particular, the Chicano movement's creative mobilization and reworking of this film is indicative of its relationship to the engagement with Mexico on the part of filmmakers and modern artists. This harnessing and reorientation of cultural production on the part of Chicana/o artists is also part of an unacknowledged history of both Latina/o cinema and nontheatrical film. First, nontheatrical or educational films were often a part of programming at Chicano cultural centers. Self Help Graphics, for instance, offered screenings of films whose subject coincided with its combined emphasis on cultural identity and arts education. One film series in 1974 featured a range of shorts that included *The Ancient Peruvian* (Julien Bryan, 1968), *Day of the Painter* (Robert P. Davis, 1960), *Yo soy Chicano*, and *Early Expressionists* (Rhoda Kellogg, Summus Films, 1965).[28] Perhaps more important, a good number of early Chicana/o films were nontheatrical shorts, and were distributed as such, as was the case with *I Am Joaquín* and *Chicana*, or they were produced for television and then subsequently distributed to educational institutions.[29]

Aside from their significant differences, a number of these Chicana/o-produced films build a visual argument through a succession of still images combined with voice-over narration. They often combine historical photography, images of Mexican murals, reproductions of preconquest art, and photographs of contemporary Chicana/os. What is particularly intriguing about films like *I Am Joaquín* and *Chicana*, aside from their largely unacknowledged status as nontheatrical or educational films, is that they, like *Day of the Dead*, function as an examination and analysis of Mexican art forms. The treatment and function of art in the Chicana/o films, however, is distinct, and might conceivably be regarded as an intervention, intentional or otherwise, in the genre of nontheatrical films about Mexican art. In this sense, they adopt a very different address, tone, gaze, and argumentation than the aforementioned educational films on Mexican art and culture. Most notably, Chicana/o artists actively rejected the exoticizing gaze directed at Mexico and Mexicans to mobilize the art in question as way of formulating historically informed conceptions of Chicana/o identity by placing historical and contemporary images in dialogue and juxtaposition. Rather than educating potential audiences about the artwork itself, these films instead posit them as illustrations and embodiments of Chicana/o cultural heritage.

Despite their significant differences, however, the Chicana/o films also bear multiple traces of their textual and conceptual connections to films like *Day of the Dead*. That is, if these earlier films present Mexico and indigenous Mexicans as timeless repositories of traditional culture, the Chicana/o films might justifiably be accused of a similar maneuver, despite their efforts to animate history by linking it to contemporary realities. In her critique of *I Am Joaquín*, for instance, Rosa Linda Fregoso argues that the film "re-invents an 'authentic' identity for Chicanos" through a "selective interpretation of the past," one that "stresses the Indian side of the equation."[30] By explicitly emulating artists like Diego Rivera, who fashioned a Mexican modernism that integrated preconquest and folk art as articulations of contemporary national identity, this early generation of Chicana/o artists and filmmakers often reproduced a

FIGURE 6.10. A young man paints a clay tree of life sculpture in *Day of the Dead* (1957).

romanticized, essentialized vision of the nation's indigenous heritage as symbol and stereotype. In this sense, their appropriation and reworking of Mexican nationalism through the selective presentation of artistic production also inherited some of the conceptual oversights and elisions perpetuated by other U.S.-based filmmakers, including the Eameses. There is consequently a palpable disconnect between the promiscuous, multifaceted travels of folk art, indigenous Mexico, and Day of the Dead that informed the production of nontheatrical films and the partial disavowal of these exchanges through a recourse to cultural authenticity. This very dilemma is at the heart of contemporary debates about the holiday; dwelling in this paradoxical tension might also provide a way of productively thinking through it.

## Conclusion

While following the origins, travels, and legacy of *Day of the Dead* provides insight into the history of the holiday and an underacknowledged lineage of representational politics, it also demonstrates how the historical study of cinema and popular culture might intervene in contemporary conversations about the celebration. So many of the debates around Day of the Dead, as Marchi points out, hinge precisely on conceptions of authenticity. Within this dynamic, critics frequently posit Day of the Dead as a pure, ancient, indigenous practice that has been adapted or appropriated by individuals, groups, and institutions in the United States. This perspective deems the indigenous population of Mexico to be a repository of authenticity and traditional practices, often placing them outside processes of modernity and cultural exchange. As such, the ahistorical fetishization of these qualities falls squarely in line with conceptions and representations of Mexican indigeneity in the twentieth century.

The polarization of modern and indigenous within these debates finds its parallels in the reliance on the supposedly oppositional dichotomy between commercialization and authenticity. These divisions are not only problematic but also overlook the role of media in the dissemination, revitalization, and durability of Day of the Dead on both sides of the border in the twentieth century. That is, the contemporary popularity and visual aesthetics of Day of the Dead can arguably be traced through twentieth-century art as transnational exchange: in the mass-produced prints of Posada at the turn of the last century; the emulation and reproduction of these by Sergei Eisenstein in his Epilogue for ¡Que Viva México! (1932); the travels of such imagery through transnational publications and tourism; the circulation and impact of *Day of the Dead*; and internationally distributed art films like *Macario* (Roberto Gavaldón, 1960) and *Under the Volcano* (John Huston, 1984). Rather than establishing these only as prominent instances of the holiday's mediation or representation, they have also served as vehicles through which Day of the Dead has circulated and transformed in the twentieth century.

Maintaining a false division between commodification and authenticity is thus not only disingenuous but also counterproductive. In other words, it may be clear that Disney's attempt to trademark the phrase "Day of the Dead," to return to a recent example, represents cultural appropriation at its most obvious, but advocating for a cleavage between the holiday and its extensive travels through popular culture is historically inaccurate. In fact, the ultimate success of Disney Pixar's *Coco* (2017)—which set box office records in Mexico—has been at least partially attributed to the strategic hiring of consultants to ensure an authentic representation of the holiday, including individuals associated with Self Help Graphics. As even this case suggests, adopting a rigid dichotomy between authenticity and commercialization does not allow us to think in a more complex or nuanced fashion about how and in what ways Day of the Dead can be meaningfully defined, celebrated, and understood in the contemporary moment. Perhaps the deceptively straightforward nature of the Eames film is also an apt metaphor for contemporary debates about Day of the Dead, which are so often premised on strict dividing lines of authenticity, ethnicity, or nationality. As a historical investigation of its production and reception reveals, however, we might instead direct our questions toward the unruly zone of inauthenticity and cultural exchange, to the decidedly gray area where Day of the Dead celebrations on both sides of the border currently reside.

FILMOGRAPHY

All available films discussed in this chapter can be streamed through the book's web page at https://www.dukeupress.edu/Features/Screening-Race.

*Chicana* (1979), 23 min., 16mm
PRODUCER: Sylvia Morales. DIRECTOR: Sylvia Morales. WRITER: Anna Nieto-Gomez. NARRATION: Carmen Zapata. MUSIC: Carmen Moreno. ACCESS: DVD, Women Make Movies.

*Day of the Dead* (1957), 15 min., 16mm
PRODUCTION: Museum of International Folk Art. DIRECTORS: Charles Eames, Ray Eames. ADDITIONAL PHOTOGRAPHY: Alexander Girard, Susan Girard, Deborah Sussman. MUSIC: Laurindo Almeida. ACCESS: DVD, *The Films of Charles and Ray Eames*, vol. 6 (Chatsworth, CA: Image Entertainment).

*Doña Rosa: Potter of Coyotepec* (1959), 10 min., 16mm
PRODUCER: Orville Goldner. DIRECTOR: Orville Goldner. ACCESS: Academic Film Archive of North America.

*I Am Joaquín (Yo soy Joaquín*, 1969), 29 min., 16mm
PRODUCTION: Teatro Campesino. DIRECTOR: Luis Valdez. MUSIC: Daniel Valdez. NARRATION: Luis Valdez. PHOTOGRAPHY: George Ballis. ACCESS: 16mm, out-of-print DVD and VHS through WorldCat.

*Mexican Village Life* (1958), 16 min., 16mm
PRODUCTION: Paul Hoefler Productions. DIRECTOR: Willard C. Hahn. ACCESS: Academic Film Archive of North America.

*Pottery Workers of Oaxaca* (1952), 14 min., 16mm
PRODUCER: Ralph Adams Productions. DIRECTOR: Ralph Adams. ACCESS: Academic Film Archive of North America.

*Yo soy Chicano* (1972), 59 min., 16mm
PRODUCTION: Jesús Salvador Treviño at KCET Los Angeles. DIRECTOR/EDITOR: Barry Nye. WRITER: Jesús Salvador Treviño. NARRATION: Victor Millan. MUSIC: Daniel Valdez, El Teatro Campesino Cultural. ACCESS: DVD, Cinema Guild, New York.

NOTES

This essay is dedicated to those who have forever shaped my own relationship to Day of the Dead: Kenny Chávez, Daniel González, Ana Guajardo, Ruth Savig, and the In Crowd. I would also like to thank Carren Kaston and Orquidea Morales for their crucial research assistance.

1  For an extensive history of the holiday in Mexico, see Claudio Lomnitz, *Death and the Idea of Mexico* (Brooklyn: Zone, 2005).

2  For coverage of this incident and the backlash it generated, see "Disney Drops Bid to Trademark Day of the Dead," *Guardian*, May 8, 2013, https://www.theguardian .com/film/2013/may/08/disney-trademark-day-dead-festival-pixar. Disney ceased the pursuit of the trademark but still produced a Day of the Dead–themed film, retitled *Coco* (2017).

3  Jacqueline Avila, "The Sounds of Mexico: Music in the OCIAA Documentaries," paper presented at the Latin American Music Center's Fiftieth Anniversary Conference, "Cultural Counterpoints: Examining the Musical Interactions between the U.S. and Latin America," Indiana University, Bloomington, October 19–23, 2011. Available from IUScholarWorks, https://scholarworks.iu.edu/dspace/handle /2022/15482.

4  These tendencies are articulated by Ana M. López, "Are All Latins from Manhattan? Hollywood, Ethnography, and Cultural Colonialism," in *Unspeakable Images: Ethnicity and the American Cinema*, ed. Lester D. Friedman (Urbana: University of Illinois Press, 1991), 404–24.

5  Haidee Wasson and Charles R. Acland, "Introduction: Utility and Cinema," in *Useful Cinema*, ed. Charles R. Acland and Haidee Wasson (Durham, NC: Duke University Press, 2011), 4.

6  Pat Kirkham, *Charles and Ray Eames: Designers of the Twentieth Century* (Cambridge, MA: MIT Press, 1995), 309–17.

7  Devin Orgeron, Marsha Orgeron, and Dan Streible, "A History of Learning with the Lights Off," in *Learning with the Lights Off: Educational Film in the United States*, ed. Devin Orgeron, Marsha Orgeron, and Dan Streible (New York: Oxford University Press, 2012), 40–41.

8  Katerina Loukopoulou, "Museum at Large: Aesthetic Education through Film," in *Learning with the Lights Off: Educational Film in the United States*, ed. Devin Orgeron, Marsha Orgeron, and Dan Streible (New York: Oxford University Press, 2012), 357.

9  Haidee Wasson, "Big, Fast Museums/Small, Slow Movies," in *Useful Cinema*, ed. Charles R. Acland and Haidee Wasson (Durham, NC: Duke University Press, 2011), 196–97. See also Haidee Wasson, *Museum Movies: The Museum of Modern Art and the Birth of Art Cinema* (Berkeley: University of California Press, 2005).

10  Rosalind Kossoff to Charles Eames, September 25, 1957, Charles and Ray Eames Papers, part 2, box 122, folder 2, "*Day of the Dead* (1957) correspondence, 1956–1960," Manuscript Division, Library of Congress, Washington, DC.

11  See Jack Lenor Larsen, "A Celebration of the Senses," in *Folk Art from the Global Village: The Girard Collection at the Museum of International Folk Art* (Santa Fe:

Museum of New Mexico Press, 1995), 12–31. See also Henry Glassie, *The Spirit of Folk Art: The Girard Collection at the Museum of International Folk Art* (New York: Harry N. Abrams, 1989).

12  Laura Gilpin, "Miss Gilpin Praises Day of the Dead Technic," *Santa Fe New Mexican*, October 27, 1957, n.p., Charles and Ray Eames Papers, part 2, box 122, folder 2.

13  Helen Delpar, *The Enormous Vogue for Things Mexican: Cultural Relations between the United States and Mexico, 1920–1935* (Tuscaloosa: University of Alabama Press, 1992). See also Marjorie Ingle, *The Mayan Revival Style: Art Deco Mayan Fantasy* (Salt Lake City: G. M. Smith, 1984).

14  Gloria Koenig, *Charles and Ray Eames, 1907–1978, 1912–1988: Pioneers of Mid-century Modernism* (Los Angeles: Taschen, 2005), 68–69; Kirkham, *Charles and Ray Eames*, 16–18.

15  Rick A. López, *Crafting Mexico: Intellectuals, Artisans, and the State after the Revolution* (Durham, NC: Duke University Press, 2010), 97.

16  Robert Redfield, *Tepoztlán, a Mexican Village: A Study of Folk Life* (Chicago: University of Chicago Press, 1931). See, for instance, the multiple articles on Day of the Dead and artistic production in *Mexican Folk-Ways* 6, no. 3 (1930).

17  Frances Toor, *A Treasury of Mexican Folkways: The Customs, Myths, Folklore, Traditions, Beliefs, Fiestas, Dances and Songs of the Mexican People* (New York: Crown, 1962), 236–44.

18  *México en el Arte*, no. 5 (November 1948).

19  See, for instance, Justino Fernández, *Mexican Folklore: 100 Photographs by Luis Márquez* (Mexico City: Eugenio Fischgrund, 1950); Patricia Fent Ross, *Made in Mexico: The Story of a Country's Arts and Crafts* (New York: Knopf, 1952); and Imgard Groth-Kimball, *The Art of Ancient Mexico* (New York: Thames and Hudson, 1954).

20  See *Mexican Popular Arts Today* [exhibition catalog] (Colorado Springs: Taylor Museum of the Colorado Springs Fine Arts Center, 1954); Ruth Elese Gardener, "An Investigative and Interpretive Study with Paintings, Drawings, and Prints of 'All Saints Day' and 'All Souls Day' in Mexico" (master's thesis, University of Denver, 1956).

21  Regina Marchi, *Day of the Dead in the U.S.A.: The Migration and Transformation of a Cultural Phenomenon* (New Brunswick, NJ: Rutgers University Press, 2009), 125.

22  Néstor García Canclini, *Hybrid Cultures: Strategies for Entering and Leaving Modernity* (Minneapolis: University of Minnesota Press, 1995), 175.

23  "U.S. Film Shorts Set for Festival," *New York Times*, February 13, 1960, 13; "Lectures, Films to Highlight Art Festival," *Los Angeles Times*, April 28, 1963, WS_A12; "Book Fair to Be Held at College," *Los Angeles Times*, November 1, 1968, F6; Richard L. Coe, "One on the Air: Hey! Let's Watch It, Eh?," *Washington Post*, February 28, 1962, C7; "Lectures and Meetings," *Observer* (London), October 29, 1961, 28; and "Calendar," *Los Angeles Times*, December 6, 1970, V28; "Art News: Colonial Works of Mexico to Be Lecture Topic," *Los Angeles Times*, November 17, 1963, B28.

24  For the most extensive examination of the holiday in California, see *Chicanos en Mictlán: Día de los Muertos in California* (San Francisco: Mexican Museum, 2000).

25 Tere Romo, "Chicanos en Mictlán: A Curatorial Perspective," in *Chicanos en Mictlán: Día de los Muertos in California* (San Francisco: Mexican Museum, 2000), 7.

26 Karen Mary Davalos and Colin Gunckel, "The Early Years, 1970–1985: An Interview with Michael Amescua, Mari Cárdenas Yañez, Yreina Cervantez, Leo Limón, Peter Tovar, and Linda Vallejo," in *Self Help Graphics and Art: Art in the Heart of East Los Angeles*, 2nd ed., ed. Colin Gunckel (Los Angeles: UCLA Chicano Studies Research Center Press, 2014), 66.

27 Marchi, *Day of the Dead in the U.S.A.*, 5.

28 See "Self Help Graphics Tuesday Nite Film Series," 1974, Self Help Graphics and Art Archives, CEMA 3, box 7, California Ethnic and Multicultural Archives, University of California, Santa Barbara.

29 See, for instance, brochure for *I Am Joaquín*, Teatro Campesino Archives, CEMA 5, series 14, box 2, California Ethnic and Multicultural Archives.

30 Rosa Linda Fregoso, *The Bronze Screen: Chicana and Chicano Film Culture* (Minneapolis: University of Minnesota Press, 1993), 6–7. For another insightful analysis of these films, including *I Am Joaquín*, see Richard T. Rodríguez, *Next of Kin: The Family in Chicano/a Cultural Politics* (Durham, NC: Duke University Press, 2009), 57–64.

# 7

## Ever-Widening Horizons?

### The National Urban League and the Pathologization of Blackness in *A Morning for Jimmy* (1960)

MICHELLE KELLEY

Your experience has nothing to do with the other fella. Just because he is discouraged, you have no right to be. You are a person, with a mind, an individual. You got to be better than the other fella. And you can be.—JIMMY'S GRANDFATHER IN *A Morning for Jimmy*

In 1960, Mrs. H. Sale of Midland, Texas, wrote to Association Films, distributor of the National Urban League (NUL) film *A Morning for Jimmy* (Barry K. Brown, 1960). In the handwritten letter, forwarded by Association Films to the league, Mrs. Sale, a white woman, lauds the film's ethos of self-help: "Today I saw a film produced for the National Urban League by your company. It was excellently produced + photographed, and put the stress on the responsibility of the Negro himself rather than expecting the white man to do something for him." Mrs. Sale proceeds to commend the NUL for espousing a by-your-bootstraps philosophy of black social uplift, which she suggests distinguishes the league from the civil rights organization with which it was often compared, the National Association for the Advancement of Colored People (NAACP). "It has seemed to me," she writes, "that the NAACP has been primarily concerned with fomenting unrest instead of educating the Negro to his own responsibility to improve his lot." Mrs. Sale concludes her letter by asserting the importance of educating both blacks and whites in order to affect social progress and curb prejudice.[1]

Described in the NUL's press release as "a vivid portrayal of the problem of guidance and incentive faced by many minority youth," *A Morning for*

A thought-provoking

documentary

presented by the

NATIONAL URBAN LEAGUE

—an interracial community service
agency conducting a program of
vocational guidance services for
young people

FIGURE 7.1. Page from a promotional brochure for *A Morning for Jimmy*. Despite the pamphlet's description of the film as a documentary, Jimmy is a fictional character. The black professionals he meets, however, are not. Box II, E1, Folder "'A Morning for Jimmy'—New Trailer. 1963," NUL records.

*Jimmy* tells the story of an African American teenager whose encounter with discriminatory hiring practices causes him to doubt the attainability of his goal to become an architect.[2] However, with the help of his teacher and an array of black professionals, Jimmy learns that if he works very hard, he may be able to achieve his dreams. *Jimmy* features a score by accomplished jazz musician Billy Taylor and a cast of both amateur and professional actors, including New York City's High School of the Performing Arts student James Pemberton as Jimmy and a young Cicely Tyson in the role of Jimmy's sister. Completed in 1960, the film was distributed nontheatrically on 16mm and broadcast on television across the country. The NUL determined that over 50 percent of those who saw *Jimmy* at a nontheatrical screening, such as a school assembly, NUL event, or civic group meeting, were African American high school students in the South, a demographic it was eager to reach with its message of expanding professional opportunities for black youth.[3] By 1962, the league estimated that roughly eight million viewers had seen *A Morning for Jimmy* either on TV or at a nontheatrical screening.[4]

Viewers reportedly responded favorably to *A Morning for Jimmy*. These viewers included both racial conservatives like Mrs. Sale, who argued that it was the responsibility of African Americans themselves to redress inequality, and black youth from Dallas to New York who drew inspiration from the film's rare depiction of black professionals and a black middle-class family.[5] Yet as I will argue, despite its appeal to viewers of varying races, ages, and social positions, *A Morning for Jimmy* is a racially conservative film that negatively characterizes black identity and solidarity. In this chapter, I trace the planning and production of what became *A Morning for Jimmy* from 1955, when screenwriter Bernard Miller submitted a script to the league called *A World for Jim*. For reasons I discuss below, the project was suspended. By the time it was resumed in 1960, profound changes had occurred, both within the broad context of U.S. race relations and, more specifically, within liberal thought on race, prejudice, and inequality. *World/Morning* bears traces of these changes, which subtly informed the project's evolution.

Both Miller's *World* script and *A Morning for Jimmy* downplay the role of systemic racism and discrimination in perpetuating racial inequality. Instead, they suggest that black people themselves have impeded racial progress by becoming embittered by their encounters with prejudice. However, *World* and *Morning* differ in their characterization of this bitterness. *World* focuses on the supposed psychological pathology of the individual black child. The script's protagonist, Jim Anderson, struggles to overcome emotional barriers within himself to achieve his vocational goals. In contrast, *Morning* focuses on the pathology not of the black child but of the black community, personified by Jimmy Carroll's father. Racial liberals of the 1950s and '60s argued that African Americans were psychologically damaged, believing that by pointing to the harm white racism causes its victims, they were helping to combat injustice. Yet these arguments stigmatized African Americans as pathological while displacing focus away from the pathology of white racism. Similarly, although both *A World for Jim* and *A Morning for Jimmy* acknowledge the very real psychic pain that systemic white racism can cause, by focusing on this pain as the primary obstacle its protagonists must overcome, they deflect from the problem of racism as such. As a result, the *World/Morning* project places the onus for racial progress on black people themselves, suggesting that what needs to change is not society at large, but rather African Americans' response to it.

## "Not Alms but Opportunity": The National Urban League

*A Morning for Jimmy* is informed by the NUL's long-standing belief that, as Miller writes in a prefatory statement to his script, "the Negro at work is his most convincing argument" against discrimination.[6] Since its establishment in 1911, the league had ascribed to the idea that the best way to overcome racial inequality in the U.S. was through displays of black merit in the work-force. Middle- and upper-class reformers, both black and white, established the league to help recent rural migrants to New York City assimilate to urban life, yet their attitude toward the new arrivals was, at best, benevolently pa-ternalistic. When, in the midst of the first wave of the Great Migration, the city implemented a series of Jim Crow laws, these reformers responded not by decrying the city's racist response to the migration, but rather by attempt-ing to reform the attitudes and behaviors of the recent migrants.[7]

The NUL's approach to black uplift changed only slightly in the context of the civil rights era. Due in part to progress made in legislative reform efforts in the 1950s, in the 1960s the league embraced legalism as a supplement to its primary, merit-based strategy of black advancement. As NUL public rela-tions executive Guichard Parris wrote in his history of the league, "For the first time . . . the NUL advanced from its traditional position of asking 'not alms but opportunity,' or simply for equal opportunity. It recognized and admitted the impossibility of blacks to compete equally because of historic handicaps and called for similar recognition from society." For Parris, this was "special pleading without apology."[8] Nevertheless, despite this acknowl-edgment of structural inequality in the 1960s, the league's members main-tained their faith in the idea that the U.S. was, in essence, a meritocracy, and they averred the notion that displays of black merit in the workforce would lead, gradually but inexorably, to racism's ultimate eradication.

*A Morning for Jimmy* was not the NUL's first foray into the use of mass media to promote its work and spread its racially moderate message. As Barbara Diane Savage has documented, the league gained unprecedented access to the nation's airwaves during World War II. The wartime emergency and its attendant increase in racial tensions created an incentive for the net-works to broadcast the league's messages of tolerance, inclusivity, and black merit.[9] In the 1950s, the league continued to work in radio while attempting to expand into film and TV, though these efforts repeatedly met with failure. It was not until *A Morning for Jimmy* that the NUL achieved its long-standing ambition of making a vocational guidance film of sufficient quality to find a wide audience outside the league.

## *Jimmy*'s Roots: Planning and Production History

The league began to plan for the production of a vocational guidance film in 1955. The project was initiated as part of the NUL's Tomorrow's Scientists and Technicians campaign, which aimed to encourage African American youth to pursue careers in skilled professions historically barred to them. Bernard Miller, a little-known writer with a background in television and nontheatrical film, wrote the preliminary script. Titled *A World for Jim*, Miller's script explores the plight of Jim Anderson, an African American youth who aspires to become an engineer. However, Jim's dreams are nearly dashed when he becomes embittered by the seemingly insurmountable career challenges he faces due to his race. A run-in with the law brings Jim face-to-face with an African American judge who challenges Jim's pessimistic worldview.

Miller submitted two detailed drafts of the script to the league, including dialogue and camera instructions. The first draft was critiqued on the levels of production feasibility and character motivation by experts in the field of nonfiction film production, including the noted documentarian Julien Bryan and the director of the American Jewish Committee's Film Section, Robert Disraeli. Miller appears to have subsequently revised the script based on Bryan and Disraeli's suggestions. As a result, Miller produced a much longer, fifty-four-page script in which he added two narrative elements: a gang of rogue youth called the Exiles, which Jim joins, and a high-achieving African American teenager named Lloyd Bender. Despite, or perhaps because of, these revisions, which would have substantially increased the production's cost, the league chose to terminate its contract with Miller, and the film project was suspended.

The project lay dormant for four years. According to an internal report on the production history of *A Morning for Jimmy*, in 1959 both Disraeli and writer Basil Beyea submitted versions of the script to the league; however, for reasons that are not revealed in the league's papers, the NUL judged both scripts to be unacceptable. Shortly thereafter, NUL board member and NBC Public Affairs Department executive Edward Stanley recommended Himan Brown to the league as a producer for the film. Brown was a noted pioneer of radio who innovated many of the medium's signature dramatic sound effects. His son, Barry K. Brown, who was just beginning to work in the film industry, was chosen to write and direct.[10] Barry K. Brown subsequently submitted an entirely new script, albeit one strikingly similar to those that Miller had drafted for the league in 1955.[11]

## A World for Jim

The script for *World* consistently emphasizes Jim's perception and vision. It describes the proposed film as opening on a close-up of a graduation cap and gown. Miller writes that the camera pulls back to reveal a young man rushing into the room and hurriedly putting the garments on. Regarding himself in the mirror, Jim chuckles sardonically at his own reflection. During his high school graduation, in an effort to escape a speaker's droning oration, Jim reflects on his youth and on recent events. Through a series of flashbacks and subjective images granting us access to his thoughts, we learn that, due to the negative influence of his peers, parents, and the actions of an "angry and prejudiced teacher," Jim has grown increasingly despairing of his prospects. Despite the intervention of a benevolent white teacher whom Jim nonetheless distrusts, Jim's grades have been falling. In a particularly striking sequence, the script describes Jim playing basketball; before a cheering crowd, he shoots. Yet in that very instant the crowd vanishes, leaving Jim alone, sobbing on the darkened court. After graduation, Jim traverses a black business district. "The Camera becomes Jim's eyes," writes Miller. "We have a continuous and panoramic view of what this boy, discouraged by what he considers to be his limited opportunity, selectively observes in his environment." Miller proceeds to identify a series of black-owned businesses ostensibly intended to represent the limited vocational opportunities afforded to African Americans.[12]

Following a brief visit home and a heated confrontation with his father, who offers to help him procure a factory job, Jim returns to the scene of his high school graduation where the senior dance is taking place. This scene is presented quite differently in the first and second drafts of Miller's scripts. In both scripts, Jim tries to enter the dance. However, a white boy collecting tickets stops him, reminding Jim that he cannot enter without a partner. Jim shouts the boy down, declaring that he has as much right to enter as anyone else. "He is reacting as though the issue in question were one of segregation," comments Miller. In the shorter of the two scripts, Jim, having forced his way in, proceeds to intervene between a white couple on the dance floor. "You'd better get used to colored guys taking a lot of things from you," Jim tells the white boy, having claimed his date. "Jim, I don't care much about your color. But your manners are lousy," the boy replies, a comment that Miller seems to have included to attest to the fact that Jim's perception of racism is, in fact, a misperception.[13] In the longer version of the script, Jim intervenes between Lloyd Bender and his date. Jim mockingly asks Lloyd, who was salutatorian at graduation, "I want to know what the secret is, Lloyd. I want to know how you got on that big white honor roll." In both script versions a fight ensues, prompting the arrival of a police officer. Jim flees the scene; however, he rather unluckily runs into yet another officer on his beat, and the two policemen tackle him.[14]

Following the incident at the dance, Jim faces charges including disorderly conduct, assault, and resisting arrest. Jim and the African American judge discuss the source of Jim's bitterness, namely, the limited opportunities he faces due to his race. The judge suggests that in fact Jim confronts two problems: the problem of the color line is one, but the other, more pressing problem concerns Jim's lack of ambition and limited job preparedness. "The fact that it may be tough for a Negro boy to get a particular job is a racial problem," admits the judge. "The fact that you're not even preparing yourself to get that job is your own personal problem . . . and has nothing to do with race." While seeming to present a balanced perspective, this statement glosses the complex relationship between limited job preparedness and racial inequality. Jim's lack of preparation has everything to do with race. Not only does the reality of racial inequality instill in Jim a profound sense of hopelessness, thwarting his ambition; it also limits his access to means of readying himself for a skilled profession, such as job training. The judge accuses Jim of complacency and ineffectual, aimless anger. When Jim asks the judge how he, a mere teenager, could possibly aid the cause of progress, the judge replies, "At age seventeen Jim . . . I'd say the best way would be to *prepare* yourself for change. What's the point of people like me working day and night for new laws . . . and civil rights . . . if people like you are not ready to accept them?"[15]

The judge's advice to Jim—specifically, that job preparedness is the best way for him to help advance the cause of equality—aptly expresses the basic tenets undergirding the league's approach to racial uplift during this era. The judge argues that his legislative efforts, though important, are meaningless if young black men like Jim fail to prove their worth in the world of work. Indeed, within the logic of the script, Jim's commitment to self-improvement and career success is of greater importance in the fight against inequality than are the judge's legal activism and reform initiatives.

Rather than sentence him to jail time, the judge offers Jim probation. However, as a condition of his probation, Jim must meet with several of the judge's friends and colleagues, all African Americans who have excelled in historically white-dominated professions. Jim's final meeting is with an African American engineer overseeing the construction of a bridge. In response to Jim's question as to whether or not he thinks Jim will succeed in achieving his career goals, the engineer asks Jim if he is "any good." "I can't really say," replies Jim sheepishly. "Well, I guess that's what it adds up to," says the engineer. "Yes, I know," replies Jim. "That's what everybody tells me." The black professionals' repeated assertion that Jim's primary obstacle to achieving success is not discrimination but rather his own as-yet-unproven merit fills him with hope. The script ends with Jim looking out over the vast expanse of a bay from the bridge as the camera recedes. *A World for Jim* thus suggests the expansion of Jim's prospects and, to borrow the title of another NUL film of the 1950s, the "ever-widening horizons" of black vocational opportunity.[16]

## Probing the Psychology of Black Youth

Miller's *World* script attests to the widespread interest at this time, manifest in both Cold War social science and popular culture, in the psychology of black youth. His script depicts Jim's psychic torment in a number of instances. For example, he describes Jim weeping alone on the abandoned basketball court. Later, appearing before the judge, Jim erupts with sudden, unexpected anger. Indeed, Miller's script displays a surprisingly complex understanding of the psychic effects of racism and inequality. Miller may have focused on exploring these effects because of the highly publicized importance attributed to them by the Supreme Court in its 1954 ruling in the case of *Brown v. Board of Education.*

The Court's decision overturned its 1896 ruling in *Plessy v. Ferguson*, which permitted the segregation of public schools based on race. The Court reversed this decision in part due to the expert testimony of many of the nation's leading social scientists, who argued that segregation causes irreparable psychic harm to African American youth. As Chief Justice Earl Warren stated in his delivery of the Court's opinion, "to separate [African American children] from others of similar age and qualifications solely because of their race generates a feeling of inferiority as to their status in the community that may affect their hearts and minds in a way unlikely ever to be undone."[17] Although *Brown v. Board* was a milestone in the history of legislative efforts to achieve a more equitable society, racial progressives have since criticized aspects of the case. Daryl Michael Scott asserts that the NAACP attorneys' focus on the psychological effects of segregation came at the expense of addressing its social and economic costs.[18] Lani Guinier argues that these attorneys stressed the psychic toll exacted by segregation on black youth in order to secure the sympathy of predominantly white middle- and upper-class liberals. In doing so, however, they failed to demand more sweeping structural changes that likely would have met with resistance from their white supporters.[19]

Both the Court ruling and *A World for Jim* reflect many of the same ideas about race, psychology, and social change prevalent among racial liberals of the 1950s. In fact, many of the criticisms that have been directed at *Brown* since 1954 can also be leveled at Miller's script. For example, Guinier observes that the Court's opinion unwittingly contributed to racial stigmatization: "Predicated on experiments purportedly showcasing blacks' low self-esteem, the opinion reinforced the stigma long associated with blacks, even as it attributed the stigma to racism rather than biology."[20] That is, the opinion characterized African Americans as psychologically damaged. True, the Court suggested that their collective psychic malady was attributable to social inequality—or, more specifically, to the fact of segregated schooling. Nevertheless, blacks were still made to bear the stigma of pathology. *World* likewise acknowledges the reality of racism and discrimination, and, like *Brown,* it attributes black youths' low self-esteem to the problem of prejudice. Yet also like *Brown,* its focus is not on white racism per se. *World* suggests that the obstacles Jim faces are not primarily those of racism and discrimination; rather, they are psychological impasses that block him from achieving success. As the judge tells Jim, "Those fancy barriers you've set up in yourself . . . are just as tough to penetrate as any color line I ever saw."[21]

It is, however, important to consider the broader social context of both Miller's *World* script and the *Brown v. Board* ruling. The Legal Defense and Education Fund attorneys' focus on the psychic pathology of the black child as a consequence of segregation may indeed have contributed to racial stigmatization, as both Scott and Guinier contend. However, the idea that segregation does, in fact, cause black children to suffer psychologically was at the time by no means widely accepted within white society at large. Undoubtedly, recognition of the real psychic costs of inequality is crucial to any effort to combat its persistence. Nevertheless, I agree with Daryl Michael Scott, who affords a powerful condemnation of the use of what he calls "damage imagery" even when the intent behind it is racially progressive. "Depicting black folk as pathological has not served the community's best interests," he writes. "Again and again, contempt has proven to be the flip side of pity."[22] Despite its progressive intent, the completed film did little to aid the cause of redressing inequality as it characterized the African American family as the locus of a deep-seated, self-perpetuating pathology.

## A Morning for Jimmy

In the completed film, *A Morning for Jimmy,* Jimmy Carroll returns home visibly upset. When questioned by his mother, he reveals that he was denied an after-school job in a downtown department store because he is black. When Jimmy's mother asks her son why he is so upset, reminding him that this encounter with racism is by no means out of the ordinary for him, he

FIGURE 7.2. Jimmy tells his mother that he was racially discriminated against. Jimmy's mother comforts her son and encourages him to continue to pursue his dreams. *A Morning for Jimmy* (1960).

responds, "I just thought with all the talk lately, that they might take me. This is a democracy, Ma, isn't it?" The film thus acknowledges the contemporary civil rights struggle and the ongoing transformation of U.S. race relations, the "talk" to which Jimmy refers. Jimmy's mother encourages her son to continue to strive to overcome racial barriers. Jimmy's father, however, is far more pessimistic about his son's prospects. "Didn't you know what to expect?" he asks Jimmy upon learning of the department store incident during dinner. "I told you enough times. You can never get as good a job as a white fella."

We later see Jimmy in an integrated classroom where he is clearly not paying attention to the lesson. When his African American teacher, Mr. Brown, calls on him, Jimmy admits that he has not heard the question asked of him, prompting Mr. Brown to request that Jimmy remain after class. During their meeting, Jimmy informs his teacher that he has decided not to work hard in school. "It's no use," he tells Mr. Brown. "What's no use?" asks his teacher. "Being colored and trying to do something. They just won't let us be anything." "Jimmy, almost every Negro at one time or another has felt what

FIGURE 7.3. Jimmy tells his teacher, Mr. Brown, that he has abandoned hope of achieving his career goals. Mr. Brown refutes Jimmy's assertion that being black in America necessarily prevents one from achieving vocational success. *A Morning for Jimmy* (1960).

you're feeling now," admits Mr. Brown. "But those of us who have made some success of our lives have done so only because we've refused to remain discouraged." "Jimmy, you're not the only one in this," Mr. Brown continues. "Are the militant students of the South beaten? Are the peoples of the new nations of Africa discouraged?" Mr. Brown thus compares Jimmy's plight to theirs, implicitly suggesting that, like these activists, Jimmy must remain steadfast in the face of adversity. Mr. Brown asks Jimmy if he would like to spend the afternoon meeting several persons who, in spite of their race, have achieved career success. One of them, he notes, happens to be an architect, precisely the profession to which Jimmy aspires. Accompanied by Mr. Brown and Taylor's upbeat, free jazz score, Jimmy traverses the city meeting African American professionals in the fields of information technology, the culinary arts, engineering, medicine, and architecture.

Upon returning home, Jimmy gushingly tells his father about his afternoon and professes his desire to pursue a career in architecture. His father, however, remains staunchly pessimistic. "Sure, son. Sure there are a few Negroes with good jobs. The ones the white folks set up to show off. But don't you realize, Jimmy, the majority of us can't get those jobs?" In the film's last scene, Jimmy discusses the dilemma he faces with his grandfather, played by retired NUL executive Robert J. Elzy. Unlike Jimmy's father, his grandfather emphatically maintains that Jimmy should pursue higher education and an architectural career. A Morning for Jimmy concludes on a mutedly optimistic note; Jimmy and his grandfather walk away from the camera alongside a set of railroad tracks accompanied by the nondiegetic sounds of Taylor's piano and lone trumpet. As in World, the film's final image is a long shot of a bridge, reminding the viewer of Jimmy's architectural aspirations.

## From World to Morning

In A World for Jim, particularly in the longer of the two drafts, Jim's bitterness is attributable to multiple influences, though perhaps none more so than that of his peers.[23] By contrast, A Morning for Jimmy identifies its protagonist's troubles as originating with his family or, more specifically, with Jimmy's father. John Carroll embodies a weakness that the film suggests is endemic among African Americans. John, we learn, had in his youth trained to be a bookkeeper; however, the prejudices of his potential employers thwarted his ambitions, instilling in him a deep-seated bitterness. Five years after the release of A Morning for Jimmy, Secretary of Labor Patrick D. Moynihan authored his controversial report The Negro Family: The Case for National Action. The Moynihan Report, as it was commonly called, argued that the disorganization of the black urban poor was self-sustaining: even if institutional racism was wholly eradicated, Moynihan claimed, this subset of the black community would remain a social underclass because of the disorder of its families. Thus, Moynihan identified the primary obstacle to black social and economic advancement as black people themselves. Moynihan acknowledged the impact that the legacy of systemic white racism and inequality had on black people. Nevertheless, he argued that these things were of less consequence for impoverished African Americans than were the ways in which they raised their children and structured their home lives.[24] A Morning for Jimmy differs in many ways from the Moynihan Report, most notably in its focus on a black middle-class family. Yet like the report, the film displaces focus away from the problem of systemic white racism through its emphasis on the shortcomings of the black father.

Despite this, however, Morning is, at least on first viewing, seemingly more politically progressive than Miller's World script. Unlike World, Morning

FIGURE 7.4. Jimmy's father, who admonishes his son for failing to accept that, as he puts it, "You can never get as good a job as a white fella." *A Morning for Jimmy* (1960).

explicitly acknowledges the persistence of white racism. Whereas *World* only alludes to the reality of racism, *Morning* makes it central to the film's narrative: Jimmy's encounter with discriminatory hiring practices is the story's instigating incident. Additionally, *Morning* references anticolonial struggle and the direct-action protest movement in the South. Thus, unlike *World*, *Morning* acknowledges, however limitedly, the emerging politicization of black identity.

Additionally, *Morning* calls into question the idea, central to the NUL's philosophy, that through displays of merit, African Americans can overcome entrenched inequality. *World* also briefly calls into question the idea that social advancement in the U.S. is based on merit. When the engineer meets Jim, he asks him if he is "any good," implying that Jim's success is contingent on his ability. However, he adds, "Sure, there are plenty of know-nothings in the field. But we're not inheriting businesses from our fathers. We've got to be a little bit better than good, if you get me." Here, the script acknowledges structural racial inequality. Jim must not only be competent at his work; he must be better than his privileged white peers to compensate for his race. Nevertheless, by the end of the script, the idea that the U.S. is, in essence, a meritocracy is strongly affirmed. *Morning*, however, offers no such affirmation. At the conclusion of the film, Jimmy discusses his situation with his grandfather, who encourages Jimmy to work hard to achieve his goals. Jimmy replies, "I guess you're right, Gramps. I guess you're right. There really isn't anything in the future for me, unless I work for it. Then there still might not be anything there. But I guess I'll have to try, and try real hard." The film thus admits the possibility that, no matter how hard Jimmy works (and, presumably, regardless of his skill and ability), he may not realize his ambitions.[25]

Despite this sober acknowledgment of the limitations of the NUL's faith in the power of hard work to overcome systemic inequality, *A Morning for Jimmy* nevertheless suggests that there is, indeed, hope for its protagonist. The film implies that Jimmy's ambitions can be achieved only if he rejects the pessimism of other African Americans, exemplified by Jimmy's father. Although their bitterness is perhaps understandable, the film implies that it is debilitating, and fathers like Jimmy's do their children a profound disservice by instilling it within them at a young age. Of course, the film includes black characters depicted as having a positive influence on Jimmy. However, characters like Jimmy's grandfather and teacher are portrayed as exceptions to the rule. Most African Americans are twisted up inside, the film suggests; their resignation is like a genetic disorder, passed from generation to generation, usually through the father. Only by steeling themselves against their influence can individual black youths like Jimmy rise above their brethren to achieve middle-class career success.

This point is made explicit in the film's concluding scene. As they talk, Jimmy's grandfather explains to his grandson that his father's sullenness and resentment are attributable to his failure to succeed as a bookkeeper. The grandfather describes his son as having been "hurt"; however, he tells Jimmy that his chances are far better than those of the boy's father. The grandfather then generalizes from the experience of Jimmy's father to African Americans collectively: Brown's script reads, "Lots of Negroes are hurt. Don't listen to them. They'll always tell you there's no chance. There may have been no chance for them, but there is one for you. . . . Your experience has nothing to do with the other fellow's. You are the only one you should be concerned with. Just because the other fellow is discouraged doesn't mean you should be. You are your own person with a mind and soul [an] individual. You got to be a bit better than the other. You can be, too."[26]

Far from suggesting that he identify his plight with black activists in the South or anticolonial protesters in Africa, *Morning* ultimately argues that it is

FIGURE 7.5. Jimmy and his grandfather. Despite his own experiences with racial prejudice, Jimmy's grandfather believes that racism in America can be overcome. He encourages Jimmy to remain optimistic despite the pessimism of men like Jimmy's father. *A Morning for Jimmy* (1960).

only by disentangling himself from the black collective that Jimmy can achieve his vocational goals. Black anger is characterized not as a motivator for political action, but rather as an impediment to individual self-advancement. In this way, despite acknowledging new forms of activism and third-world solidarity movements across the globe, *Morning* is arguably less invested in the emerging politics of black solidarity and black identity than is Miller's *World* script. In *World*, the engineer tells Jimmy he must be better than his white peers, acknowledging the structural inequality that defines the ideally meritocratic world of work. By contrast, *Morning* focuses not on the obstacles African Americans face in competing with whites but on the need for black youth to compete with and overcome the influence of other blacks. In this way, *Morning* is a profoundly reactionary film, suggesting that inequality is perpetuated not by racism per se, but rather by the pathological bitterness of African Americans. In keeping with the league's ethos, the film characterizes black solidarity as little more than a potential impediment to individual achievement.

*A Morning for Jimmy*'s racial conservatism clearly resonated with white viewers like Mrs. Sale, who responded favorably to the film's strategic effort to displace responsibility for racial inequality from whites to African Americans. But why was the film also well received by black youth? In correspondence from NUL Associate Director Otis E. Finley to Director of Vocational Guidance Ann Tanneyhill, Finley reported, "Audience reaction at all showings was highly favorable. In Tulsa and Oklahoma City the student audiences reacted with loud applause when they saw the Negro hotel food supervisor give orders to a white chef."[27] In May 1961, a school administrator at PS 139 in Harlem wrote to Tanneyhill about a screening of the film for the school's 1,700 pupils: "[The students] were enlightened to see a family sit down to dinner + eat together," he told Tanneyhill. "Expressed surprise to really see this and questioned me as to whether this really happened. So small and yet so very big!"[28] Although I have argued that *A Morning for Jimmy* was a product of postwar racial liberalism's effort to disavow white responsibility for systemic racial inequality, African American viewers were clearly able to ascribe progressive and even radical meanings to the film's sounds and images. Undoubtedly, despite its conservatism, elements of *A Morning for Jimmy*, such as its use of nonprofessional black actors and Billy Taylor's jazz score, imbued the film with political potency. That black audiences were able to focus on these elements, however, is a testament not to the essential progressivism of the film's message; rather, it suggests the agency of black audiences well practiced in culling emancipatory significance from even the most racially regressive works of popular culture.[29]

FILMOGRAPHY

All available films discussed in this chapter can be streamed through the book's web page at https://www.dukeupress.edu/Features/Screening-Race.

*A Morning for Jimmy* (1960), 29 min., 16mm
PRODUCTION: National Urban League and Association Films, Inc. DIRECTOR/WRITER/EDITOR: Barry K. Brown. PRODUCER: Himan Brown. SOUND: Morgan Smith. MUSIC: Billy Taylor. ACCESS: National Archives and Records Administration.

*A World for Jim* (1955), script (two versions)
WRITER: Bernard Miller. ACCESS: NUL records, Library of Congress, Washington, DC.

RELATED FILMS

*This Is Worthwhile!* (c. 1956), filmstrip

WRITER/PRODUCER: Otis E. Finley Jr. DISTRIBUTION: National Urban League. NOTE: The proposed film *Ever-Widening Horizons* was adapted into this filmstrip, or series of still slides to be shown accompanied by scripted narration. The filmstrip promoted the NUL's Vocational Opportunity Campaign, intended to aid African American youth in gaining employment and pursuing careers.

NOTES

1   Mrs. H. Sale to Association Films, June 13, 1961, box I, E4, "A Morning for Jimmy" film project, 1959–1962, folder 2, "A Morning for Jimmy," National Urban League records, Library of Congress, Manuscript Division, Washington, DC (hereafter NUL).

2   *A Morning for Jimmy* press release, November 19, 1960, box I, E4, folder 2, "'A Morning for Jimmy,'" NUL.

3   National Urban League 1962 Summary Report Education and Youth Incentives, 2 pp., n.d, box II, E1, folder "A Morning for Jimmy"—New Trailer, 1963, NUL.

4   National Urban League 1962 Summary Report Education and Youth Incentives.

5   For more on the reception of *A Morning for Jimmy*, see box I, E4, folder 2, "'A Morning for Jimmy,'" NUL. The folder contains letters to the league responding to the film as well as typewritten accounts of viewer responses at NUL screenings. I also discuss *A Morning for Jimmy*'s reception in the conclusion of this essay.

6   Bernard Miller, *A World for Jim*, version one (thirty-three-page version), n.d., box I, G11, folder "'A World for Jim' (film) 1956–1960," NUL.

7   Touré F. Reed, *Not Alms but Opportunity: The Urban League and the Politics of Racial Uplift, 1910–1950* (Chapel Hill: University of North Carolina Press, 2008).

8   Guichard Parris and Lester Brooks, *Blacks in the City: A History of the National Urban League* (Boston: Little, Brown, 1971), 415.

9   Barbara Diane Savage, "The National Urban League on the Radio," in *Broadcasting Freedom: Radio, War, and the Politics of Race, 1938–1948* (Chapel Hill: University of North Carolina Press, 1999), 157–93.

10  "Background and Historical Development of 'A Morning for Jimmy.'" Note that this document refers to Barry K. Brown as Himan Brown's brother; however, he was his son.

11  Barry K. Brown claims that the dialogue for the film was improvised; however, a fully drafted script that deviates only slightly from the completed film is contained in the league's papers. Brown shot the film on 35mm using an eighty-pound Arriflex camera and edited the film himself. Barry K. Brown, email message to author, August 14, 2016. The film was distributed in 16mm.

12  Miller, *A World for Jim*, version one, 6, 9.

13  Miller, *A World for Jim*, version one, 10, 11.

14  Bernard Miller, *A World for Jim*, version two (fifty-four page version), n.d., 23, box I, G11, folder "'A World for Jim' (film) 1956–1960," NUL.

15  Miller, *A World for Jim*, version one, 15, 16.

16  Miller, *A World for Jim*, version one, 21, 31. *Ever-Widening Horizons* was the original title of a proposed film project documenting the league's activities that subsequently yielded the filmstrip *This Is Worthwhile!* Box I, G11, folder "Working Together for Tomorrow's Jobs" (film), 1952–1953, NUL.

17  *Brown v. Board of Education of Topeka*, 347 U.S. 483 (1954). For a discussion of the role social science played in the Supreme Court case and ruling, see John P. Jackson Jr., *Social Scientists for Social Justice: Making the Case against Segregation* (New York: NYU Press, 2005); and Daryl Michael Scott, "Justifying Equality: Damage Imagery, *Brown v. Board of Education*, and the American Creed," in *Contempt and Pity: Social Policy and the Image of the Damaged Black Psyche* (Chapel Hill: University of North Carolina Press, 1997), 119–36.

18  Scott, "Justifying Equality," 119–36.

19  Lani Guinier, "From Racial Liberalism to Racial Literacy: *Brown v. Board of Education* and the Interest Divergence Dilemma," *Journal of American History* 91, no. 1 (June 2004): 101.

20  Guinier, "From Racial Liberalism to Racial Literacy," 109.

21  Miller, *A World for Jim*, version one, 16.

22  Scott, *Contempt and Pity*, xviii.

23  As noted above, in the longer draft, Jim joins a teenage gang called the Exiles. In both drafts of the script, Jim first learns of the reality of white racism from other black youth who mock his career aspirations.

24  For an excellent discussion of the social and political contexts in which the report appeared, its reception, and its legacy, see James T. Patterson, *Freedom Is Not Enough: The Moynihan Report and America's Struggle over Black Family Life* (New York: Basic Books, 2012).

25  *A Morning for Jimmy* shooting script, n.d., 14, box II, A50, folder "Taconic Foundation Project—Film proposal, 1959–1961," NUL.

26  *A Morning for Jimmy* shooting script, 13. Note that the line in the script is slightly different than that uttered by Elzy in the role of the grandfather in the film, which I cited at the outset of this essay.

27  Otis E. Finley to Ann Tanneyhill, April 19, 1961, box I, E4, "A Morning for Jimmy" film project, 1959–1962, folder 2, NUL.

28  Administrator of PS 139 (name illegible) to Ann Tanneyhill, January 31, 1961, box I, E4, "A Morning for Jimmy" film project, 1959–1962, folder 2, "A Morning for Jimmy," NUL.

29  For more on the complexities of African American reception of dominant representations of racial difference, see, for example, Jacqueline Najuma Stewart, "'Negroes Laughing at Themselves'? Black Spectatorship and the Performance of Urban Modernity," in *Migrating to the Movies: Cinema and Black Urban Modernity* (Los Angeles: University of California Press, 2005), 93–113; and Christine Acham, "Reading the Roots of Resistance: Television of the Black Revolution," in *Television Revolutionized: Prime Time and the Struggle for Black Power* (Minneapolis: University of Minnesota Press, 2005), 1–23.

8

## "A Touch of the Orient"

Negotiating Japanese American Identity
in *The Challenge* (1957)

TODD KUSHIGEMACHI AND DINO EVERETT

The University of Southern California (USC) student film *The Challenge* (Claude V. Bache, 1957) offers one of the earliest known film representations of a Japanese American social and cultural movement in the post–World War II era. As an expository documentary, *The Challenge* discusses nineteenth-century immigration from Japan, the incarceration of Japanese Americans in prison camps during World War II, and the state of the Little Tokyo enclave in 1950s Los Angeles.[1] The film first became available for rental and purchase in the 1960–61 supplemental catalog from USC's film sales division.[2] Twelve minutes in length, *The Challenge* touches upon crucial issues of culture and identity that continue to resonate in the Asian American community and that received virtually no attention in film, theatrical or otherwise, until decades later. In this regard, *The Challenge* takes important steps toward an articulation of Asian American subjectivity by placing the past, present, and possible future of Japanese Americans front and center. This educational student film provides a rare depiction and expression of Japanese American history and identity; the fact that it was created more than a decade before the oft-cited beginning of Asian American cinema in the 1970s makes it all the more remarkable.

This chapter situates *The Challenge* in the context of Asian American cinema.[3] The film clearly fits two of the three characteristics Renee Tajima-Peña identifies in her exploration of Asian American filmmaking. First, *The Challenge* is an example of "socially committed cinema," exploring the history of an oppressed people and their political struggles. Second, the film is "characterized by diversity shaped through . . . the constant flux of new immigration flowing from a westernizing East into an easternizing West." Specifically, *The Challenge* narrativizes Japanese immigrants' experiences and considers the lasting implications of international exchange. However, *The Challenge* does not readily satisfy Tajima's third criterion, because of the student filmmaker's racial identity: director and cowriter Claude V. Bache's parents were of American and European descent, and Tajima states that Asian American cinema is "created by a people bound by 1) race; 2) interlocking cultural and historical relations; and 3) a common experience of western domination."[4] Although Bache had served in Japan and Korea as an American officer before studying film production at USC, he was looking in at an Asian American community from an outside position.[5] Thus, *The Challenge*'s authorship might inspire questions about who is speaking and for whom.

Such an assumption about Bache's authorship, however, does not account for the richness and complexity of *The Challenge*'s production. In a 2008 interview, Bache remembered pitching the project to his USC adviser as a sort of representational intervention, saying, "These people have been terribly maligned and I could make a film about their story."[6] The film's complete roster of collaborators and supporters suggests that many Japanese Americans influenced the film's at first seemingly outsider perspective. Ken Miura, a member of USC's faculty who had been incarcerated in the concentration camps with his family during World War II, oversaw and guided the film's production.[7] In addition, Judge John F. Aiso, who was the highest-ranking Japanese American military officer in World War II, and the Japanese American Citizens League (JACL) provided "production assistance" and financial support.[8] The JACL touted itself as the voice of the Japanese American community, and indeed, *The Challenge* is ideologically consistent with the agenda of community elites at the time of the film's production. Clearly on display in *The Challenge*, the JACL's conservative, assimilationist perspective in the 1950s suggests ways in which Asian American authorship may not necessarily be politically progressive.

By reframing the authorship of this film, this chapter reclaims a piece of Asian American cinema history and uncovers a prehistory of independent Asian American filmmaking, typically dated as starting in the late 1960s. Scholarship has largely focused on independent films, including fictional features, documentaries for festivals and/or public broadcasting, or experimental film and video.[9] As a nontheatrical educational and student film previously outside the primary scope of study, *The Challenge* problematizes

FIGURE 8.1. The final credit for *The Challenge* (1957) highlights the contributions of Japanese American institutions and individuals.

Jun Okada's claim that the film collective Visual Communications "by 1973, produced the first Asian American films about the Japanese American internment."[10] If *The Challenge* is, as we argue, an Asian American film, the 1957 student project may actually be the first of its kind to discuss the incarceration of Japanese Americans in concentration camps.

As Bache's student film explores Japanese American history, the film resonates with Asian American cinema's institutional contingency and its themes of identity and collective memory. But perhaps most importantly, *The Challenge* exemplifies the state of ambivalence and process of negotiation at the heart of not only Asian American cinema but of Asian American identity. Scholars such as Peter X Feng and Celine Parreñas Shimizu focus on Asian American spectatorship and performance-as-authorship to recuperate films such as *The World of Suzie Wong* (Richard Quine, 1960), and thus, they accept both the pains and pleasures of representation.[11] This ambivalence extends to the very notion of "Asian American" itself. Feng argues that to self-identify as Asian American is to "both accept and critique the externally imposed label that denies the specificity of one's cultural heritage and defines one's otherness in racial terms."[12] *The Challenge* (un)comfortably fits into this tradition, with the Japanese American community using the film to strategically position itself as both Japanese and American, and as both a model minority and an oppressed people. In a sense, this essay itself is an expression of ambivalence, wrestling with the problematic authorship and lessons of *The Challenge* just as it recuperates an important piece in a community's history of self-definition.

## Japanese and American

*The Challenge* highlights the parallels between the functions of institutions in Asian American film and in educational film more broadly. Okada argues that institutionality is a defining element of Asian American cinema, that institutions of education, filmmaking, and public television together shaped the ideological attitudes and the formal strategies of the movement's films for decades.[13] Just as Okada looks to sources of funding and avenues of distribution to better understand the form and contexts of Asian American films, the history of the USC film school reveals how *The Challenge* came to exist, including why it took shape as a message-based educational film and why the JACL had such a significant influence on the nature of that message. Ultimately, *The Challenge* and the JACL more broadly advocate a position that simultaneously asserts cultural difference and successful assimilation, an ambivalent state of Japaneseness and Americanness.

An educational film, *The Challenge* was typical of the USC film school's output during this period, as the school had financial incentives to prioritize nontheatrical films. Documentaries and sponsored instructional films made it easier for USC to secure funding from sources outside the school itself, and these films could then be rented and sold to other institutions. Because of this established distribution avenue, USC encouraged students to produce films such as *The Challenge*, rather than narrative films, which had few screening possibilities at the time. In particular, Herbert Farmer, USC director of audiovisual services and Department of Cinema professor, understood nontheatrical films as a revenue stream for the school.[14] In 1959, Farmer wrote in the *Journal of the University Film Producers Association* that in the Graduate Student Workshop, "the emphasis is shifted from the study of techniques and procedures to the message and audience of the film."[15] Indeed, the first credit after *The Challenge*'s title cards reads, "Produced in the Graduate Student Workshop[,] Department of Cinema," linking *The Challenge* to the larger push toward message-oriented nontheatrical films.

This historical context of USC's Graduate Student Workshop also offers a possible explanation for the participation of Japanese American organizations in the making of *The Challenge*. If the context of USC helps to explain why the film takes an instructional approach, the Japanese American community's involvement helps explain what precisely the film was attempting to teach. Titles in the opening credits signal the prominent role of the JACL in the making of this film. The first superimposed words after the completion of the film's technical credits read, "Grant in aid by East Los Angeles and Southwest Los Angeles Chapters of the Japanese American Citizens League." This is followed by the credit "Production Assistance by The Regional Office Japanese American Citizens League[,] The Japanese Art and Culture Institute and The Honorable John F. Aiso[,] Judge of the Superior Court of Los Angeles." These are the final words of the opening credits; student filmmaker Bache is not credited until the end of the film. This placement highlights the input of leading Japanese American organizations and individuals in the film. Such a connection legitimizes the film as an authentic depiction of the Japanese American community.[16]

Although the organization lends credibility to the film's message, the JACL is controversial. Established as a national organization in 1929 by existing community groups in California and Washington, the JACL historically touted itself as the social and political voice of the Japanese American community. However, critics then and now have targeted the group's political positions, particularly its narrow, assimilationist agenda and its role in actively supporting Japanese American cooperation in their own incarceration during World War II. During the war, the JACL not only encouraged the Japanese American community to quietly accept their incarceration but also reportedly aided federal authorities in identifying Issei who were possible national security threats.[17] Additionally, the organization barred draft resisters from membership, a position consistent with their patriotic assimilationist perspective.[18] The JACL worked during and after the war to position itself as the singular voice of the Japanese American community, even though historian Ellen D. Wu points to cries of resistance that "laid bare the divergent possibilities of Japanese American identity that JACL had labored carefully to suppress."[19]

The prominent placement of the JACL in *The Challenge*'s opening credits suggests that the organization likely influenced the film's messages about political and ethnic identity. Indeed, the film articulates many of the JACL's talking points from the 1940s and 1950s. Awareness of the JACL's controversial history is not meant to condemn or criticize *The Challenge* but instead

FIGURE 8.2. The title card briefly superimposes the film's English title over Japanese kanji characters, and the kanji later fades, leaving only the English.

to contextualize it in contemporaneous discourses about Japanese American identity. In some ways, this history complicates the possible reading of this film as simply a white, dominant view of Japanese Americans and suggests how intracommunity debates impacted this film.

In addition to establishing the film's institutional context, *The Challenge*'s opening credits, through their design, suggest the simultaneity of Japanese identity and American identity that is a key issue in this film, as well as in Asian American cinema more broadly. Directly after the image of the USC seal, the film announces its title in a manner that visualizes this negotiation of identity, first featuring the film's title in bright red Japanese kanji characters. After five seconds, the English translation is superimposed over the Japanese characters in all-capitalized white letters. After a few more seconds, the Japanese title fades away, leaving only the English. In this subtle use of superimpositions and fades, the scene visually represents issues related to the assimilation of Japanese people into American culture, including the question of whether Americanism necessitates the erasure of national and cultural origins. Although this opening sequence could be read as suggesting the necessity of such racial and cultural denial, *The Challenge* and the

JACL more broadly advocate a position that simultaneously asserts both cultural assimilation and difference.

The relationship between Asian and American identities is a defining issue throughout Asian American cinema and related scholarship. As Peter X Feng observes, Asian Americans exist in the cultural imaginary as "perpetual foreigners," with the racially based denial of belonging related to a "crisis in the definition of what it means to be American."[20] Despite the presence of Asian Americans with deep roots in the United States throughout the twentieth century, commercial film and television has historically depicted Asians as non-Americans and/or inassimilable. This characterization extends back to Sessue Hayakawa's villainous character in *The Cheat* (Cecil B. DeMille, 1915) and Richard Barthelmess's benevolent but tragic Cheng Huan in *Broken Blossoms* (D. W. Griffith, 1919), and this Othering of Asian characters persisted in the 1950s. Films in the 1950s continued to focus on recent Japanese and Asian immigrants. Interracial romance melodramas such as *Japanese War Bride* (King Vidor, 1952) and *Sayonara* (Joshua Logan, 1957) largely centered around white American military men falling in love with Japanese women overseas.[21] Even though second-generation Japanese Americans were legally citizens, they simply did not exist in Hollywood's cultural imaginary.

The negotiation of Japanese American identity suggested by the Japanese and English letters of *The Challenge*'s title sequence continues throughout the film, including its opening voice-over and photographic images. Narrator Robert Kino's first words set the scene: "This is Little Tokyo in Downtown Los Angeles. There is a touch of the Orient in the old shops and restaurants that line the streets, but here life is the same as it is anywhere else in America." In just these opening lines, we have two seemingly opposed descriptions: the exoticized description of Little Tokyo as embodying "the Orient" and the assimilating discourse of its normalcy, "the same as it is anywhere else in America." These words resonate with both theoretical interrogations of the contradiction of Asian American identity and, more importantly for this film, the Japanese American community's navigation of its own image in the decades leading up to the 1950s.

The images that accompany this narration similarly express a negotiation of Otherness and Americanness. One medium long shot shows a black kimono through a Little Tokyo storefront window. This setup suggests how aspects of Japanese culture might be on display and for sale—the "touch of the Orient in the old shops." However, the film then cuts to an image of two young Japanese American women stepping out of a shop, just as Kino notes

FIGURE 8.3. Japanese American women walk out of a shop in downtown Los Angeles's Little Tokyo, as narrator Robert Kino says the district is "the same as it is anywhere else in America."

the sameness of American life. The two women wear blouses and long skirts, suggesting continuity with mainstream, white American fashion. Through both its narration and editing, *The Challenge* starts its expository look at Japanese America with a statement about the simultaneous Japaneseness and Americanness of this community.

The message conveyed in *The Challenge*'s opening minutes echoes the JACL's agenda to portray the Japanese American community in a fashion that Wu describes as "assimilating Others."[22] Wu argues that that the JACL wanted to depict Japanese Americans as "*both* the same and different from whites . . . in order to simultaneously vindicate its political decisions, make claims on the state, and shore up its hegemony as *the* voice of the ethnic community."[23] On the one hand, the JACL depicted Japanese Americans as successfully adopting white middle-class norms of American identity to ensure their place in the national fabric. At the same time, they strategically positioned themselves as Japanese because they had an interest in brokering U.S.-Japan relations and, more importantly, because they understood they would never look American, even if they acted American.

FIGURE 8.4. A white couple looks in on a Little Tokyo store, with the camera positioned on the opposite side of the window.

*The Challenge*'s negotiation of Japaneseness and Americanness becomes especially pronounced when the film features clearly staged shots of white Americans visiting Little Tokyo. After several shots of Japanese Americans, the film cuts to a young white male and female walking past the community's shops. Kino's narration proclaims, "The colorful display of the old and the new is a constant attraction to curious people." The young couple enters from screen right, with a slight reframing movement to keep them at the center of attention. The couple stops in the middle of the frame at a storefront window, and the film then cuts to a shot from inside the shop looking outward through the window. In a way, these shots reinforce an objectification of Japanese culture, something to be displayed for and consumed by white Americans who visit Little Tokyo.

Despite the possible reading of Japanese culture as object in this scene, the shot looking out through the window briefly positions the viewer as Other, as well as the potential source of the Anglo couple's curiosity. On a very practical level, the shot further suggests that the Japanese American community cooperated with the filmmakers, granting access inside stores to shoot the film. On an aesthetic level, the shot is also a momentary reversal for a white viewer, an attempt to duplicate the uncomfortable position of being reduced to an object of curiosity. This interpretation suggests ways in which *The Challenge* gestures toward Japanese American subjectivity as it implicitly and explicitly thematizes the community's own negotiation of Japanese and American identities.

## Suppression and Success

In its opening scenes, *The Challenge* focuses on the role of Little Tokyo and Japanese culture in brokering a peaceful relationship between Japanese Americans and "curious people," an apparent euphemism for tolerant white Americans. After a brief discussion of Nisei Week, Little Tokyo's annual cultural festival established in 1934, the film shifts in tone and in time to discuss Japanese immigration in the nineteenth century. Here the viewer is given the first indication that the assimilation of Japanese Americans included serious obstacles. The film's second section discusses hardships endured by Japanese families, including difficulties in Japan that prompted individuals to migrate as well as the mass Japanese American incarceration during World War II. Similar to how *The Challenge* emphasizes both Japaneseness and Americanness, the film's historically oriented second section reiterates notions of Asian Americans as a model minority while also recognizing the impact of systemic racism.

After a somewhat upbeat passage focusing on Japanese immigrants' early success finding work in the United States, the music shifts from a bright celebratory tone to a far more somber sound. This modulation occurs just before the voice-over narration begins to discuss California's Webb-Haney Act of 1913, also known as the Alien Land Law, which prohibited Japanese immigrants from owning land.[24] *The Challenge* acknowledges how these discriminatory laws pushed Japanese immigrants to crowded areas in the cities, leading them to "[retreat] into a little world of their own." Thus far in *The Challenge*, Little Tokyo has been depicted as a place of cultural contact between Japan and the U.S., between Japanese America and white America. By acknowledging how institutional segregation led to the creation of community enclaves in the first place, *The Challenge* complicates the notion of Little Tokyo as an innocent place of cultural celebration and exchange.

The connection between this early segregation and the present community is made even more powerful by the film's use of contemporary color footage to accompany the narration, an anachronistic touch that connects past and present. In an extreme long shot with two Japanese men entering a store across the street, the film briefly shows the Fugetsu-Do confectionery, originally founded in 1903 and considered the oldest business in Little Tokyo. *The Challenge*'s brightly colored images consistently remind the viewer that, thus far, the film has opted for staged scenes rather than archival materials to visually represent the historical moments discussed in the voice-over. With narration discussing institutionalized racism in the early twentieth century and images showing Little Tokyo in the 1950s, the film counters the earlier narration about cultural assimilation with a darker narrative of racial exclusion.

After depicting the transition from Japan to American farmland, and then from there to the cities, *The Challenge* cuts to an interview with Judge Aiso to elaborate on institutional limits to Japanese American social and economic mobility. This is the first of the film's four shots of Japanese American subjects speaking directly to the camera. Aiso explains that Japanese Americans "couldn't buy property or obtain good jobs or even attend the same schools as some Americans. They felt the reason they were not accepted was because they were uneducated, so the Issei gave his son or Nisei an opportunity to get an education hoping this would open the doors to opportunity. The Nisei was a citizen by birth and an American by choice. But in spite of this political heritage he often found himself where he was when he began." Although *The Challenge* highlights Japanese Americans' cultural assimilation, Aiso expresses uncertainties about the promise of socioeconomic mobility in the United States.

The JACL's advocacy for Japanese American assimilation was not simply cultural. The organization's agenda was also tied to socioeconomic ideals concerning middle-class American life. Indeed, the organization's assimilationist position was a prototype of the model minority myth. This conception of Asian Americans lives on to this day and is often criticized as a less blatantly malicious form of racism. Although the term was coined in 1966, the JACL itself campaigned to create the image of a patriotic, hard-working Japanese American decades earlier.[25] The narrative suggests that Asian Americans attained success in the United States through hard work and because of compatible value systems. Although the discourse supposedly offers a positive representation of Asian Americans, this stereotype offers a narrow view of a diverse community of people, overlooks the existence of continued prejudice against Asian Americans, and also implicitly denies the role of systemic racism in the socioeconomic status of other communities of color. Thus, if the very notion of a model minority is premised upon the denial of systemic racism's persistence, Aiso's comments in *The Challenge* instead highlight the

FIGURE 8.5. In a staged scene, two Japanese Americans listen in on a radio broadcast about Japan's bombing of Pearl Harbor on December 7, 1941.

institutional and legal barriers that have limited Japanese American socio-economic mobility.

The model minority myth suggests that Asian Americans attained their socioeconomic status without resisting the dominant political order, a conclusion often explicitly tied to critiques of black political activism.[26] The issue of Japanese American compliance becomes especially significant as *The Challenge* shifts from the early history of Little Tokyo to World War II, including the mass incarceration of Japanese Americans. Although Aiso first appears in a talking head interview, his words conclude over a shot of a grocer handing a piece of fruit to a child. After a match on action to a closer shot of the grocer, the camera pans over to a radio in the store. After the grocer is shown increasing the volume on the radio, the sound of the film switches to the diegetic radio playing a news broadcast announcing the bombing of Pearl Harbor on December 7, 1941. Having used color reenactment footage to this point, the film here switches to black-and-white stock footage taken from the Office of War Information film *Japanese Relocation* and the *Army-Navy Screen Magazine #45* from 1945.[27] By incorporating state-sponsored footage into a film about the Japanese American experience, *The Challenge*

FIGURE 8.6. *The Challenge* incorporates black-and-white footage from World War II government films, including images of the Japanese American concentration camps.

reclaims these pieces of a broader American historical record for the story of a specific ethnic community.

*The Challenge*'s characterization of the camps reflects a discourse prevalent within the Japanese American community that denies political resistance and affirms American power. Narrator Kino uses the term "isolated relocation camps," a euphemism designed to deny the severity of racist federal action. In addition to using the prevailing semantics of the dominant culture, the narrator states, "instead of rebelling, the Japanese Americans wore their indignity with grace and understanding." This is partly true; the JACL advocated for compliance with the government's actions at the time of the mass incarcerations. However, Japanese Americans were far from uniform in their response to the incarceration. Journalist Jimmie Omura, for example, openly spoke out against Executive Order 9066 and was consequently dubbed JACL's "Public Enemy Number One." Later, other Japanese Americans turned to violence against JACL officials who actively campaigned for the enlistment of Nisei into World War II.[28] These and other instances of resistance suggest that *The Challenge*'s claim about what individuals did "instead of rebelling" elide more progressive strands of the Japanese American community, those that might problematize the JACL's preferred self-image of a politically docile model minority.

Although *The Challenge* refuses to condemn the Japanese American concentration camps, any mention of the incarceration, especially in 1957, is a remarkable and rare recognition of how the U.S. government violated the civil rights of more than 100,000 individuals. Indeed, Bache used the troubled history of Japanese Americans as a primary justification in his pitch for *The Challenge*, as a story about people who "have been terribly maligned."[29] Hollywood had only incidentally referenced the mass incarceration in films such as *Japanese War Bride* and *Bad Day at Black Rock* (John Sturges, 1955).[30] As Karen L. Ishizuka found in the process of researching the incarceration to create the Japanese American National Museum's historical exhibit, which opened in 1994, even Japanese Americans who had gone through the incarceration "were still separated from the facts and historical analyses that would allow them finally to understand the history they were a part of but not privy to."[31] That is, decades after World War II and even *The Challenge* in 1957, many Japanese Americans were not given the opportunity to remember and reflect, precisely because of the collective trauma and the pervasive denial of the government's wrongdoing. *The Challenge*'s discourse often reflects complacent talking points of 1950s community leaders, but the very mentions of segregation and incarceration were and remain powerful. To have these addressed in a film, one produced in part by Japanese Americans and marketed as an educational film, suggests a move toward the widespread recognition of Japanese American history as a part of American history.

This chapter previously mentioned that, in *The Challenge*, there are four shots of Japanese American subjects speaking directly to the camera. Two of these are black-and-white footage of soldiers during World War II. The JACL often referenced and continues to reference the military service of Japanese Americans despite the incarceration as an example of the community's assimilation into the United States. The fourth shot features the Yamato Employment Agency's Chester Yamauchi, who talks about the increased employment opportunities for Japanese Americans after the war. Thus, both of these instances are consistent with the film's problematic message about socioeconomic and political change without radicalism, one consistent with the model minority myth. At the same time, it is stunning to see any Japanese American speaking about himself and his community in a film made at this time. These images are emblematic of *The Challenge*'s contradictions, giving voice to a flawed historical narrative but also giving members of the

Japanese American community the space to develop and negotiate this image themselves. By considering nontheatrical films such as student projects, we can expand our understanding of Asian American cinema and also find different avenues through which the discourses of the Japanese American community circulated in moving image culture.

FILMOGRAPHY

The film discussed in this chapter can be streamed through the book's web page at https://www.dukeupress.edu/Features/Screening-Race.

*The Challenge* (1957), 12 min., 16mm
PRODUCTION: Department of Cinema, University of Southern California, School of Performing Arts. DISTRIBUTOR: USC. DIRECTOR: Claude Bache. WRITERS: Richard A. Malek, Claude Bache. CAMERA: Kishor Parekh. MUSICAL SUPERVISION: Tak Shindo. SPECIAL ORCHESTRATION: David Zea, Robert Greenwell. EDITOR: Robert Roxanne. SOUND: Ted Gomillion. NARRATOR: Robert Kino. ACCESS: USC Hugh M. Hefner Moving Image Archive.

RELATED FILMS

*Army-Navy Screen Magazine #45* (1945), 7 min.
PRODUCTION: U.S. Army Pictorial Services. SUMMARY: Depicts the situation involving Japanese Americans being held in concentration camps from the perspective of the U.S. military.

*Bad Day at Black Rock* (1955), 81 min.
PRODUCTION/DISTRIBUTION: Metro Goldwyn Mayer. DIRECTOR: John Sturges. SUMMARY: A Hollywood attempt to showcase the shame and horror of the United States' actions toward Japanese Americans during World War II.

*Broken Blossoms* (1919), 90 min.
PRODUCTION: D. W. Griffith Productions. DISTRIBUTION: United Artists. DIRECTOR: D. W. Griffith. SUMMARY: The friendship of a Chinese shopkeeper toward a young girl is challenged by the racism of her brutal father.

*Chan Is Missing* (1982), 80 min.
PRODUCTION: Wayne Wang Productions. DISTRIBUTION: New Yorker Films. DIRECTOR: Wayne Wang. SUMMARY: A mystery involving some stolen money reveals the struggles faced every day by Chinese Americans.

*The Cheat* (1915), 59 min.
PRODUCTION: Jesse L. Lasky Feature Play Company. DISTRIBUTION: Paramount Pictures. DIRECTOR: Cecil B. DeMille (uncredited). SUMMARY: The spoiled wife of a stockbroker steals charity money and clandestinely turns to a Japanese trader to help replace the money undetected.

*History and Memory: For Akiko and Takashige* (1991), 32 min.
PRODUCTION/DISTRIBUTION/DIRECTOR: Rea Tajiri. SUMMARY: A personal account of the filmmaker's family experience of incarceration during World War II.

*Japanese Relocation* (1942), 10 min.
PRODUCTION: Office of War Information, Paramount Pictures. DISTRIBUTION: War Activities Committee of the Motion Pictures Industry. SUMMARY: Propaganda film putting forth reasons why Japanese Americans were put into concentration camps during World War II.

*Japanese War Bride* (1952), 91 min.
PRODUCTION: Joseph Bernhard Productions, Inc. DISTRIBUTION: Twentieth Century Fox Film Corporation. DIRECTOR: King Vidor. SUMMARY: A Korean War veteran returns home to the U.S. with a Japanese wife and faces racist responses from neighbors.

*Manzanar* (1971), 16 min.
PRODUCTION/DISTRIBUTION: Visual Communications. DIRECTOR: Robert A. Nakamura. SUMMARY: An artistic look back on what it was like to be Japanese and held in the concentration camps during World War II.

*Minority of Youth: Akira* (1971), 14 min.
PRODUCTION: Veriation Films. DISTRIBUTION: BFA Educational Media. DIRECTOR: David Espar. SUMMARY: A college-aged Japanese American man describes what it is like to be caught between two cultures.

*Sayonara* (1957), 147 min.
PRODUCTION: Pennebaker Productions, William Goetz Productions. DISTRIBUTION: Warner Bros. DIRECTOR: Joshua Logan. SUMMARY: A U.S. serviceman struggles internally when he falls for a Japanese woman while stationed in Japan.


NOTES

1   For more on expository and other modes of documentary filmmaking, see Bill Nichols, *Representing Reality: Issues and Concepts in Documentary* (Bloomington: Indiana University Press, 1991).
2   USC *Cinema Film Catalog* (Los Angeles: Film Distribution Division, 1961).
3   The panethnic conception of Asian Americans emerged in the late 1960s and 1970s, a political construct recognizing shared histories and experiences of oppression in the United States. Thus, the application of the term to a 1957 film might appear anachronistic, but we find it useful. First, most of the scholarship on film and cinema uses the notion of Asian American identity to ground its understanding of race in the media, whether it is engaging representation before or after the 1960s. Second, as historian Ellen D. Wu has argued, the histories of Japanese and Chinese Americans in the early and mid-twentieth century reveal strong parallels in how different ethnic communities negotiated their racial identity. Ellen D.

Wu, *The Color of Success: Asian Americans and the Origins of the Model Minority* (Princeton, NJ: Princeton University Press, 2014).

4   Renee Tajima, "Moving the Image: Asian American Independent Filmmaking 1970–1990," in *Moving the Image: Independent Asian Pacific American Media Arts*, ed. Russell Leong (Los Angeles: UCLA Asian American Studies Center, 1991), 12; Claude V. Bache, interview by Sandra Stewart Holyoak, Rutgers Oral History Archives, August 12, 2008, http://oralhistory.rutgers.edu/interviewees/30 -interview-html-text/741-bache-claude-v.

5   Co-writer Richard A. Malek was also an American with no Japanese heritage.

6   Bache, interview by Holyoak.

7   This chapter specifically opts for words such as "incarceration" and "concentration camps" rather than "internment" or "relocation camps." The latter terms are now considered euphemisms that were designed to deny the severity of the federal government's affronts to Japanese Americans' civil rights. For more on the "semantics of suppression," see Karen L. Ishizuka, *Lost and Found: Reclaiming the Japanese American Incarceration* (Urbana: University of Illinois Press, 2006), 8–13.

8   Judge John F. Aiso biography, Judicial Council of California, accessed July 21, 2016, http://www.courts.ca.gov/documents/AisoJ.pdf.

9   An exception to scholarship's focus on theatrical film is Karen L. Ishizuka's work on home movies. Japanese Americans were not legally allowed to bring cameras to the concentration camps, and yet individuals smuggled in still and moving image cameras, resulting in representations of the camps that were not only nontheatrical but also extralegal. Home movies are generally discussed in terms of their appropriation in documentary and experimental film. As Peter X Feng has demonstrated, Asian American filmmakers including Lise Yasui and Rea Tajiri have integrated home movies into their own documentaries to suggest the complex relationships between history and memory, between the personal and the collective. Ishizuka, *Lost and Found*, 15–16, 118–38; Karen L. Ishizuka and Patricia R. Zimmermann, eds., *Mining the Home Movie: Excavations in Histories and Memories* (Berkeley: University of California Press, 2008); Peter X Feng, "Articulating Silence: Sansei and Memories of the Camps," in *Identities in Motion: Asian American Film and Video* (Durham, NC: Duke University Press, 2002), 68–100.

10  Jun Okada, *Making Asian American Film and Video: History, Institutions, Movements* (New Brunswick, NJ: Rutgers University Press, 2015), 2.

11  Peter X Feng, "Recuperating Suzie Wong: A Fan's Nancy Kwan-Dary," in *Countervisions: Asian American Film Criticism*, ed. Darrell Y. Hamamoto and Sandra Liu (Philadelphia: Temple University Press, 2000); Celine Parreñas Shimizu, *The Hypersexuality of Race: Performing Asian/American Women on Screen and Scene* (Durham, NC: Duke University Press, 2007).

12  Peter X Feng, "Being Chinese American, Becoming Asian American: *Chan Is Missing*," in *Screening Asian Americans*, ed. Peter X Feng (New Brunswick, NJ: Rutgers University Press, 2002), 185–216.

13  Okada, *Making Asian American Film and Video*.

14  In 1955, Farmer published an article in the *Society of Motion Picture and Television Engineers Journal* titled "A Survey of the Distribution of Non-theatrical Motion Pictures." The actual article was a 3-page synopsis of a 195-page master's thesis submitted by Farmer in June 1955 to earn a master of arts degree while continuing to act as a faculty member and associate dean of business affairs. Herbert E. Farmer, "A Survey of the Distribution of Non-theatrical Motion Pictures" (master's thesis, University of Southern California, 1955), Hugh M. Hefner Moving Image Archive collection.

15  Herbert E. Farmer, "USC Cinema in Perspective," *Journal of the University Film Producers Association* 11, no. 2 (winter 1959): 11.

16  The film includes contributions from several other individuals of Japanese descent, including Stone Ishimaru (technical advisor), John Miyauchi (title cards), and Tak Shindo (music supervisor).

17  Wu, *The Color of Success*, 77.

18  Wu, *The Color of Success*, 73.

19  Wu, *The Color of Success*, 102.

20  Peter X Feng, introduction to *Screening Asian Americans*, ed. Peter X Feng (New Brunswick, NJ: Rutgers University Press, 2002), 1.

21  For more on how Hollywood has perpetuated Asians as Other at the intersection of race and sex, see Gina Marchetti, *Romance and the "Yellow Peril": Race, Sex, and Discursive Strategies in Hollywood Fiction* (Berkeley: University of California Press, 1993).

22  Wu, *The Color of Success*, 108.

23  Wu, *The Color of Success*, 108.

24  California's Webb-Haney Act of 1913 was essentially designed to curtail immigration from Japan to California by prohibiting noncitizens from owning agricultural land. Given that many of the immigrants at this time were farmhands, the law attempted to confine them to low-paid work, unable to better themselves and their families. Subsequent amendments and additional laws were voted throughout the 1920s in order to counteract loopholes that allowed Nisei to purchase land and put it in their parents' names. The California Supreme Court struck down the law in 1952.

25  William Petersen coined the term "model minority." In a 1966 *New York Times* article, he suggests that "by any criterion of good citizenship that we choose, the Japanese Americans are better than any other group in our society, including native-born whites. They have established this remarkable record, moreover, by their own almost totally unaided effort. Every attempt to hamper their progress resulted only in enhancing their determination to success." William Petersen, "Success Story, Japanese-American Style," *New York Times*, January 9, 1966.

26  Wu quotes a September 1957 *Chicago Daily News* letter that suggests African Americans should see Japanese Americans as an example because they achieved success through "hard work, honesty and clean living" but "not pressure groups." Wu, *The Color of Success*, 165.

27  The *Japanese Relocation* footage was licensed from a company called International Film Foundation, and the *Army-Navy Screen Magazine* was licensed from the

Department of the Army. Some paperwork detailing each is located in the production file for *The Challenge* held in the Student Film Collections, USC Hugh M. Hefner Moving Image Archive.

28 Wu, *The Color of Success*, 80, 95.

29 Bache, interview by Holyoak.

30 For a thorough analysis of the former, see David Palumbo-Liu, *Asian/American: Historical Crossings of a Racial Frontier* (Stanford, CA: Stanford University Press, 1999), 225–32.

31 Ishizuka, *Lost and Found*, 7.

# 9

## "I Have My Choice"

Behind Every Good Man (1967) and the Black Queer
Subject in American Nontheatrical Film

NOAH TSIKA

To imagine historical subjects as "gay," "lesbian," or as "transgender" ignores the radically different understandings of self and the contexts that underpinned the practices
and lives of historical subjects.—DAVID VALENTINE, *Imagining Transgender*

As far as I'm concerned, a person has the right to be opaque.—ÉDOUARD GLISSANT

Queer histories of audiovisual media tend, like their heterocentric counterparts, to ignore nontheatrical film—except, perhaps, when it can be con-
strued as a campy source of misinformation, a ludicrous means of peddling
stereotypes and propagandizing against sexual and gender "minorities." Indeed, the *longue durée* of queer-themed nontheatrical film is often presented
in terms of a protracted initial stage of reactionary production that was only
eclipsed with the popularity of video formats for activist uses in the lib-
erationist 1970s and AIDS-plagued 1980s. This binary understanding of pre-
liberation didacticism and postliberation experimentation and community
building has emerged at the expense of a more nuanced recognition of the
capaciousness of nontheatrical film as a category of production, distribution, and exhibition.[1]

A student film completed in 1967 and immediately exhibited in a variety of
nontheatrical venues, Nikolai Ursin's *Behind Every Good Man* offers a formally
heterogeneous depiction of a black subject whose queerness—identifiable
as a principled opposition to normative expectations and categories of
personhood—indicates the importance of peering beyond conventional

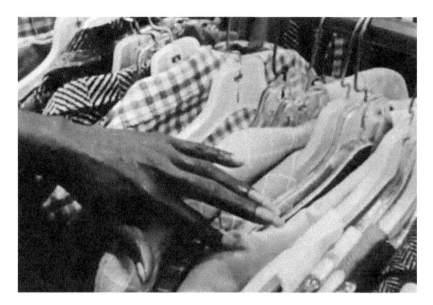

FIGURE 9.1. The subject of *Behind Every Good Man* (1967) handles "women's" clothes in the film's opening scene.

accounts of film history.[2] *Behind Every Good Man* examines the experiences of a young, unnamed person of color who identifies as neither straight nor gay, neither male nor female, and whose fluid conceptions of gender and sexuality lend this eight-minute hybridized documentary a queer expansiveness that relatively few films of its era could legitimately claim—a sort of politics of genderqueerness *avant la lettre*. In presenting some of the strategies of self-fashioning of a black subject who eschews fixed identity categories, Ursin refrains from providing confining interpretations of his own, marking *Behind Every Good Man* as a major contribution to filmic efforts to resist essentialism. In place of the detached, didactic third-person exposition of classical documentary, *Behind Every Good Man* offers a confessional, first-person voice-over commentary, complicating the conventions of cinéma vérité even as it embraces them. Framed by obviously staged sequences in which the film's protagonist interacts with the camera (as well as with a range of other social actors), the central section of *Behind Every Good Man* provides a far less reflexive glimpse of its subject preparing for a romantic evening, donning "women's" clothes, and carefully applying makeup, while a voice on the soundtrack (presumably the subject's own) says, "I have my choice"—that is, the choice to self-identify in a multiply resistant, idiosyncratic manner.

It is impossible for the viewer to know for sure whether these central scenes were staged—whether the subject is performing "naturally" (albeit with the knowledge of being filmed) or according to Ursin's specific instructions. It is perhaps equally impossible to know whether the surrounding sequences were, in fact, as staged as they seem—as much the product of dramaturgical convention as they appear (as when, for example, the subject must melodramatically cut short a romantic encounter in order to catch a bus, tripping and falling on the sidewalk in the process). In any case, *Behind Every Good Man* is clearly invested in exploring the agency of its subject in relation both to specific historical markers (such as the 16mm camera that records that subject's urban mobility, or the popular recordings of Dionne Warwick and the Supremes that provide part of the soundtrack of the subject's life) and to self-constructions that continue to resist classification.

The significance of *Behind Every Good Man* is inextricable from its ambiguity as well as from the sheer difficulty of defining it in relation to notions of race, gender, and sexuality. In addressing its subject as queer, I am in fact imposing a term that is neither used in the film nor cited in any of the extant discourses surrounding it—and thus perpetuating the very object of my critique here, which is the historical capacity of various nontheatrical exhibition sites to restrict the meanings of works that seem to queerly evade classification. However anachronistic, my use of the term "queer" is intended to express and honor this process of evasion—what Barbara Hammer terms "the politics of abstraction"—in keeping with queer's dominant theoretical associations with definitional elasticity and a critique of the disciplinary effects of identity categories.[3] E. Patrick Johnson has advanced a powerful critique of queer theory for its tendency to exclude the experiences of people of color, offering, in its place, "something with more 'soul,' more 'bang,' something closer to 'home'" that he calls "quare studies."[4]

It is one of my goals in this chapter to suggest how *Behind Every Good Man*, in pointing toward the emergence of queer theory, also suggests ways of redressing what Johnson, following Gloria Anzaldúa, reads as the homogenizing capacity of "queer."[5] While many queer theorists of color have, like Cathy Cohen, rejected "queer theorizing which calls for the elimination of fixed categories," arguing that essentialism "can, in fact, be important to one's survival," *Behind Every Good Man* suggests quite the opposite.[6] It seems important—indeed, crucial—to the survival of Ursin's subject to embrace fluidity and indeterminacy, to reject fixed categories in a way that predicts, by at least two decades, the central thrust of queer theory as developed

FIGURE 9.2. Selecting a dress.

by the likes of Lauren Berlant, Judith Butler, Michael Warner, Annamarie Jagose, and Eve Kosofsky Sedgwick.

*Behind Every Good Man* suggests ways of contesting the notion that the antiessentialist, anti-identitarian core of queer theory is purely a product of white privilege—exclusively a function of willful ignorance of race and class. While Ursin's own whiteness raises key questions regarding possibly distortive privileges of authorship, his documentary techniques serve to communicate radical strategies of self-fashioning that his black queer subject voluntarily employs, proudly declaring, "I have my choice." Throughout this chapter, I refer to Ursin's protagonist as "the subject" not because I wish to convey an impersonal, clinical impression of this figure as a nameless ethnographic object but because of the anonymity that the film itself encodes, and that no surviving document can supplant. Available information pertaining to Ursin and his production methods indicates, in fact, that the director's goal was to honor the chosen anonymity of a black queer subject even as his filming of that subject signals an instance of uncloseting—a way of exposing certain lived experiences to the scrutiny of the film camera as well as to potential viewers.

Anonymity also served a more practical purpose, offering a measure of protection to the film's subject at a time when so-called cross-dressing was illegal in Los Angeles, owing to antimasquerade laws introduced in the late nineteenth century. Punishable by up to six months in jail and a fine of $500, the crime of masquerading is one to which *Behind Every Good Man* alludes through voice-over narration, as the subject describes being detained by a police officer after electing to use a bathroom designated for men. In this telling, the officer and his colleagues, after determining that the subject had no previous criminal record, decided to let "him" go, lamenting that "he" wasn't a "real" woman. If I cannot name the subject of *Behind Every Good Man*, then neither can I identify that subject with the gendered pronouns that these police officers reportedly used—with words that are simply not a part of the subject's spoken self-description. Thus my very writing style, in this chapter, reflects the queer textuality of *Behind Every Good Man*—the film's remarkable resistance to the potential violence of naming.

The relative lack of documentation surrounding the production of *Behind Every Good Man* might seem emblematic of the challenges associated with the study of nontheatrical film, but it has also constituted a curious provocation for many who have distributed and exhibited Ursin's film for the past fifty years—an inducement to naming that has involved the application not merely of conventionally gendered pronouns but also of questionable, and often downright offensive, sexological models.[7] Scholars of nontheatrical film have long been alert to the multiple constraints inherent in this form of cinema, particularly where it intersects with state and corporate interests. Heide Solbrig, for instance, has examined how a subsidiary of Western Electric developed an infrastructure for nontheatrical film "in the image of corporate managerial expertise," while Victoria Cain has shown how the American Film Center, in formulating a course of action for nontheatrical motion picture production and distribution, "attempted to collaborate, rather than compete, with Hollywood studios," thereby reproducing certain representational norms and cultivating orthodox reading strategies.[8] However, it is precisely the breadth of nontheatrical film—its inclusion of more than just state-sponsored propaganda or industrial didacticism—that permits and indeed demands attention to how the category has, at various times and in a range of guises, accommodated representations that seem identifiably queer.

Alluding to these practices of accommodation, Marsha Gordon and Allyson Nadia Field enumerate some of the key justifications for studying nontheatrical films made during the greater part of the twentieth century, noting that "their very different and less centralized means of production, distribution, and exhibition allowed for a fascinating diversity that was never possible in the more controlled, corporate environment of Hollywood."[9] In

FIGURE 9.3. *Behind Every Good Man* features several moments of direct address. Here, the film's subject smiles at the camera from a city sidewalk.

this essay, I understand such diversity as encompassing challenging depictions of black queer subjects, including the central figure—the ostensible biographical focus—of *Behind Every Good Man*, a film that suggests an early form of resistance to long-standing popular discourses designed to quarantine blackness (especially black masculinity) from queerness. Indeed, recovering key histories of nontheatrical film enables us to understand how these critical cinematic interventions anticipated—and perhaps laid some of the discursive groundwork for—such later, canonical works as Isaac Julien's *Looking for Langston* (1989) and Marlon Riggs's *Tongues Untied* (1989), two documentaries that have generated an abundance of scholarship in the field of queer studies. Describing "the rise of essentialist black thinking" in his classic essay "Black Is, Black Ain't," Julien laments the erasure of countervailing historical discourses.[10] Contesting "the notion of a black essence," Julien recognizes that the suppression of the black queer subject—the dogmatic refusal to see queerness in blackness—depends on certain historiographic blind spots and archival limitations.[11]

Recent developments in the academic field of transgender studies are indispensable to an analysis of *Behind Every Good Man*. Describing the emergence and institutionalization of the term "transgender" as a tool intended

FIGURE 9.4. The joys of flânerie.

to "incorporate all and any variance from imagined gender norms," David Valentine presents it as a site of contestation—the discursive locus "where meanings about gender and sexuality are being worked out."[12] While understanding "transgender" as a capacious, potentially limitless identity category, Valentine cautions against its overuse—particularly its retroactive application to (or imposition on) those who have not themselves chosen it—noting the "inability of discrete analytic categories" to adequately describe the experiences of all marginalized subjects.[13] Queer theory, for its part, similarly rests upon a suspicion of the regulatory effects of certain terms—even those (like "queer" itself) embraced as radical and oppositional, often in contrast to their pathologizing deployment in popular and clinical discourses. Many of queer theory's earliest intersections with so-called gender-variant subjects, however, seemed to reproduce key aspects of those very discourses, sharing feminist concerns regarding the capacity of a diversity of male-bodied feminine people to sustain and reproduce male privilege, as though maleness were an inescapable ontological given for those born with penises.

As Jay Prosser argues in *Second Skins*, queer theory developed through a pronounced investment in camp and drag as paradigmatic of gender performativity, simultaneously consigning questions of transsexual embodiment

FIGURE 9.5. Challenging the camera's capacity to recognize all potentialities.

to the realm of a much-maligned essentialism, wherein a "pure" gender identity may be sought through surgical intervention, or a purportedly superficial femininity might serve to smuggle in an "inherent" masculinity defined as hegemonic. According to the logic of early queer theory, then, transsexual embodiment represented, by definition, the achievement of a gender identity that is ontologically separate from the masculinity or femininity assigned to a subject at birth, thus reproducing conventional categories of personhood and sustaining a binary understanding of gender. Rather than radically occupying two expressive spaces at once, juggling differential markers of gender through the practice of drag, transsexual embodiment suggests, in this telling, a refusal of hybridity and intermediacy—a rejection of what Sandy Stone calls "the potentialities of mixture."[14] Transsexual subjects as constructed through autobiography and, later, through queer theory thus "go from being unambiguous men, albeit unhappy men, to unambiguous women," indexing, in Stone's account, "no territory in between."[15] It is this very "territory in between"—this productive and potentially permanent liminality—that concerns me here, and that is central to the representational strategies of *Behind Every Good Man*, a film whose nontheatrical presence has, for half a century, continuously occasioned efforts to contain its human subject according to a stable, ideologically overdetermined set of identity categories.

Unlike other student films that have attained canonical or near-canonical status in documentary studies, such as Mitchell Block's . . . *No Lies* (1973) and George Lucas's *Look at Life* (1965), *Behind Every Good Man* has not been cited in any previous scholarly publication, and its director has been similarly occluded despite numerous, conspicuous contributions to cinema history. Ursin made *Behind Every Good Man* some four years before earning a master's degree in film and video production at UCLA, and while it is unclear whether the university provided production support of any kind, the film did not serve as Ursin's thesis. (The term "student film" is thus a bit of a misnomer in this instance.) In any case, Ursin established an early commitment to queer documentary that would characterize his decades-long career as a filmmaker. With his partner, fellow UCLA student Norman Yonemoto, Ursin would go on to direct the groundbreaking 1969 documentary *Second Campaign*, about the People's Park rebellion in Berkeley. In the 1980s and early 1990s, Ursin was director of photography on a number of experimental videos that Yonemoto made with his brother Bruce, including *Green Card* (1982), *Spalding Gray's Map of L.A.* (1984), *Kappa* (1986), and *Made in Hollywood* (1990), which Ursin completed shortly before his death in 1990. In 1979, Ursin was the cinematographer on Rosa von Praunheim's film *Army of Lovers, or Revolt of the Perverts* (1979), a landmark social documentary that atomizes gay and lesbian activism beyond familiar assimilationist frameworks, revealing the diversity of experiences (including "homosexual Nazism") that subtended gay liberation.

Working under the name Nick Elliot (sometimes spelled "Eliot" and "Elliott"), Ursin also enjoyed considerable success in the realm of gay pornography, directing three films (including 1975's *Snowballing*) and serving as cinematographer on the hardcore classics *Kansas City Trucking Co.* (Joe Gage, 1976) and *A Night at Halsted's* (Fred Halsted, 1980), among a dozen others. Ursin's body of work thus spans discrepant yet similarly alternative or underground cinematic forms, but it is his first known contribution to nontheatrical nonfiction that concerns me here, particularly its loose, unbounded, anti-identitarian presentation of a black queer subject—a presentation that has rarely been recognized in efforts to bring the film to various audiences. Despite its outlier status and seemingly radical textual methods, *Behind Every Good Man* is hardly anomalous, however, and an overview of its relationship to a number of alternative film practices of the 1960s is necessary for a more comprehensive understanding of its place in cinema history.

FIGURE 9.6. The power of portraiture in *Behind Every Good Man*.

## The Portrait Film

*Behind Every Good Man* provides an intimate portrait of the sort that informed much underground film production in the 1960s, including Andy Warhol's *Screen Tests* (1964–66). Silent, static medium close-ups of various subjects—famous and unknown individuals whom Warhol and his associates typically instructed to refrain from acting—the *Screen Tests* both fulfilled and defied expectations engendered by decades of documentary portraits, suggesting complex tensions between revelation and concealment. Jonathan Flatley has described the *Screen Tests* in terms of their shared capacity to display "the radical instability of recognizability," and it is this aspect that *Behind Every Good Man* captures, compelling the viewer to question assumptions regarding a range of gendered practices and artifacts.[16] The affinities between *Behind Every Good Man* and Warhol's *Screen Tests* is arguably most evident at the conclusion of Ursin's film, when the subject, having prepared for a romantic evening by dressing up and setting a table for two (complete with a pair of candles), sits on a sofa and stares in the direction of the camera. In Paul Arthur's reading, the *Screen Tests* critique the portrait film's promise "to illuminate an irreducible core of being," revealing the sheer performativity of simply staring into a camera while providing a minimum of facial expressions.[17] *Behind Every Good Man* reproduces and extends this critique in its fusion of typically segregated documentary and avant-garde styles, troubling any clear distinctions between the two and thus further confounding the epistemological promise of what Arthur terms "the portrait film." In his exploration of the genre, Arthur traces a telling trajectory from the celebrity profiles of the early 1960s (such as the Drew Associates films *Primary* [Robert Drew, 1960], about John F. Kennedy and Hubert Humphrey, and *Jane* [D. A. Pennebaker, 1962], about Jane Fonda) to the anticelebrity or outcast portraits produced later in the decade (such as Shirley Clarke's *Portrait of Jason* [1967]). *Behind Every Good Man* suggests its own sort of bridge between these two phases of documentary portraiture, providing yet another reminder of the capacity of nontheatrical film to complicate even the most sophisticated (and seemingly exhaustive) practices of periodization.

Ursin's protagonist, however marginal, is less a definable social type than a kind of celebrity—a subject whose singularity derives from a unique enactment of self. *Behind Every Good Man* provides numerous links between its subject and a more recognizable celebrity culture, perhaps especially through the use of various pop songs: Dionne Warwick's "Reach Out for Me" (1964), which accompanies a dramatic sequence in which the subject picks up a young man on the street and follows him to a diner; Warwick's "Wishin' and Hopin'," which plays during an observational sequence in which the subject applies makeup (and which competes, at one point, with a first-person voice-over describing the subject's willingness to use bathrooms marked for both men and women—a habit that once led to an encounter with the LAPD); and the Supremes' "I'll Turn to Stone" (1967), which accompanies shots of the subject dancing (and appearing to lip-sync) to a phonograph record—a juxtaposition of sound and image that, more than any other device in the film, suggests Ursin's interest in presenting his subject as a celebrity (not unlike, say, the equally glamorous Diana Ross). Consciously performing for the camera, Ursin's subject escapes the conventions of the outcast portrait, becoming more "Miss Ross" than social misfit, as *Behind Every Good Man* troubles its own ties to objective urban ethnography.

Ursin's film resists the representational impulses common to conventional accounts of transgender embodiment, especially as surveyed by Sandy Stone in "The Empire Strikes Back: A Posttranssexual Manifesto." *Behind Every Good Man* can scarcely be considered what Stone terms a "stereotypical male account of the constitution of woman."[18] In the first shot of the film's subject, many of the conventional markers of womanhood are dominant, providing the impression of female embodiment or, at the very least, of

FIGURE 9.7. Applying makeup.

feminine identification. The film's temporal construction—its organization of shots—thus hardly suggests a trajectory from unambiguous man to unambiguous woman. The subject may use the word "woman" when quoting the famous saying that lends the film its title, but that does not necessarily suggest a feminine self-identification, much less an eagerness to be the proverbial woman standing behind a mythical good man. In quoting this aphorism, the subject offers a digressive account of modern romance and the pressure to settle down, thus raising important questions about what, exactly, precipitated these musings. Is, for instance, the subject responding to direct questions, or simply extemporizing with a minimum of prompting? If questions are being asked, we do not hear them; only the answers are part of the film's soundtrack.

Even in the aural absence of interrogation, however, the subject's audible responses may evoke the intake interviews by which, in Stone's telling, gender dysphoria clinics of the 1960s attempted to determine the acceptability of candidates for gender-reassignment surgery. In hearing this voice-over narration, it may be difficult to escape the impression that the speaker is struggling to justify personal strategies of self-fashioning, perhaps to a resistant interlocutor. There is, however, simply no way of knowing for sure if this voice belongs to the human subject that we see, given the film's reliance on

FIGURE 9.8. Dancing like Diana Ross.

nonsynchronous sound. If certain documentary conventions invite us to assume that a nonsynchronous, first-person voice-over belongs to the images
that it accompanies—that it emanates from the individual at the center of
those images—then queer questions suggest different possibilities. Ursin's
relative inexperience and probable budgetary restrictions likely demanded
that he shoot silent film, later dubbing in "wild lines" recorded separately,
but this technological-determinist explanation obscures the potential artistic
and political justifications for nonsynchronous sound, which include a commitment to questioning documentary's authority as a mode of biographical
pedagogy.

Ursin's soundscape suggests Christian Metz's account of the ambiguity
of film sound—the difficulty of decisively determining the sources of what
one hears.[19] *Behind Every Good Man* indicates that identity is necessarily
multiple and thus resistant to the epistemological drive of classical documentary—to a particular juxtaposition of sound and image that seeks to
ground the former in the latter, and vice versa. As we hear a disembodied
voice describe the pleasures of sidestepping the historically specific illegality of drag and confidently using public restrooms designated for both men
and women, we see an embodied subject standing as well as sitting before a
mirror. This motif of self-recognition is not, however, necessarily a source

of insight for the spectator: the film's subject gazes into a mirror, but we know neither who nor what that subject sees, even—perhaps especially—if we infer an intimate correspondence between sound and image, between autobiographical voice-over narration and visible self-fashioning. After all, the narration escapes the limitations of identity politics, whether through Ursin's editorial elisions or the speaker's own, inveterate rhetorical style—an evasion process that has been ignored or misrepresented in every available account of the film produced in the past fifty years.

## Early Misrepresentations

However much we may wish to idealize nontheatrical film as a vehicle for alternative cinematic expressions—a riposte to the regulatory schemas of Hollywood studios and their attendant modes of distribution and exhibition—it remains necessary to consider the disciplinary effects on this category of various intermediaries. Bringing *Behind Every Good Man* to far-flung audiences under a variety of banners, these intermediaries invariably classified the film—and, by extension, its elusive subject—according to rigid conceptions of gender and sexuality. Many of the discursive mechanisms that seemingly pigeonhole Hollywood films through the deployment of generic labels and established marketing strategies are perhaps equally applicable to nontheatrical nonfiction, but they may seem particularly distortive when applied to *Behind Every Good Man*, a film that announces no taxonomic intentions, whether in relation to its own textuality or to the identities (racial, sexual, gendered) of its subject.

In the late 1960s, long before the academic establishment of queer studies, numerous nontheatrical contexts of reception for *Behind Every Good Man* reflected the theoretical tensions that Stone and Prosser have described, vacillating between an inflexible understanding of the film's subject as a gay male drag performer and an equally obstinate presentation of this figure as a transsexual (to take the term most frequently employed at the time)—as, that is, an individual who would gladly change "his" gender identity, if only "he" could afford gender reassignment surgery. The latter interpretation hinged on a particular reading of the film's images—specifically, those few shots of the subject in a state of undress, which appear to reveal masculine musculature (tight pectorals in place of plush breasts, boyishly narrow hips, and so on), along with a genital protuberance suggestive of penis and testicles. Viewed in terms of their shared fixation on this particular protuberance, which a pair of constricting white underwear does little to diminish, the two major approaches to interpreting *Behind Every Good Man* may seem more similar than dissimilar, their affinities pivoting around the perception of a penis—the belief that Ursin's images bear the indexical traces of a bulge that is both biologically generated and proof of masculinity.

Both approaches define the subject as emphatically male, and both, in addition, indicate equivalent understandings of race and class, reading the film's black subject as poor and thus unable to afford either gender reassignment surgery or the privilege of sustaining a purportedly frivolous, unsalaried attachment to drag. Neither approach, however, is responsive to the film's own strategies—to the indeterminacy of its sounds and images, which evokes a broader epistemological crisis in documentary film, an increasing lack of trust in the typical documentary contract, with its promise to reflect and reproduce the realities of historical events, places, and personages. For D. N. Rodowick, cinema in its narrative, theatrical iterations did not begin to assimilate (and engender a popular acceptance of) the inexplicable and the undecidable until the politically charged (and perhaps retroactively overdetermined) year 1968.[20] *Behind Every Good Man*, completed in the previous year, suggests that nontheatrical film may have been ahead of the curve.

It was in 1968 that Genesis Ltd., the nontheatrical distribution branch of Filmways Productions (best known as the company behind the sitcoms *Mister Ed* [1961–66], *The Beverly Hillbillies* [1962–71], and *Green Acres* [1965–71]), acquired *Behind Every Good Man* as part of its inaugural film program, Genesis I. Collecting mostly student films for distribution to American college campuses, Genesis was meant to function as the nontheatrical counterpart to Sigma III Corp., the Filmways division in charge of distributing foreign films—such as Roman Polanski's *Cul-de-sac* (1966) and Jiří Menzel's *Closely Watched Trains* (1967), along with the occasional American experimental film such as *Dionysus in '69* (Brian De Palma, Bruce Rubin, and Robert Fiore, 1970)—to American art-house cinemas. Publicizing its nontheatrical film program, Genesis prepared synopses of each of the works included in Genesis I (including for publication in the trade journals *Audio-Visual* and *Film Society Review*), and its questionable characterization of *Behind Every Good Man* would establish a precedent—a set of rhetorical norms—for subsequent accounts of Ursin's film.

Presenting it as "a sensitive, behind-the-scenes glimpse into the life of a young male transvestite," Genesis staff members revealed not merely their own willingness to identify maleness and transvestism, but also their apparent eagerness to set aside these descriptors in order to allege the film's "universal" appeal: "Honest and compassionate, this short documentary dramatization transcends its subject to become a moving reminder of our own loneliness and alienation, of the futility of our own aspirations." Deploying the language of sameness and difference—of normality and abnormality, "us" and "them"—Genesis seemed to presuppose an audience of conventionally gendered individuals, prescribing a particular, universalizing mode of interpretation. Further defining *Behind Every Good Man* as a "documentary dramatization," Genesis provided no indication of what, exactly, that term might entail, or of how, precisely, it might apply to a film that appears to be equal parts docudrama and—in keeping with the style and ideals most fashionable during its period of production—cinéma vérité. Whatever the intentions behind it, the Genesis synopsis of *Behind Every Good Man* became widely influential. In fact, it is by far the most recurrent description of a film that seems to defy such description, and it is quoted to this day, including by the Film-Makers' Cooperative, which uses the Genesis text verbatim on its website, where it also classifies *Behind Every Good Man*—a film that it currently distributes—according to the keywords "erotic" and "queer/bi/trans."

Equally questionable were the taxonomic techniques of Canyon Cinema, a foundation promoting independent, noncommercial films and their nontheatrical exhibition. Established in the San Francisco Bay Area in 1961, Canyon Cinema acquired a distribution branch in 1967 and began promoting *Behind Every Good Man* in 1969, mainly through its monthly journal *Canyon Cinema News*. Borrowing the Genesis I synopsis, the publication, which enjoyed a nationwide readership, thus drew quasi-ethnographic attention to the subject of *Behind Every Good Man* while touting the film for screenings in "basements and backyards" as well as at Glide Memorial, a United Methodist church in North Beach.[21] Despite its conspicuous commitment to radical critique and nontraditional spectatorship, Canyon Cinema succumbed to what Judith Butler terms "the regulatory requirements of diagnostic epistemic regimes," actively assigning a gender identity (and suggesting a sexual one through the use of the term "transvestite"), in the process simplifying the techniques of self-expression that *Behind Every Good Man* appears to record and violating the film's ethic of indeterminacy.[22] Conceivably, Glide Memorial, a radically inclusive church rooted in the Methodist philanthropy and social reform movements of the 1920s, further complicated these rhetorical strategies by hosting screenings of *Behind Every Good Man* in the late 1960s. During this period, Canyon Cinema enjoyed a special arrangement with Glide, organizing film screenings in the church's basement and thereby furthering its commitment to eccentric exhibition sites. At the time, a black minister named Cecil Williams presided over Glide, helping to form the Council on Religion and the Homosexual, a Bay Area organization devoted to establishing lines of communication between local churches and gay and lesbian activists. When *Behind Every Good Man* was screened in Glide's basement in the late 1960s, the church's association with the council was well established. While it is unclear whether these site-specific screenings of Ursin's film were understood as continuous with the aims of the organization, they would have been experienced—quite literally—under the banner of Glide's intersections with gay and lesbian activism.

Early readings of *Behind Every Good Man* presupposed masculinity as its subject's original state, seeing "him" as either longing to undergo gender reassignment surgery or simply enjoying, on occasion, the erotic and social affordances of women's clothes. Still other strategies involved presenting the film as a universally relevant docudrama—an account of the human condition that could conceivably appeal to any audience. Advertising the film in conjunction with Ursin and Yonemoto's *Second Campaign*, a 1969 issue of *Canyon Cinema News* contextualized *Behind Every Good Man* in terms of Ursin's budding career, suggesting that the film, far from anomalous in its account of a "marginal" subject, was in fact consistent with the director's other explorations of "universal basic needs." Turning the film into an index of loneliness, alienation, and futility, *Canyon Cinema News* suggested the difficulty of recognizing Ursin's radical strategies—a difficulty that has not abated in the decades since, as a series of more recent encounters attests.

## Contemporary Agendas

Despite the emergence of transgender studies and an associated terminological expansion in academic and popular accounts of queer subjects, contemporary platforms for *Behind Every Good Man* continue to employ limited, even archaic rhetorical strategies, repeatedly identifying the film's subject as a gay man or aspiring male-to-female transsexual. Take, for instance, the program notes of the Museum of Contemporary Art Detroit (MOCAD), which hosted a screening of *Behind Every Good Man* in June 2010, classifying it as "a brief encounter with a transsexual black man who shares his experiences as a woman through snagging a 'good man.'" For MOCAD, the film's significance is more musicological than sexological: included as part of its film series House of Sound, *Behind Every Good Man* was situated as one of many experimental investigations of "sound as a harbinger of change," merging "the popular and the perplexing," and finally signaling "control gained, control lost." It is unclear precisely how this interpretation applies to Ursin's work: What change does *Behind Every Good Man* promise? What aspects of the film are popular and perplexing, and what control is gained and lost? Ursin's own rhetorical strategies—his own ways of describing *Behind Every Good Man*—are unavailable as fodder for museum copy, and the terms "transsexual," "man," and "woman" are among the few that recur in descriptions of the work, indicating, perhaps, queer theory's lack of purchase on the very institutions that circulate queer nontheatrical film.

Efforts to identify the film's relationship to race are perhaps as contestable as those designed to establish the sexual and gender identity of its subject. If masculinity and femininity are, as specifically gendered markers, scarcely mentioned in *Behind Every Good Man*, blackness as a category of racial identity is even less acknowledged at the level of voice-over commentary. Nevertheless, and despite Ursin's own whiteness, *Behind Every Good Man* is often exhibited as an example of black cultural production and situated alongside the films of Isaac Julien and Marlon Riggs, which are more explicitly invested in deconstructing various formulations of blackness. For instance, in September 2009, the Canadian film series Early Monthly Segments (EMS), which boasts a commitment to "historical and contemporary avant-garde 16mm films in a salon-like setting," hosted a screening of *Behind Every Good Man* at the Art Bar in Toronto's Gladstone Hotel, where Ursin's film occupied a triple bill with *Tongues Untied* and Warren Sonbert's *Short Fuse* (1992). A thirty-seven-minute experimental film that includes footage of ACT UP demonstrations, *Short Fuse* is an expression not simply of Sonbert's long-standing commitment to representing gay men (as in his first film, *Amphetamine* [1966], which features an extended same-sex kiss), but also of his own mortality and growing frustration regarding the (federally stymied) battle against HIV/AIDS. Grouping *Behind Every Good Man* with two such firmly gay-identified films, EMS seemed to revive earlier justifications for positing the gayness of Ursin's subject, which similarly evoked a wide swath of social problems, particularly as explicitly explored in other documentaries. The three films have something else in common, however: their gay-identified makers all died of complications from AIDS—a detail that the EMS program notes omit even as they emphasize Riggs's own battle with the disease, pointing out that he "succumbed to AIDS in 1994."

Classifying *Behind Every Good Man* as a gay film, then, may represent an auteurist reading, reflecting an awareness not only of Ursin's preferred self-definition but also, perhaps, of his longtime association with gay pornography. But it also suggests, in this instance, an equivalence of cultural critique among films that are, in fact, differently positioned in relation to blackness, both textually and extratextually. When screened alongside *Tongues Untied*, Ursin's film is typically returned to its earliest associations with male homosexuality, indexing, as the EMS program notes put it, "how it is to be both black and gay." Not only does *Behind Every Good Man* offer no such direct engagement with an ontology of blackness, but this conflation of Ursin's film and *Tongues Untied* serves to efface some of the crucial differences between the two texts. Recall, for instance, Jackie Goldsby's influential reading of Riggs's alleged transphobia, his presentation of gender fluidity as pathetic and productive of loneliness—a presentation that Ursin's film does not share, except, perhaps, in its concluding seconds, when the film's subject sits alone, staring somberly in the direction of the camera.[23]

If the otherness of nontheatrical film presents innumerable challenges to typical historiographic methods, so does the indeterminacy of *Behind Every Good Man*—the opacity that it shares with its subject—require us to complicate received knowledge about gender and sexuality. Opacity is not an obstacle to intellect, as decades of queer theoretical writing has argued; it is not an occasion for silence. In *Epistemology of the Closet*, Eve Kosofsky Sedgwick famously championed "particular opacities"—"a plethora of *ignorances*" that, if honestly articulated, could constitute an ethic, even an episteme, enabling the evasion of misrecognition and other forms of discursive violence.[24] Promoting knowledge of a film like *Behind Every Good Man* hardly requires that we fix its subject according to rigid conceptions of race, gender, and sexuality. In fact, we stand to learn more about the work—and, by extension, about nontheatrical film and its specific contexts—by embracing its indeterminate aspects.

Whenever *Behind Every Good Man* is revived for a museum or festival screening, the film is subjected to the unwarranted confidence of those who claim, in keeping with whatever terms seem to serve their institutional affiliations or political allegiances, that its subject is transgender, or a transsexual, or a gay man, or an African American. It is precisely because of its careful avoidance of categorization that the film, like its subject, can seemingly accommodate all of these labels and, conceivably, many more, remaining a projection screen for multiple strategies of signification. As Édouard Glissant argues, a person has the right to be opaque—a statement that seems especially relevant to a consideration of *Behind Every Good Man*. Glissant's concept of opacity represents, in the words of Zach Blas, "an ethical mandate to maintain obscurity, to not impose rubrics of categorization and measurement, which always enact a politics of reduction and exclusion." Opacity, in other words, "does not concern legislative rights but is rather an ontological position that lets exist as such that which is immeasurable, nonidentifiable, and unintelligible in things."[25] *Behind Every Good Man* embraces opacity in multiple ways, at once resisting the impulse to categorize its subject and producing ambiguity through the union of seemingly discrepant stylistic devices. The film's formal hybridity has obvious affinities with the strategies of self-fashioning of its elusive subject, presenting the viewer with a particular documentary contract only to rescind it in a subsequent scene, replacing the apparently observational with the ostensibly staged, in the process blurring distinctions between the two approaches and providing the groundwork for a much-needed reappraisal of cinema history.

FILMOGRAPHY

All available films discussed in this chapter can be streamed through the book's web page at https://www.dukeupress.edu/Features/Screening-Race.

*Army of Lovers, or Revolt of the Perverts* (1979), 107 min., 35mm
PRODUCTION: Rosa von Praunheim Filmproduktion. DIRECTOR: Rosa von Praunheim. ACCESS: None known.

*Behind Every Good Man* (1967), 8 min., 16mm
PRODUCTION: Independent. DIRECTOR: Nikolai Ursin. ACCESS: UCLA Film and Television Archive, Film-Makers' Cooperative.

*Green Card: An American Romance* (1982), 79 min., VHS
PRODUCTION: KYO-DAI. DIRECTORS: Bruce Yonemoto, Norman Yonemoto. ACCESS: Electronic Arts Intermix.

*Jane* (1962), 53 min., 16mm
PRODUCTION: Drew Associates. DIRECTOR: D. A. Pennebaker. ACCESS: Pennebaker and Hegedus Films.

*Kansas City Trucking Co.* (1976), 67 min., 16mm
PRODUCTION: Joe Gage Films. DIRECTOR: Joe Gage. ACCESS: HIS Video.

*Kappa* (1986), 26 min., VHS
PRODUCTION: KYO-DAI. DIRECTORS: Bruce Yonemoto, Norman Yonemoto. ACCESS: Electronic Arts Intermix.

*Look at Life* (1965), 1 min., 16mm
PRODUCTION: Independent. DIRECTOR: George Lucas. ACCESS: USC Hugh M. Hefner Moving Image Archive.

*Looking for Langston* (1989), 42 min., Super 16mm/35mm
PRODUCTION: Sankofa Film and Video. DIRECTOR: Isaac Julien. ACCESS: British Film Institute.

*Made in Hollywood* (1990), 56 min., VHS
PRODUCTION: KYO-DAI. DIRECTORS: Bruce Yonemoto, Norman Yonemoto.
ACCESS: Electronic Arts Intermix.

*A Night at Halsted's* (1980), 76 min., 16mm
PRODUCTION: COSCO Studio, Kevin Kramer Productions. DIRECTOR: Fred Halsted.
ACCESS: HIS Video.

*. . . No Lies* (1973), 16 min., 16mm
PRODUCTION: Independent. DIRECTOR: Mitchell Block. ACCESS: Direct Cinema
Ltd.

*Portrait of Jason* (1967), 105 min., 16mm
PRODUCTION: Shirley Clarke Productions, Graeme Ferguson Productions.
DIRECTOR: Shirley Clarke. ACCESS: Milestone Films.

*Primary* (1960), 60 min., 16mm
PRODUCTION: Robert Drew Associates. DIRECTOR: Robert Drew. ACCESS: Criterion
Collection, DVD and Blu-ray.

*Second Campaign* (1969), 19 min., 16mm
PRODUCTION: Independent. DIRECTORS: Norman Yonemoto, Nikolai Ursin.
ACCESS: None known.

*Short Fuse* (1992), 32 min., 16mm
PRODUCTION: Independent. DIRECTOR: Warren Sonbert. ACCESS: Warren Sonbert
Collection, Harvard Film Archive, Fine Arts Library, Harvard College Library.

*Snowballing* (1975), 60 min., 16mm
PRODUCTION: Selo Films. DIRECTOR: Nick Elliot (Nikolai Ursin). ACCESS: The Porn
Classic.

*Spalding Gray's Map of L.A.* (1984), 27 min., VHS
PRODUCTION: KYO-DAI. DIRECTORS: Bruce Yonemoto, Norman Yonemoto.
ACCESS: Electronic Arts Intermix.

*Tongues Untied* (1989), 55 min., 16mm
PRODUCTION: Signifyin' Works. DIRECTOR: Marlon Riggs. ACCESS: California
Newsreel.

NOTES

1  For more on the campy pedagogy of nontheatrical educational films, see Harry M.
   Benshoff, *Monsters in the Closet: Homosexuality and the Horror Film* (New York:
   Manchester University Press, 1997). For more on the emergence of queer art video,
   see Julianne Pidduck, "New Queer Cinema and Experimental Video," in *New
   Queer Cinema: A Critical Reader*, ed. Michele Aaron (New Brunswick, NJ: Rutgers
   University Press, 2004), 80–97.

2   Contradictions abound regarding the film's year of completion and release. The Film-Makers' Cooperative, which distributes the film, lists the year as 1966. But the finished version of the film, the only version known to have ever existed, features a song ("I'll Turn to Stone," by the Supremes) that was not released as a single until 1967. No records survive that indicate when, exactly, Ursin shot the film, but it first began circulating in 1967.

3   Barbara Hammer, "The Politics of Abstraction," in *Queer Looks: Perspectives on Lesbian and Gay Film and Video*, ed. Martha Gever, Pratibha Parmar, and John Greyson (New York: Routledge, 1993), 70–75.

4   E. Patrick Johnson, "'Quare' Studies, or '(Almost) Everything I Know about Queer Studies I Learned from My Grandmother,'" in *The Routledge Queer Studies Reader*, ed. Donald E. Hall and Annamarie Jagose (New York: Routledge, 2013), 97.

5   Johnson, "'Quare' Studies," 98.

6   Cathy Cohen, "Punks, Bulldaggers, and Welfare Queens: The Radical Potential of Queer Politics?," in *The Routledge Queer Studies Reader*, ed. Donald E. Hall and Annamarie Jagose (New York: Routledge, 2013), 84.

7   These include categories (such as that of the "invert") inherited from as far back as Richard von Krafft-Ebing's *Psychopathia Sexualis* (1886) and Havelock Ellis and John Addington Symonds's *Sexual Inversion* (1897).

8   Heide Solbrig, "Dr. ERPI Finds His Voice: Electrical Research Products, Inc. and the Educational Film Market, 1927–1937," in *Learning with the Lights Off: Educational Film in the United States*, ed. Devin Orgeron, Marsha Orgeron, and Dan Streible (New York: Oxford University Press, 2012), 213; Victoria Cain, "'An Indirect Influence upon Industry': Rockefeller Philanthropies and the Development of Educational Film in the United States, 1935–1953," in Orgeron, Orgeron, and Streible, *Learning with the Lights Off*, 245.

9   Marsha Gordon and Allyson Nadia Field, "The Other Side of the Tracks: Nontheatrical Film History, Pre-Rebellion Watts, and *Felicia*," *Cinema Journal* 55, no. 2 (winter 2016): 3.

10  Isaac Julien, "Black Is, Black Ain't: Notes on De-essentializing Black Identities," in *Black Popular Culture*, ed. Michele Wallace and Gina Dent (Seattle: Bay Press, 1992), 258.

11  Julien, "Black Is, Black Ain't," 263.

12  David Valentine, *Imagining Transgender: An Ethnography of a Category* (Durham, NC: Duke University Press, 2007), 14.

13  Valentine, *Imagining Transgender*, 172.

14  Sandy Stone, "The Empire Strikes Back: A Posttranssexual Manifesto," in *The Transgender Studies Reader*, ed. Susan Stryker and Stephen Whittle (New York: Routledge, 2006), 226.

15  Stone, "The Empire Strikes Back," 225.

16  Quoted in Douglas Crimp, *"Our Kind of Movie": The Films of Andy Warhol* (Cambridge, MA: MIT Press, 2012), 8.

17  Paul Arthur, "No Longer Absolute: Portraiture in American Avant-Garde and Documentary Films of the Sixties," in *Rites of Realism: Essays on Corporeal Cinema*, ed. Ivone Margulies (Durham, NC: Duke University Press, 2003), 108.

18  Stone, "The Empire Strikes Back," 227.

19  Christian Metz, "Aural Objects," trans. Georgia Gurrieri, in *Film Sound: Theory and Practice*, ed. Elisabeth Weis and John Belton (New York: Columbia University Press, 1985), 154–61.

20  D. N. Rodowick, *Reading the Figural, or, Philosophy after the New Media* (Durham, NC: Duke University Press, 2001).

21  *Canyon Cinema News* 69, no. 1 (1969): 56.

22  Judith Butler, "Imitation and Gender Insubordination," in *Inside/Out: Lesbian Theories, Gay Theories*, ed. Diana Fuss (New York: Routledge, 1991), 27.

23  Jackie Goldsby, "Queens of Language: *Paris Is Burning*," in *Queer Looks: Perspectives on Lesbian and Gay Film and Video*, ed. Martha Gever, Pratibha Parmar, and John Greyson (New York: Routledge, 1993), 108–15.

24  Eve Kosofsky Sedgwick, *Epistemology of the Closet* (Berkeley: University of California Press, 2008), 8.

25  Zach Blas, "Informatic Opacity," *Journal of Aesthetics and Protest*, no. 9 (summer 2014), http://www.joaap.org/issue9/zachblas.htm.

## 10

## Televising Watts

Joe Saltzman's *Black on Black* (1968) on KNXT

JOSHUA GLICK

Joe Saltzman's *Black on Black* challenged staid conventions of broadcast journalism and stereotypical representations of Watts when it premiered on Los Angeles station KNXT on July 18, 1968. Shot in the thick of urban uprisings sweeping the country, the documentary took aim at prestige public affairs specials' depiction of Watts as a site of poverty, a crime-ridden neighborhood, or a war zone. Saltzman, a white liberal documentarian from the nearby suburb of Alhambra in the San Gabriel Valley, sought to provide a platform for black residents to speak for themselves and to reorient mainstream television audiences' understanding of South Central Los Angeles. *Black on Black* portrayed Watts as a community of people with deep ties to their neighborhood. Residents reflected on the meaning of black identity and spoke openly about their struggles living within a city that marginalized their presence.

Cinema and media studies scholars have written extensively on the television industry's engagement with the Black Power movement, most often analyzing nationally broadcast situation comedies (*Sanford and Son* [NBC, 1972–77]), variety shows (*The Flip Wilson Show* [NBC, 1970–74], *Soul Train* [1970–2006]), and public affairs series (*Black Journal* [NET, 1968–77]). However, the expanding field of local programming constituted a crucial site of innovation and resistance to the whitewashed mainstream media.[1] *Black on Black* directly addressed topics such as systemic racism and black cultural expression. Investigating Saltzman's documentary demonstrates how social forces in Los Angeles shaped a national debate about the fraught relationship between minorities and the film and television industry, as well as how this debate influenced on-the-ground media production and race relations in the city. The documentary was widely seen and discussed within Los Angeles and was broadcast in St. Louis, Chicago, New York, and Philadelphia. But like many films primarily intended for local exhibition, it quickly fell out of circulation, only to resurface decades later for occasional retrospectives.[2]

*Black on Black*'s enthusiastic reception in the news, entertainment, and African American press encouraged stations across the country to devote more resources to reporting on inner-city neighborhoods. At the same time, the documentary revealed broader tensions within cultural liberalism concerning the limited role of a film's subjects in the conceptualization, creation, and outreach of the film itself. Just as *Black on Black* anticipated future television documentaries that took an in-depth and nuanced look at minority communities, it also marked a pivot within broadcasting institutions toward supporting projects where minorities asserted more authorial control in front of and behind the camera.

## Station Renegade

Saltzman's experiences as an undergraduate at the University of Southern California gave rise to his interests in alternative kinds of social documentary. Saltzman studied nonfiction with film critic Arthur Knight and also served as editor in chief of the school newspaper, the *Daily Trojan*. After pursuing a graduate degree in journalism at Columbia University, he returned to Los Angeles in 1962. Saltzman covered the crime beat for the *San Fernando Valley Times* and worked as news editor for the *Palisadian Post*. He then took a job at the CBS-owned and -operated station KNXT as an interviewer and researcher for *Ralph Story's Los Angeles* (1964–70), a popular magazine-style series that covered the city's cultural milieu. For example, programs looked at the exotic decor of Clifton's Cafeteria, the immigrant history of Boyle Heights, and the biographies of movie stars. Saltzman enjoyed the valuable training in on-location filmmaking; however, the fact that the series typically avoided pervasive issues of racism, government corruption, and displacement left him wanting to work on other kinds of programs.[3]

When the Watts Uprising erupted on August 11, 1965, it was depicted by print and broadcast journalists from the point of view of the police and city officials. This skewed portrayal heightened Saltzman's conviction that television programming needed to address the views of the city's minorities. While the protests were triggered by the arrest of the African American resident Marquette Frye at the intersection of 116th Street and Avalon Boulevard, the unrest stemmed from a sense of injustice concerning the persistence of police brutality, the choking off of public utilities from the neighborhood, exploitation by business owners, neglect by absentee landlords, and the lack of employment opportunities.[4] Occurring only five days after the signing of President Lyndon B. Johnson's Voting Rights Act, which outlawed discriminatory practices that disenfranchised minorities, the Watts Uprising signaled a rupture in the Great Society and prefaced the wave of nationwide street protests in cities throughout the late 1960s.

In KTLA's *Hell in the City of Angels* (1965), the reporter Hugh Brundage describes the heated summer confrontations as "hoodlums" committing "indiscriminate" acts of "violence" that brought about rampant destruction. Flyover views from the station's telecopter surveyed burning commercial establishments along Avalon Boulevard, police officers dispersing crowds and making arrests, and individuals carrying stolen objects moving quickly down alleys and sidewalks. In an interview within a bustling newsroom, cameraman Ed Clark spoke about Watts as a "war zone" that was "worse than Korea" and Mayor Sam Yorty confidently declared that the only effective way to meet the "mob" was with "overwhelming power." Throughout the documentary, Watts residents were talked about rather than listened to.

Coverage by KTLA was consistent with the alarmist headlines of the *Los Angeles Times*, stories in *Time* and *Newsweek*, and Universal's newsreel *Troops Patrol L.A.* (1965). The CBS Reports documentary *Watts: Riot or Revolt* (1965) reinforced the recently published *Violence in the City—an End or a Beginning?*, authored by Governor Edmund Brown's Commission on the Los Angeles Riots. Members of the commission did not take seriously the fact that widespread police prejudice and excessive use of force was a direct cause of the tension and considered the uprising a detestable act of anger rather than a protest. In the documentary, Police Chief William Parker blamed members of the black community for the current crisis, stating that a criminal element in Watts, stirred up by civil rights leaders, created unreasonable demands and had promoted widespread disrespect for law enforcement. The lack of black voices in the show resonates with how scholar Devorah Heitner describes public affairs programs of the era, in which an "emphasis on the expertise of people in power meant an overwhelming exclusion of Black points of view."[5]

Saltzman proposed a documentary on South Central residents in which the film's subjects would be the only voices heard. He believed that the program would be meaningful for black viewers as well as educational for white

Angelenos who would constitute the program's main viewing demographic. Saltzman thought that the documentary would increase awareness of and dialogue about what life was like for African Americans in South Central and urban America more generally.[6] But KNXT rejected the idea, arguing that the absence of an in-house anchor would give viewers the impression that the station lacked control over its content. Flagrant racism also prevented the program from getting off the ground. The show was frequently called "Saltzman's N***** Project" by staff.[7] It was not until 1968, when two factors contributed to a climate of media reform, that KNXT greenlit the film.

The first of these factors was a report issued by the National Advisory Commission on Civil Disorders and chaired by Illinois governor Otto Kerner. The report was the upshot of the Johnson administration's July 27, 1967, mandate to explore the motivations behind four years of urban unrest.[8] The Kerner Commission researched the mass media's interpretation of these events and investigated the larger relationship between minorities and the film, television, and newspaper industries. The document stated that these outlets "have not shown understanding or appreciation of—and thus have not communicated—a sense of Negro culture, thought, or history."[9] The report elaborated on the need to bring more minority personnel into the culture industries and also claimed, "the news media must find ways of exploring the problems of the Negro and the ghetto more deeply and more meaningfully."[10]

The second major factor involved the efforts of lawyers, advocacy groups, civil rights leaders, and entertainment personnel to make television stations more responsive to their minority constituencies. Their fight led to a 1966 court case with the station WLBT in Jackson, Mississippi, that established the right of citizens to participate in a station's license-renewal proceeding. A 1969 court decision stripped the same station of its license because of its failure to address the views of the area's black community. Media historian Allison Perlman has argued that the WLBT case showed that a station's racist programming and lack of attention to minority audiences could serve as reason for revocation.[11] This climate of media reform touched down in Los Angeles, the nation's fastest-expanding multiracial metropolis that was also the country's film and television capital. The owned-and-operated status of KNXT encouraged station executives to shift their position on Saltzman's program from rejection to reluctant acceptance. On the one hand, the station was distant from the New York–based corporate oversight of the CBS network. On the other hand, KNXT was defined by its identity as a flagship

FIGURE 10.1. Donnell
Petetan, 1968, Herald-
Examiner Collection/
Los Angeles Public
Library.

Southern California station, and thus was under pressure to respond to issues
facing Los Angeles.

## Listening to Los Angeles

Saltzman and his producer, Dan Gingold, convinced KNXT to give their documentary a ninety-minute (rather than the standard sixty-minute) slot and
a more flexible budget. The small crew spent approximately three months
working on the film, including three weeks on location during the spring
and early summer of 1968. Saltzman's main liaison with Watts was Truman
Jacques, a community organizer and aspiring broadcast journalist. Through
Jacques, Saltzman met Donnell Petetan, a resident who worked for the Concentrated Employment Program helping to provide services to job seek-
ers. Petetan became Saltzman's main interlocutor with Watts, showing him

around, introducing him to various business owners, and helping to set up interviews with family and friends.[12]

The race prejudice harbored by some of the crew made filming difficult, forcing Saltzman to think of ways to routinely remove them for periods of time during production.[13] Radio engineers for KNX proved to be more congenial collaborators. Saltzman worked with them for the editing of ambient noises, individual testimony, and music. He was more drawn to the 1930s British and American social documentary practice of recording interviews and overlaying voice-over onto observational footage, rather than the 1960s direct cinema techniques that stressed mobile, immersive cinematography and sync-sound recording. "I was far more concerned with audio than video," Saltzman would later recall, for sound could document "the things that were happening inside the heart and the mind of the people."[14]

*Black on Black* foregrounds sound from the outset. The film begins by way of Lou Rawls's "Southside Blues" monologue playing against a black screen that gradually becomes dotted with perforation marks. This musical opening marked a point of divergence from standard television documentaries, which seldom used nondiegetic music based on the notion that it compromised the program's ability to dispassionately communicate information. *Black on Black* encourages emotional connections to its subject. Rawls's incantatory monologue, recorded live at Capitol Studios in Los Angeles in 1966, maps black neighborhoods within cities, before announcing the particularity of Watts and the belief that it is in a state of change. Rawls's chant, "*Burn* Baby . . . *Burn* Baby . . . *Burn* Baby . . ." then transitions to the opening of his song "Tobacco Road." The illuminated dots can be interpreted as corresponding to individual black enclaves. Or, considering that protestors of the Watts Uprising appropriated local DJ Magnificent Montague's phrase "Burn, Baby! Burn!" as a militant rallying cry, the perforation marks can also be interpreted as referring to the intensity of the urban unrest or even bullet holes.

As the monologue comes to a close, the camera focuses on one of the dots, which dissolves into the headlight of an oncoming train rolling through Watts. Next, a cut to a tracking shot follows Petetan driving past small homes, the Watts Towers, housing projects, weed-filled vacant lots, children playing, and adult men and women walking down the street. Petetan explains that "Tobacco Road" is slang for the "black ghetto" that exists in every American city. Watts at once shares characteristics of other black urban working-class neighborhoods and is also distinct in its makeup and relationship to its metropolitan area. People reside in all sorts of single-family homes; however, "there is very little ownership here of houses" and landlords are most

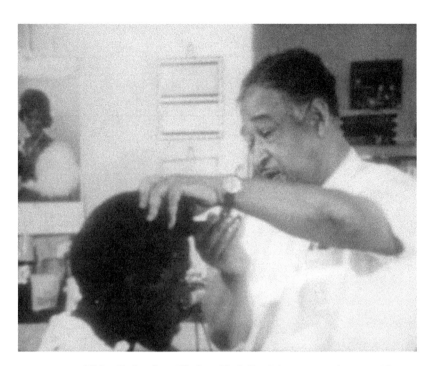

FIGURE 10.2. Walter Butler, from *Black on Black* (Joe Saltzman, 1968), DVD, with thanks to Joe Saltzman.

often absentee and neglectful. Landlords live elsewhere, as do those who own many of the businesses, ensuring that money flows out of the community. But Petetan contends that Watts is not simply a blighted terrain or a problem for urban planners to solve. Residents feel affection for and draw psychological support from the environment. The film then proceeds by examining a range of topics that coalesce around black self-identification, cultural practices, oppression, and hopes and anxieties for the future. Saltzman explores these subjects in one-on-one interviews where his own presence is beyond the frame. These segments are then interwoven with observational sequences matched with voice-over narration from the interviewees.

Speaking from within his bedroom in his East 112th Street home, Petetan asserts that cultivating a black identity begins with embracing the word "black." Popular culture has for so long attached negative connotations to "black" and positive connotations to "white." It is important to resituate the former as affirmative and beautiful. Male and female interviewees then extend the discussion of identity through reflecting on the significance of wearing clothing that

FIGURE 10.3. Ethel Petetan, from *Black on Black* (Joe Saltzman, 1968), DVD, with thanks to Joe Saltzman.

relates to one's ancestral heritage or styling their hair to express racial pride. Talking as he cuts a young man's hair in his own shop, barber Walter Butler explains how at one time black people were urged by the cosmetic industry to process, curl, and straighten their hair, emulating that of whites. He claims that wearing a "Natural" allows African Americans to develop a more acute sense of self. A woman getting her hair washed describes, "This is the way I came into the world. I didn't come into it pressed and curled. I came into it nappy."

Ethel Petetan (Donnell's mother) provides a more in-depth reflection on black culture through the preparation of chitterlings in her kitchen. While washing and plucking the hair off the intestines, seasoning them, and cooking them in a pot, she shares that she learned everything observing her mother when she was a child growing up in rural Texas. Making and eating food is something that bolsters family ties, Ethel explains. Cooking is a way of passing on knowledge from one family member to another, and preparing a big meal is an occasion for bringing the whole family together. Petetan's own voice-over commentary during this scene notes that racial prejudice and

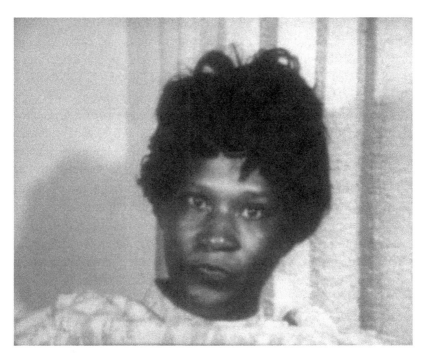

FIGURE 10.4. Ethel Petetan, from *Black on Black* (Joe Saltzman, 1968), DVD, with thanks to Joe Saltzman.

substandard material conditions shaped the evolution of his family's food. Petetan discusses that black families have had to be creative with the vegetables and meat more easily accessible to them.

Additional scenes in *Black on Black* explain that conflict is part of everyday life. This conflict can take the form of television's psychological attack on people of color. "Why does TV make fool[s] out of other races?" Petetan asks. The white man is "always the supreme being," while minorities are always the butt of jokes or absent from television all together. Conflict can also involve face-to-face indignities, such as being pulled over by police who look for any kind of minor violation. Footage of policemen interrogating a black driver on the side of the road followed by a quick shot of a squad car with the LAPD's official slogan, "To Protect and to Serve," prominently in view, underscores the disconnect between the LAPD's ostensibly virtuous mission and its treatment of minorities. One young woman shares an aggravating story of a time when her boss discouraged her from applying for a higher-paying position because he thought she wouldn't "enjoy working in this office where there are all white people." Petetan's sister says that a boss she once had lied to her about there not being an opening within her company and then ultimately gave the job to a white woman. Criticizing a racially divided workforce, Ethel looks directly at the camera and states, "I tell you why the white man is a snake in the grass. The white man will train you for any kind of job that he wants you to do. . . . He won't train you for the better jobs. He'll save his better jobs, his best-paying jobs, for the whites."

While numerous interviewees share common frustrations, *Black on Black* does not try to build consensus or to provide a monolithic view of Watts. Religion, for example, is a divisive issue. Inside a service at the Garden of Eden Church of God in Christ, where Reverend W. D. Willis is seen preaching and teenagers sing "The Lord Is Blessing Me Right Now," a woman shares with the congregation how the church offers a safe space for children. Another woman recounts how the church has helped provide a moral compass for her family. By contrast, Petetan speaks of religion as "the biggest hustle of all," a form of economic exploitation and even mind control. He proudly asserts that agency lies with humans rather than an abstract entity.

The film's individual perspectives, often framed in intimate close-ups, humanize Watts for network audiences. However, *Black on Black*'s focus on individuals speaking about their lives ignores the efforts to build institutions devoted to progressive change in South Central. The documentary eschews the impact of grassroots organizing as well as broader economic and political forces affecting life on the ground in Watts. Saltzman might have tried to document the initiative to bring Watts its much-needed hospital, course offerings in political theory at the Mafundi Institute, and the films and theatrical productions by the Performing Arts Society of Los Angeles. Additionally, the film could have examined corporate disinvestment from the central city and the industrial growth of suburban Los Angeles, factors that ultimately hurt job opportunities for Watts residents. Expanding the purview of the documentary might have more clearly connected distinct experiences to the social infrastructure of the region.[15]

Instead, *Black on Black* stays focused on particular individuals through its conclusion, where it presents residents' desires and predictions for the future. Voice-over plays against evenly paced medium and long shots of the younger generation of South Central going about their daily routines: children amusing themselves on the playground and walking to school, young adults going to work, and groups of friends hanging out near commercial establishments. One woman declares that the ultimate goal is to become part of society, to have equal opportunities, and that violence never yields tangible benefits. Petetan and his friend argue that violence is an American tradition that stretches back to the country's founding. In the context of sustained oppression, violence has been the only thing that gets the attention of those in power and forces the government and civic elites in Los Angeles to recognize and address the needs of the black community. These perspectives in *Black on Black* pointed to a debate between the liberal belief in nonviolence and the militant nationalist interest in physical force as a tool of self-defense and protest. At the same time, presenting these voices as stand-alone opinions made Black Power seem less threatening, as if it was a view held by select individuals rather than a political movement.

Still, *Black on Black*'s final song gives the documentary a defiant tone. Whereas "Southside Blues"/"Tobacco Road" takes the viewer from black enclaves across America to Watts, the film's conclusion moves from the local to the national through soul singer Nina Simone's incendiary "Four Women." The song, in which Simone takes the first-person perspective of four black women, plays against a montage of figurative paintings by art students at Watts's Fremont High School.[16] The searching gaze of the camera explores painterly surfaces, at times rendering much of the canvas in view, at other times highlighting a detail of a face or body part. First, the slave Aunt Sarah, whose "back is strong, / strong enough to take the pain / inflicted again and again," strikes a rebellious posture. The mixed-race Safronia, whose "rich and white" father raped her mother, appears with flowing, multicolored hair and faces the viewer with eyes closed. Sweet Thing, a prostitute forced to sleep with anybody with "money to buy," stands tall and looks directly at the viewer, refusing to be submissive or objectified. The militant Peaches proclaims, "My skin is brown, / my manner is tough, / I'll kill the first mother I see, / my life has been rough." She is depicted with a steely glare, wearing a broken handcuff emblematic of her body and mind breaking free of imposed shackles. The pairing of song and paintings foregrounds how black women in particular, and black people in general, have resisted oppression throughout U.S. history, reinforcing the importance of these struggles for present-day conceptions of black identity.

### Broadcasting *Black on Black*

As the airdate for the documentary approached, producer Dan Gingold battled KNXT executives to prevent them from inserting Jerry Dunphy, the prominent white anchor of the nightly public affairs program *The Big News*, as *Black on Black*'s narrator. Gingold also fought to ensure the film's music remained intact.[17] Finally cleared for broadcast, *Black on Black* premiered on July 18 at 7:30 p.m. The station placed an advertisement in the *Los Angeles Times*, announcing the film's innovative approach to representing race on television and touting the program's wide appeal.[18] An article in the African American newspaper the *Los Angeles Sentinel*, expressed, "*Black on Black* will be a departure from standard 'documentary' presentations because it will be structured by black citizens of Los Angeles. There will be no reporter, narrator, or writer to give it traditional documentary form. Rather, it will be presented in the faces and voices of those who know black people best—black people."[19]

Saltzman was not the only broadcast journalist going into inner-city neighborhoods, but his approach to documentary differed from that of many of his contemporaries. *Television* critic Sherman Brodey cataloged the efforts of broadcasters to intensify coverage of black communities in San Francisco, Denver, New Orleans, Little Rock, Chicago, Baltimore, New Haven, and Boston. He noted that Saltzman's *Black on Black* both was part of and distinguished itself from this trend.[20] *Variety* stated that *Black on Black* "transcended any previous effort to picture the black people as they are, without the embellishments of extraneous dramatization." Saltzman's hometown paper, the *Alhambra Post-Advocate*, echoed this sentiment. Journalist Bonnie Epstein wrote that the man who "spent five years washing 'some of the best windows' in Alhambra" made an important film that takes a "unique" approach to its subject. In his *Hollywood Reporter* review, Bob Hull wrote that black subjects speaking for themselves was a breakthrough, providing a more penetrating account of the dual presence of hope and hopelessness that currently exists. Following up on their previous story on the film, the *Los Angeles Sentinel* commented that most news programs provide a "recitation of statistics on crime, violence, poverty and despair," but *Black on Black* shows residents "articulat[ing] what it's like to be black as it is to them."[21]

*Black on Black* received an encore broadcast on September 8 and was then sent to other CBS-owned and -operated stations. The documentary won two local Emmys as well as numerous national awards.[22] Station KNXT gave the Los Angeles Public Library (LAPL) a 16mm print, and Saltzman frequently appeared in person with the film during its exhibition in schools and churches. Letters of support streamed into KNXT headquarters at 6121 Sunset Boulevard. The film found a welcome audience among middle-class white liberals, who affirmed that the documentary increased awareness about social issues. For example, San Pedro resident Barbara Wasser wrote, "*Black on Black*, which appeared last night, offered me more insights

For the first time, Blacks in South Central Los Angeles tell it like it is, frankly talking about themselves in their own homes and neighborhoods. No reporter. No interviews. A broadcast no white —or black person should miss! Tonight! 90 minutes! "BLACK ON BLACK" A KNXT Special!

# 7:30PM CBS◉2

29

into Negro problems than any TV show I've seen to date. I find it incredible and gratifying that you would devote 90 mins. to such a worthwhile, probing show." Activist and UCLA philosophy professor Tom Robischon wrote to the station, saying, "I must say I found this one of the most enlightened and hard-hitting things I have seen whites do. . . . I think you ought to turn [Saltzman] loose on other similar zones of ignorance and misapprehension in our society." Rowena Boylan of North Hollywood exclaimed that the documentary was "spellbinding" and implored KNXT to broadcast the film again so that others who missed it could see it. Producer-director and animator Chuck Jones of MGM had this to say about the program: "*Black on Black* is a remarkably tight, retina-searing, cortex-lashing documentary. . . . We were not glued to the set; we were glued to the idea."[23]

The film was also used to teach black history. Horace Mann Elementary School in Glendale hosted a screening with Saltzman, after which students sent him letters. Mike Acosta wrote that he "wasn't so much aware that black[s] had so much against them." Cindy Evans mentioned that she gained knowledge of "how black people feel now." Following Saltzman's screening the film at Markham Junior High School in Watts, English teacher Allen Gross sent Saltzman a letter noting that *Black on Black* was a favorite of the class and also enclosed short student reflections on the film. Freddie Howard agreed with Ethel's testimony that supermarket food was better quality in the white neighborhoods. McKinney Ferry wrote, "The main thing that I like about this film was th[at] black people could express their feeling[s] towards white people."[24]

Despite the positive reception, *Black on Black* inspired some hateful backlash. Saltzman later recounted that following the broadcast, calls came in through the CBS switchboard slamming the program as liberal propaganda and grossly inaccurate.[25] Attorney Maurice Mac Goodstein wrote in a letter that he could not see any value in the program and that he, as a white man, felt offended that *Black on Black* did not even consider the white perspective and the "doctrine of self-help." Rena Rogers of Downey mailed a six-page angry rant about the program, asserting that the same opportunities were open to black people as white people. San Fernando Valley resident George Donahue wrote that the program was most likely "communist inspired and communist paid for." Shortly after a copy of *Black on Black* was donated to the LAPL, it was mutilated by a patron. The LAPD even demanded that KNXT add a disclaimer to the end of the film for the rebroadcast stating that police officers in the city were working to improve community relations.[26]

Saltzman spent a significant amount of time speaking with Watts residents about their reaction to the documentary. In an early August memo to Gingold, he wrote that many people he talked to were extremely positive about the show. Seeing their own faces and voices represented in the mass media made them feel listened to and recognized. One interviewee said, "It made me proud to see it. I'm not saying it made me hate less, but it made me feel very good to see something like that on television for everyone to see." In many cases, people expressed disbelief that a white man had created *Black on Black*. Saltzman remembers that while many had kind words to share, some claimed that *Black on Black* did not capture enough of a cross-section of the community, that the documentary was an isolated program created by outsiders, and that the broadcast would not lead to any kind of positive change for Watts.[27] Such comments point not only to the limitations of *Black on Black* as a standalone program on individual experiences, but to a more entrenched tension within the film's production: the documentary was created by a white crew, and editorial control remained with Saltzman.

To be sure, Saltzman's interests and expertise in providing a platform for black people to talk candidly about their lives resulted in a critical intervention in standard network programming and put pressure on mainstream journalism outlets to create more socially conscious films. *Black on Black* also enabled Saltzman to make future hard-hitting documentaries throughout the early 1970s.[28] However, the dissatisfaction with the program voiced in Saltzman's informal postbroadcast survey signaled a desire for a more sustained effort for homegrown media primarily produced by and intended for the people it was representing. This perspective was not unique to those in the survey. As the minority liberation movements of the late 1960s intersected with activist calls for media reform, representation became an increasingly politicized issue. Minority groups argued for the ability to assert authorial control over projects, and the public and private broadcasting sectors were at times amenable to providing new channels of access to the means of production. For example, the Performing Arts Society of Los Angeles collaborated with KTTV to create the documentary series *From the Inside Out* that focused on community issues in South Central. The Human Affairs Department within Los Angeles public television station KCET provided a home for black and Chicano filmmakers. Jesús Salvador Treviño worked on *¡Ahora!* (1969–70), a documentary series broadcast out of East Los Angeles that concentrated on such topics as Chicano history, contemporary mural art, job-training programs, and protests against the deplorable conditions of local high schools. Sue Booker set up a KCET satellite studio at 4211 South Broadway that took a similarly inclusive view of the African American community in South Central. Her series *Doin' It!* (1972) and then *Doin' It at the Storefront* (1972–73) included profiles on cultural establishments, avant-garde musicians in the Black Arts movement, and pressing issues such as the horrific conditions for black inmates in prison.

Examining the production and reception of *Black on Black* reveals how the film resonated with viewers within and beyond Los Angeles as well as contributed to a turning point in social documentary practice. The broadcasting industry's representation of minority communities during this politically heated period was not confined to a few flagship network series. Analyzing *Black on Black* makes visible the increasingly central role of local television in forging new understandings of racial identity.

The film discussed in this chapter can be streamed through the book's web page at https://www.dukeupress.edu/Features/Screening-Race.

*Black on Black* (1968), 90 min., 16mm
PRODUCTION: KNXT. DIRECTOR: Joe Saltzman. NARRATOR: Donnell Petetan. EXECUTIVE PRODUCER: Dan Gingold. PHOTOGRAPHY: Jack Leppert. EDITOR: Robert Heitmann. PRODUCTION ASSISTANT: Ruth Fleishman. MUSIC: Lou Rawls, Nina Simone. ACCESS: UCLA Film and Television Archive, Los Angeles. NOTE: Transferred to two-inch videotape for broadcast.

NOTES

I would like to thank Mark Quigley at the UCLA Film and Television Archive, who kindly showed me a valuable collection of Los Angeles–related television programs. Deep gratitude goes to Joe Saltzman for making his personal archive available. This essay addresses themes and subjects that I expand on in Joshua Glick, *Los Angeles Documentary and the Production of Public History, 1958–1977* (Berkeley: University of California Press, 2018).

1  Television's engagement with Black Power came after its coverage of civil rights sit-ins, marches, and rallies. In this former period, networks covered the civil rights movement to grow a national television audience, legitimize themselves as experts on topical issues, and offset claims concerning television's status as simply a for-profit medium of entertainment. Civil rights programming tended to depict industrious, respectable black and white citizens working together to bring about integration through nonviolent protests. For this earlier history, see Aniko Bodroghkozy, *Equal Time: Television and the Civil Rights Movement* (Champaign: University of Illinois Press, 2012). For accounts of television and Black Power, see Tommy Lee Lott, "Documenting Social Issues: *Black Journal*, 1968–1970," in *Struggles for Representation: African American Documentary Film and Video*, ed. Phyllis R. Klotman and Janet K. Cutler (Bloomington: Indiana University Press, 1999), 71–98; Christine Acham, *Revolution Televised: Prime Time and the Struggle for Black Power* (Minneapolis: University of Minnesota Press, 2004), 24–169; Devorah Heitner, *Black Power TV* (Durham, NC: Duke University Press, 2013).

2  For *Black on Black*'s fortieth anniversary, USC Annenberg School for Communication and Journalism screened the film on October 27, 2008. The Ralph J. Bunche Center for African American Studies at UCLA screened the film for a Black History Month event on February 25, 2009.

3  Email correspondence between Joe Saltzman and Joshua Glick, June 19, 2011; March 5, 2014; May 29, 2016. Joe Saltzman, interview by Joshua Glick, May 28, 2014, Los Angeles. "Valleyites Land 'Trojan' Posts," *Pasadena Independent*, May 13, 1959, 12. For more on local broadcasting during this period, see A. William Bluem, *Documentary in American Television: Form, Function, Method* (New York: Hastings House, 1965),

221–39; Michele Hilmes, *Only Connect: A Cultural History of Broadcasting in the United States* (Boston: Wadsworth, 2011), 207–85.

4    I use "Uprising" to imply that the unrest in Watts constituted a form of social protest against abusive state power. This line of interpretation follows how journalists, intellectuals, and scholars used "Uprising" or "Rebellion" to write about the unrest, in contrast to how much of the mainstream media used "riot" to imply a chaotic and irrationally violent expression of rage. See Gerald Horne, *Fire This Time: The Watts Uprising and the 1960s* (New York: Da Capo, 1997), 45–167.

5    John A. McCone, chairman, *Violence in the City—an End or a Beginning? A Report by the Governor's Commission on the Los Angeles Riots* (Los Angeles: The Commission, 1965), 1–37; Heitner, *Black Power TV*, 7.

6    *Black on Black*'s effort to inform a mainstream white audience about black life in South Central Los Angeles through the perspective of neighborhood residents followed important pre-Uprising projects. Alan Gorg, Robert Dickson, and Trevor Greenwood's 16mm film *Felicia* (1965) documented the aspirations and concerns of a female African American high school student living in Watts. Marsha Gordon and Allyson Nadia Field, "The Other Side of the Tracks: Nontheatrical Film History, Pre-Rebellion Watts, and *Felicia*," *Cinema Journal* 55, no. 2 (2016): 1–24; Joe Saltzman, "Guest Columnist," *TV Week, Pasadena Independent Star-News*, July 14, 1968, 6, Joe Saltzman Papers (JSP), private collection of Joe Saltzman, Palos Verdes Estates, Los Angeles.

7    The quotation is from Saltzman's written introduction to the film at USC. Joe Saltzman, "An Introduction to *Black on Black*," presented by IJPC and Visions and Voices, USC Annenberg School for Communication and Journalism, October 27, 2008, 3–4.

8    Otto Kerner, chairman, and David Ginsburg, executive director, *Report of the National Advisory Commission on Civil Disorders* (New York: Bantam, 1968), 1–29.

9    Kerner and Ginsburg, *Report of the National Advisory Commission*, 383.

10   Kerner and Ginsburg, *Report of the National Advisory Commission*, 384. Also see Nicholas Johnson, "'White' Media Must Meet Challenge of Negro Antipathy and Disbelief," *Variety*, January 3, 1968, 1.

11   Allison Perlman, *Public Interests: Media Advocacy and Struggles over U.S. Television* (New Brunswick, NJ: Rutgers University Press, 2016), 46–51. For additional coverage, see Leonard Zeidenberg, "The Struggle over Broadcast Access," *Broadcasting*, September 20, 1971, 32–43; Leonard Zeidenberg, "The Struggle over Broadcast Access II," *Broadcasting*, September 27, 1971, 24–29.

12   *Variety* reported that the program cost "more than $25,000." "*Black on Black* Now Rescheduled," *Los Angeles Sentinel*, June 20, 1968, C11; Saltzman, "Guest Columnist," 6; Helm, "*Black on Black*," *Variety*, July 24, 1968, 38; Joe Saltzman, "Shooting Notes and Schedule," n.d., JSP.

13   Saltzman, "An Introduction to *Black on Black*," 6.

14   Saltzman, interview by Joshua Glick, June 19, 2011; Saltzman, interview by Joshua Glick, May 28, 2014; Saltzman, "An Introduction to *Black on Black*," 5; John Luter, "Investigative Reporting, 1968–1969," in *The Alfred I. duPont–Columbia University*

*Survey of Broadcast Journalism, 1968–1969*, ed. Marvin Barrett (New York: Grosset and Dunlap, 1969), 75.

15  Josh Sides, *L.A. City Limits: African American Los Angeles from the Great Depression to the Present* (Berkeley: University of California Press, 2003), 169–97; Daniel Widener, *Black Arts West: Culture and Struggle in Postwar Los Angeles* (Durham, NC: Duke University Press, 2010), 90–218.

16  Art Peters, "B'Cast Stations Ban 'Bold' Tune by Nina Simone," *Philadelphia Tribune*, September 13, 1966, 11; Joe Saltzman to Bob Malcolm, Fremont High School Principal, May 12, 1968, JSP.

17  Dan Gingold, phone interview by Joshua Glick, September 30, 2014.

18  Advertisement, *Los Angeles Times*, July 14, 1968, P29. Similar advertisements appeared in African American newspapers. Advertisement, *Los Angeles Sentinel*, July 18, 1968, B8.

19  "*Black on Black* KNXT-TV Special," *Los Angeles Sentinel*, May 9, 1968, B8.

20  Sherman Brodey, "In Local Television the Eye Begins to Open on the Ghetto," *Television*, August 1968, 40.

21  "*Black on Black* Special," *Los Angeles Sentinel*, June 9, 1968, B8; "*Black on Black*," *Variety*, 38; "*Black on Black*: S. Central L.A. Negroes Tell Own Story," *Independent Press-Telegram*, July 14, 1968, 17; Aleene MacMinn, "*Black on Black* Show Airs Tonight," *Los Angeles Times*, July 18, 1968, F17; Bonnie Epstein, "AHS Grad Now TV Producer," *Post-Advocate*, July 18, 1968, 1; Bob Hull, "Television Review: *Black on Black*," *Hollywood Reporter*, July 19, 1968, 3; Robert A. Malone, "Local TV: Public Service with a Capital P," *Broadcasting*, June 22, 1970, 50, 58.

22  See, for example, "WCAU TV Presents Black Documentary on Life in Ghetto," *Philadelphia Tribune*, December 9, 1969, 24; "KNXT Is Awarded Two Local Emmys," *Los Angeles Sentinel*, February 19, 1970, B2A.

23  "KNXT to Donate '*Black on Black*' to L.A. Library," *Los Angeles Sentinel*, March 6, 1969, F4; Barbara Wasser to CBS Programming Dept., Beverly Hills, July 19, 1968; Rowena Boylan to Ray Beindorf, July 19, 1968; Tom Robischon to KNXT Offices, July 18, 1968; Chuck Jones to Joe Saltzman, July 19, 1968. All letters are included in the JSP.

24  Compiled letters from students at Horace Mann School to Joe Saltzman, dated January 16–17, 1973. Allen Gross to Joe Saltzman, June 23, 1972. Reflections by Markham Junior High School students, compiled by Allen Gross, sent to Joe Saltzman, JSP.

25  Saltzman, "An Introduction to *Black on Black*," 6; Joe Saltzman, email interview by Joshua Glick, March 5, 2014.

26  Saltzman, "An Introduction to *Black on Black*," 6, 14; Maurice Mac Goodstein to KNXT, July 19, 1968; Rena Rogers to KNXT, July 19, 1968, 1–6; George Donahue to CBS, July 19, 1968, JSP. Saltzman remembered that the day after the donation of the 16mm print of the film to the LAPL, a librarian called him to say that someone had checked out the documentary and scratched swastikas all over the frames, distorting the print beyond recognition. Joe Saltzman, email interview by Joshua Glick, October 2, 2016.

27  Joe Saltzman to Dan Gingold, memorandum, CBS, August 5, 1968, 1–5, JSP.

28 Saltzman's later films focused on American Indians and Red Power (*The Unhappy Hunting Ground*, 1970), the plight of elderly pensioners (*The Very Personal Death of Elizabeth Schell Holt-Hartford*, 1972), abuses of power in junior high school (*The Junior High School*, 1971), and sexual violence against women (*Rape*, 1972). Many of these programs, along with episodes of *Ralph Story's Los Angeles*, are available for viewing at the UCLA Film and Television Archive. Saltzman left KNXT in the mid-1970s to help create the broadcasting sequence at the journalism school at USC. Saltzman, email correspondence and interview by Joshua Glick, June 19, 2011.

# 11

## "A New Sense of Black Awareness"?

### Navigating Expectations in *The Black Cop* (1969)

TRAVIS L. WAGNER AND MARK GARRETT COOPER

*The Black Cop* (1969) abruptly begins with sounds of wailing sirens mixed with a bass line laid down by the John Coltrane Quartet. The image track delivers close-ups of police lights, the city at night seen from a moving patrol car, and a black officer in uniform, introduced in voice-over as New York City patrolman David Walker. One of the NYPD's very few black officers, the unnamed narrator explains, Walker is on the beat in Harlem, "a community bursting at the seams with a new sense of black awareness." "As a black cop," the voice-over continues, "Walker's allegiance to this ideal is constantly under question." Coltrane's saxophone takes up the siren's wail over shots of officers responding to a car wreck. The handheld camera follows Walker helping a limping African American woman to one patrol car while a group of white officers clusters defensively around another. An all-black crowd looks on.

In this opening sequence, the narrator—who sounds male and white—proclaims from a position outside the world of the film that there is a conflict between the cop's role and his black identity. Camera, music, and editing explore the same conflict, but from a position within, although not necessarily part of, the black community. Writer-producer Kent Garrett's fifteen-minute documentary develops and nationalizes this theme by comparing Walker's experience with that of Los Angeles police veteran Harrison Bailey in the film's second half. Throughout, visual style conspires with and sometimes against interviews and voice-over to create the black cop as a figure symptomatic of complex U.S. race relations during the period.

FIGURE 11.1. Frame enlargement from *The Black Cop* (Kent Garrett, 1969).

The film's documentary address exposes complex problems rather than advocating specific remedies; this might make it seem an unlikely candidate for use as a police training film in the U.S. South of the late 1960s and early 1970s. Yet it was. Following the initial release of *The Black Cop* (hereafter *Black Cop*) as a documentary feature on the Detroit-based public broadcast show *Black Journal*, National Educational Television (NET) distributed it as a stand-alone 16mm film. The PBS precursor NET had handled content produced for television in this way from the early 1950s, when film offered the only means to recirculate broadcast material. Through 16mm distribution, *Black Cop* reached an audience very different from the one Garrett imagined: the relatively small Spartanburg, South Carolina, police department. This seems a likely explanation for why a print appeared as part of the Spartanburg Police Training Film Collection now held by the University of South Carolina's Moving Image Research Collections. Precisely because it suggests unexpected uses, the rediscovery of this particular print in an archive a half-century after the documentary first aired underscores a complex, perennial theme in U.S. race relations: not only do nonwhite citizens view police as instruments of white power, but the police have long been aware of that perception as a problem to be managed.

*Black Cop* thus provides occasion to reexamine entanglements of race, community, and police power in America. In 1969, Garrett was an emerging African American filmmaker who, by his account, set out to explore the conflicted psychology of black officers for black audiences. As critical appraisal and his own recollections make clear, the film extends a variety of stylistic precedents to balance a critique of racialized violence at the hands of white systems of power with sympathetic representations of African American officers who are identified as part of those systems by their large urban communities. Intriguingly, the film's potential use as an educational tool to teach race relations to a predominantly white police force in predominantly African American Spartanburg is very different from, though not opposed to, its initial intent. Spartanburg's officers may well have appreciated the film's revelation that black cops could face unique challenges in merely attempting to enforce the law. At the very least, *Black Cop* reflected a growing sentiment that black experiences needed acknowledgment by white America, and especially by those institutions tasked with maintaining order. At the intersection of these trends, Garrett turned his lens critically on this shifting terrain.

## *Black Cop*, *Black Journal*, and Kent Garrett's Early Production Work

*Black Cop* originated as part of a series of works exploring black experiences on the television show *Black Journal*. Produced by African American filmmaker William Greaves, the goal of *Black Journal* was "to report and review the events, the dreams, the dilemmas of Black America."[1] Film historian Mark A. Reid explains that *Black Journal* emerged out of NET's perceived need for programming that "respon[ded] to the social activism of both the civil rights movement and the sporadic urban uprisings," while being exclusively created by African Americans.[2] Reid also notes that because of the show's immediate popularity and critical acclaim, *Black Journal* became a place for aspiring black media producers to hone their craft.

Kent Garrett was key to *Black Journal* from its beginnings, working primarily as a producer of documentary segments for the show. Reflecting on the predominantly white filmmaking community in the mid-1960s, Garrett notes that "there were not many black technicians in the field." In Garrett's recollection, *Black Journal* was the first time that there was a "broadcast for blacks" with a national scope so as to allow "blacks in Los Angeles to see what was happening with blacks in New York and Boston."[3] While *Black Journal*'s topics ranged from socioeconomic housing investigations to explorations of political candidates, Garrett's major contributions were *Black Cop* and *The Black GI* (1970). Similar in style and thematic organization to *Black Cop*, *The Black GI* focuses on black soldiers in Vietnam, who find themselves hesitant instruments of white institutions.[4]

*Black Cop* develops its argument by juxtaposing scenes of neighborhood life with talking-head interviews, primarily with officers Walker and Bailey. The interviews often recontextualize the neighborhood scenes. For example, in the initial interview with Walker, he sits in what looks like his living room as he explains that his job entails an education in "all phases of life" that he finds fulfilling. This is followed by shots of Walker assisting a man who is convulsing on the sidewalk, probably due to a drug overdose, as crowds look on. The short sequence concretizes what Walker might have in mind when describing his work as an education in life.

A later sequence employs sound and image more ambitiously to probe Walker's experience as a specifically black cop. His interview transitions to voice-over as we see him on the street at a call box: "I'm just as loyal as any other cop." "It's hard to explain," the voice-over continues, with a cut to a domestic interior as Walker and his white partner in the background appear to confront an unidentified black man in the foreground: "White officers feel that because you're black working in a black community, you should be in front. You should be the front-runner in the suppression of crime." This last phrase comes over a shot of a dressing table mirror with the citizen reflected at frame right, the white officer at frame left, and Walker squarely in the middle. While doing nothing to indicate the nature of the complaint that brings the officers here, the sequence frames the black cop standing between his white partner and the black community member. This allows the audience to hear Walker's concern with "them feeling for [his] loyalty" as an expression of his conflicted position between a white police force and the black community.

The structure of the film encourages viewers to derive more abstract points from the juxtaposition of particulars. By including similar statements from the more senior Los Angeles officer after examining Walker's situation, *Black Cop* indicates a persistent national dilemma. "I've been called an Uncle Tom more than once," Bailey says in voice-over at the end of a sequence showing what looks like a positive encounter at a community center. Bailey and his white partner listen attentively to an older African American man while younger black men play pool. As the voice-over delivers the Uncle Tom line, the camera draws back from a tight close-up of Bailey's smile to show him in conversation with one of these young men. He looks completely at home in this community, yet we hear that often he is not treated with

FIGURE 11.2. Frame enlargement from *The Black Cop* (Kent Garrett, 1969).

"respect." As with the Walker sequence near the start of the film, combination of voice-over and image draws out the psychological struggle entailed by the black cop's daily encounters on the beat.

Garrett claims that creating *Black Cop* seemed "obvious" because it allowed viewers to grasp the experiences faced by black officers daily.[5] Media historian Devorah Heitner has remarked on the importance of style to this objective. She observes "long cross-fades that linger to show doubled exposures of urban landscapes" and that "by intentionally not editing for narrative consistency [the film] emphasizes the challenging position of the officer caught between allegiances," a technique noted in the aforementioned sequences.[6] Garrett claims a stylistic debt to cinéma vérité, which is evident in the highly mobile camera, location sound, and expository editing. The film possesses an experimental bent, evident in many unconventional visual compositions and especially in sequences where John Coltrane's free jazz soundtrack seems to direct the editing and camera movement. The combined strategies go beyond indicating "conflicting allegiances" to convey a feeling of psychological distress and to locate its causes not in individuals, but in systematic distortions of U.S. race relations.

The distorting force of racism becomes most evident in a sequence interweaving a Bailey interview with on-street interviews in which black men describe black cops as especially brutal. One man, mid-manicure, asserts that the black officer "mingle[s] with us because he's black, and then he takes advantage of us." The film does not discredit this point but follows it with a statement from Bailey that partly rebuts it. Bailey describes people who "take the attitude that just because they are black, the law doesn't apply to them equally as well as somebody else. And I think this is where part of the problem lies. They want to be exempt from the law because I am of color." Bailey speaks with the voice of experience and reason. Significantly, we never see any officer acting brutally in the film. Yet repetition gives weight to the testimony from community members. The film presents black people using the word "brutal" to describe black officers three different times (a woman in a car, a man on a sidewalk, and the man in the manicurist's chair). Through this collision of police and citizen viewpoints, Garrett gives the impression that the history of race relations has so colored perceptions that black communities may be unable to see black cops as the film presents them, that is, as complex human beings struggling to serve their communities while retaining legitimacy as officers of the law.

The film punctuates both the New York and the Los Angeles segments with interviews with higher-ranking African American officers. From behind desks, these administrators speak in the voice of official policy about challenges faced by black beat cops. Deputy Inspector Arthur C. Hill concludes the New York segment by suggesting that black officers might, in general, be expected to understand black communities better than their white counterparts. Edward C. Henry, Los Angeles's "highest-ranking Negro officer," asserts that the perception of being an "Uncle Tom" would be "lessened or even completely eliminated" were the black officer to "identify his role as a policeman as opposed to his role as a Negro." These contradictory statements support the narrator's conclusion, read over nighttime shots of a patrol car in motion, a Harlem sidewalk, and Walker's close-up profile: "The black cop is the man in the middle. He seeks acceptance in the police community, which reflects the white society and the status quo. On the other hand, he is a black man from a black community, which is demanding change, a community which continues to ask him: Which side is he on?" This final question rings over Walker's silhouette suspended in freeze frame, using backlight and contrast to obscure Walker's facial expression and forcing the question back onto the audience. Insofar as the audience has seen and heard, this question places the black cop in a psychologically uncomfortable position,

FIGURE 11.3. Frame enlargement from *The Black Cop* (Kent Garrett, 1969).

and they may misrecognize the quality of his service as simultaneously a cop and a member of the community.

This voice-over sums up the film, but it also flattens the more complex layers and textures introduced by the juxtaposition of relative rookie Walker with the more seasoned Bailey, as well as of those beat cops with administrators Hill and Henry. What the voice-over presents as a singular "black cop," the film reveals as an abstraction describing more concrete multiplicities of experience. In the abstract, the "which side" dilemma is an old one. At the end of the nineteenth century, W. E. B. Du Bois termed it double consciousness, by which he meant the internalized sense that becoming more American meant being less black. Du Bois's famous wish "to make it possible for a man to be both a Negro and an American without being cursed and spit upon" responds to this internalized dilemma.[7] *Black Cop* does more than reassert this proposition mutatis mutandis with regard to black officers. It imagines how double consciousness felt to particular individuals in communities demanding change in 1969.

*Black Cop*'s production is itself historically specific, depending not only on the forum provided by *Black Journal* but also on enlisting police support. In a 2015 interview, Garrett emphasized the effort required to record the daily work of police officers in New York and Los Angeles. It "took a long time to get permission from the police," he noted, and even longer to find two sets of partners who were white and black.[8] Despite these challenges, the level of access and the freedom to present the story as he saw fit struck Garrett as remarkable (in an interview with the author he noted that government entities no longer provide anything like the access he was allowed).[9] On location, his African American crew included cinematographer Leroy Lucas and sound technician Andrew Ferguson. They felt themselves to be conducting a timely examination not "for a police community," but for the black community.

Documentary historian Jonathan Kahana has characterized cinéma vérité technique as "a kind of domestic spying" due in part to its debt to more portable filmmaking technologies developed for military surveillance in World War II. He also notes that oppositional documentaries, like Cinda Firestone's *Attica* (1973), have sometimes reworked surveillance footage to challenge state power.[10] On this continuum, Garrett's film often seems closer to the uncritically surveilling end of the spectrum. Lucas's camera feels intrusive when it hovers over the convulsing man, follows Walker and his partner into an apartment, or captures a distraught, inebriated man being taken into custody. In such moments, it is clear that Garrett's access is secured by agreement with the police and that the camera is an ally of their disciplinary power. Awareness of this alliance need not undermine the critique, in on-street interviews and the narrator's voice-over, that the police are instruments of white oppression. Inasmuch as the documentary records a racialized conflict between the community and the cops, *Black Cop* also presents thoughtful black voices on the force who are attempting to understand and ameliorate conflict.

Latent still is the question of whether the film is complicit in a strategy of tokenization. Literature from the time suggests that the introduction of black officers had a performative purpose. James Wilson, a Harvard professor in 1968, acknowledged racial discrimination on the nation's police forces, but argued that whites should continue to control them because white officers were allegedly "more civil" and thus able to enact their "duty" more appropriately. Wilson felt that, though "no less important," black officers served a "symbolic" function on the force, cloaking the white dominance that he advocates.[11] In this context, recruitment of black officers looks like a way to manage racial inequality rather than to rectify it. *Black Cop* shows this strategy at work. For instance, we first see Bailey as the only black face in room full of white officers, and Walker speaks of his role as "guide" for proper community conduct. Nonetheless, the film avoids developing a commentary

FIGURE 11.4. Frame enlargement from *The Black Cop* (Kent Garrett, 1969).

on tokenization as a policing strategy. The attitudes of the black community, more than those of unseen and unheard white superiors, seem responsible for putting the black cop "in the middle."

That authoritative voice-over thus has a particularly complex function in this film. Historically marked and immediately intelligible as the kind of voice that speaks on behalf of official institutions, that defines problems and proposes solutions via the state, the voice has in this instance been given the job of criticizing the normative whiteness that more consistently legitimizes.[12] It summarizes the internalized experience of black officers while also providing a statistical context for that experience: "6 percent" of NYPD officers are black, relative to a "20 percent" black population of New York City. Relating the trauma of black cops to their proportional underrepresentation, the film proclaims both as equally objective realities.

The surveilling camera sometimes seems to be an extension of the authoritative voice-over and at other moments provides a vantage that contextualizes it. It invades black houses, but it also catches white officers looking defensively over their shoulders and shows the black cop as the odd man out. Throughout the soundtrack, moreover, many voices compete for attention. Importantly, those voices are not limited to human speech.

Cultural historian Amy Abugo Ongiri suggests that "African American culture after 1964 blurred the lines between popular culture and high art even as it attempted to delineate notions such as realism, authenticity, experience, and commercially driven expression."[13] By merging a version of cinéma vérité style with a Coltrane soundtrack on a public television show for black audiences, *Black Cop* places itself squarely within this tendency and anticipates the commercial blaxploitation film genre. Garrett's use of music to convey the pace and texture of the black urban experience is similar to *Sweet Sweetback's Baadasssss Song* (music by Melvin Van Peebles performed by Earth, Wind and Fire, 1971), *Shaft* (music by Isaac Hayes and Johnny Allen, 1971), and *Super Fly* (music by Curtis Mayfield, 1972). Each of these films thematizes police racism. None focuses on black officers, although *Sweet Sweetback* does highlight the problem of the black token cop and includes a shot that might recall Bailey's introduction amid a room of white faces in Garrett's film. The siren wail, close-ups of police lights, and a restless camera that roams the city in *Black Cop* have even stronger echoes in *Sweet Sweetback*. Viewers familiar with blaxploitation films are liable to find the documentary an uncanny forebear.

Garrett asserts that he included Coltrane's free jazz soundtrack simply because he felt "it worked."[14] The acoustical resemblance between the thematically important police siren and Coltrane's saxophone may have suggested this fit, as it does help to meld the musical soundtrack with the location recording. Film scholar Paula Massood urges another explanation for why this strategy works. In *Black City Cinema*, she argues that black musical forms function not only to unify audiences from disparate ages and locations, but also to highlight the city's influence "in shaping black life" and even to "speak for the struggles faced by" black communities.[15] Massood sees black music as central to depictions of African American urban spaces. Such spaces, she argues, feel black because of their soundtracks. While *Black Cop* can be said to anticipate blaxploitation, it is more relevant to suggest that blaxploitation retrospectively indicates how Garrett's film communicates urban sensibilities.

*Black Cop*'s score extends its reach beyond its nominal topic. When the saxophone echoes the siren, audiences can hear the documentary as an exploration not just of policing but also of black life. Film scholar Courtney Bates sees the disjointed narrative of *Sweet Sweetback* as a means to decenter Hollywood's conventional white masculinity.[16] Likewise, *Black Cop*'s score

FIGURE 11.5. Frame enlargement from *The Black Cop* (Kent Garrett, 1969).

often provides nonnarrative coherence to images of urban life. Van Peebles's Sweetback runs through Los Angeles at night in a sequence punctuated by flashing lights and wailing sirens held together by pulsing bass and the lyrical injunction to run: the effect is not to move the character from point A to point B, as would be typical for a Hollywood hero. Rather, the effect is to render black life as the permanent condition of feeling on the run from the law. Similarly, Garrett's opening sequence neither asks nor answers where the patrol cars are headed. Underscored by the bass line, they become an inescapable part of the mise-en-scène of black America. Unlike *Black Cop*, blaxploitation films present clear oppositions between the community and the man. When Isaac Hayes scores Shaft's defiant strut, he does not render a man in the middle: we know what side he's on. Nonetheless, in *Black Cop* Coltrane's improvisational saxophone explodes into scenes to say what the black cop cannot, which is that his community defines, masters symbolically if not legally, the space through which he moves. We cannot know if this point connected with an audience the filmmakers did not anticipate. However, we can reasonably assume that the priority of the Spartanburg police force was not just to see and hear the black experience, but instead to make sense of their racially charged workspace.

Asked about the print of *Black Cop* found in the Spartanburg Police Training Film Collection, Garrett expressed surprise that his film had circulated beyond *Black Journal*.[17] Distribution by NET not only provided the documentary an unanticipated audience but also placed it in dialogue with nontheatrical films specifically designed to educate the police about race relations.

Garrett's stylistically adventurous television documentary is, in fact, surprisingly similar to contemporary educational films. As nontheatrical film historian Marsha Orgeron suggests, race relations films from the late 1960s took up the challenges of acknowledging the race riots occurring across the country, while also positing racial harmony as a possibility. This description fits *Black Cop* as well. In the film, when pushed to talk about Black Power movements, Walker chuckles and says that such organizations are "tricky," but he favors "anything that can help [his] community." Orgeron explains that educational films with young, black male protagonists, like *Joshua* (Bert Salzman, 1968) and *Who Cares* (Lumin Film, 1968), while encouraging conversation about integration, employed rhetorics serving predominantly white classroom discourses at a time when America "was anxiously observing escalating disparities and dissatisfaction" in "cities across the country."

In turn, the "dissatisfied minority" was made more palatable to white classrooms through a delegitimization of black angst, for example, as inappropriately expressed in rioting. In contrast, Orgeron identifies *220 Blues* (Richard Gilbert, 1970) as a work that legitimizes, or at the very least accepts, a potentiality for black anger.[18] In doing so, *220 Blues* employs techniques similar to Garrett's. Like *Black Cop*, for instance, *220 Blues* ends with a freeze frame that poses a question to the audience, in this case about the effects of integrating a high school track team. Orgeron observes that the film does not "celebrate integration as an unproblematic ideal" while also giving "voice to the ideas behind black separatism and militancy."[19] With this point of comparison in mind, one can imagine *Black Cop* being used to launch a classroom (as opposed to a living room) discussion of the role of law enforcement in either reforming or reifying race relations.

Late 1960s films made specifically to educate the police remain relatively unexplored by scholars, but the Spartanburg collection makes it possible to isolate a few examples. Like the educational films discussed by Orgeron, many of these films acknowledge racial strife and propose ameliorations. Several examine the role of white cops in a postintegration police force, considering how these officers might best prepare for engagement with black communities and partners. *Help I'm a Cop* (1969) uses a view-and-respond approach, with segments designed for interruption by group discussion to urge white officers to consider issues they might face on the beat, while also instructing them to avoid certain behaviors. For example, audiences are reminded that it is unacceptable for white officers to refer to black community members with racial epithets.

Other films tend either to idealize friendship between white officers and black community members or to stoke fear of black militancy. *Let's Work Together* (1969) takes the former approach. It focuses on white police officers in Chicago attempting to foster camaraderie between the department and the black community. The central scene depicts a group of young black men discussing concerns regarding white law enforcement, including accounts of harassment and distrust. The white cops look on with apparent indifference before assuring the group that they aim to change their feelings of animosity. Like *Black Cop* and *220 Blues*, the film ends with a freeze frame, in this case of a black teen begrudgingly shaking a white cop's hand. Presumably, viewers could discuss whether they thought this approach likely to succeed.

In contrast, friendship, no matter how ambivalent, is not the goal for films like *April '68* (1968). This film presents black political thinkers like Malcolm X not as community advocates but as threatening agents of black militancy. Consistent with overarching ideological objectives to present racial harmony as ideally possible, it stops short of openly criminalizing black leaders or groups, but it clearly implicates them in many riots.

*Black Cop* is both like and unlike these films. Like them, it could be seen to advocate for healing the breach that puts African American communities and law enforcement into irreconcilable binaries. Unlike them, it articulates the problem from a series of black viewpoints. This makes a difference in how the issue is framed, as when Walker voices suspicion of Black Power while also describing its potential productivity. Of those interviewed in Garrett's film, Deputy Inspector Hill, who is identified as one of NYPD's highest-ranking African American officers, provides the most integrationist perspective. He presents racism as an effect of socialization and geography. The white cops tend to come from the suburbs, he observes, while black cops hail from urban communities like those they patrol. Accordingly, while Hill knows white officers who have been socialized to "dig black people" and would never suggest that a white cop should not patrol a black community "based on skin color," he observes that "black men can empathize and understand black problems better," which is why NYPD was working to recruit more black officers. Seen alongside this sociological explanation of racism and defense of affirmative action policy, the tense interracial handshake that concludes *Let's Work Together* might well have looked like a naive solution. The conclusion of the Hill segment also overreaches the mandate that seems typical of the police training film. The voice-over explains, "We asked Deputy Inspector Hill whether civilians should be in control of the police," and Hill strongly asserts the need for civilian oversight. Given the larger context, it seems like *Black Cop* might have been receivable by police audiences familiar with training films like *Let's Work Together* and *April '68*, but would likely have been seen as a distinct, and perhaps divergent, perspective.

## Conclusion

Though records of use for the Spartanburg Police Collection do not exist, the very fact that it includes *Black Cop*, *April '68*, and *Let's Work Together* suggests that the department faced challenges similar to those documented in larger cities. The city of Spartanburg did not commit to desegregation until 1963, on the eve of the landmark 1964 Civil Rights Act.[20] In 2016, it remained a predominantly African American community and had a black police chief (Alonzo Thompson).[21] Throughout the 1970s, white chief W. T. Ivey ran the department. Ivey's obituary mentions nothing of his stance on desegregation.[22] In 1970, the state police investigated Spartanburg police officer James Ward (presumably white) for shooting Raymond Cross, "a Spartanburg Negro . . . following a high speed chase through the city."[23] Perhaps that incident, along with others like it, prompted the department to seek training on how to ease racial tension.

The Spartanburg Police Department evidently committed resources to the proposition that films could help prepare white officers to work with both officers and communities of color. *Black Cop* might have proved a conversation starter. Perhaps the least challenging interpretation of the film would have laid the blame for the black cop's dilemma at the door of the black community, suggesting that black officers should embrace their roles first as cops and not as Negroes. The most challenging interpretation of the film, urged by its musical score, would discover that the gulf separating black communities from law enforcement cannot be easily bridged, and certainly not resolved simply by hiring additional black officers. Rather, music symbolically reclaims the city from the law and seeks extralegal allies in the blaxploitation mode.

Kent Garrett's *Black Cop* would certainly not have had a singular reception. The documentary asked viewers to consider seriously how race shaped perceptions of policing, not least among officers themselves. Primarily an attempt to paint a sympathetic picture of the struggles of black officers for black audiences, it also activated a potent acoustical strategy for symbolically reclaiming the black city from white law. Nonetheless, it could also be understood as a tool, albeit an atypical one, to educate white officers as they worked their way through the epochal change of desegregation.

Garrett may well be right that such a film could not be made today due to lack of unfiltered access to the daily life of officers. Yet for that very reason it remains relevant at a time when body cams and cell phones regularly document police violence toward black men. In 2015, Los Angeles, Harlem, and even Spartanburg, South Carolina, were sites of contested police shootings of persons of color.[24] Then, 2016 brought Charlotte, North Carolina, and the nation the spectacle of an African American officer shooting Keith Scott, a black man.[25] It seems reasonable to conclude that police training films, including Garrett's, did little in the long term to alter the fear and suspicion with which African American communities must face the police. Even so, when seen alongside today's instantly circulated, minutely parsed, and, on the part of the police, carefully guarded media representations, Garrett's complex and self-conscious examination of the roles and struggles of black cops provides a welcome reminder that it was possible to have a different kind of conversation. Perhaps it would be useful to continue it.

FILMOGRAPHY

All available films discussed in this chapter can be streamed through the book's web page at https://www.dukeupress.edu/Features/Screening-Race.

*April '68* (1968), 10 min., 16mm
PRODUCTION: Government Adjustment Bureau. ACCESS: University of South Carolina, Moving Image Research Collections.

*The Black Cop* (1969), 15 min., 16mm
PRODUCTION: National Educational Television. DIRECTOR: Kent Garrett. CAMERA: Leroy Lucas, Andrew Ferguson. MUSIC: John Coltrane. ACCESS: University of South Carolina, Moving Image Research Collections.

*The Black GI* (1970), 54 min., 16mm
PRODUCTION: National Educational Television. DIRECTOR: Kent Garrett. CAMERA: Leroy Lucas, Andrew Ferguson. ACCESS: New York Public Library.

*Help I'm a Cop* (1969), 31 min., 16mm
PRODUCTION: Bell and Howell Distributors. ACCESS: University of South Carolina, Moving Image Research Collections.

*Let's Work Together* (1969), 31 min., 16mm
PRODUCTION: Henry Ushijima Films. ACCESS: University of South Carolina, Moving Image Research Collections.

NOTES

1   Devorah Heitner, *Black Power TV* (Durham, NC: Duke University Press, 2013), 85.
2   Mark A. Reid, *Redefining Black Film* (Berkeley: University of California Press, 1993), 126.
3   Kent Garrett, phone conversation with Travis Wagner, November 6, 2015.
4   *The Black GI* possesses a parallel existence with *Black Cop* inasmuch as it was screened on *Black Journal* and subsequently redistributed for educational reasons. However, the film's circulation presumably mirrors that of *Black Cop*. Only two copies are recorded in WorldCat: one film copy at the New York Public Library and a DVD copy at the library at the University of München in Germany, in comparison to *Black Cop*, which shows two copies on film and DVD in WorldCat.
5   Heitner, *Black Power TV*, 98.
6   Heitner, *Black Power TV*, 100–101.
7   W. E. B. Du Bois, "Strivings of the Negro People," *Atlantic Monthly* 80 (1897).
8   Garrett, phone conversation, November 6, 2015.
9   Garrett, phone conversation, November 6, 2015.
10  Jonathan Kahana, *Intelligence Work: The Politics of American Documentary* (New York: Columbia University Press, 2008), 13.
11  James Q. Wilson, "Dilemmas of Police Administration," *Public Administration Review* 28, no. 5 (1968): 407–17.
12  On the historical connection between documentary voice-over and state power, see Kahana, *Intelligence Work*, 89–140.
13  Amy A. Ongiri, *Spectacular Blackness: The Cultural Politics of the Black Power Movement and the Search for a Black Aesthetic* (Charlottesville: University of Virginia Press, 2000), 8.
14  Garrett, phone conversation, November 6, 2015.
15  Paula J. Massood, *Black City Cinema: African American Urban Experiences in Film* (Philadelphia: Temple University Press, 2003), 124.
16  Courtney E. J. Bates, "Sweetback's 'Signifyin(g)' Song: Mythmaking in Melvin Van Peebles' Sweet Sweetback's Baadasssss Song," *Quarterly Review of Film and Video* 24, no. 2 (2007): 176.
17  Garrett, phone conversation, November 6, 2015.
18  Marsha Orgeron, "'A Decent and Orderly Society': Race Relations in Riot-Era Educational Films, 1966–1970," in *Learning with the Lights Off: Educational Films in the United States*, ed. Devin Orgeron, Marsha Orgeron, and Dan Streible (New York: Oxford University Press, 2011), 439.
19  Orgeron, "'A Decent and Orderly Society,'" 437–38.
20  Walter Edgars, *South Carolina: A History* (Columbia: University of South Carolina Press, 1998), 544.

21  U.S. Census Bureau, "Annual Estimates for the Residential Population for Incorporated Places: April 1, 2010 to July 1, 2014," accessed February 4, 2019, https://web.archive.org/web/20170217160844/http://www.census.gov/2010census/popmap/ipmtext.php?fl=45.

22  A. J. Weichbrodt, "Police Chief Ivey Dead at 77," *Herald-Journal* (Spartanburg, SC), January 14, 1987.

23  "Report Received from SLED Probe in Spartanburg," *State*, March 6, 1970, 34.

24  Samuel Sinyangwe, "Mapping Police Violence," *Mapping Police Violence*, July 9, 2016, http://mappingpoliceviolence.org/.

25  Erik Ortiz, "Keith Lamont Scott, Fatally Shot by N.C. Cops, Warned Repeatedly to Drop Gun: Chief," NBC News, September 21, 2016, http://www.nbcnews.com/news/us-news/keith-lamont-scott-fatally-shot-n-c-cops-warned-repeatedly-n651846.

# 12

## "Don't Be a Segregationist: Program Films for Everyone"

The New York Public Library's Film Library
and Youth Film Workshops

ELENA ROSSI-SNOOK AND LAUREN TILTON

"The New York Public Library, as a modern educational institution, should use all recognized media of communication, including film," argued NYPL librarian Robert S. Ake in his 1948 proposal for the incorporation of 16mm film within the New York system.[1] Although a reference service for 16mm had existed since 1948, and a small collection of films was acquired in 1952 through the American Heritage Project of the American Library Association (ALA), the Film Library proper was not inaugurated until 1958. Recognizing the potential of 16mm to educate the public through nontheatrical circulation, the Film Library opened with a dedicated staff, budget, policies, and space at the newly constructed Donnell Library Center at 20 West Fifty-Third Street in Manhattan.[2] Drawing on existing models like that at the Cleveland Public Library Film Bureau, NYPL's film center was inspired by a growing generation of media-savvy librarians and, most importantly, demand by New Yorkers for expansion into full film-circulation service.[3]

By the 1960s, NYPL negotiated how to situate the public institution in relationship to the struggle for civil rights. In the city, activists like the NAACP's Ella Baker organized to desegregate public schools as the Congress on Racial Equality (CORE) challenged the city to realize the promises of liberalism by ending discrimination in city services such as garbage removal.[4] Under the leadership of William "Bill" Sloan, the Film Librarian from 1958 until 1980, NYPL grappled with civil rights. Rather than offering films already available in classrooms, the library system acquired films that represented the freedom struggles in New York and beyond. Sloan advanced a broad definition of educational film that allowed for a liberal acquisition policy.[5] Enacting the politics of integration they were projecting through film, NYPL purchased, distributed, and programmed films about issues such as segregation, housing discrimination, voter registration, and the Vietnam War.

In particular, NYPL identified local youth as a constituency in which to invest. They partnered with the Young Filmaker's Foundation (YFF), a community organization on the Lower East Side dedicated to youth filmmaking, to further diversify their film catalog and public programming while supporting communities of color.[6] Sloan supported area teenagers' struggle for visibility and voice by purchasing and programming YFF films on the pressing issues of the day. In doing so, NYPL funded filmmaking by local youth of color while building a more inclusive public institution. Through its relationship with YFF, NYPL circulated moving images by, about, and for people of color, thereby supporting and disseminating nontheatrical film that enacted and supported civil rights politics.

## Outside the Classroom: Film at the Public Library

Beginning in the early twentieth century, public libraries identified film as an important educational resource. Library film advocates reasoned that if the overwhelming majority of the population were seeking out commercial entertainment films while only a fraction of Americans were regular book readers, then the public library should add audiovisual materials in order to reach a segment of the public through its preferred medium. In order to reach their constituents, librarians experimented with using motion pictures in conjunction with reading initiatives as early as 1910.[7] Numerous studies, reports, and publications on motion picture efficacy in education buttressed efforts to acquire film in the public library throughout the 1920s and 1930s. World War II solidified film's role as an educational tool as the federal government, Hollywood, and independent production companies worked to galvanize the nation behind the war.[8] Public libraries helped spread information and cultivate knowledge of national and global matters through 16mm programming. With the success of library film programming and the growth in the postwar educational film industry, public libraries solidified their position as a prominent site for acquiring, accessing, and lending educational film.

Like 16mm collections in peer American public library systems, NYPL set out to provide audiovisual educational resources for communities in Manhattan, the Bronx, and Staten Island. Adopting the popular notion that public libraries were "The People's University," NYPL decided in 1940 to add film programming in order "to reach the greatest number of people possible."[9] They began circulating film prints in 1952. The November 1953 issue of NYPL's *Branch Library Book News* announced, "The Library has a small, highly selected collection of films to lend to non-profit groups and organizations within New York City for other than purposes of instruction and classroom use."[10] The film service department relocated in 1955 to the new Donnell Library Center, located across the street from the Museum of Modern Art. Circulation steadily increased, with the number of films passing through the doors of Donnell each month growing from approximately 100 to 200 in 1955 to over 1,400 in 1961.[11]

Debates ensued over which kinds of films qualified as educational. In 1942, NYPL librarian Gerald D. McDonald published his seminal study for the ALA, *Educational Motion Pictures and Libraries*, defining educational films as "films of 16 mm. width which deal with fact rather than fiction, and which are intended to reach an audience outside the theatre and to contribute to the process of learning."[12] As film librarians established their profession and began working with community members and groups, they expanded upon this definition to include a variety of filmmaking styles. In its formative years, the film department of NYPL sought out works that would be "most effective stimulants to discussion."[13] Sloan wrote in 1961 that "the purpose of the Library's film collection is to service the educational and cultural needs of the community outside of and beyond formal classroom instruction."[14] Meeting "the educational and cultural needs" resulted in a topically, stylistically, and aesthetically diverse film collection. The library subscribed to a broad definition of what constituted "educational" and embraced independently produced films for programming and circulation. While NYPL may have been comparatively late in joining the ranks of public library 16mm film departments, it was part of an effort to embrace avant-garde, independent, and local film as educational.

## Circulating Marginalized Voices

As NYPL redefined and expanded the boundaries of educational film, it also negotiated how to use film to address social issues. In this effort NYPL was not alone, as moving images were increasingly a tool used both for and against civil rights. As televised coverage of violence against African Americans in the North and South were reframing how the country understood the liberation struggle, Sloan and his peers strove for ways to serve their

FIGURE 12.1. William Sloan with a young patron (c. 1960–65). Courtesy of Jennifer Sloan.

community and address contemporary social issues in an educational capacity.[15] If the purpose of a library's 16mm film collection is to meet the needs of a diverse community, NYPL determined, then films and related programs that addressed these experiences were necessarily a part of the institution's work. The critiques of media circulation, which often rendered the experiences of people of color invisible, resonated at NYPL. They sought a shift in public library services to become more responsive to communities of color. The Film Library subscribed to civil rights integration politics thanks to Sloan's leadership, thereby integrating into the institution a policy of using motion pictures to serve those members of the community who were culturally and politically under- or misrepresented.

Of particular concern was how to grow NYPL's film offerings. Sloan identified integration films as an area for acquisition. In the 1964 issue of the *Journal of the Society of Cinematologists*, he published a history of the "integration film," a term used for films intended to improve race relations in the U.S.[16] They were "aimed primarily at preparing the white community for integration," he explained, following the 1954 Brown decision.[17] Sloan noted at the conclusion of his essay that "one of the most startling developments" by the early 1960s in this genre was young, independent filmmakers producing low-budget, politically invested, candid documentary films. Film Library staff selected and secured films such as *An Interview with Bruce Gordon* (1964) and *The Streets of Greenwood* (1963), both of which were celebrated by Sloan for their "total commitment to the cause of integration."[18]

Others joined Sloan in calling for a new and improved use of film to engage with patrons of color. Wendell Wray, director of NYPL's North Manhattan Project and the first African American man to graduate from the Carnegie Tech Library School, wrote in 1967 that library patrons in Harlem "want to see films showing black faces."[19] He explained, "This is neither paranoid, discrimination in reverse or being anti-white. It is the need to fill a tremendous psychological void in their lives. They often feel they are invisible, neuter, nonentities, and they want to be visible and have a feeling of real worth."[20] Tired biopics on historic leaders were no longer acceptable for outreach. Kenneth W. Axthelm, head of the Audio Visual Department of the Brooklyn Public Library, argued that "Booker T. Washington and George Washington Carver are no longer heroes. . . . These men do not speak the words that young people want to hear."[21]

Recognizing this necessity for communities to see themselves reflected in their local public institution, the Film Library built up the collection through collaboration with branch librarians and the independent film community. Wray, who oversaw programming at the Countee Cullen Branch in Harlem, remarked on the new acquisition policies, "Statistics released by our Film Library [at the Donnell Library Center] show a higher rate of use of films in Harlem than in any other area of the city. . . . This may be due in part to a very fine collection which has had strong emphasis placed on the acquisition of films dealing with subjects of current interest, among them civil rights, desegregation, Africa and Negro history."[22] Recognizing the role of branch librarians, Sloan wrote in his 1970 "Film Library Annual Report," "Indeed, I feel NYPL is a leader in using films in neighborhood libraries so that they may take an activist role in community life."[23]

The desire for connection through outreach—not just showing "black faces" but making a public library's film service a "force in the community"— led Sloan to champion independent filmmakers uniquely positioned to create works that resonated with their communities. His support came in the form of independent film acquisition and programming, which turned the library into a public outlet for their works. At a time when the ALA filled their "Films for a Great Society" program at the 1965 conference with titles like *Chartres Cathedral* (1963) and the Alitalia-sponsored *Variations on an Italian Theme* (1961), NYPL acquired films such as *Committee on Un-American Activities*

(1962), a protest against the House Un-American Activities Committee, and *Felicia* (1965), a portrait of an African American teenager.[24] When the ALA conference came to New York the following year, Sloan programmed films that addressed poverty, education inequality, and social services.

Film programs in the Donnell Library Center auditorium highlighted the growing collection. One section of the regular weekly Films at Noon series from 1967 is emblematic of the department's aim to educate the public through provocative curation. Films included the aforementioned *Felicia*, a documentary by UCLA students capturing a fifteen-year-old girl's perspective on living in the Watts neighborhood in Los Angeles just before the rebellions; *A Time for Burning* (1966), a documentary on attempts by the Lutheran Church to combat racism in Nebraska; *How Do You Like the Bowery?* (1964), future Academy Award–winning documentary filmmaker Alan Raymond's NYU student project on the homeless in New York's Bowery neighborhood; and *Abortion and the Law* (1965), Walter Cronkite's presentation of "the case for and against legalized abortion."[25] In addressing controversial topics, NYPL risked a backlash that could have harmed the public institution.

## Seeing Youth: Young Filmaker's Foundation and NYPL

In the 1960s, NYPL identified youth as an underserved constituency. They sought more inclusive and representative films that could expand their youth audience while integrating their public programs and collection. The Film Library shifted from simply buying and showing works for children and teens to include films made by children and teens. A key partnership ensued with the Young Filmaker's Foundation, a community organization that supported film workshops among youth of color, and the Youth Film Distribution Center (YFDC), YFF's film distribution wing. Through this process NYPL—as a purchasing entity, event programmer, and film community leader eager to procure independent works made in and by the communities which it served—encouraged the production of films by local youth.

In part, NYPL's interest was supported by the local youth film workshops, which used film as a mechanism for communities to create and speak on their own terms. Started by arts educators in the early 1960s, the workshops offered a flexible, open space to create film by and for youth, including middle-class Jewish communities and low-income communities of color. They argued that filmmaking was an important creative art to which youth should have access and control in an effort to democratize media making and wrangle it from the hands of Hollywood and corporate entities. The

workshops allowed young people to communicate their concerns, conditions, desires, and fantasies through 8mm and 16mm.[26]

By the late 1960s, the collective struggles of people of color to gain greater
community control and self-determination informed the film workshops.
The workshops created a physical and creative space for youth to contemplate and experiment with self-representation through film, creating
a counternarrative to mainstream media that either rendered them invisible or was marred by negative racial stereotypes.[27] These films illustrated
how youth of color interpreted and negotiated their daily conditions such
as drugs, racism, and the Vietnam War.[28] "They [the youth] are creating a
revolution in the way we see," argued acclaimed documentarians Edward
Pincus and David Newman in WNET's *The Way We See It* (1969). The "revolution" percolated in community centers and settlement houses such as the
92nd Street Y, Lillian Wald Recreation House, and Henry Street Settlement,
where art educators opened youth film workshops beginning in the early
1960s.

Many of the workshops used federal monies to promote expression and
visibility by and for participants. This visibility assumed new meaning as
those involved in the freedom struggles sought control of media to articulate
and circulate their calls for equal citizenship.[29] For example, the Southern
civil rights movement harnessed television to expose the violence used by
white people, often with the help of the state, to maintain Jim Crow–era segregation practices. Concurrently, new forms of public television led by African
Americans such as Tony Brown and William Greaves (who was a close friend
of Sloan) emerged with the understanding that without control of the camera, they were subject to the white perspective of network television.[30] White
control of mass media also impacted TV coverage of inner-city revolts in
places such as Chicago, Newark, and Watts in the mid- to late 1960s. The media's role in fostering inequality became the subject of the Kerner Commission, which lodged a damning critique in February 1969. The commission's
report concluded, "The press has too long basked in a white world, looking
out of it, if at all, with white men's eyes and a white perspective. The painful
process of readjustment that is required of the American news media must
begin now. They must make a reality of integration—both their product and
personnel."[31]

In response, the federal government and organizations such as the NAACP
increased pressure on corporate media to cease circulating stereotyped and
racist images of people as grassroots organizations worked to remake moving images on the ground. Film workshops in New York City often became

open spaces for youth to experiment with filmmaking as they pleased, with little oversight or control over content and form. Recounting his experience at YFF, Luis Vale stated, "He [instructor Rodger Larson] just gave us a camera and said, 'Go to it.' As we started editing, they showed us a little bit on how to edit, how to splice, and things like that. They said, 'Do your thing.'"[32] Workshop participants produced hundreds of films, with at least fifty films circulating through the YFDC. Thus NYPL became a prominent customer of YFDC, who in turn shared the revenue with the community film workshops whose films they circulated.

The relationship between NYPL and YFF/YFDC created a means by which the Film Library could serve its patrons, especially those in the emerging young adult demographic, through its most important activities: circulation and programming. In January 1969, the popular Donnell Noon Film Programs series featured for the first time a YFF film. In a program called "Filmmakers and Filmmaking," Alfonso Sanchez Jr.'s The End (1968), made at YFF's Film Club and among the library's first acquisitions from YFDC, was presented along with films ranging from Willard Van Dyke's The Photographer (1948) to A Day with Timmy Page (1967). Of the six films shown, The End exemplified NYPL's commitment to purchasing and circulating youth social commentary films in order to build a more inclusive institution and society.[33]

The film opens with a close-up on Bob Dara's 1962 "Harley Bird" poster: an illustration of a man mounted on a motorcycle, his "Me" button prominently displayed along with the letters B-U-L-L tattooed across his knuckles. The soundtrack is filled with the sound of the engine revving as the camera pans up, revealing a caricature of President Lyndon Johnson as the rider. The camera moves again to show the film's title, "The End," imposed over an American flag. The film then cuts to fast, disjointed editing and camera pans accompanied by Dave Brubeck's "Take Five," a revolutionary jazz track recorded in the late 1950s, its five-four time a conscious break from the symmetrical, standard four-four time signature. The protagonist, a Puerto Rican teenager, smokes a joint and enters an altered state where he negotiates his version of America with the realities of the current condition. A short sound bite cuts in of a man stating "America's Wonderful," likely lifted from Frank Zappa's 1968 song "The Return of the Son of Monster Magnet," which would also be used in Haskell Wexler's Medium Cool, released the following year.

The pot-induced dream slowly turns into a nightmare. The camera spins and then cuts to the protagonist getting into a stripped car chassis on the

FIGURES 12.2–12.3. *The End* (Alfonso Sanchez Jr., 1968). Frame enlargements taken from preservation release print, New York Public Library (preserved with funding from the Carnegie Corporation of New York).

FIGURE 12.4. *The End* (Alfonso Sanchez Jr., 1968). Frame enlargement taken from preservation release print, New York Public Library (preserved with funding from the Carnegie Corporation of New York).

side of the street. He drives to the park where a graffitied wall reads "The End." Tom Paxton's anti-Vietnam song "Lyndon Johnson Told the Nation" plays:

> Lyndon Johnson told the nation
> Have no fear of escalation
> I am trying everyone to please
> Though it isn't really war
> We're sending fifty thousand more
> To help save Vietnam from the Vietnamese[34]

Optimistically, the teenager tries to ignore the reality the lyrics represent. Rather than being drafted and sent to fight in an increasingly controversial war, he opens his newspaper to read that pot has been legalized. He jumps around the park in ecstasy.

The film then cuts to him on a New York City street on the Lower East Side. An older man walks up to offer him a Bible while another offers him LSD, both possible escapes from Vietnam. The two men begin to fight each other as Country Joe and the Fish's anti-Vietnam song plays. Joe McDonald sings:

FIGURE 12.5. *The End* (Alfonso Sanchez Jr., 1968). Frame enlargement taken from preservation release print, New York Public Library (preserved with funding from the Carnegie Corporation of New York).

> And it's one, two, three, what are we fighting for
> Don't ask me I don't give a damn, next stop is Viet Nam
> And it's five, six, seven, open up the pearly gates
> Ain't no time to wonder why, whoopee we're all gonna die[35]

The protagonist's fatalism has set in. Whether drugs, religion, or war, all lead down the same road to death. The film cuts to him running as gunshots inundate the soundtrack. He awakes from his lucid dream, startled by knocks on his door. Yet the dream is not simply the result of a drug-induced paranoia, for through the peephole he sees a montage of images including pictures from Vietnam, drugs, and a skull with crossbones. He backs away, refusing to open the door. The film ends with the words "life" and then "peace" on the screen.

Sanchez's astute critique of American politics and society is indicative of topics that NYPL increasingly programmed and circulated, films that revealed the inequitable conditions that communities of color experienced daily and their struggles for full, equal citizenship. Yet the Film Library was careful with how it promoted such films and their progressive politics. The program coyly described *The End* in these terms: "The sounds and music of today are background to this mad-cap view of today's 'scene' involving a phantasy in which pot is legalized. Made by teenager Alfonso Sanchez Jr. with Rodger Larson's University Settlement group."[36] The next month, in February, the Noon series featured a program dedicated to adolescence, including YFDC films *That Rotten Tea Bag* (1964), which used humor to address ethnic and racial discrimination, and *The Thief* (1969), made by fifteen-year-old Paul Gunn at the Studio Museum in Harlem. Despite the series taking place on Thursdays at midday, 143 people attended the January program, and 234 came for the February screening, nearly filling the 278-seat auditorium.[37]

This growing attention to the works of young filmmakers at NYPL created an ecosystem wherein the Film Library functioned as a hub for those seeking and producing youth filmmaking. A press release issued by NYPL in 1972 on the Film Library cited data collected by the department that teenagers favored "black history and films created by young people."[38] And those teenagers, presumably youth of color interested in seeing something of their own existence presented outside of the racial clichés propagated by commercial filmmaking, became a significant patron base for the library. In a speech, Bill Sloan offered statistics on the Film Library's users: under "Special Groups," "Negro" made up 40 percent and "Teenager" was 40–60 percent.[39] Encouraged by program attendance and patron statistics, the Film Library continued to focus its purchasing and programming priorities on these topics and users, with the YFDC serving as a significant supplier of "movies for young people," as its works were described in a 1972 YFDC print ad.[40] More film programs featuring youth films purchased from YFDC followed in 1973, including a special Saturday program called "Films by New Independents" in which the filmmakers presented their works. Donnell staff went as far as to host a Movie Box installation, a stand-alone playback system for Super 8mm reduction prints of films made at YFF, and a video workshop that encouraged students to join YFF.

By the mid-1970s, New York's nontheatrical film community's emphasis shifted to media centers focused on equipment rental. Workshops closed. No longer able to sustain itself financially, YFDC was shuttered. Then YFF followed suit, keeping its media center that focused on access to equipment while choosing to close its workshops. However, this change in the nontheatrical film landscape had less impact on NYPL, which had, thanks to YFDC and YFF, established itself as a place to give voice to its constituents through film while realizing civil rights integrationist politics.

In 1968, Barbara Bryant, an African American public librarian who went on to form and serve as vice president of educational film producer and distributor Phoenix Films, captured the field's growing sentiment with her aptly titled presentation at the University of Wisconsin-Milwaukee School of Library Science Colloquium, "Don't Be a Segregationist: Program Films for Everyone."[41] Ten years later, Euclid Peltier would revisit the definition of "the public library film," writing that independent films "present a fresh point of view on many important social issues ignored by earlier film-makers and therefore cannot be overlooked by today's public libraries."[42] Her call in the late 1970s to look to independent film to find fresh points of view reflected a continued priority for public libraries to identify, purchase, and circulate films about the communities they served. These ideals of diversity and inclusion were exemplified by NYPL.[43]

Having embraced the YFF at a critical juncture in American culture and politics, the Film Library, which was renamed the Donnell Media Center in the late 1970s and then the Reserve Film and Video Collection in 2008, earned a national reputation as uniquely committed to community and independent film. It became a trusted partner in the nontheatrical film world, among the first places independent filmmakers would go to have their work previewed for purchase. This was the case with Julia Reichert and Jim Klein, founders of New Day Films, a cooperative distribution group for feminist films, when they were shopping around *Growing Up Female* (1971), one of the first films of the modern women's movement and now on the Library of Congress's National Film Registry. According to Reichert and Klein, "The whole first year we were distributing, we made hardly any sales. . . . The New York Public Library saw it and immediately bought it on the third day we took it around."[44]

It is because of this role and these relationships that the YFDC library came to reside at NYPL. In 1976, at a conference in Minnewaska, New York, Rodger Larson described the languishing materials of the defunct YFDC as a "Youth Film Archive," a collection which he adamantly wished not be "destroyed or lost" but remain accessible in perpetuity.[45] In 1999, the remains of the collection, mostly 16mm prints and production elements, were transferred to the Donnell Media Center, catalyzing a film preservation program that continues today. The conservation and preservation by NYPL of the YFDC library, in addition to those prints originally purchased in the 1960s and 1970s, has ensured the inclusion of marginalized voices as part of the historic record. These ongoing actions continue to provide NYPL's community, as Bill

Sloan advocated during his illustrious career, access to "horizon widening films that provoke the imagination and provide new insights."[46]

FILMOGRAPHY

In collaboration with NYPL, a selection of films from YFDC will be available on Participatory Media, a platform for participatory community media during the 1960s. The project is funded by the National Endowment for the Humanities and the University of Virginia in partnership with the University of Richmond. For more, visit participatorymediaproject.org.

*The End* (1968), 9 min., 16mm
PRODUCTION, DIRECTOR: Alfonso Sanchez Jr. ACCESS: New York Public Library (http://catalog.nypl.org/record=b17120382~S1). NOTE: Preserved by the Reserve Film and Video Collection of the New York Public Library for the Performing Arts, with funding from the Carnegie Corporation of New York.

*That Rotten Tea Bag* (1964), 3 min., 16mm
PRODUCTION, DIRECTOR: Andy Gurian. ACCESS: New York Public Library (http://catalog.nypl.org/record=b17655587~S1). NOTE: Preserved by the Reserve Film and Video Collection of the New York Public Library for the Performing Arts, with funding from the Carnegie Corporation of New York.

*The Thief* (a.k.a. *The Surprised Thief*) (1969), 3 min., 16mm
PRODUCTION, DIRECTOR: Paul Gunn. NOTE: Archival elements held by the Reserve Film and Video Collection of the New York Public Library for the Performing Arts.

*The Way We See It* (1969), 57 min., 16mm
DIRECTOR: Ed Pincus, David Neuman. ACCESS: Harvard Film Archive, Harvard University. NOTE: Commissioned by Public Television to document a Hispanic film project for youth on the Lower East Side of New York City.

RELATED FILMS

*Abortion and the Law* (1965), 57 min., 16mm
PRODUCTION: CBS News. ACCESS: DVD, Princeton Films for the Humanities and Social Sciences.

*Chartres Cathedral* (1963), 30 min., 16mm
PRODUCTION: Encyclopaedia Britannica. ACCESS: New York Public Library (http://catalog.nypl.org/record=b17542680~S1).

*Committee on Un-American Activities* (1962), 45 min., 16mm
PRODUCTION, DIRECTOR: Robert Cohen. ACCESS: New York Public Library (http://catalog.nypl.org/record=b17550670~S1).

*A Day with Timmy Page* (1967), 18 min., 16mm
DIRECTOR: David Hoffman. ACCESS: New York Public Library (http://catalog.nypl .org/record=b17560368~S1).

*Felicia* (1965), 13 min., 16mm
DIRECTORS: Trevor Greenwood, Alan Gorg, Bob Dickson. ACCESS: New York Public Library (http://catalog.nypl.org/record=b17570451~S1).

*Growing Up Female* (1971), 60 min., 16mm
DIRECTORS: Julia Reichert, James Klein. ACCESS: New York Public Library (http:// catalog.nypl.org/record=b17135997~S1).

*How Do You Like the Bowery?* (1964), 14 min., 16mm
DIRECTOR: Dan Halas, Alan Raymond. ACCESS: New York Public Library (http:// catalog.nypl.org/record=b17137842~S1).

*An Interview with Bruce Gordon* (1964), 17 min., 16mm
PRODUCTION: Harold Becker Productions. ACCESS: New York Public Library (http:// catalog.nypl.org/record=b17592125~S1).

*The Photographer* (1947), 30 min., 16mm
DIRECTOR: Willard Van Dyke. ACCESS: New York Public Library (http://catalog.nypl .org/record=b17179149~S1).

*The Streets of Greenwood* (1963), 20 min., 16mm
PRODUCTION, DIRECTORS: Jack Willis, John Reavis, Fred Wardenburg. ACCESS: New York Public Library (http://catalog.nypl.org/record=b17199391~S1).

*A Time for Burning* (1966), 58 min., 16mm
DIRECTOR: William Jersey, Barbara Connell. ACCESS: New York Public Library (http://catalog.nypl.org/record=b17652349~S1).

*Variations on an Italian Theme* (1961), 28 min., 16mm
PRODUCTION: Alitalia. DIRECTOR: Carson Davidson. ACCESS: New York Public Library (http://catalog.nypl.org/record=b17337365). NOTE: Preserved by the Reserve Film and Video Collection of the New York Public Library for the Performing Arts, with funding from the Carnegie Corporation of New York.

NOTES
1  New York Public Library, *Proposed Use of Film and Film Information* (1948), 56.
2  William J. Sloan, "The Donnell Center Film Library Busily Serves New York City," *Film News* 18, no. 4 (April 1961): 14; "Job Description," January 9, 1958, Bill Sloan Papers, New York Public Library for the Performing Arts; "Film Policy Meeting Minutes," January 2–3, 1958, William Sloan Papers, New York Public Library for the Performing Arts. NYPL opened the Film Library sixteen years after the founding of the Cleveland Public Library Film Bureau, which was among the first in the country to develop an independent department within a library system.

3   A lengthy explanation by Mrs. Mildred V. D. Mathews, supervisor of Adult Services at NYPL, was published in the March 15, 1949, issue of *Library Journal* detailing how many times a day she had to explain why the library had no circulating film collection. See Mildred V. D. Mathews, "Supplies Film Information," *Library Journal* 74 (March 15, 1949): 473–75.

4   Clarence Taylor, *Civil Rights in New York City* (New York: Fordham University Press, 2013).

5   For more on the debate about the definition of educational film, see Devin Orgeron, Marsha Orgeron, and Dan Streible, eds., *Learning with the Lights Off: Educational Film in the United States* (New York: Oxford University Press, 2012).

6   While some contemporary sources use "Young Filmmakers Foundation," we have chosen to use the spelling that was established on the organization's original charter and common during the 1960s and 1970s.

7   "Moving Pictures in Library Work," *Wisconsin Library Bulletin* 6, no. 6 (November–December 1910): 138–40.

8   Elena Rossi-Snook, "Continuing Ed: Educational Film Collections in Libraries and Archives," in *Learning with the Lights Off: Educational Film in the United States*, ed. Devin Orgeron, Marsha Orgeron, and Dan Streible (New York: Oxford University Press, 2012), 457–77. For more on Hollywood's role in World War II, see Thomas Doherty, *Projections of War: Hollywood, American Culture, and World War II* (New York: Columbia University Press, 1999).

9   New York Public Library, *Proposed Use of Film and Film Information*, 36. While film was generally considered an excellent resource, there were those librarians who were not quite convinced, and essays supporting the use of film in the library continued well into the 1970s. See Orgeron, Orgeron, and Streible, *Learning with the Lights Off*.

10  New York Public Library, *Branch Library Book News: Films for Learning* 30, no. 9 (November 1953).

11  William Sloan to Miss Leona Durkes, November 28, 1956, William Sloan Papers; Sloan, "The Donnell Center Film Library," 14.

12  Gerald D. McDonald, *Educational Motion Pictures and Libraries* (Chicago: American Library Association, 1942), 7.

13  New York Public Library, *Branch Library Book News*.

14  Sloan, "The Donnell Center Film Library."

15  For more on TV and the African American civil rights movement, see Christine Acham, *Revolution Televised: Prime Time and the Struggle for Black Power* (Minneapolis: University of Minnesota Press, 2004); Aniko Bodroghkozy, *Equal Time* (Urbana: University of Illinois Press, 2013); Donald Bogle, *Primetime Blues: African Americans on Network Television* (New York: Farrar, Straus and Giroux, 2015); Alan Nadel, *Television in Black-and-White America: Race and National Identity* (Lawrence: University Press of Kansas, 2005); Sasha Torres, *Black, White, and in Color: Television and Black Civil Rights* (Princeton, NJ: Princeton University Press, 2003). For more on civil rights in the North, see Thomas Sugrue, *Sweet Land of Liberty: The Forgotten Struggle for Civil Rights in the North* (New York: Random House, 2009).

16  William J. Sloan, "The Documentary Film and the Negro: The Evolution of the Integration Film," *Journal of the Society of Cinematologists* 4/5 (1964/1965): 66–69. The journal was the precursor to *Cinema Journal*, the publication of the Society for Cinema and Media Studies.

17  Sloan, "The Documentary Film and the Negro," 67.

18  Sloan, "The Documentary Film and the Negro," 69.

19  Wendell Wray, "Hey Mister, When's the Movies?," *Film Library Quarterly* 1, no. 1 (winter 1967–68): 11.

20  Wray, "Hey Mister, When's the Movies?," 11. The argument over visibility animated the twentieth century. See Brian J. Distelberg, "Visibility Matters: The Pursuit of American Belonging in the Age of Moving Images" (PhD diss., Yale University, 2015).

21  Kenneth W. Axthelm, "Minority Groups: Our Majority Audience," *Film Library Quarterly* 1, no. 3 (1968): 27.

22  Wray, "Hey Mister, When's the Movies?," 11.

23  "Film Library Annual Report 1969–1970," Bill Sloan Papers.

24  *Committee on Un-American Activities* (1962) was a protest of HUAC and is considered the first film made by an American citizen that questioned the legitimacy of a U.S. governmental agency. For more on *Felicia*, see Marsha Gordon and Allyson Nadia Field, "The Other Side of the Tracks: Nontheatrical Film History, Pre-Rebellion Watts, and *Felicia*," *Cinema Journal* 55, no. 2 (February 2016): 1–24.

25  William Sloan, "Films at Noon Program Notes for January 19–March 2, 1967," William Sloan Papers.

26  For more on community film workshops and participatory media, see Lauren C. Tilton, "In Local Hands: Participatory Media in the 1960s" (PhD diss., Yale University, 2016).

27  For a selection of work on representation in mass media, see Janet K. Cutler, *Struggles for Representation: African American Documentary Film and Video* (Bloomington: Indiana University Press, 1999); Edward Guerrero, *Framing Blackness: The African American Image in Film* (Philadelphia: Temple University Press, 1993); Jacquelyn Kilpatrick, *Celluloid Indians: Native Americans and Film* (Lincoln: University of Nebraska Press, 1999); Paula Massood, *Black City Cinema: African American Urban Experience in Film* (Philadelphia: Temple University Press, 2003); Chon A. Noriega, *Shot in America: Television, the State, and the Rise of Chicano Cinema* (Minneapolis: University of Minnesota Press, 2000); Amy Abugo Ongiri, *Spectacular Blackness: The Cultural Politics of the Black Power Movement and the Search for a Black Aesthetic* (Charlottesville: University of Virginia Press, 2009); Beverly R. Singer, *Wiping the War Paint Off the Lens: Native American Film and Video* (Minneapolis: University of Minnesota Press, 2001).

28  Approximately two hundred films from YFDC are held by the Reserve Film and Video Collection, the current name of the Film Library, many of which are accessible to any patron or visitor. In collaboration with NYPL, a selection of films will be available on Participatory Media—a platform for participatory community media during the 1960s.

29   Distelberg, "Visibility Matters."

30   For more on TV, see Devorah Heitner, *Black Power TV* (Durham, NC: Duke University Press, 2013); and Nadel, *Television in Black-and-White America*.

31   Kerner Commission, *Report of the National Advisory Commission on Civil Disorders* (Washington, DC: U.S. Government Printing Office, 1968), 383.

32   Luis Vale, interview by Elena Rossi-Snook and Lauren Tilton, August 19, 2014.

33   New York Public Library, "Noon Film Program," December 6, 1968, William Sloan Papers.

34   Tom Paxton, "Lyndon Johnson Told the Nation," on *Ain't That News*, 1965.

35   Country Joe and the Fish, "The 'Fish' Cheer/I-Feel-Like-I'm-Fixin'-to-Die Rag," on *Rag Baby Talking Issue No. 1*, 1965.

36   "Part of Ten Noon Hour Programs. Donnell Library Center," January 9, 1969, William Sloan Papers.

37   New York Public Library, "Program Attendance Statistics for 1969," William Sloan Papers.

38   New York Public Library Press and Communications Office, "Press Release," 1972, William Sloan Papers.

39   William Sloan, "Speech on Film Library," William Sloan Papers.

40   Marilyn Iarusso, "Adult Specialty Training Seminar Program, Report on a Special Collection: The Film Library," 1972, William Sloan Papers.

41   Ronald F. Sigler, "A Rationale for the Film as a Public Library Resource and Service," *Library Trends* 27 (1978): 23.

42   Euclid Peltier, "The Public Library Redefined," *Library Trends* 27 (1978): 33.

43   NYPL's liberal acquisition policy continued into the 1980s, even after Bill Sloan's tenure, with films such as Liz White's adaptation of *Othello* (1980), made exclusively with black talent and starring a young Yaphet Kotto; *Grey Area* (1981), a UCLA thesis film now considered part of the L.A. Rebellion film movement; Kathleen Collins's *Losing Ground* (1982); Camille Billops's *Suzanne, Suzanne* (1982); Debra Robinson's *I Be Done Been Was Is* (1983); and seminal works by Ayoka Chenzira and Julie Dash.

44   Julia Lesage, Barbara Halpern Martineau, and Chuck Kleinhans, "Interview with Julia Reichert and Jim Klein New Day's Way," *Jump Cut* 9 (1975): 21–22.

45   1976 Minnewaska Conference recording, tape #1, collection of DeeDee Halleck.

46   William J. Sloan, "Films in the Sixties: The Search for Excellence," *Illinois Lib.* 48 (February 1966): 96.

## 13

## Teenage Moviemaking in the Lower East Side

The Rivington Street Film Club, 1966–1974

NOELLE GRIFFIS

In the opening of the eighteen-minute 16mm film *The Growing of a Young Filmmaker* (Raymond Esquilin, 1969), a New York City teenager describes his new passion: "I like shooting a gun." Over a long shot of a young Puerto Rican male walking away from the Chelsea Vocational School in Manhattan, the narrator goes on to share that he recently dropped out of high school due to difficulties with his classes and teachers, noting that some "wouldn't even let me wear a moustache." The introduction of a troubled teen with a penchant for crime is revealed to be deliberately misleading when the young man explains, "And by a gun, I mean a camera. A camera is the best gun in the world." In the next shot, the same teenager sits on a bed with his prized Bolex camera and offers a friendly greeting: "Hi, I am Raymond Esquilin." Esquilin, also the film's director, then discusses his development as a film-maker by introducing clips of the films he has made with the support of the Young Filmaker's Foundation (YFF).[1] His work ranges greatly in style and genre, from a stop-animated fantasy, *The Dream* (c. 1967–68), to a live-action exploration of crime and regret, *The Thief* (c. 1967–68).[2] Esquilin proclaims that he is most proud of his latest film, *The Camp* (c. 1968), which juxtaposes the clean, spacious grounds of an upstate retreat with the squalor of a Lower East Side city slum, depicted by the young filmmaker as a dangerous cesspool of junk-filled empty lots and lecherous old drunks. According to Esquilin, *The Camp* displays his best camera work, but he is sure that his next project will be even better because, he proclaims, "this is one school I won't quit."

FIGURE 13.1. Raymond Esquilin and his Bolex. Frame enlargement from *The Growing of a Young Filmmaker* (Raymond Esquilin, 1969).

Esquilin made *The Growing of a Young Filmmaker* in 1969 along with friends and fellow filmmakers Alfonso Sanchez Jr. (camera) and Jesus Cruz (sound) at a filmmaking workshop founded in 1966 by Rodger Larson in New York City's Lower East Side. With funding from the Neighborhood Youth Corps, a Great Society program that supported education and employment opportunities for low-income sixteen-to-twenty-one-year-olds, art teacher–turned–film instructor Rodger Larson founded the workshop in the kitchen pantry of the University Settlement House, established in 1896, on the corner of Rivington Street and Eldridge.[3] The location had been the flagship of the settlement house movement in the United States, boarding wealthy, educated social reformers to help settle impoverished immigrant communities populating the Lower East Side at the turn of the century. By the 1960s, the University Settlement House functioned primarily as a community center, providing recreational facilities and social services to the area's low-income and immigrant populations—or migrants in the case of Puerto Ricans. Prior to taking the position at the University Settlement House, Larson had introduced filmmaking into his art classes at the Mosholu-Montefiore Community Center and the 92nd Street Y, both working-class and middle-class community centers at the time, but he recognized that the goals of his

Settlement House/Youth Corps program were different: "in sharp contrast to my other projects, the emphasis here was on rehabilitation for 'hard-core' high school drop-outs through the use of film."[4] The young men who made *The Growing of a Young Filmmaker* were part of the first cohort to frequent the Settlement House workshop, which the participants named Film Club. By 1968, Film Club included twenty teenagers from the neighborhood who regularly attended, most of whom identified as Puerto Rican, and ten others from various backgrounds who traveled from other parts of the city.[5]

Defined geographically by Houston Street on the north, Grand Street on the south, Bowery on the west, and Essex Street on the east, the Lower East Side became and remained the locus of Film Club's identity and its mission throughout its nearly twenty-year life from 1966 to 1984.[6] With the goal of setting up a permanent, independent youth filmmaking center, Larson teamed with educator Lynne Hofer and Chilean filmmaker Jaime Barrios to found the Young Filmaker's Foundation in 1968. They moved the workshop a few blocks from the Settlement House to storefronts at 8 and 11 Rivington Street with financial support from the New York State Council of the Arts and the Helena Rubinstein Foundation.[7] While Film Club would eventually attract a diverse group of male and female filmmakers to the area from throughout the city, ranging in age from preteen to young adult, its origins as a Youth Corps/Settlement House initiative placed the older Puerto Rican teens like Esquilin, Sanchez, and Cruz at the forefront of the instructor's mission to prove "that filmmaking meant more to many teen-agers than any of the creative arts being offered to them."[8] In turn, these young men became the case studies and the spokespersons for the creative, communicative, and rehabilitative potential of youth filmmaking throughout New York City and state.

Esquilin's story, as told in *The Growing of a Young Filmmaker*, is personal, yet typical of the first Film Club members: a young man turned off by school, marginalized by his socioeconomic status, and isolated by racial and cultural difference, finding a new source of pride and motivation through filmmaking. Funded by Eastman Kodak, *The Growing of a Young Filmmaker* gave the teens their first opportunity to work with sync-sound in the service of producing "a vivid case study of the impact of filmmaking on a youngster."[9] The sponsorship also meant a larger budget for the teens to accomplish their objective, providing a degree of professionalism. Film Club participants usually shot silent, black-and-white, five-to-ten-minute 16mm narrative shorts, like *The Thief* and *The Dream*, which were to be written, directed, and edited by a single filmmaker. Although the films that Esquilin produced at Film

Club are important to his story, it is the transformative effect of filmmaking—an activity that can turn a high school dropout into a skilled movie director—that provided the impetus for the Kodak-sponsored film. *The Growing of a Young Filmmaker* thus offers a generative introduction to Film Club, presenting visual evidence of the program's success through the presentation of one young filmmaker's accomplishments, while its production and funding sources point to the popular discourses and institutional support behind what *Variety* once referred to as the "phenomenon" of "ghetto filmmaking" in the late 1960s.[10]

As the YFF grew, assisting with the development of youth filmmaking workshops throughout the city and state, the Rivington Street Film Club would serve as the organization's model for other youth film initiatives to emulate. New York City's Department of Cultural Affairs named Larson as the city's film consultant and commissioned his first book on filmmaking, *A Guide for Film Teachers to Filmaking by Teenagers* (1968).[11] The following year, E. P. Dutton published Larson's expanded mass-market guide for aspiring filmmakers, *Young Filmmakers*, which he coauthored with Ellen Meade. The Film Club members and their works figured prominently in Larson's books, providing examples of filmmaking techniques and production methods for other young people who encountered the films and Larson's books at both a local and national level.[12]

The production and exhibition history of Film Club provides a remarkable example of "useful cinema"—in this case for teens, by teens—which Charles Acland and Haidee Wasson have conceptualized as "a body of films and technologies that perform tasks and serve as instruments in an ongoing struggle for aesthetic, social, and political capital"—a definition that applies fully to the YFF and the works produced at Film Club.[13] But the story of Film Club is first and foremost about the perceived utility of filmmaking beginning in the late 1960s when, as David E. James has noted, "if only for a moment, the concept of popular culture was redefined from one of consumption to one of praxis."[14] The YFF promoted filmmaking as an activity that could bridge racial and socioeconomic divides through a common interest, while the Rivington Street Film Club provided an example of how film production could be tailored and adapted to address the needs and concerns of a specific community through its focus on the Puerto Rican youth of the Lower East Side. In this context, Film Club's history broadens our understanding of the way that small-gauge, nonprofessional filmmaking came to be seen as a tool for addressing complex urban and racial problems.

The Young Filmaker's Foundation grew from a small workshop in a Settlement House pantry to a citywide movement that gained national attention because its status as both a youth filmmaking initiative and a minority arts program placed the organization at the intersection of several strands of thought regarding the value of media arts and communications in the late 1960s. The proliferation of youth filmmaking programs during this period stemmed from what Michael Zryd has described as "the powerful and widespread idea that film was the new mode of individual youth expression."[15] While the white, male university student became emblematic of the generation's new film enthusiast—drawn from the countercultural champions of the avant-garde, New Left filmmakers, and Hollywood's so-called film school generation—this popular image overshadows the diversity of the period's youth film movement, which included women, minorities, and children of all ages. During this time, there was a demonstrable concern for the number of hours kids were watching television or the latest "box office smash"—with "pseudo-espionage, beach party, and fantasy" films cited as egregious examples—which motivated the development of media literacy initiatives and production instruction.[16] One of the underlying ideas for this movement was that as media makers, young people would develop a more active and responsible relationship to film and television.

Larson, Hofer, and Barrios stressed the communicative potential of youth media making, and the desire for young people "to make their own statements through film," but the idea of empowering children and teenagers through filmmaking took on an additional significance when programs were implemented for teenagers struggling not only with the generational divide but also with racial, cultural, or linguistic difference.[17] The urgency to find new approaches for reaching minority youth was especially felt in cities at a time when events such as the Watts Rebellion of 1965 and the 1967 civil disturbances in Newark, and the volatile period following Martin Luther King Jr.'s assassination in 1968, brought national media attention to the economic disparity and the growing frustration of African Americans living in inner cities.[18] In "A Decent and Orderly Society," Marsha Orgeron sheds light on a series of educational films made during this period (1966–70) that revealed "a real desire, perhaps even a sense of desperation, for educational films that would speak to, rather than alienate, a black (and presumably urban) audience."[19] The YFF took the execution of the idea a step further: instead of relying on films produced for this demographic, they addressed young urban minority audiences through films made by teenagers from within their communities. Making movies offered young people who had been cast as dropouts, addicts, and small-time criminals to both see themselves and present themselves as complex human beings who dealt with the challenges of poverty, identity, and youth with passion, creativity, and humor.

However, the films made by Film Club participants were neither professionally produced nor created with an explicitly educational intent. Although some of the filmmakers made social problem documentaries and politically motivated films, just as many drew inspiration from popular film and television—creating their own versions of the "pseudo-espionage, beach party, and fantasy" films. As first works, Film Club projects frequently left narrative gaps and could be inconsistent in tone. It was up to the YFF organizers, then, to interpret and creatively program the films for nontheatrical venues such as schools, social service organizations, and libraries; city-sponsored screenings; and film festivals. The filmmakers contributed to the programming and exhibition process by introducing their films at screenings geared toward youth audiences, foregrounding their learning process and personal development through filmmaking. The screenings performed double duty when presented for an audience of the filmmaker's peers: providing relatable content for discussion and a means for recruitment.

Larson, Hofer, and Barrios sought and created exhibition opportunities for the completed works and assisted with the development of new filmmaking programs throughout the city and state, many of which were implemented for minority outreach. Part of this work included joint ventures with New York's elite cultural institutions such as the Metropolitan Museum of Art, the Museum of Modern Art, the Whitney Museum, and the New York Film Festival to screen films and host filmmaking classes.[20] Hofer, the designated liaison to schools and libraries, also spearheaded Movie Bus—a VW bus rigged to project films for young audiences that traveled throughout the city during the summer months, blasting pop songs from its sound system in city parks and streets to attract a crowd. A YFF report claimed that over fifty thousand people were able to see the films and that Movie Bus "brought to the street youngsters who had never seen themselves or their activities as screen-worthy."[21] Hofer also introduced Movie Box, a mobile exhibition site in city libraries for films that had been transferred to 8mm cartridges. Movie Box allowed audiences to program, play, and review their favorite films—a novelty and convenience in an era before readily available commercial playback machines.[22]

By creating both filmmaking programs and interactive exhibition programs to engage and entertain minority youth, the YFF contributed to and benefited from New York City and state initiatives to decentralize the arts as part of a larger strategy to address inequality and to deter civil uprisings. As Mariana Mogevilich's "Arts as Public Policy" and Susan Cahan's *Mounting Frustration: The Art Museum in the Age of Black Power* have shown, art decentralization programs became one way that New York City's government and its elite cultural institutions worked to address race- and class-based tensions in the city—by bringing art to underserved areas through mobile exhibition sites and community-oriented art spaces, such as the Studio Museum in Harlem and El Museo Del Barrio, and through exhibitions designed to make Manhattan's central institutions, such as the Metropolitan Museum of Art and Lincoln Center, more inclusive.[23] The YFF not only set up a permanent neighborhood art space geared toward disadvantaged minority residents but also brought a diverse group of films and filmmakers into the city's top cultural institutions. Additionally, Movie Bus and Movie Box brought youth-made art to underserved neighborhoods and the outer boroughs. For the YFF, this mobility gave their current filmmakers a platform and helped to inspire future filmmakers. For the city, programs in city parks and streets helped to "keep the city cool" in the summertime, which officials described in their fiscal reports as a necessary form of riot prevention.[24]

## *The Potheads*: Making Movies in the Lower East Side

Movie Box, Movie Bus, and other film screenings in schools, libraries, and community centers were organized, most often, for young African Americans and Puerto Ricans throughout the city, but Film Club itself was attuned to the geographic and culturally specific needs of the Lower East Side. The midcentury mass migration of Puerto Ricans to New York City, and the subsequent loss of manufacturing jobs, especially in the textile industry, contributed to high rates of unemployment and poor prospects for economic mobility for the city's Puerto Rican communities by the mid-1950s.[25] In this way, Puerto Ricans faced many of the same socioeconomic obstacles as the city's African American population, including substandard housing, underemployment, and neglected neighborhoods. However, Puerto Ricans in New York also experienced distinct challenges due to cultural difference and, for some, a language divide. For many, life in New York also gave Puerto Ricans their first brush with racism.[26] City leaders in the 1950s and early 1960s, including Mayor Robert Wagner and urban planner Robert Moses, blamed the recent wave of Puerto Rican migrants for rising rates of juvenile delinquency, street gangs, and crime, without recognizing how their own policies contributed to economic disparity and slum creation.[27] While these officials blamed young males, in particular, for creating what they referred to as "The Puerto Rican Problem," social services organizations such as settlement houses and Mobilization for Youth, an antipoverty youth organization headquartered in the Lower East Side, worked to find ways to address the problems that New York's Puerto Rican communities were actually facing.[28]

DeeDee Halleck ran the neighborhood's first youth filmmaking workshop from 1960 to 1966 at the Henry Street Settlement House, just a few blocks from the University Settlement House. Her film about the program, *Children Make Movies* (1961), was screened and distributed by Jonas Mekas, champion of the underground film scene, at the Film-Makers' Cooperative.[29] The Ford Foundation purchased a copy of Halleck's film around the time that it funded Mobilization for Youth in 1962.[30] Mobilization for Youth also experimented with a film collaboration between an adult filmmaker, Roberta Hodes, and a group of African American and Latino children and teenagers who acted out a scenario about poverty and social isolation. The resulting film, *The Game*, earned an award at the Venice Biennale. The interest in youth filmmaking from both the area's avant-garde scene and social service organizations set the stage for Larson's arrival and the development of Film Club.

According to Larson's recollections, the University Settlement House workshop began with a group of young Puerto Rican men, each around seventeen years old, who had come to the University Settlement House to play basketball.[31] Larson asked if they would like to shoot a film. The boys all looked to their unofficial leader, Alfonso Sanchez Jr., who took the camera in hand. After showing them how to thread the film and use the light meter, Larson gave the group a one-hundred-foot roll of film (approximately three minutes) and the freedom to take the camera, unsupervised, to the roof and experiment. They returned thirty minutes later with their first film, completed through in-camera editing. They needed a title, so with a Scrabble set available at the Settlement House, they spelled out and shot the final title card, which reads, "The Potheads in 'Let's Get Nice.'"[32] They added a soundtrack, and their first 16mm project was in the can. Larson has called *The Potheads*, "not only a film, but a documentation of the beginning of Film Club."[33]

In a loosely vérité style, *The Potheads* is an attempt by Sanchez and his friends Jesus Cruz, Ismael Otero, Raymond Esquilin, Rafael Esquilin, Ivan Quilis, Benny Hernandez, Willy Mercado, and Angel Martinez to evoke the

FIGURE 13.2. Frame enlargement from *The Potheads in "Let's Get Nice"* (Alfonso Sanchez Jr., 1967).

feeling of being stoned through cinematic technique. *The Potheads* also explores the relationship between identity and geography through the juxtaposition and layering of images. Double exposure is used to place the transparent bodies of the young men over the New York City skyline and an American flag, making a subtle commentary about the tenuous relationship between the Puerto Rican males and their status as New Yorkers and as citizens. The use of superimposition, cutaways, and rapid in-camera editing suggests that Sanchez had received at least some training in 16mm production beyond film threading and light reading, but the simplicity of the theme (let's film ourselves getting stoned on the roof) and the lack of story or structure marks *The Potheads* as a preliminary Film Club project.

As the program expanded, guidelines were implemented that required more planning. After learning the basics of 16mm production, new members were encouraged to write, cast, direct, and edit their first film. The members of Film Club did not pay dues, but they did have to prove their commitment to the workshop by showing up, seeing their films through from start to finish, and assisting other filmmakers on their projects. The teachers would act as producers and approve projects before turning over equipment; however, Larson emphasized that the only requirement was for the filmmaker to come up with an original idea and a plan for execution, which could range from a "detailed description of the movie to a few hieroglyphics scribbled hastily."[34] Nearly all of the young men who appeared in *The Potheads* completed at least one or two original works. Sanchez Jr., Cruz, and Raymond Esquilin became three of the most prolific Film Club regulars, along with a few others, including Alfonso Pagan and Luis Vale, who joined around the same time.

The works by the first cohort often bear a striking resemblance to one another. This is in part due to technical and aesthetic parameters—the majority of films are short, black-and-white, 16mm works, shot silently with soundtracks composed of popular music (a mix of jazz, rock, and Latin fusion). Most were filmed in close proximity to the workshop: on the street, in nearby parks, on rooftops, and inside the Film Club locations. But in addition to technical similarities, the films by this first group display an unmistakable machismo. Women and girls, when they occasionally appear onscreen, are victims of violence and drug abuse, or the catalyst for a street fight. Due to the location shooting and the prominence of drug use, knife fights, and gang activity, some of the films reproduce negative stereotypes associated with the slums. Still others draw on tropes common to popular film and television depictions of New York City's rougher neighborhoods and are reminiscent of—if not explicitly derived from—*The Naked City* (both Jules Dassin's 1948 film and the 1958–63 television series) and *West Side Story* (Jerome Robbins, 1961). Films like Jose Colon's *Flash* (1968), a sci-fi adventure shot at an upstate location, offer notable exceptions, but the typical film presents a loosely structured narrative, often a day-in-the-life scenario of teenagers on the streets of New York City.

Jesus Cruz's *A Park Called Forsyth* (1967) exemplifies the mix of social message and pop culture references common to many of the early works. Cruz's film opens with a title card that reads, "The story you are about to see is about boys who have nothing to do but destroy themselves in the city." The film presents a tough-looking group of Latino males, all wearing identical white T-shirts and jeans, hanging out on a park bench until a violent dispute over a girl leads to a full-fledged rumble. In his book *Young Filmmakers*, Larson profiles *A Park Called Forsyth* as an impressive work of visual storytelling and describes Cruz's film as a "nostalgic look at the gangs that have now passed into folklore and myth" that "also demonstrates how boredom can lead to gratuitous violence."[35] The theme, as interpreted by Larson, provided a social message ready-made for postfilm discussion and offered pursuits like filmmaking as an antidote to the problems of isolation and boredom. The film's stylistic nod to popular films about street gangs made it a popular choice for the young people who saw the film at Movie Bus and Movie Box screenings. For example, Hofer quoted one fan who called *A Park Called Forsyth* her favorite because it was "the *West Side Story* of the Lower East Side."[36] *The Potheads* and *A Park Called Forsyth* were among the films described by Hofer and Barrios as the "crowd pleasers," particularly with minority audiences, which they attributed to the audience's identification with the people and places that appeared in the films and the familiar generic styles and narrative tropes employed.[37] These films often had a moral or topical message—even *The Potheads*, which otherwise celebrates marijuana, ends with an image of a young man hanging from a noose; however, the meanings were often obscured by the more entertaining elements—especially in the case of filmmakers experimenting with fight scenes, car chases, and other stunt work.

In other cases, filmmakers developed an interest in creating explicitly political cinema. Jaime Barrios, who was not much older than his students, may have influenced some to create socially conscious documentaries about the neighborhood, as he did in his own films, *Chileans in New York* and *La Calle*, a film about Rivington Street that he was working on in 1968.[38] Commissioned works gave advanced filmmakers additional resources to draw attention to community issues or local services (examples include Homemaker's Association, American Youth Hostel, New York City Parks Department/ Sixth Street Block Association). Alfonso Pagan and Luis Vale's *Life in New York*, a rare color sound film funded by CBS, presents the trash-filled streets of the Lower East Side in comparison to the clean, well-manicured sidewalks of Park Avenue, not unlike Esquilin's approach for *The Camp*. The film is a documentary that incorporates a staging of someone shooting heroin on the street and a more fanciful heist scene. Though the filmic re-creations of street crime draw similarities to gang films like *A Park Called Forsyth*, Pagan and Vale make clear that their film is a statement to the local Puerto Rican community. The film opens with a voice-over—first in Spanish and repeated in English—that introduces the neighborhood to the outsider while making a plea to local residents: "this is the ghetto of the LES; one of many slum neighborhoods in New York. This community must unite to do something about this filth." Using political language familiar to Third World Cinema, Pagan claimed that they wanted to make a film about three of their main concerns—garbage, theft, and drug use—using shock tactics to "inspire his neighbors to take action."[39] Pagan expressed that the discomfiting elements

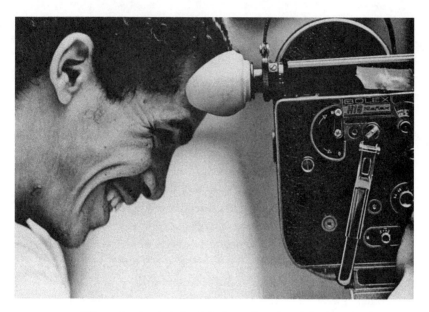

FIGURE 13.3. Alfonso Sanchez Jr. behind the lens. Photo by Michael Fredericks Jr.

of the film were necessary to inspire protests, declaring, "Puerto Ricans should learn a lesson from the blacks if they want a better life."[40]

Pagan, who received another commission from the city's parks department shortly after completing *Life in New York*, would become one of the foundation's great success stories. According to an organizational history, the Puerto Rican–born youth had a passion for filmmaking but showed little interest in learning English, due to his wish to retain his cultural identity and eventually return to Puerto Rico. Through his experiences with YFF, however, he began to improve his English skills and became a salaried film teacher with the organization.[41] Alfonso Sanchez Jr., who directed *The Pot-heads* and shot *The Growing of a Young Filmmaker* for Esquilin, had a history of drug abuse but emerged as Film Club's most promising artistic film-maker. Sanchez's films also explore the neighborhood, revealing its bustling streets along with its less desirable elements of drugs and trash, but he was singular among the group for his more avant-garde approach and counter-cultural themes.[42] Although he would later fall on hard times (statements by Larson imply a drug relapse), for a brief period Sanchez demonstrated that filmmaking could prove transformative for even the hardest of cases.[43]

Sanchez's aptly titled final film, *The End*, called "the true dream" in the shooting script, further developed his subjective, experimental style hinted

FIGURE 13.4. Frame enlargement from *The End* (Alfonso Sanchez Jr., 1968).

at in *The Potheads*. While Film Club works most often screened for young audiences in nontheatrical settings, *The End* crossed over into art house and film festival circuits. In addition to playing in special programs at the Cannes Film Festival and the New York Film Festival, *The End* also won a silver medal at the Tenth Muse International Contest, Amsterdam. Like *The Potheads*, *The End* begins with a celebration of marijuana, but this time firmly rooted in countercultural themes and imagery. The film visualizes a young man's anxieties, stemming from the deadly temptations of street life and the looming threat of the Vietnam draft. Sounds from a motorcycle continuously revving its engine accompany a rapid-cut montage of hand-rendered images of a menacing man on a motorcycle, a Lyndon B. Johnson caricature, protest signs, and drug paraphernalia. A young man lies on his bed smoking a joint and slips into a dream state. A series of episodes unfolds through his reverie, first joyous but increasingly ominous. The protagonist walks through burned-out abandoned lots, filled with a bizarre collection of debris—including two giant stuffed giraffes, simultaneously comic and heartbreaking amid the urban decay and trash. While this slum imagery was typical of what could be seen in social problem documentaries and urban exploitation films, *The End* creatively makes use of and reimagines urban blight. Sanchez may be the only person in New York who benefited from the infamous garbage strike of 1968, discovering in the excess a visually provocative home for a flashy devil wearing a white tuxedo.

## Conclusion

Although Film Club developed and, in fact, thrived as a minority-focused art- and skill-training program during a time when the government (federal and state) and philanthropic foundations actively supported novel and experimental programs created for African American and Puerto Rican youth, Larson and the Young Filmaker's Foundation would push back against the segregation, and in some cases romanticization, of ghetto filmmaking. In the introduction to his first filmmaking guide, created for the city's Department of Cultural Affairs, Larson wrote, "Too often, because of the newness of the idea, film making is viewed as a panacea for all social ills. 'Telling it like it is' does little to enrich the lives of the young filmmakers. When the novelty of presenting slum conditions in film wears off, the effectiveness of film making with ghetto youth should remain."[44] Alternately, by promoting Film Club as a model workshop and bolstering its first members as experienced young filmmakers for others to follow, Larson worked to desegregate youth filmmaking by reversing the norm—foregrounding the experiences of a marginalized group to introduce filmmaking to a more diverse community of interested teens who attended screenings in the city, whether on an underserved street or at the Metropolitan Museum of Art. YFF implemented this integrated approach on a national scale with the introduction of the Youth Film Distribution Catalog, which allowed educational organizations across the country to rent Film Club projects alongside films from other New York workshops including the 92nd Street Y, Union Settlement House, Mosholu-Montefiore Community Center, and the Studio Museum in Harlem.

In Larson's mass-market guide, *Young Filmmakers*, stories of Film Club members like Esquilin, Sanchez, Pagan, and Cruz appeared alongside a coed group of white, middle-class filmmakers from the Upper East Side and African American filmmakers in Harlem to demonstrate to other young people how to draw from their own experiences and surroundings for ideas, and employ a range of strategies and techniques for making their personal statements through film—regardless of whether their specific interests were rooted in exposing the conditions of inner-city poverty, protesting Vietnam, or navigating teenage dating rituals. In putting the films and the filmmakers of Film Club to work, the Young Filmaker's Foundation reframed the educational use of film as a mode of practice, rather than one of consumption. By emphasizing the value of making movies, while also utilizing the completed works as evidence of the program's success, as teaching and training tools, and as artistic works to be discussed and appreciated, they empowered young people to be students, producers, artists, and educators.

The organization's most visible and well-funded period was 1966 to approximately 1974. However, the Film Club and the Young Filmaker's Foundation outlasted the ghetto film phenomenon, soldiering on after Great Society funding dried up and remaining a presence in the downtown film scene for the next two decades, in large part by adapting their language regarding the function of filmmaking (from communication to rehabilitation to skill training) without significantly changing their methods or limiting the possibilities available to the young filmmakers.[45] Today, these films are best viewed within the context of the larger YFF Youth Film Distribution Catalog in order to see a broader picture of amateur and student filmmaking in the 1960s, and the intersections of the youth film craze and minority arts initiatives. But the individual works produced in the early years of Film Club should also be considered on their own terms. Through these short films, we encounter a significant but underseen contribution to New York City's cinematic history, and, in the words of youth film instructor DeeDee Halleck, "some of the best images of the Lower East Side in the 1960s."[46]

FILMOGRAPHY

All available films discussed in this chapter can be streamed through the book's web page at https://www.dukeupress.edu/Features/Screening-Race.

*The Dream* (c. 1967), 7.5 min., 16mm
PRODUCTION: Film Club. DIRECTOR: Raymond Esquilin. DISTRIBUTOR: Youth Film Distribution Center. ACCESS: New York Public Library, Reserve Film and Video Collection, Young Filmaker's Foundation Collection (original elements only, no access print currently available).

*The End* (1968), 9 min., 16mm
PRODUCTION: Film Club. DIRECTOR: Alfonso Sanchez Jr. DISTRIBUTOR: Youth Film Distribution Center. ACCESS: New York Public Library, Reserve Film and Video Collection, Young Filmaker's Foundation Collection. Access print available for onsite screening. NOTE: Won silver medal, Tenth Muse International Contest, Amsterdam. Also screened on NET, "Film Generation," in special programs at Cannes Film Festival and the New York Film Festival, and as part of a Cineprobe series at the Museum of Modern Art.

*Flash* (1968), 11 min., 16mm
PRODUCTION: Film Club. DIRECTOR: Jose Colon. DISTRIBUTOR: Youth Film
Distribution Center. ACCESS: New York Public Library, Reserve Film and Video
Collection, Young Filmaker's Foundation Collection. Access print available for onsite
screening.

*The Growing of a Young Filmmaker* (1969), 18 min., 16mm
PRODUCTION: Young Filmaker's Foundation, sponsored by Eastman Kodak. DIRECTOR:
Raymond Esquilin. CAMERA: Alfonso Sanchez Jr. SOUND: Jesus Cruz. EDITOR: Jaime
Barrios. DISTRIBUTOR: Youth Film Distribution Center. ACCESS: Indiana University, IU
Libraries Moving Image Archive—Educational Film Collection.

*Life in New York* (1969), 6 min., 16mm
PRODUCTION: Film Club, sponsored by CBS. DIRECTORS: Alfonso Pagan, Luis Vale.
DISTRIBUTOR: Youth Film Distribution Center. ACCESS: New York Public Library,
Reserve Film and Video Collection, Young Filmaker's Foundation Collection. Access
print available for onsite screening.

*A Park Called Forsyth* (1967), 10 min., 16mm
PRODUCTION: Film Club. DIRECTOR: Jesus Cruz. DISTRIBUTOR: Youth Film
Distribution Center. ACCESS: New York Public Library, Reserve Film and Video
Collection, Young Filmaker's Foundation Collection (original elements only, no access
print currently available).

*The Potheads in "Let's Get Nice"* (c. 1967), 5 min., 16mm
PRODUCTION: Film Club. DIRECTOR: Alfonso Sanchez Jr. DISTRIBUTOR: Youth
Film Distribution Center. ACCESS: New York Public Library, Reserve Film and Video
Collection, Young Filmaker's Foundation Collection (original elements only, no access
print currently available); Internet Archive.

*The Thief* (1967), 7 min., 16mm
PRODUCTION: Film Club. DIRECTOR: Raymond Esquilin. DISTRIBUTOR: Youth
Film Distribution Center. ACCESS: New York Public Library, Reserve Film and Video
Collection, Young Filmaker's Foundation Collection. Access print available for onsite
screening.


RELATED FILMS
*Children Make Movies* (1961), 9 min., 16mm
DIRECTOR: DeeDee Halleck. DISTRIBUTION AND ACCESS: Film-Maker's
Cooperative.

*Film Club* (1968), 26 min., 16mm
PRODUCTION: Film Club. DIRECTOR: Jaime Barrios. DISTRIBUTION AND ACCESS:
The Film-Makers' Cooperative.

NOTES

I would to like to express my appreciation to those who generously offered their time and resources to assist with this project: Elena Rossi-Snook, collection manager at the Reserve Film and Video Collection of the New York Public Library, who provided not only the films but also invaluable insight into their histories; Alex Kelly Barman, who kindly shared oral histories from her personal research; and Mary Ann Quinn, archivist at the Rockefeller Archive Center.

1   All official documents from the organization, including grant reports and letterhead, use the spelling Young Filmaker's Foundation, which I use throughout.
2   The Young Filmaker's Foundation Collection is held at the Reserve Film and Video Collection of the New York Public Library, located at the New York Public Library for the Performing Arts (hereafter New York Public Library, Reserve Film and Video Collection). Several of the titles discussed in this essay are accessible through the New York Public Library catalog. See filmography for more details.
3   "Report on the Activities of Young Filmaker's Foundation, Inc.," December 1968, Taconic Foundation Files, box 169, folder 1680, Rockefeller Archive Center (hereafter RAC).
4   Rodger Larson, *A Guide for Film Teachers to Filmaking by Teenagers* (New York: Cultural Affairs Foundation, 1968), 10.
5   Larson, *A Guide for Film Teachers*, 20.
6   From 1984 to 1996, Larson ran an offshoot of the program under the name Film/ Video Arts on Twelfth Street and Broadway. Rodger Larson, "Young Filmmakers," in *Captured: A Film/Video History of the Lower East Side*, ed. Clayton Patterson (New York: Seven Stories Press, 2005), 5.
7   Larson, "Young Filmmakers," 5.
8   Rodger Larson and Ellen Meade, *Young Filmmakers* (New York: E. P. Dutton, 1969), 11.
9   "Report on the Activities of Young Filmaker's Foundation," RAC, 9G.
10  The October 9, 1968, *Variety* article "Seedbed for Ghetto Film" discusses "ghetto filmmaking" as a "phenomenon of the past few years." The article briefly alludes to Film Club.
11  Doris Freedman, foreword to Larson, *A Guide for Film Teachers*, 8.
12  Larson, Hofer, and Barrios also published *Young Animators and Their Discoveries* (New York: Praeger, 1974). However, the first Film Club cohort, who did not work in animation (with the exception of some stop-animation experimentation) are not discussed in that book.
13  Haidee Wasson and Charles R. Acland, "Introduction: Utility and Cinema," in *Useful Cinema*, ed. Charles R. Acland and Haidee Wasson (Durham, NC: Duke University Press, 2011), 3–5.
14  David E. James, "The Movies Are a Revolution: Film and the Counterculture," in *ImagineNation: The American Counterculture of the 1960s and '70s*, ed. Peter Braunstein and Michael William Doyle (London: Routledge, 2002), 193.

15   Michael Zryd, "Experimental Film and the Development of Film Study in America," in *Inventing Film Studies*, ed. Lee Grieveson and Haidee Wasson (Durham, NC: Duke University Press, 2008), 184.

16   Peter Bradley, "Film Project," *New York State Council of the Arts 1966–1967 Annual Report* (NYPL), 26.

17   Lynne Hofer to Mr. Dana S. Creel, director of the Rockefeller Family Fund, January 22, 1970, Rockefeller Brothers Fund Records, 1969–70, RAC.

18   Similar conditions led to the University of California at Los Angeles's Ethnocommunications initiative, aka the L.A. Rebellion, and what Devorah Heitner has dubbed "Black Power TV," which included public-access black news programs like *Black Camera* and *Soul!* Heitner argues that in addition to answering the call for black media perspectives, these shows were given air time as a way to provide African Americans with "a place to let off steam without rioting." See Devorah Heitner, *Black Power TV* (Durham, NC: Duke University Press, 2013), 11. See also Allyson Nadia Field, Jan-Christopher Horak, and Jacqueline Najuma Stewart, *L.A. Rebellion: Creating a New Black Cinema* (Berkeley: University of California Press, 2015). For an overview of the period's urban history, see Janet L. Abu-Lughod, *Race, Space, and Riots in Chicago, New York, and Los Angeles* (New York: Oxford University Press, 2012).

19   Marsha Orgeron, "'A Decent and Orderly Society': Race Relations in Riot-Era Educational Films, 1966–1970," in *Learning with the Lights Off: Educational Film in the United States*, ed. Devin Orgeron, Marsha Orgeron, and Dan Streible (New York: Oxford University Press, 2012), 429.

20   For example, Larson designed a student film teacher program for the Whitney Museum and ran a Movies by Teenagers series at the Metropolitan Museum of Art.

21   "Distribution of Workshop Productions," in "Report on the Activities of Young Filmaker's Foundation," RAC.

22   Lynne Hofer, "Films on Demand," *School Library Journal*, November 1970, 27.

23   Susan E. Cahan, *Mounting Frustration: The Art Museum in the Age of Black Power* (Durham, NC: Duke University Press, 2016); Mariana Mogilevich, "Arts as Public Policy: Cultural Spaces for Democracy and Growth," in *Summer in the City: John Lindsay, New York, and the American Dream*, ed. Joseph P. Viteritti (Baltimore, MD: Johns Hopkins University Press, 2014), 195–224.

24   Barry Gottehrer, Mayor's Urban Action Task Force Report of the Citizen's Summer Committee, Report to Mayor John V. Lindsay, August 7, 1967, 8, New York Public Library, SASB M2—General Research Room 315.

25   Gottehrer, Mayor's Urban Action Task Force Report.

26   See Harold Weissman, "Introduction," in *Community Development: In the Mobilization for Youth Experience*, ed. Harold Weissman (New York: Association Press, 1969), 12–30.

27   Christopher Mele, *Selling the Lower East Side* (Minneapolis: University of Minnesota Press, 2000), 130–39.

28   Mele, *Selling the Lower East Side*, 130.

29 Halleck's film is available to rent through the Film-Maker's Cooperative Distribution Catalog. See Filmography.

30 Weissman, "Introduction," 12–30.

31 Rodger Larson, oral history conducted by Alexandra Kelly, recording provided by Elena Rossi-Snook.

32 Alfonso Sanchez Jr., *The Potheads in "Let's Get Nice,"* black and white, 16mm, 1968, Youth Film Distribution Center. It was more likely filmed in 1966–67.

33 Larson, oral history.

34 Larson and Meade, *Young Filmmakers*, 94.

35 Larson and Meade, *Young Filmmakers*, 59.

36 Hofer, "Films on Demand," 28.

37 In his documentary *Film Club*, Barrios mentions that the black and Latino teens did not respond to the more experimental works by many of the white filmmakers. In "Films on Demand," Hofer confirmed that the films by black and Puerto Rican filmmakers had greater appeal to audiences from similar backgrounds.

38 "Report on the Activities of Young Filmaker's Foundation," RAC.

39 Rockefeller Brothers Fund Records, 1971–73, box 1106, March 29, 1971, RAC.

40 Rockefeller Brothers Fund Records, 1971–73.

41 Rockefeller Brothers Fund Records, 1971–73.

42 "Case histories of Juan P. and Carlos S., pseudonyms for Alfonso Pagan and Alfonso Sanchez Jr. (identifiable by the films discussed)," Rockefeller Brothers Fund Records, 1971–73.

43 Larson, oral history.

44 "Report on the Activities of Young Filmaker's Foundation," RAC.

45 According to Larson, the organization changed its name to Film/Video Arts in 1984 and moved to Twelfth Street and Broadway. Larson, "Young Filmmakers," 5.

46 DeeDee Halleck, "Making Movies with Kids on the Lower East Side," in *Captured: A Film/Video History of the Lower East Side*, ed. Clayton Patterson (New York: Seven Stories Press, 2005), 3.

# 14

## Ro-Revus Talks about Race

### South Carolina Malnutrition and Parasite Films, 1968–1975

DAN STREIBLE

In the twenty-first century, a short educational film with the curious title *Ro-Revus Talks about Worms* (1971) became a minor cult film. With its titular character—a frog puppet with a South Carolina accent—telling children in his comic basso voice how to avoid getting intestinal worms and its bare-boned production values, the hygiene film typically draws laughter from audiences encountering this decontextualized ephemeral work. Whether viewers are amused, bewildered, disturbed, or indifferent, most remember the essential lesson of the film, which the wise frog Ro-Revus states plainly: "Never use the out-of-doors for a bathroom." In schooling Nutty the squirrel, his naive puppet sidekick, the raspy-voiced bullfrog repeats variations on the dictum throughout. That contemporary viewers still come away quoting the phrase testifies to the film's effectiveness. The uncanny voice of Ro-Revus maintains a curious staying power a half century on.

### Rediscovering Ro-Revus

In 2005, collector Skip Elsheimer discovered *Ro-Revus Talks about Worms* among a jumble of 16mm prints deaccessioned from the University of South Carolina (USC).[1] He found receptive audiences at his A/V Geeks screenings, and its popularity spread. When USC's 2006 Orphan Film Symposium projected his print, it again proved a crowd pleaser. However, among the viewers was venerable documentarian and North Carolinian George Stoney, then eighty-nine, who had begun his career at the Southern Educational Film Production Service more than sixty years prior. He rose to defend *Ro-Revus* as a "good film" that did its work effectively. Further, he pointed out that to make a state-funded film showing racially integrated schools was practically unheard of in the South in 1971.

Inspired by Stoney's trenchant remarks, this reexamination of the film's history builds upon his two points. First, contrary to first impressions, *Ro-Revus Talks about Worms* is a well-made educational film, one that accomplished its goal with laudable effect. It was one of three classroom shorts produced by South Carolina Educational Television (ETV) with scientists at USC's Malnutrition and Parasite Project (MPP), both in Columbia. *Who Lives with You?* (1969) features "Carrie Ascaris," a cartoon rendition of the menacing roundworm (*Ascaris lumbricoides*), while the sequel short *Ascaris, a Human Parasite* (1972) is a conventional science documentary aimed at high school students. *Ro-Revus* proved the most popular and long-lived. After the grant-funded university project concluded in 1973, the state's health department commissioned three more Ro-Revus films in 1975. Along with a multimedia kit, *The Amazing Ro-Revus Educational Packet and Learning Circus*, they were integrated into the public school curriculum. The health campaign worked. The incidence of roundworm infestation among Palmetto state children fell. Among schools participating in a mass treatment and education drive, infection rates fell from more than 70 percent in some areas to single digits.[2]

Second, *Ro-Revus Talks about Worms*, like its companion films, presented a relatively progressive depiction of racially integrated schools, playgrounds, bathrooms, and medical facilities. In a state notorious for its history of de jure racial segregation, white-dominated power structures, and the pernicious treatment of African American citizens, this unassuming little film of 1971 nevertheless offered viewers images of black and white children playing and learning together. The images of people, however, are confined to silent B-roll footage, which alternates with animation while Ro-Revus talks throughout. By casting a green frog as its defining voice and face, the film was able to distance itself somewhat from the issue of race and, for a moment, defuse the politics of race that otherwise vexed the place and time in which it was produced.

*Ro-Revus Talks about Worms* merits scholarly attention because understanding its origins makes its ephemeral negotiation with issues of race and class more legible. This film and its nontheatrical companions made between 1968 and 1975 entered into intense state and national debates about race and poverty. They did so in idiosyncratic ways specific to their place of origin and their ability as nontheatrical films to travel outside of mass media.

The War on Worms: South Carolina and Ascaris
in the National Spotlight

It is worth recalling the defining social experiences of 2.5 million South Carolinians, circa 1970, nearly a third of whom were African American. Intestinal worms were a perennial affliction in the warm climate, but ascariasis had reached alarming levels, especially among the rural poor. Many families lacked clean water, toilets, or even outdoor privies. The 1970 census revealed the state had the lowest life expectancy in the nation. Racial desegregation of the infamously separate and unequal public schools in South Carolina had barely begun to take effect when these films went into production in 1968.

The seriousness and racial complexity that generated the parasite prevention films become clear when considering the political events of their moment. South Carolina received national attention for its roundworm and malnutrition crisis in the months leading up to the release of the ascaris films. Doctors and scientists became immersed in a mounting campaign to fight worm infestation, which was tied to economic and racial inequalities. Beaufort County, at the state's southeastern tip, became the epicenter of attention.

Throughout 1967–68, Donald E. Gatch, a white physician serving the county, garnered national attention and local opprobrium when he spoke out about a social order that kept African Americans in poverty, with high worm infestation a major factor in their malnutrition. When his findings met with attack, the "Hunger Doctor" increased his activism. In November 1967, he spoke at a forum convened in Columbia by the national Citizens' Board of Inquiry into Health and Malnutrition, telling them about coastal Carolina's hunger problems and the toll parasites took on black children in particular. Among those present were Dr. James P. Carter, the first African American faculty member at Vanderbilt University, and white civil rights leader Leslie Dunbar, head of the Field Foundation. (The foundation soon thereafter funded USC scientists to study parasitism with Carter.) The Citizens' Board of Inquiry published its influential report *Hunger, U.S.A* (1968), which in turn prompted the landmark CBS *Reports* television documentary "Hunger in America," broadcast in May of the same year.[3]

In June, *Esquire* magazine lionized the doctor's work in "Let Us Now Praise Dr. Gatch." Photographs by Diane Arbus showed him visiting impoverished black families. On June 6, he testified to a U.S. House of Representatives committee about the impact of intestinal worms in Beaufort.[4] In 1969, yet another photograph of Gatch treating an African American child appeared on the front page of the *New York Times*. In "the first of a series" of reports on hunger, the reporter followed Gatch on a "tour of Negro shanties."[5] The doctor diagnosed a variety of severe health problems, correlating them to intestinal parasites and charging that a treatable condition was being ignored because the victims were black.

The article also previewed the three days of hearings that Sen. George McGovern's new Senate Select Committee on Nutrition and Human Needs devoted to testimony about South Carolina. Those testifying often cited Gatch's work, including USC professors whose work led to the educational films about worms, parasitologist Felix Lauter, and nutritionist E. John Lease. Joining their panel was coresearcher Carter, as well as Robert Coles, prominent author and child psychiatrist at Harvard. All had visited Beaufort County, then enduring what their state senator earlier told the committee was "the harsh glare of publicity which has fallen on my district because of the discovery of the ascaris worm."[6] Press follow-up mentioned Lease and Carter's finding that an alarming 73 percent of children carried either roundworm or whipworm.[7] The four experts presented their evidence with a call for educational campaigns. "We are going to try to feed these children and job No. 1 is to get rid of all these intestinal parasites," Lease argued. He framed his scientific presentation with a plea for funding production of "visual aids and other education materials geared to the educational level of these victims." Finding the printed material ineffective, Lease reported, "We are, therefore, preparing educational films at the level that they can understand."[8]

Lauter presented a slide show that was, in effect, a preview of how Ro-Revus talked about worms and how all three films visualized the worm problem. He led with a photograph of a male and female worm alongside a twelve-inch ruler; such a shot appears in all three films. As in the later productions, Lauter showed microphotography of ascaris eggs, emphasizing "her" ability to produce thousands of eggs when "she lives with" a host. Other slides were charts of the ascaris life cycle, its migration through the human stomach, intestines, and lungs; illustrations of dooryards contaminated by human feces; and pictures of worm transmission via pets, as well as children putting dirty fingers in their mouths. Lauter's slide presentation to senators was sequenced and narrated much like the films that followed. He described his concluding slides as points to be taught via a "massive program on hygiene

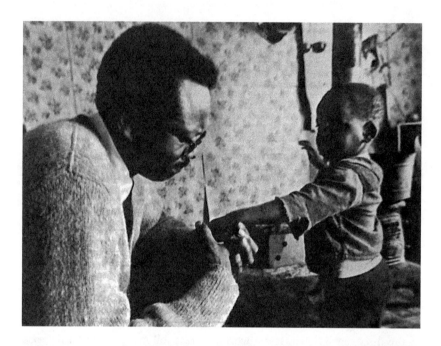

FIGURES 14.1–14.2. Dr. James P. Carter during his December 1968 fieldwork with children in Beaufort County, South Carolina. He supplied photographs to the McGovern committee for his testimony February 19, 1969. "Hearings before the Select Committee on Nutrition and Human Needs," 1969, 1418. Photographer unidentified.

education and sanitation," a five-year project for which the university had not yet found funding.

The McGovern committee hearings affirmed lead witness Sen. Ernest Hollings's opening statement: "There is hunger in South Carolina." While an obvious fact, his pronouncement signaled a political departure from the state's culture of white denial and silence. Hollings even confessed that as governor (1959–63) he had been guilty of perpetuating that silence. His 1968–69 hunger tours across the state followed Sen. Robert Kennedy's example. "Hookworm Hollings," as his opponents dubbed him, brought reporters to rural and urban sites of poverty, including a visit to Beaufort and Dr. Gatch.[9] Eight of the fifteen Carolinians testifying referred to the ascaris infestation as an urgent problem. Charles E. Fraser, a real estate developer in Hilton Head, Beaufort County, had privately funded a local public health project. He too urged a mass education campaign, telling senators, "We know of no lesson plans, pamphlets, or visual aids which would be useful." The federal government's catalog, *Selected Films on Child Life*, he testified, included "not a single film" on intestinal parasites among its 480 titles.[10]

## Nontheatrical Precursors

Although teaching films appropriate for the time, place, topic, and audience were lacking in 1969, both the U.S. government and public health professionals had a long history of effectively addressing worm problems via nontheatrical films. *Unhooking the Hookworm* (1920) and *Exit Ascaris* (1921) were created as the educational film movement entered its initial heyday. The latter, produced by the U.S. Department of Agriculture, addressed Midwestern farmers, then seeing heavy losses due to roundworms infecting swine. Its scenario depicted a farmer with a failing herd learning from an agent how to eliminate the intestinal worm. The two-reeler was widely seen in small towns across the Midwest for a decade, accompanied by USDA field agents offering further instruction. While few people might know the word "ascaris," the Linnaean genus name was long in use.[11]

As Kirsten Ostherr's account of *Unhooking the Hookworm* demonstrates, the South Carolina productions closely parallel its form and approach. In 1909 the Rockefeller Foundation launched a hookworm eradication campaign. Its International Health Board funded this one-reel film as part of its public health work in the 1920s. Used in many countries for fifteen years, *Unhooking* addressed the hookworm epidemic then afflicting up to 40 percent of Southerners. The USC team may not have known the film, but they replicated its technique, which mixed animation, microcinematography, and live action. These films also bear other similarities: a dangerous, fanged worm enemy invades a child's body, grows, and multiplies, with its movements through organs represented in animated diagrams. Direct address warns viewers that the microscopic eggs are found in ground soiled with human feces, repeatedly stressing the need for sanitary outhouses and instructing viewers to follow medical authorities' orders for cure and prevention.

Ostherr also points to an issue that begs comparison with the South Carolina films, the "principle of racial identification." The narrative portion of *Unhooking the Hookworm* features only white actors. Responses from nonwhite viewers in Latin America, Asia, and the Southern states—ranging from laughter to disengagement—led Rockefeller administrators to believe, as Ostherr puts it, "racial and cultural similarity between spectators and actors seemed vital to ensuring that a film's 'message' was received." Finding African American viewers in the rural South indifferent to white-cast educational films, a white physician explained it aptly. "No one realizes better than a southern negro the vast gulf that exists between the whites and the negroes," Dr. Mark Boyd wrote. "Consequently the negro is not much impressed by scenes dealing with whites." He replaced the "human interest scenario" in one Rockefeller health film with new footage of black actors and reported enthusiastic reception among African American viewers.[12] Others in the organization followed this practice, on the principle of racial identification. A half-century later, the makers of the ascaris and Ro-Revus films found a more efficient and arguably progressive way to address spectators in a historical moment of contested racial desegregation.

## Making the Malnutrition and Parasite Films

The state's inglorious moment in the national spotlight soon led to funding ($57,000) from the Office of Economic Opportunity, which allowed USC to create the MPP, which operated from 1970 to 1973. The university had been linking grant-funded research with educational film production since 1968. The Beaufort field research began with a $15,000 grant from the Field Foundation, matched by Lease's federal grant for a pilot education campaign to elevate "health and nutrition standards of disadvantaged pre-school children in Beaufort County." Lease funded *Food and Drugs* (1968), which lecturers would show to county officials, teachers, and families to demonstrate "the incontrovertible causal relationship" between poor sanitation and parasitic infection, as well as subsequent malnutrition.[13] The movie's generic title masked the contested premise as well as Lease's collaboration with Gatch. After the 1969 pilot's success, USC and ETV produced a short film annually, rolling out the campaign statewide. The first ascaris film, *Who Lives with You?*, was followed by *What You Eat, You Are* (1970), which replicated the *Food and Drugs* message, teaching low-income homemakers how to get nutritious food. *Ro-Revus Talks about Worms* reinforced the ascaris and hygiene lessons for children ages four through nine.

Lease headed the initiative, with Lauter and researcher Bettye W. Dudley extensively involved. Although her only screen credits are as writer of two films, she played a role in the deployment of all five. (Her three children are among those seen in the films.) A biochemist, Dudley published in medical journals and authored three editions of *Malnutrition and Intestinal Parasites: An Instructional Guide for Control and Eradication* during 1971–73.[14] These books outlined a rudimentary curriculum to educate children and the public about hygiene and nutrition. Dudley described the films and their suggested uses, understanding them as only one tool in the kit, which included pamphlets for parents, technical information for health professionals, and a battery of classroom items for preteens such as puzzles, quizzes, and art projects. Lauter also devised a filmstrip and audiotape with novel accessories that encouraged children to playact routines of good hygiene. The three-dimensional tabletop objects were designed for different domestic environments: "dolls representing both black and white families," buildings with indoor toilets or outdoor privies, electrical or manual water pumps. The *Instructional Guide* went to every public school library in the state, with information on how to obtain 16mm prints from USC or the state's departments of education or health.

Dudley scripted the text for teachers with imperatives. "You must follow your doctor's directions." "Listen to your teacher . . . and never, never put dirt or dirty objects into your mouth." "WASH YOUR HANDS."[15] The language closely resembles the narration she wrote for *Who Lives with You?* and *Ro-Revus Talks about Worms*. The *Instructional Guide* is notable for its earnest tone, but steers clear of naming the issue of race that was both beneath and at the surface of the problem it addressed. The films show African American citizens more positively and frequently—and address them more directly—than other media in the state in the 1960s and '70s. But this aspect is muted in curricular materials and newspaper mentions.

*What You Eat, You Are* is the most striking example. The *Instructional Guide* says only that the film is "designed for the low-income or disadvantaged homemaker" but also serves "any adult or teen-ager." Yet the producers chose to center on an African American family. Throughout the fifteen minutes, we see an unidentified black woman, in a well-furnished home, making and serving dinner for a man and three children. The nutrition worker who visits is also an African American woman, as are the smart shopper with kids we see in a supermarket and other makers of home and garden. The cutaways to children at play intermix white and black faces. However, we never hear them. The unseen narrators are a white male and female pair of voices (local television personalities), alternately conveying banal facts about diet, thrift, and sanitary habits.

Dudley, who cowrote *What You Eat, You Are*, adds a conspicuous comment in her *Instructional Guide*, its rare reference to racial identity literally tucked in a footnote: "The family scenes were filmed locally [in Columbia] in the residence of one such person whose home is situated in the center of an infamous poverty slum. This mother through diligent effort and pride has upgraded her home, educated her children, and serves as an inspiration and example to her community." The footnote tells us that "the Camp Fornance area, long known [disparagingly] as 'Black Bottom,' had about 150 white and Negro families living in conditions that were labeled 'a public disgrace.'"[16] The passage stands apart from the rhetoric of the MPP grants and manuals, which consistently identify their subjects and audiences in socioeconomic terms. To be sure, this allowed for recognition that both white and black citizens suffered when trapped in cycles of poverty, but it also avoided the issue of race that determined how the films were cast.

While his parasite research and treatment efforts continued in low-income areas statewide, Lauter brainstormed with students about how to convey the dangers of intestinal worms to children.[17] However, Dudley led the education project, designing a comic book format and coloring sheets to teach the evils of roundworm. Carrie Ascaris, the female, dragon-like cartoon, was then animated for the film. "Carrie is a bad worm, ugly, and very mean," says the alarmist voice-over narrator. The seven-minute movie previewed for a legislative committee chaired by the Beaufort senator who had testified before the McGovern committee.[18] Beyond this press mention of the then-untitled film, documentation of its use is scant. That would change greatly when much of the footage was repurposed in 1971 to make *Ro-Revus Talks about Worms*.

FIGURE 14.3. Carrie Ascaris, as seen in *Who Lives with You?* (1969) and *Ro-Revus Talks about Worms* (1971).

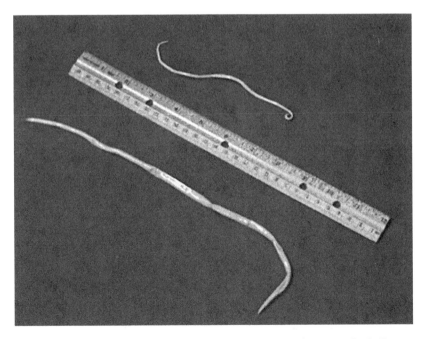

FIGURE 14.4. *Ascaris lumbricoides* measured against a ruler, also seen in both films.

*Who Lives with You?* intercuts two minutes of limited animation with some five minutes of live action sequences, both produced by professionals at ETV. The animated foot-long Carrie invading major organs and the microscopic images of slithering worms are aided by a conventional narration performed in a mellifluous baritone. Locals would have recognized the voice of a popular kiddie TV host and radio announcer praised for his "perfect" voice.[19] However, the otherwise banal footage of playgrounds, yards, schools, offices, and housing contains a powerful representation of black and white bodies, the significance of which may be lost on many latter-day viewers. The film's original Carolina audiences would rarely have seen such casual social interaction between African American and white schoolchildren, either on screen or in daily life. Excerpts from this footage were repurposed in *What You Are, You Eat* and *Ro-Revus.*

The camerawork is remarkable only in that it deliberately stages scenes of children and adults of both races. When not on camera together, they are strategically intercut. In the first sequence, two white boys interact with a pet dog in a backyard and at a veterinarian's office. When the narrator asks, "Did you know that worms can get inside of you too?" we see a close-up of one boy reacting with surprise. The first black person we see is of like age, shown rubbing his aching belly. "And here's a boy who looks as though he has a lot of these worms inside him." But after this initial racial difference, the rest of the film abandons the principle of racial identification: "Many people have these worms inside them." A series of shots depicts kids black and white, playing in the dirt. Later seen clean and well dressed, they happily interact on a racially integrated school playground.

The same filmic desegregation applies to the adult authority figures. Health care workers are white, but the classroom teacher we see is an African American woman. Not only do these children play and go to school together, they also share public bathrooms. The most important lessons to be taught in the worm eradication program were to wash hands and to use a "toilet or privy." In *Who Lives with You?*, the narrator stresses, "Watch! When you use the out of doors, your yard, behind the bushes near your door, or the dirt under your doorstep for a bathroom you are asking for trouble." The B-roll shots of ramshackle houses, junk-filled yards, and a dilapidated wooden privy show no people. This contrasts with the many documentary photographs, films, and television newsfilms of the period that consistently show African Americans in South Carolina living in extreme poverty. Media

FIGURE 14.5. Ro-Revus schools Nutty in *Ro-Revus Talks about Worms* (1971).

FIGURE 14.6. A racially integrated bathroom in *Ro-Revus Talks about Worms* (1971). This shot was also used in *Who Lives with You?* (1969).

coverage of the Hollings hunger tour and Gatch patients in Beaufort were uniform in showing large African American families living in unsanitary housing. An NBC *Nightly News* package that aired the night before the Mc-Govern committee hearings, for example, showed Hollings talking with a black mother of eleven in her home, which they note had neither toilet nor privy. The children "go down to the woods," she says. Hollings repeats her phrase, as if aware of his national television audience's need to understand the continuing practice among the rural poor.[20]

In light of this, Ro-Revus's advice to children about the outdoors stands as straightforward schooling. Outhouses remained fixtures of daily life in some areas through the 1970s. Moreover, the idealized footage of racially integrated social spaces seen in both films was an unconventional and even bold choice. Rather than create separate films for white and black viewers to identify with, as some Rockefeller films had, they imagined (however naively) teaching tools that gave both black and white viewers points of identification.

Although Dudley referred to *Ro-Revus Talks about Worms* as simply a "revised edition," the sequel's use of the talking frog is what makes it far more engaging. In 1971, Ro-Revus was familiar to South Carolina families. He appeared regularly on ETV's daily children's program *The June Bugg Show*, which aired late afternoons from 1966 to 1974. In 1967, teenage production assistant Joe Bowie happened upon a hand puppet among the studio props and improvised a deep-throated frog character. Producer and on-camera host June Timmerman soon added him to interact with the kids who joined her in the studio. Bowie was already doing the puppetry and high, squeaky voice for Nutty the squirrel. The plywood tree prop in which his puppets appear in *Ro-Revus Talks about Worms* was part of the *June Bugg* set. Of the show's many videotaped episodes, only one survives. The Ro-Revus in that extant 1969 segment about good manners is a bad-boy comic figure, not yet the "wise frog" Dudley scripted. To everyone's surprise, ETV received growing amounts of fan mail for the character. Producers recorded Bowie/Ro-Revus singing covers of hit pop songs. College students tuned in, no doubt amused in ways similar to latter-day viewers.[21]

Given the MPP's aim for films that spoke to both black and white viewers, how might Ro-Revus have served that end? Would children be more likely to listen to or identify with a bass-voiced frog than the conventional voice-of-God baritone in *Who Lives with You?* Certainly casting an animal figure offers a point of identification without race. American children's television, both national and local, has always had a multitude of frog characters. *Captain Kangaroo*'s Miss Frog puppet and Froggy the Gremlin on Andy Devine's

Saturday kid's show were among the first in the 1950s. However, none approached the popularity of Ro-Revus's contemporary on public television, Kermit the Frog. In 1969, Jim Henson's Muppet began his run on *Sesame Street*, a program that addressed children with a multicultural spirit and cast. A frog might not have race, but in the first season Kermit debuted "It's Not Easy Bein' Green" (1970), an introspective ballad about embracing one's color. Many heard it as a song about blackness. Singers immediately started covering the song in that black-is-beautiful moment. Lena Horne and Ray Charles did duets with Kermit on the program. *The June Bugg Show* did not present a diverse cast, but ETV stations programmed it with *Sesame Street*, allowing viewers to see Ro-Revus and Kermit in one sitting.[22]

Watching Ro-Revus in my university classes over the past decade, a few students have wondered aloud if his voice was an antiquated black racial caricature. Some note the rhyme with Uncle Remus, associating it with Negro folktales. Joe Bowie's origin stories tell us his sound was a natural imitation of a frog (who originally said only "ribbit"). However, he acknowledges he drew upon voices from popular culture, white and black: Frog Millhouse (Smiley Burnette), Gene Autry's film and TV sidekick with a comic croak, and Clarence "Frogman" Henry, with his R&B hit "Ain't Got No Home" (1956). The name came from Bowie's friend with a penchant for dishing out nonsensical nicknames, something he might have heard from an "old black gentleman who told stories" in his hometown outside of Columbia.[23] A more certain point of identification for South Carolinians hearing Ro-Revus is his regional Southern inflection.

Returning to the films, how might schoolchildren have experienced educational films in South Carolina in 1969? Would they have reached low-income rural populations, particularly the African American children the Beaufort studies showed were most in need? Evidence is scarce, but a white Beaufort County teacher who taught black preteens at the time is one suggestive source. Pat Conroy's fictionalized memoir *The Water Is Wide* (1972) recounts his 1969–70 school year teaching Gullah children, ages ten to thirteen, on Daufuskie Island. The 16mm film projector, he writes, was as valuable as "gold bullion" in the classroom, with students wanting daily screenings, sometimes watching a reel twice. The Beaufort County Library and the State Film Library, Conroy says credibly, allowed him to keep a variety of prints on hand. Conroy's account is embellished but verifies active use of educational films even in remote classrooms in the era of Ro-Revus.[24]

Beaufort County children, like those in other parts of the Palmetto state, experienced notable declines in roundworm disease before the MPP ceased.

The educational campaign of which the films were a part received some credit, although medical treatment and other poverty-fighting efforts more directly ameliorated the suffering. The hazards of intestinal parasites did not go away, of course. Seeing the end of the university project without an elimination of the worm problem, the press noted the MPP's legacy was the availability of the USC films and guidebooks.[25] Although Lease retired and Dudley moved on to other research, their *Instructional Guide* was certainly aspirational and even multicultural. The final edition in 1973 concluded with *Ranita Habla de Gusanos*, Ro-Revus and Nutty's dialogue translated into Spanish.

## Ro-Revus Reborn

With the MPP gone, in 1973 the state legislature appropriated an annual $100,000 to the Department of Health and Environmental Control (DHEC) to battle human parasites. Consequently, DHEC increased funds for classroom materials. Staff scripted a three-part series of new Ro-Revus films, written with teachers, scientists, and health educators. A journeyman nontheatrical filmmaker won the state contract to produce them. More intelligibly than the MPP productions, *Ro-Revus Act 1*, *Act 2*, and *Act 3* squarely present an idealized interracial cast of kids joyfully playing together while learning hygiene lessons in recurring visits from their smart frog friend.

Director Bob Brabham's films took an entirely different form. These too used only local talent, but Brabham was an experienced producer of sponsored films, nontheatrical documentaries, and television ads (including a national TV spot for the Slinky toy). Each lively production features an original number, sung by Ro-Revus, as well as a funky theme song during the opening and closing credits. "DHEC has some slickly produced Ro-Revus films," a journalist noted during 1977 coverage of the continuing parasite problem.[26] But the most striking departure from *Talks about Worms* is that this Ro-Revus is a different puppet with a higher voice. (Brabham did not know of the ETV character, and Bowie was unaware of the new productions.) Accomplished puppet maker Jean Cornwall created the new frog, who makes magical costume changes (garbed as a doctor, professor, drum major, song-and-dance man, jester, and Sherlock Holmes). Her ten-year-old son became the puppeteer.[27]

The titles of the three short films suggest their light tone: *As the Worm Turns*, *Wash Wash, Scrub Scrub*, and *Don't Take a Worm to Lunch*. Their style is marked by rapid cutting among close-ups of the white and black faces of the playmates with whom Ro-Revus visits in each episode. The nonprofessional

FIGURE 14.7. Frame from *Ro-Revus . . . Act 2 (Or . . . Wash Wash, Scrub Scrub)* (1975). The new Ro-Revus appears with a poster for *The Amazing Ro-Revus Educational Packet and Learning Circus* at the beginning of all three films of 1975.

FIGURE 14.8. Frame from *Ro-Revus . . . Act 2 (Or . . . Wash Wash, Scrub Scrub)* (1975), in which the frog hero rides on Willie's shoulder.

child actors speak with distinctive regional accents, far thicker than Bowie's. The zippy pace, comic cutaways, whip zooms, substitution edits, and location shooting are reminiscent of the era's interstitial films for *Sesame Street.* After the opening theme song, during which we see Ro-Revus and children among nature and farmland, each film begins with our host addressing the camera while sitting next to a poster for *The Amazing Ro-Revus Educational Packet and Learning Circus.*

"Can anybody get worms?" a child asks in *Act 1.* Yes, Ro-Revus replies. "Rich people, poor people; black people, white people; boys, girls. Animals, too." Although the series otherwise does not name racial difference, the films equitably intermix close-up reaction shots and speaking parts between African American and white kids. In longer shots, the cast groupings are consistently interracial and free of stereotyping. Our protagonist's closest bond is with the eldest black character, the only one he calls by name. Ro-Revus rides on Willie's shoulder.

The *Educational Packet and Learning Circus* also scrupulously integrates images of children, even encouraging interracial friendship. Its game board's illustrations exactly alternate black and white faces. The playing cards, which we see being used on-screen in *Act 2*, include a drawing of an African American girl showing a white boy how to write the name "Ro-Revus." The card's caption reads, "Tell friends about worms." Whether or not such media succeeded in teaching across racial lines, there is evidence they were used in the way intended. A 1976 newspaper account, for example, included a photograph of a health educator playing the board game with black and white fourth graders at Hilton Head Elementary School. They discuss a Ro-Revus film. Students affected by worms were "embarrassed," their teacher says, "until they realized that people aren't singled out because of race or socioeoncomic level."[28]

Unlike the ETV Ro-Revus, the rebranded character was created solely to be "the 'Smokey-the-Bear' of the roundworm world."[29] Both were creatures of state-funded agencies, but South Carolina's interracial dynamics shifted in the decade between them. The state legislature had no African American representative in the twentieth century until 1970, and most public schools did not implement desegregation until then. Yet national battles for black representation on screen were visible in the state too. In 1971, when *Ro-Revus Talks about Worms* quietly worked its way into the slowly desegregating educational sector, Columbia moviegoers turned out for a ten-week run of Melvin Van Peebles's *Sweet Sweetback's Baadasssss Song,* the movie that catalyzed the blaxploitation boom.[30]

FIGURES 14.9–14.10. Gameboard and playing cards from *The Amazing Ro-Revus Educational Packet and Learning Circus* (South Carolina Department of Health and Environmental Control, 1975). South Carolina Department of Archives and History. Photographs by the author.

## Conclusion

Clearly some contemporary viewers have genuine affection for *Ro-Revus Talks about Worms*, taking pleasure in the vocal performance of its singular star. But any laughter it elicits need not be mingled with condescension toward region, class, or race. Seeing this film only as a curio to be enjoyed ironically as dated or bad would be to miss its powerful qualities. The little film had a positive impact on a big health problem, one that was bound up with injustices of class and race.

George Stoney was of course right in calling *Ro-Revus Talks about Worms* a good film. These movies communicated clearly to rural and low-income families lacking basic needs. They spoke in a regional inflection shared by their audiences. And they found a way to address black viewers their producers knew to be disproportionately affected by poverty in a state governed by a white power structure. As Jennifer Zwarich argues in her analysis of USDA agents using films such as *Exit Ascaris*, the unsung filmmakers working on educational campaigns should be recognized as "bureaucratic activists." The term, she writes, "captures the nature of an enterprise"—state-supported nontheatrical film education—that could seek "social change from within the confines of the status quo."[31] Major health and hunger problems continued after the Malnutrition and Parasite Project. Educational inequities persisted after these ephemeral films. Yet these good films made important strides in the midst of hard times.

FILMOGRAPHY

All available films discussed in this chapter can be streamed through the book's web page at https://www.dukeupress.edu/Features/Screening-Race.

*Ascaris, a Human Parasite* (1972), 12 min., 16mm
PRODUCTION: Malnutrition and Parasite Project, University of South Carolina; S.C. State Board of Health; Medical University of South Carolina. DIRECTOR: Dan Givan. ACCESS: University of South Carolina Cooper Library; Virginia Commonwealth University Libraries.

*Ro-Revus . . . Act 1 (Or . . . Don't Take a Worm to Lunch)* (1975), 9 min., 16mm
CAST: Bobby Brabham, Mario Rowe, Paula Harris, Brad Kneece (kids). ACCESS: University of South Carolina, Moving Image Research Collections.

*Ro-Revus . . . Act 2 (Or . . . Wash Wash, Scrub Scrub)* (1975), 7 min., 16mm
CAST: Dana Danielsen, Dotty Danielsen, Mark Derrick, Gail Martin (kids). ACCESS: University of South Carolina, Moving Image Research Collections.

*Ro-Revus . . . Act 3 (Or . . . As the Worm Turns)* (1975), 8 min., 16mm
SPONSOR: South Carolina Department of Health and Environmental Control,
Division of Child Heath, Intestinal Parasite Program; Peter Lee, coordinator.
PRODUCER: RCB Productions. WRITER: Jim Bostwick. PUPPETEER: Danny Cornwall.
GRAPHICS: Marianne Soufas. MUSIC: Jay Knowles; "RoReVus Theme" sung by Big
George Collier, words by Joyce Covington. CAST: Jim Seay ("voice of RoReVus");
Carol Rivers, Bobby Brabham, Lori Brabham (kids). ACCESS: University of South
Carolina Moving Image Research Collections. NOTE: Robert C. Brabham shot, edited,
and directed each film, without screen credit.

*Ro-Revus Talks about Worms* (1971), 7 min., 16mm
PRODUCTION: Malnutrition and Parasite Project, University of South Carolina, with
South Carolina ETV Network. VOICES: Joe Bowie (Ro-Revus the frog, Nutty the
squirrel), Tom Shirk (uncredited voice-over introduction). ACCESS: University of
South Carolina Cooper Library; *Orphans 7: A Collection of Orphan Films*, DVD (NYU
Orphan Film Project, 2010); *Kids and Kritters*, DVD (A/V Geeks, 2011).

*Unhooking the Hookworm* (1920), 10–12 min., 35mm
SPONSORS: International Health Board, Rockefeller Foundation. PRODUCTION:
Coronet Pictures. DIRECTOR: George Skinner. ACCESS: Rockefeller Archive Center
(12 min.) and U.S. National Archives and Records Administration (10 min.).

*What You Eat, You Are* (1970), 15 min., 16mm
PRODUCTION: Malnutrition and Parasite Project, University of South Carolina, South
Carolina ETV Network. NARRATORS: Mackie Quave, Lynn Nevius. DIRECTOR: Tom
Shirk. SCRIPT: E. John Lease, Bettye W. Dudley. ACCESS: A/V Geeks.

*Who Lives with You?* (1969), 7 min., 16mm
PRODUCTION: University of South Carolina, Department of Biology and School of
Pharmacy, with South Carolina ETV Network. PRODUCER/DIRECTOR: Dave Smalley.
WRITER: Bettye W. Dudley. ADVISORS: Felix H. Lauter, E. John Lease. EXECUTIVE
PRODUCER: Bob Frierson. ANIMATION: Bob Ray. ANIMATION CAMERA: Bob
Ray, John Coles. DIRECTOR OF CINEMATOGRAPHY: Ed Garrigues. FILMED AND
EDITED: Aubrey Vance. NARRATOR: Mackie Quave. ACCESS: University of South
Carolina Cooper Library.


RELATED FILMS AND VIDEO
*Exit Ascaris* (1921), 20 min., 35mm
PRODUCTION: U.S. Department of Agriculture. DIRECTOR: B. H. Ransom, Fred W.
Perkins. CAMERA: George R. Goergens, H. K. Sloat. ACCESS: National Archives and
Records Administration.

*Food and Drugs* (1968), 12 min., 16mm
PRODUCTION: University of South Carolina, with South Carolina ETV Network.
ACCESS: A/V Geeks.

*Parasites: A User's Guide* (2011), 27 min., digital
PRODUCTION: Sharon Shattuck. NOTE: Includes footage from *Ro-Revus Talks about Worms*. ACCESS: Sweet Fern Productions DVD.

NOTES

1   While I was teaching at the University of South Carolina, the library shared its unpublished 1999 inventory of 3,767 16mm prints marked for deaccession. Among them were multiple copies of *Ro-Revus Talks about Worms* and related South Carolina films.

2   Bettye W. Dudley and E. John Lease, creators of the films, published data at the conclusion of the MPP's research. Their three-year case study of one county reported that ascaris infestation fell from 27.6 percent in 1970 to 0.6 percent in 1973. "Intestinal Helminths in Children in Coastal South Carolina: Follow-Up Report," *Southern Medical Journal* 66, no. 10 (1973): 1100; Roger G. Sargent et al., "Intestinal Helminths in Children in Coastal South Carolina," *Southern Medical Journal* 65, no. 3 (1972): 294–98.

3   Citizens' Board of Inquiry into Hunger and Malnutrition in the United States, *Hunger, U.S.A.* (Boston: Beacon, 1968); "USC Receives Three Grants," *Greenville News*, May 30, 1968.

4   Bynum Shaw, "Let Us Now Praise Dr. Gatch," *Esquire*, June 1968, 108–11; "Dr. Gatch Backing Freedom Physicals; against 'Racist Army,'" *Columbia Record*, February 6, 1969. Gatch was coauthor with Geoffrey M. Jeffery et al., "Study of Intestinal Helminth Infections in a Coastal South Carolina Area," *Public Health Reports* 78, no. 1 (1963): 45–55. See his testimony in U.S. Congress, House, Committee on Education and Labor, "Malnutrition and Federal Food Service Programs: Hearings," 19th Cong., 2d Sess., Part 2, 1968, 966–76. See also Robert Coles and Harry Huge, "The Way It Is in South Carolina," *New Republic*, November 30, 1968, 17–21; and David Nolan, "The Hunger Doctor," *New York Review of Books*, March 11, 1971.

5   Homer Bigart, "Hunger in America," *New York Times*, February 16, 1969.

6   James Waddell testimony, U.S. Congress, Senate, Select Committee on Nutrition and Human Needs, "Hearings before the Select Committee on Nutrition and Human Needs," 19th Cong., 2d sess., February 18–20, 1969, 1182 (hereafter "Hearings").

7   David E. Rosenbaum, "U.S. Ready to Spur Carolina Food Aid . . . Senators Told of Children Infested with Worms," *New York Times*, February 20, 1969. The 73 percent statistic was presented to the Senate committee ("Hearings," 1199) and published a year later. Carter, Lease, Lauter, and Dudley were among the nine authors of "Nutrition and Parasitism among Rural Pre-school Children in South Carolina," *Journal of the National Medical Association* 62, no. 3 (1970): 181–91.

8   "Hearings," 1200–1201.

9   Ernest F. Hollings, *The Case against Hunger: A Demand for a National Policy* (New York: Cowles, 1970), 174.

10  "Hearings," 1283. *Selected Films on Child Life* (Washington, DC: U.S. Department of Health, Education, and Welfare, 1959), updated 1962 and 1969.

11 "Roundworm in Swine Subject of New Film," *Educational Film Magazine*, January–February 1922, 20.

12 Kirsten Ostherr, "Cinema as Universal Language of Health Education: Translating Science in *Unhooking the Hookworm* (1920)," in *The Educated Eye: Visual Culture and Pedagogy in the Life Sciences*, ed. Nancy Anderson and Michael R. Dietrich (Hanover, NH: University Press of New England, 2012), 132–34 (including Boyd quote). For an excellent class-based analysis, see Anna Rothschild's video *Hookworms and the Myth of the "Lazy Southerner"* (2016), youtube.com/watch?v =7BwgpYexMjk. Rothschild incorporates footage from *Unhooking the Hookworm*.

13 "Development of a Demonstration and Education Program on Nutritional Health Improvement for Pre-school Children of Low-Income Families in Beaufort County, South Carolina," *State of South Carolina Triennial Report for Fiscal Years 1966–1967–1968* (Washington, DC: ERIC Clearinghouse, 1969), 75–77; and *Community Service and Continuing Education Program Conducted by Institutions of Higher Education in South Carolina* (Washington, DC: ERIC Clearinghouse, 1971).

14 Bettye W. Dudley, *Malnutrition and Intestinal Parasites: An Instructional Guide for Control and Eradication* (Columbia, SC: Malnutrition and Parasite Project, USC, 1971–73).

15 Dudley, *Malnutrition and Intestinal Parasites* (1973), 6–7, 27, 70.

16 Dudley, *Malnutrition and Intestinal Parasites* (1972), 2–3. See *Hollings' Poverty Tour: Camp Fornance Neighborhood* (WLTX, January 11, 1968), TV news film, USC Moving Image Research Collections (http://mirc.sc.edu). The unidentified woman seen with the senator is community activist Lugenia K. Hammond (1897–1991), whose story inspired *What You Eat, You Are*. "'Big Mama' Left Mark," *The State* (Columbia), April 17, 1991. The only reference to *What You Eat, You Are* as a film about "black families" is in *Journal of Nutrition Education* 2, no. 3 (1971): 117.

17 Thomas Buckelew, "A Tribute to Felix H. Lauter, PhD," *Australian Society for Parasitology Newsletter*, April 2005, 25.

18 "Researchers Find Worms in Children," *Greenville News*, August 12, 1969.

19 "Salley Sidelights," *Aiken Standard*, July 11, 1951.

20 *NBC Nightly News*, February 17, 1969, Vanderbilt Television News Archive. Other photographs of South Carolina poverty by Maurice Sorrell illustrate Simeon Booker, "Hunger in the United States," *Jet*, March 1969, 17–28.

21 Joe Bowie, phone interviews and email correspondence, 2008–16. Margaret Compton identified the surviving episode of *The June Bugg Show* ("Buggs Visit Airport," December 15, 1969) in the Peabody Awards Collection, Walter J. Brown Media Archives, University of Georgia. Additional information from Columbia native Lee Tsiantis and ETV veterans Terry Pound, Betsy Newman, Mimi Wortham-Brown, and Linda DuRant by email, April 28, 2008.

22 "Bein' Green," Muppet Wiki, 2006, muppet.wikia.com/wiki/Bein%27_Green. Television schedules listing *The June Bugg Show* and *Sesame Street* programmed together appeared in newspapers statewide from 1969 to 1972, beginning with "'Sesame Street' Looks Promising," *Greenville News*, November 15, 1969, 12.

23 Bowie interview by Eric Kohn, *Orphans 7: A Collection of Orphan Films* (DVD, 2010). Ro-Revus tells Nutty about "ooly-gooly animals." Uncle Remus uses the phrase "gooly-ooly" in "How Brer Rabbit Raised the Dust," *Uncle Remus's Magazine* 1, no. 4 (1907).

24 Pat Conroy, *The Water Is Wide: A Memoir* (1972; Kindle ed., New York: Open Road Media, 2010), 55, 98–101. Craig Kridel, USC Museum of Education, showed me William Keyserling's photographs that document the 16mm projector and film cans in Conroy's classroom.

25 "Parasite Problem Is Still with Us," *The State*, February 25, 1973.

26 "S.C.'s Problem of Worms Is Far from Solved," *The State*, January 2, 1977, says "the internationally known Ro-Revus was born" with the campaign, forgetting his birth at ETV.

27 Bob Brabham, phone interview, January 2, 2017. Brabham said he received no instructions on casting but understood it was industry practice to have representation of African American talent. Interview with Dan Cornwall, May 25, 2017.

28 "Intestinal Parasites Remain Health Problem," *Gaffney Ledger*, May 12, 1976.

29 "'Wanta Play, Go Croak!,'" *Gaffney Ledger*, November 19, 1975.

30 Orville Vernon Burton, "Civil Rights Movement," *Digital South Carolina Encyclopedia*, 2016, www.scencyclopedia.org/sce/entries/civil-rights-movement. Ads for *Sweet Sweetback* in *The State* and *Columbia Record*, May 7–July 14, 1971.

31 Jennifer Zwarich, "The Bureaucratic Activist: Federal Filmmakers and Social Change in the U.S. Department of Agriculture's Tick Eradication Campaign," *The Moving Image* 9, no. 1 (2009): 26–27.

## 15

# Government-Sponsored Film and *Latinidad*

*Voice of La Raza* (1971)

LAURA ISABEL SERNA

In 1970, the *Albuquerque Journal* announced "Actor [Anthony] Quinn, [producer Lou] Adler May Hoist Banner of Minority Group."[1] *Journal* readers learned that the Oscar-winning actor was filming "a scene" for a "government sponsored study of Mexican-American work opportunities." That "study" was the film *Voice of La Raza* (1971), a sponsored film produced and directed by African American documentary and experimental filmmaker William (Bill) Greaves (1926–2014) under the auspices of the Equal Employment Opportunity Commission (EEOC).[2] Quinn, born in Mexico to an Irish father and a Mexican mother and raised in the Mexican immigrant barrio of Boyle Heights in Los Angeles, starred in the film, which was written by Greaves in collaboration with Nuyorican documentary filmmaker José García Torres.[3] Referred to in the press as an example of cinéma vérité, the film combines techniques including direct observation, staged interviews, and dramatizations to educate viewers about the unequal treatment of "Spanish-speaking Americans"—as Latin American immigrants and their children were commonly referred to during this period—in the labor market.

The film premiered in May 1971 at an EEOC celebration honoring Quinn, and then screened at numerous film festivals and on television.[4] It won awards at the Atlanta International Film Festival and the Columbus Film Festival and an Emmy nomination in 1972 after it screened on public television in the New York area.[5] The film also circulated in community centers, libraries, union halls, and military bases, initially as part of efforts to increase awareness about labor discrimination and later as part of Hispanic heritage celebrations.[6]

In the context of the EEOC's activities in the late 1960s and early 1970s, *Voice of La Raza* was conceived of as an effective way to educate audiences about labor discrimination. The film mobilizes aesthetic strategies associated with politically committed filmmaking, including shooting on location and showcasing the voices and faces of everyday people in lieu of experts. At the same time, the film employs experimental techniques including dramatizations and psychodramatic confrontations that, understood in the context of Greaves's work in the late 1960s, highlight the increasing radicalization of Latinos in the U.S. and call attention to the need for social change. Thus, while some elements of the film align with the federal government's project of constructing an ethnoracial group, Hispanic, whose needs could be addressed by agencies like the EEOC, others draw attention to relationships of power between and within racial groups and the role of media in effecting social change.

To date, neither this film nor any of the other films about Latino issues made by Greaves for the EEOC have been analyzed. Scholarship on documentary treatments of Latino subjects and themes made in the late 1960s and early 1970s focuses primarily on films made by Chicano and Puerto Rican filmmakers. That work, much of which was produced in the context of the broader movement for civil rights, is most frequently discussed as a step toward feature film production.[7] At the same time, *Voice of La Raza* and the other films that Greaves made for the EEOC are generally absent from considerations of his career, which focus primarily on his experimental work and documentaries related to African American history and culture. This chapter situates *Voice of La Raza* at the intersection of African American documentary, government-sponsored film, and films about the Latino experience.

## Government-Sponsored Film and the EEOC

In the late 1960s, U.S. federal agencies charged with addressing discrimination began to use film in their work. Federal agencies had produced films to support programs and policies, train military personnel, and document important events. However, government-sponsored films did not take up race relations and discrimination to a significant extent until the late 1960s.[8] Both the Commission on Civil Rights, formed as part of the Civil Rights Act of 1957, and the EEOC, which was created after the passage of the Civil Rights Act of 1964, saw film as crucial to their missions. The Commission on Civil

Rights, which made one film in 1971 and two in 1972, justified the expense by declaring, "Motion pictures present an attractive medium for the dissemination of information about Commission programs. They have the potential to reach a much larger audience than publications, particularly if they can be made suitable for presentation on T V."[9] Reaching a large audience was also crucial to the EEOC, which was established to support legislation forbidding discrimination in employment, but lacked any enforcement mechanism for the first six years of its existence.

During this period, film and television constituted an important field of civil rights activism.[10] Activists from African American, Chicano, and Puerto Rican communities protested the film and television industries that marginalized minority perspectives, traded in stereotypes, or ignored communities of color altogether. This activism led to some changes, especially in public television, where government and foundation support facilitated minority media professionals' participation and subsidized many of the documentaries that became the mainstay of public affairs programs aimed at minority audiences. Some of these media professionals received their training in two important but short-lived university-based programs designed to increase minority participation in film and media production, while others trained on the job.

In this context, William Greaves found opportunities.[11] Born in New York, Greaves trained as an actor in the 1940s before turning to filmmaking. Dismayed by the lack of opportunities for African Americans in the U.S. film industry, he moved to Canada. There he worked his way up at the National Film Board and eventually directed a well-received portrait of a public hospital, *Emergency Ward* (1959). Greaves returned to New York in the early 1960s as a public information officer at the United Nations, where he produced and directed a documentary about civil air flight, *Cleared for Take Off* (1963).

Throughout the 1960s, Greaves made documentaries about African American culture, public figures, and everyday life, worked in public television, and ventured into experimental docu-fiction with a feature-length film, *Symbiopsychotaxiplasm: Take One* (1968). Many of the documentaries Greaves made during this period were government-sponsored projects. As Rick Prelinger notes, in the postwar period sponsored film "production companies and 16mm distribution outlets proliferated," especially in New York where Greaves was based.[12] In 1964, Greaves founded William Greaves Productions, which promptly received contracts from the United States Information Agency to make a film about freedom of expression in the United States, *Wealth of Nations* (1964), and document the global gathering of black artists in Dakar, Senegal, *The First World Festival of Negro Arts* (1966).[13] In 1968, Greaves was signed to cohost the national black public affairs program *Black Journal*, where he served as executive director for the last two years he was affiliated with the show. It was in the context of *Black Journal* and public television that Greaves mentored younger filmmakers and likely met José García Torres, who had been a central force in the creation of a New York–based Latino public affairs program, *Realidades*.[14]

Greaves was more than qualified to produce the types of films the EEOC required, but also benefited from personal connections and government programs. Greaves came to the attention of the EEOC via Olivia Stanford, the successful black businesswoman who served as the commission's information specialist from 1967 to 1970 and whom *Jet* magazine credited with being a "leading force" in Greaves landing agency contracts.[15] In addition to Stanford's advocacy, he benefited from a provision of the Small Business Act (originally signed into law in 1954), SBA 8(a), that strove to help businesses owned by women and minorities, like William Greaves Productions, obtain government contracts.[16]

The films Greaves made for the EEOC reflect a documented shift in the federal government's attitude toward Chicano and Puerto Rican communities. Under Lyndon Johnson and then Richard Nixon, the federal government worked to popularize the designation "Hispanic" to signify a broad ethnic group composed of diverse Latino populations. As Cristina Mora explains, the promotion of this term was part of a larger political project: "Fearing the rise of militancy and sensing the opportunity to win more votes both Johnson and Nixon created agencies that would purportedly represent Mexican American and Puerto Rican needs within the federal government."[17] In this context, the EEOC, which appointed its first Mexican American commissioner in 1967, began to examine and hold hearings about the question of labor discrimination against Puerto Ricans in New York and Mexican Americans in the Southwest.

The EEOC engaged Greaves's services to help document this work. In fiscal year 1971, the EEOC reported that it had paid Greaves for four films: *The EEOC Story*, a film describing the "machinery of the EEOC and how it serves both the minority community and women," narrated by African American actress Ruby Dee; *Power versus the People*, which consisted of footage from the EEOC's hearings in Houston, Texas, in 1970; *Struggle for Los Trabajos*, a film depicting the "investigation and conciliation process of a violation of the rights of a Mexican American white collar worker," and the most expensive of all these productions, *Voice of La Raza*.[18]

FIGURE 15.1. Anthony Quinn listens to a group gathered in East Los Angeles. *Voice of La Raza* (William Greaves, 1971). Frame enlargement courtesy of Dino Everett, USC Hugh M. Hefner Moving Image Archive.

## Voice of La Raza

*Voice of La Raza* cost $87,000 to make and featured the star power of not only Anthony Quinn but also fellow Academy Award winner Rita Moreno. Beyond utilizing the exceptional visibility of these two Latino stars, the film appeals, beginning with the term *la raza* or "the people" in its title, to the spirit of the radical movements that had emerged in Mexican American and Puerto Rican communities during the late 1960s. Chicano activists had taken up the term as a way of expressing shared experiences of conquest, colonialism, and imperialism amid regional struggles such as land reform in New Mexico or education in Southern California.[19] The title also gestures toward a fundamental strategy for achieving social change that emerged out of this activism: allowing the Chicano community to speak for itself.[20]

Shot in 16mm on the streets of Los Angeles, New York, and Albuquerque, *Voice of La Raza* focuses on everyday people. Descriptions of the film suggest it emerged organically "out of conversations and questions asked by Quinn in his travels across the country concerning the plight of Spanish-speaking Americans."[21] Characterized as an example of cinéma vérité or

FIGURES 15.2–15.4. (*Opposite, top to bottom*) A young man on the streets of Spanish Harlem in New York; the film's sole female voice on Pico Boulevard in Los Angeles; (*above*) a white-collar Puerto Rican worker in New York. *Voice of La Raza* (William Greaves, 1971). Frame enlargements courtesy of Dino Everett, USC Hugh M. Hefner Moving Image Archive.

direct cinema, the film is structured around a series of interviews with "witness-participants," a strategy that Bill Nichols argues characterizes politically committed films of the 1970s.[22] Significant portions of the film are devoted to sequences of Quinn engaged in conversation with young people. In heavily accented English, street slang, or with traces of regional accents, these men (and one young woman) shown in close-up recount their experiences of being discriminated against by employers or educators. These interviews take place most frequently on the street but also in other public spaces like a church courtyard or a campus quad where ambient noise such as traffic, music from a passing band, and other conversations lends an immediacy and authenticity to the scenes. Some people speak timidly, having to be coaxed into speaking by Quinn, while others engage him with confidence.

Though the audience hears the voices of these everyday people, our experience of them is mediated by a series of narrators whom the film grants varying degrees of authority. The first and most important narrator is Quinn. When the camera focuses on crowds or groups of people on the street, the camera seeks him out and shows him listening intently, head cocked to one side, eyes on whoever is speaking. He reinforces his listening role when he declares, "It doesn't matter if you are in the barrios of Los Angeles or streets of New York, I found there is much to learn if you just listen." At the same time, his mellifluous voice dominates the film, and he is granted interpretive authority as he places his interviewees' comments in broader social and cultural context in voice-over that follows each interview or in scenes of Quinn himself being interviewed. Phrases such as "I can relate to" and "I have to personalize" and his consistent use of "we" emphasize his connection to the experiences of the people he interviews even as he seeks to explain them to the film's viewers.

Quinn was well suited to play the role of mediator between the film's informants and audience. An international star, he was well known to the filmgoing public, for whom his Irish surname and a career built playing Mediterranean types obscured his Mexican roots. But Quinn, as the press frequently noted in passing, grew up in Boyle Heights, a barrio of East Los Angeles. Beginning with the Sleepy Lagoon case in the 1940s, Quinn became an increasingly visible advocate for the Mexican American community. In the early 1970s, he lent his name to a range of causes related to education and other issues.[23] He was not, however, considered a radical. As one article phrased it, he was "opposed to nationalism of any sort, but . . . equally concerned with equality for minority groups."[24] Thus, Quinn's politics and public persona were well calibrated to the concerns of the federal government.

Three other voices serve a similar, if secondary, mediating function. A nameless male voice that speaks grammatically correct English with a Spanish accent offers factual commentary in an expository mode at different points in the film. For example, over footage of Spanish Harlem, this voice explains the different Latino groups living in New York and how Puerto Ricans came to constitute a significant ethnic group there. Later, the same narrator explains the work of the EEOC and introduces a brief sequence on filing a complaint. Two other voices belonging to EEOC regional commissioners Vicente Jimenez and Tom Robles likewise explain and contextualize. Their white-collar jobs, signaled by office buildings, meeting tables, and desks flanked by American flags, mark them as educated, and they are presented as experts on both the issue of labor discrimination, by virtue of their roles at the EEOC, and Spanish-speaking populations in the United States, by virtue of their personal backgrounds. Jimenez, the EEOC commissioner in Houston, speaks at length to what the viewer assumes are fellow EEOC employees about the degree of alienation Mexican American children encounter in public schools. Robles, the EEOC commissioner in Albuquerque, recounts that when he left the military he could only find work as a manual laborer, experiencing the problem of discrimination in the workplace firsthand. Like Quinn's, their voices, positioned as native informants and experts, contextualize the experiences of the film's working-class interviewees. While the film eschews the "voice of God" narration of classical documentary, it offers not the voice of la raza but rather multiple voices that speak from distinct social positions: uneducated, educated, unknown, famous, blue collar, white collar, and so on. Commonalities emerge within this diversity, the most salient being the experience of discrimination in the labor market.

The film uses other formal elements, most notably montage, to construct a shared identity out of historical and regional diversity. Establishing shots of Spanish Harlem, East Los Angeles, and Albuquerque, New Mexico, are marked by street signs or other written text to locate sequences at specific geographic coordinates. Montage sequences bind those spaces together. For example, EEOC officer Jimenez's declaration that the nation's ten million Spanish-speaking Americans need to be "treated as a national group in national terms" is accompanied by a montage of workers in various settings: cooks preparing food in hotel kitchens, men clocking in at factory gates and rail yards and pushing carts on urban streets. Another slower and longer montage sequence, with no establishing shot to ground it geographically, shows children, young women, and older people sitting on top of cars, on front porches, at bus stops, or entering their modest homes. Vicente Jimenez, whose voice we hear over the images, invokes Mexican writer Octavio Paz's description of Mexicans in the United States as "beauty in tatters." The Spanish guitar music that accompanies this sequence (and most of the film's transitions) suggests a shared cultural identity regardless of geographic location. Finally, another brief montage sequence composed of a series of photographs of pre-Columbian pyramids and other built structures with paintings of the conquest illustrates Jimenez explaining Latino history and culture to a group of colleagues. This sequence brings to mind the primary visual strategy of Luis Valdez's film adaptation of the important Chicano movement poem by Rudolfo "Corky" Gonzales, *Yo soy Joaquín* (1969), which is composed entirely of filmed still images. In different ways, these montage sequences propose connections across geographical space and historical time, educating viewers—Anglo and Latino alike—about Latinos' shared historical, cultural, and social experiences.

What is more, despite the fact that the film is almost entirely spoken in English, it proposes language as a central axis for a shared ethnic identity.[25] In an extended sequence, Quinn speaks with young children in New Mexico. For the first time in the film, we hear Spanish spoken. The camera moves in closely to their slightly dirty faces, while Quinn asks repeatedly, "Are you Spanish?" They reply that that they do not know or that they are English. A dismayed Quinn asserts, "You have to speak Spanish," a sentiment he reinforces in voice-over that ties language to identity. These combined strategies—erasing geographical space and proposing a shared history and language as binding forces—offers a cultural rather than political model of ethnic identity. In this way, the film seems to participate in the federal government's project of developing a "bureaucratized category" that could encompass disparate Latino groups in order to "extend and further legitimate, instead of threaten, government policies."[26] While these strategies appear to hold radical politics at bay, Greaves uses experimental techniques to underscore the growing militancy of Chicano and other Latino youth.

## The Message

Toward the end of *Voice of La Raza*, Tom Robles, the EEOC officer from Albuquerque, declares forthrightly, "The message of this film is you either do it within the law, within the legal system that [*sic*], within what we have now. And this is a message to employers. Or else. . . . Let's get rid of this discrimination bit or you're going to have chaos." His statement raises the specter of civil unrest and recontextualizes the voices we have heard over the course of the film—the dejected young Puerto Rican actor in New York, the frustrated unemployed Chicano in Los Angeles, the Chicano students at the University of New Mexico skeptical about their future employment prospects—as more than expressions of personal experience; their voices are the rumblings of radicalization.

While the film links labor discrimination to racism, primarily through the multiple narrators' explanations and analyses, at key moments in the film Greaves stages conflict to suggest the need for reflection and dialogue. Sociodrama and psychodrama, therapeutic techniques that use role-playing and dramatization to address group or personal issues, had become popular in mental health circles and were being used at the Actors Theatre in New York, where Greaves was a director, actor, and teacher.[27] Greaves had used such techniques before. In *Symbiopsychotaxiplasm*, his widely hailed experimental documentary that captured the filming of a scene repeated and improvised on, Greaves used the principles of psychodrama to explore the relationship between director, cast, and crew and also to investigate how conflict emerges among members of a group, in this case his crew.[28] *In the Company of Men* (1969), a management training film sponsored by *Newsweek*, depicted a sociodramatic encounter between "hardcore unemployed" (as the description of the film on the William Greaves Productions website phrases it) working-class African American men and white auto industry executives. The film sought to facilitate communication between the two groups and thus to generate understanding and eliminate preconceptions. In 1970, Greaves wrote a *New York Times* editorial in which he hailed "psychodramatic and sociodramatic encounter television" as a means of "improving mass mental health and social reform."[29]

Greaves's commitment to these techniques explains key elements of *Voice of La Raza* that deviate from the film's assumed pedagogical function. The film makes use of both dramatization and sociodramatic techniques to raise awareness of the subjective and social dimensions of race-based labor discrimination. The opening sequence of the film consists of a dramatization in which an Anglo supervisor discourages a Puerto Rican worker from applying for a promotion. In conversation with Quinn after the dramatization ends with José the electrician going back to Puerto Rico, José the actor reflects on his own experiences of labor discrimination in the film and television industry. In the process of playing this role and subsequently reflecting on that process, José and the viewer gain insight into his personal experience and what he might have in common with other Latinos.

FIGURES 15.5. A Puerto Rican mail room attendant, boxed in by his workplace. *Voice of La Raza* (William Greaves, 1971). Frame enlargement courtesy of Dino Everett, USC Hugh M. Hefner Moving Image Archive.

This dramatization is mirrored by the penultimate sequence of the film, in which Greaves stages a sociodramatic encounter between a young Chicano and a group of fathers who represent older, middle-class Mexican Americans. Over the course of the film, Greaves establishes the theme of passivity—José the fictional electrician quietly accepts his supervisor's dismissal of his capabilities. A Puerto Rican mail room attendant asked by Quinn if he had hopes of finding a better job replies, "The boss like that I take care of here." The image accompanying his reply shows him literally hemmed in by the walls of his small office, trapped behind the desk where he has worked for fourteen years. Both Quinn and Moreno recall their parents' fears of any government official, a fear Moreno attributes to Puerto Ricans being a "sweet and passive people."

This passivity contrasts sharply with the militancy of the young Chicanos featured in a long sequence shot on the campus of the University of New Mexico. Throughout the sequence, the camera lingers on scenes of Chicano youth engaged in political organizing in a classroom, grilling Quinn about his own politics, and finally in a smaller, mixed-gender group that discusses the failure of agencies like the EEOC to adequately address the issue of labor discrimination. The problem, one young man declares forcefully, is that employers fail to see past race, "what you represent," as he phrases it. He contends that racial thinking contaminates encounters with employers regardless of an applicant's professional or educational qualifications.

The phrase "take away his suit" functions as a sound bridge to a shot of a man with close-cut hair wearing a suit and tie. With this image, the viewer enters a different generational and social space. Jeans and T-shirts have been traded for suits and ties and the words "Chicano" and "Black" replaced by "Spanish" and "Negro." The film's secondary narrator describes this group of parents (fathers actually) seated on sofas in a sterile, institutional room as "willing to work within existing structures." A voice that we learn is that of Greaves asks, offscreen, "Do you have any thoughts on this?" The camera swings left to focus on a young man wearing glasses, a black armband, and a United Farmworkers pin, who had not appeared in the previous shots. He challenges the group of suit-clad men, pointing his finger and raising his voice. The camera captures this conflict, moving back and forth from speaker to speaker. While the fathers assert that things have improved, the young man insists, in ever more heated language, that things are in fact still quite bad. Finally, with an American flag off to the left of the frame just behind him, he shouts, "If caring about my people makes me a radical, a communist, I am a fucking communist." One of the men stands up, clearly provoked.

At this point Greaves himself appears on screen, breaking the fourth wall and any illusion of objectivity. With his sound tech standing just behind him, Greaves intervenes, urging the man, who accuses him of planning this confrontation, to see the impact the heated exchange will have on the film's future viewers. This encounter visualizes in microcosm two approaches to addressing racial inequality: one gradual and conciliatory and the other militant. While it dramatizes the film's principal message to employers—make change or you will have social unrest—it also throws into high relief tensions within the Latino community and suggests, by modeling such communication, the need for intragroup dialogue.

Setting up and facilitating this encounter also gestures toward the role Greaves imagined for the media in helping communities and individuals navigate the divide between activists and the institutions they sought to do away with or reform, between racial groups, and between militant and more mainstream political orientations within racial groups. The latter was a topic he had explored in his 1968 film *Still a Brother: Inside the Negro Middle Class*, made for National Educational Television. As in that film, the question about

FIGURES 15.6–15.7. A young Chicano student challenges members of his parents' generation. *Voice of La Raza* (William Greaves, 1971). Frame enlargements courtesy of Dino Everett, USC Hugh M. Hefner Moving Image Archive.

FIGURE 15.8. The filmmaker makes an appearance in the middle of a heated conversation. *Voice of La Raza* (William Greaves, 1971). Frame enlargement courtesy of Dino Everett, USC Hugh M. Hefner Moving Image Archive.

whether to adopt a radical nationalist stance or take a more accommodationist approach was set against mainstream media's circulation of images of so-called race riots and protests. While Chicano and Puerto Rican activists received far less media attention than their black counterparts, when their actions were covered they were framed in predictable negative ways. As Randy Ontiveros has written, the mainstream media, when it deigned to cover the Chicano movement, "positioned Mexican Americans as radicals while discursively linking the Chicano movement to other perceived threats, including black militancy, war unrest, the youth counter culture, and Latin inflected communism."[30] Similarly, the Young Lords, a radical leftist organization that emerged in Puerto Rican New York and Chicago, was frequently the object of sensational media coverage.[31] These images of militant urban activists hover offscreen in *Voice of La Raza*. Compliance with antidiscrimination legislation, the film suggests, would ensure that violence, protests, and civil unrest stayed offscreen. At the same time, the film pushes less radicalized segments of the Latino community toward an understanding of the motivations of militant young activists.

## Conclusion

In 1975, Chicano filmmaker Francisco X. Camplis dismissed *Voice of La Raza* as "little more than an exploration of the problem of job discrimination and unemployment."[32] In part, this dismissal stemmed from his own conviction that only a Chicano filmmaker was qualified to make films about the Chicano experience or the Chicano community. Setting to one side the question Camplis raises about a filmmaker's identity as a prerequisite for representation, a close analysis of *Voice of La Raza* demonstrates that Greaves, even within the confines of sponsorship by a government agency, sought to do more than merely educate or inform his audience about a given topic. Instead he sought to portray the impact of racial discrimination on individuals, carve out a role for middle-class figures (as well as film stars), and model the way that confrontation could generate inter- and intragroup understanding of social issues. While Greaves combines techniques such as montage, direct address, and multilayered narration to construct a shared identity that would fit more readily into the federal government's framework for addressing inequality, he also employs experimental techniques to explore tensions within the Latino community and express the urgency of communication between and within racial groups.

### FILMOGRAPHY

The film discussed in this chapter can be streamed through the book's web page at https://www.dukeupress.edu/Features/Screening-Race.

*Voice of La Raza* (1971), 53 min., 16mm
PRODUCTION: Equal Employment Opportunity Commission and William Greaves Productions. DIRECTOR: William Greaves. WRITERS: William Greaves, Jose Garcia. CAMERA: Jose Garcia, William Greaves. ASSISTANT CAMERA: Steve Garcia, Bill Johnson. MUSIC: Vicente Saucedo. EDITORS: John Dandre, William Greaves. SOUND CREW: David Greaves, Ned Judd, Juan Rodriguez. UNIT MANAGER: Bob Gonzalez. PROJECT SUPERVISOR: Olivia Stanford. CAST: Anthony Quinn, Rita Moreno. ACCESS: Texas Archive of the Moving Image.

### RELATED FILMS

*The EEOC Story* (1970), 38 min.
PRODUCTION: Equal Employment Opportunity Commission and William Greaves Productions.

*In the Company of Men* (1969), 52 min.
PRODUCTION: Newsweek and William Greaves Productions.

*Power vs. the People* (1970), 36 min.
PRODUCTION: Equal Employment Opportunity Commission and William Greaves Productions.

*Still a Brother: Inside the Negro Middle Class* (1968), 90 min.
PRODUCTION: National Educational Television and William Greaves Productions.

*Struggle for Los Trabajos* (1970), 35 min.
PRODUCTION: Equal Employment Opportunity Commission and William Greaves Productions.

*Symbiopsychotaxiplasm* (1968), 75 min.
PRODUCTION: William Greaves Productions.

NOTES

1   "Actor Quinn, Adler May Hoist Banner of Minority Group," *Albuquerque Journal*, November 21, 1970, A14.
2   The film's release date has been cited as 1972, but the film was finished and had been screened by the spring of 1971. The film is available on a number of websites including Texas Archive of the Moving Image, http://www.texasarchive.org/library /index.php/Voice_of_La_Raza, and is listed on the William Greaves Productions website as available for purchase, http://www.williamgreaves.com/catalog.htm.
3   Surprisingly, García Torres, an active documentarian in the 1960s and 1970s and producer of the WNET public affairs program *Realidades*, has received scant scholarly attention. He is mentioned in overviews of New York–based Puerto Rican filmmakers by Chon Noriega in *Shot in America: Television, the State, and the Rise of Chicano Cinema* (Minneapolis: University of Minnesota Press, 1993), 150–51; and Lillian Jiménez, "From the Margin to the Center: Puerto Rican Cinema in New York," *Centro de Estudios Puertorriqueños Bulletin* 2, no. 8 (spring 1990): 28–43.
4   "Actor Honored for Battling Discrimination," *Progress-Index* (Petersburg, VA), May 22, 1971, 12. Television listings in local papers indicate that the film was shown by Los Angeles station KTTV (Channel 11) in the greater Southern California area and subsequently, presumably via cable broadcast of KTTV programming, in Illinois, Northern California, New Mexico, Arizona, Colorado, and even Pennsylvania. See, for example, *Redlands Daily Facts*, July 22 1972, 6; *Pomona Progress Bulletin*, July 23, 1972, 9; *San Antonio Light*, March 12, 1972, 28; *Oxnard Press Courier*, July 23, 1972, 11; and *Newsday*, August 20, 1972, E35.
5   "Black Producer's Film about Chicanos a Winner," *Los Angeles Sentinel*, July 15, 1971, B2A; "Anthony Quinn in Movie," *New York Amsterdam News*, September 25, 1971, B9; and "Greaves Nominated Thrice," *Back Stage*, December 15, 1972, 7.
6   "Awareness Workshop Set in TF," *Times-News* (Twin Falls, ID), March 28, 1973, 2; "Hispanic Week," *Press-Courier* (Oxnard, CA), September 11, 1972, 8; "Cinco de Mayo Films," *Arcadia Tribune* (Arcadia, CA), May 5, 1974; "Activities Slated for Hispanic Week," *Press-Courier*, September 11, 1972, 8; and "Hispanic Film Set at Library," *Colorado Springs Gazette Telegraph*, September 13, 1975.

7 See Charles Ramirez Berg, *Latino Images in Film: Stereotypes, Subversion, Resistance* (Austin: University of Texas Press, 2002); Noriega, *Shot in America*; and Rosa Linda Fregoso, *The Bronze Screen: Chicana and Chicano Film Culture* (Minneapolis: University of Minnesota Press, 1993). It is rare to find sustained treatment of specific documentary films from the 1960s and '70s beyond a handful of key film texts such as *Requiem 29* (Raul Ruiz and David García, 1971); *Yo soy Joaquín* (Luis Valdez, 1969); and *Chicana* (Sylvia Morales, 1979).

8 In a 1963 catalog of government films available for public use, only one film from 1947 touched on the topic of race relations. That film was listed under three different headings: Discrimination, Minorities, and Race Problems. U.S. Department of Health, Education, and Welfare, Office of Education, *US Government Films for Public Educational Use 1963*, OE-34006-63, Circular No. 742 (Washington, DC: U.S. Government Printing Office, 1964). Richard Dyer McCann notes only two examples of films with a focus on race in *The People's Films: A Political History of U.S. Government Motion Pictures* (New York: Hastings House, 1973), 55 and 192.

9 U.S. Congress, Senate Subcommittee on Departments of State, Justice, Commerce, the Judiciary and Related Agencies, Hearings before a Subcommittee on Appropriations, 92d Congress, 1st sess., 438.

10 On the African American civil rights movement and television, see, for example, Aniko Bodroghkozy, *Equal Time: Television and the Civil Rights Movement* (Champaign: University of Illinois Press, 2012); Steven Classen, *Watching Jim Crow* (Durham, NC: Duke University Press, 2004); and Sasha Torres, *Black, White, and in Color: Television and Black Civil Rights* (Princeton, NJ: Princeton University Press, 2003).

11 For a general account of Greaves's life and career, see Noelle Griffis, "'This Film Is a Rebellion!': Filmmaker, Actor, *Black Journal* Producer, and Political Activist (1924–2014)," *Black Camera* 6, no. 2 (spring 2015): 7–16; Adam Knee and Charles Musser, "William Greaves, Documentary Film-Making, and the African-American Experience," *Film Quarterly* 45, no. 3 (spring 1992): 13–25; Kay Eastman and Brenna Sanchez, "Greaves, William 1926–2014," in *Contemporary Black Biography*, vol. 123, ed. Margaret Mazurkiewicz (Farmington Hills, MI: Gale, 2015), 66–69; and Steven Otfinoski, "Greaves, William," in *African Americans in the Visual Arts* (New York: Facts on File, 2011), 88–90.

12 Rick Prelinger, *The Field Guide to Sponsored Films* (San Francisco: National Film Preservation Foundation, 2006), vii.

13 On the United States Information Agency's development of its film production program in the 1960s, see Sonke Kunkel, *Empire of Pictures: Global Media and the 1960s Remaking of American Foreign Policy* (Oxford: Berghahn, 2016), 45–46. Letter from William Greaves to Hon. Joseph P. Addabbo, April 17, 1981, reprinted in *Hearings before the Subcommittee on SBA and SBIC Authority, Minority Enterprise and General Small Business Problems, Washington DC May 21; June 4 and 10, 1981* (Washington, DC: U.S. Government Printing Office, 1981), 71.

14 See Lillian Jiménez, "Puerto Rican Cinema in New York: From the Margin to the Center," *Jump Cut*, no. 38 (June 1993): 60–66; and Noriega, *Shot in America*, 150–52.

15 *Jet* magazine claimed that Stanford was "the leading force in Greaves' firm winning the unusual contract to produce the film [*Voice of La Raza*]." "Ex-TV Producer, Anthony Quinn Team in Job Bias Film," *Jet*, June 10, 1971, 52. In the Virgin Islands, Stanford's adopted home to which she returned in 1971, the local newspaper gave her production credit for *Voice of La Raza* and other unnamed films, including television spots. "Local Director's Film Deals with Prejudice," *Virgin Islands Daily News*, June 12, 1971.

16 U.S. Congress, House, *An Act to Amend the Small Business Act of 1953*, 15 U.S.C. 631 et seq.; 72 Stat. 384 et seq. Public Law 85–536, 384, 85th Congress, 1st sess., July 8, 1958.

17 G. Cristina Mora, *Making Hispanics: How Activists, Bureaucrats, and Media Constructed a New American* (Chicago: University of Chicago Press, 2014), 46.

18 These descriptions are drawn from an appendix attached to a 1988 hearing and William Greaves Productions' list of films. *The EEOC's Performance in Enforcing the Age Discrimination in Employment Act: Hearing before the Special Committee on Aging*, U.S. Senate, 100th Congress, 2d sess., Washington, DC, June 23, 24, 1988 (Washington, DC: U.S. Government Printing Office, 1989), 510–11. *Voice of La Raza* cost $87,000 to produce. *Departments of State, Justice, and Commerce, the Judiciary and Related Agencies Appropriations for 1973 Part 4* (Washington, DC: U.S. Government Printing Office, 1972), 857.

19 For an overview of the historiography on the diverse manifestations of the movement, see Mario T. Garcia, ed., *The Chicano Movement: Perspectives from the Twenty-First Century* (New York: Routledge, 2014).

20 Dennis López, "Good-Bye Revolution—Hello Cultural Mystique: Quinto Sol Publications and Chicano Literary Nationalism," *MELUS* 35, no. 3 (fall 2010): 198. See the primary sources collected in Darrel Enck-Wanzer, *The Young Lords: A Reader* (New York: New York University Press, 2010). On media representations in particular, see Lillian Jiménez, "Moving from the Margin to the Center: Puerto Rican Cinema in New York," in *The Ethnic Eye: Latino Media Arts*, ed. Chon A. Noriega and Ana M. López (Minneapolis: University of Minnesota Press, 1996), 22–37.

21 "Greaves Film Cops 2nd Festival Nod," *Afro-American*, September 25, 1971, 9.

22 Bill Nichols, "The Voice of Documentary," in *The Documentary Film Reader: History, Theory, Criticism*, ed. Jonathan Kahana (New York: Oxford University Press, 2016), 640.

23 Anthony Quinn Script Collection, California State University Northridge, Special Collections, box 41, folder 16. Among his papers are numerous reports and pamphlets regarding Chicano land rights claims and activism in New Mexico, the EEOC's hearing on discrimination in the film industry, and the Chicano movement in Los Angeles.

24 "Actor Quinn, Adler May Hoist Banner."

25 Rafael Pérez-Torres notes that for Latinos (Chicano/as in his analysis), "ethnic identity can be tied to linguistic skills." Rafael Pérez-Torres, "Chicano Ethnicity, Cultural Hybridity, and the Mestizo Voice," *American Literature* 70, no. 1 (March 1998): 155.

26 Mora, *Making Hispanics*, 49.

27 Maria San Filippo, "What a Long, Strange Trip It's Been: William Greaves' 'Symbiopsychotaxiplasm': Take One," *Film History* 13, no. 2 (January 2001): 217. On the relationship between psychodrama and Method acting in the 1950s and '60s, see Shonni Enelow, *Method Acting and Its Discontents* (Evanston, IL: Northwestern University Press, 2015). She devotes the last chapter to *Symbiopsychotaxiplasm*.

28 *Symbiopsychotaxiplasm* has received a great deal of scholarly attention since its wide release in 2001 and the release of a Criterion Collection DVD in 2006. Insightful readings of the film's relationship to jazz can be found in Akiva Gottlieb, "'Just Another Word for Jazz': The Signifying Auteur in William Greaves's Symbiopsychotaxiplasm: Take One," *Black Camera* 5, no. 1 (October 2013): 164–83; and Charles P. Linscott, "In a (Not So) Silent Way: Listening Past Black Visuality in Symbiopsychotaxiplasm," *Black Camera* 8, no. 1 (October 2016): 169–90.

29 William Greaves, "100 Madison Avenues Will Be of No Help," *New York Times*, August 9, 1970, 13.

30 Randy Ontiveros, "No Golden Age: Television News and the Chicano Civil Rights Movement," *American Quarterly* 62, no. 4 (December 2010): 908.

31 Ángel G. Flores-Rodríguez describes the way that mainstream media portrayed the Young Lords in Chicago as "an undisciplined street gang." Ángel G. Flores-Rodríguez, "On National Turf: The Rise of the Young Lords Organization and Its Struggle for the Nation in Chicago," *Op. Cit.*, no. 20 (2011–12): 136.

32 Francisco X. Camplis, "Towards a Raza Cinema," in *Chicanos and Film: Representation and Resistance*, ed. Chon Noriega (Minneapolis: University of Minnesota Press, 1992), 297.

## 16

## An Aesthetics of Multiculturalism

Asian American Assimilation
and the Learning Corporation of
America's *Many Americans* Series (1970–1982)

NADINE CHAN

From the early 1970s to the early 1980s, the Learning Corporation of America (LCA) produced a ten-part series, *Many Americans*, aimed at promoting intercultural understanding in the classroom and beyond. As a subsidiary of Columbia Pictures, the LCA produced some of the most insightful and timely social education films for both the classroom and television during the company's existence from 1968 to the mid-1980s. These short films on controversial subjects such as race and immigration were intended to help educators manage new demands for diversity in youth education. Films in the LCA's *Many Americans* series range from twelve to twenty-eight minutes and feature an immigrant, racial, or ethnic minority child and his or her attempts at navigating the challenges of everyday life. Of the ten films in the series, half were about new immigrant families and their struggles with racial discrimination, societal expectations, learning the English language, and economic survival. As suggested by the title of the series, these dramatic narrative shorts brought the stories of America's marginalized peoples to the screen in an effort to redefine a national imaginary based on the promising idea of an inclusive multiculturalism.

The *Many Americans* series was part of a larger movement advocating for film's usefulness in educating American youth about multiculturalism in the 1970s and '80s. Following the civil rights movement, changes in immigration policy, the Vietnam War, and other events that marked dramatic shifts in America's racial politics, many educational film companies began producing ethnic-conscious films aimed at helping teachers address the need for multicultural awareness in the curriculum. Recent scholarship has observed the centrality of race relations in postwar educational films and vice versa, focusing particularly on African American and Anglo American integration following the 1954 *Brown v. Board of Education* decision to abolish racial segregation in public schools and the 1964 Civil Rights Act.[1] While the politics of black-white integration and civil rights certainly initiated the move toward civic education in the 1950s and '60s, teaching ethnic consciousness in the decades that followed increasingly meant rethinking the boundaries of what and who would be considered American in the first place. Ongoing immigration crises (as they were repeatedly called throughout the history of nonwhite immigration to the U.S.) not only raised concerns about racial integration but also elicited anxieties about the very notion of an authentic American identity. As more new immigrants began partaking in public culture, Americans were faced with hard questions about what modern American society ought to look like.

A study of how the politics of immigration were entangled with those of film deepens and extends our understanding about how the educational film industry responded to shifting racisms and mutable structures of racial exclusion. Focusing on the LCA's *Many Americans* series, this chapter demonstrates how the educational film industry in the 1970s and '80s was attuned to changes in immigration policy during a transformative period in U.S. ethnic politics. This chapter begins by situating the 1960s educational film industry amid a broader marketplace of Cold War cultural politics, paying particular attention to the crisis of national identity caused by the new wave of non-European immigration that followed the 1965 Immigration and Nationality Act and the 1975 Indochina Migration and Refugee Assistance Act. The representation of multiethnic citizens in educational films was the direct result of new markets for multiracial education that emerged from Cold War federal grants and nationwide policies intent on furthering visions of American democracy. The camera's ability to capture the ethnoscapes of America's multiple ethnic groups, combined with the wider availability of projectors in schools and a developed system of educational film distribution, allowed nontheatrical films to render nonwhite America visible.

While the *Many Americans* series sought to teach multiculturalism, racial equality, and diversity, a closer look at how multiculturalism was aestheticized in its films brings out ideological frictions about assimilation and the place of nonwhite immigrants in the new American citizenry. The second part of this chapter discusses *Siu Mei Wong: Who Shall I Be?* (1970) as an example of how film aesthetics were entangled with Asian American immigration politics and Cold War progressivism in the 1970s. The film's hybrid style and deeply humanist narrative questioned the singularity of American identity even as it upheld problematic racializations of Asians in America. Indeed, while the cinematic apparatus enabled the visual projection of America's multiple races and ethnicities, its outcomes were as fraught as contemporary understandings of what it meant to be multicultural. Even as the educational film industry met strong support for the production of films that taught intercultural understanding, unresolved debates about the place of assimilation amid shifting ideas of Americanness produced an aesthetics of multiculturalism that existed in tension between ideas of desirable difference versus cultural essentialism, and shared identity versus the erasure of cultural histories.

## Race, Immigration, and the Flourishing of the Educational Film Industry

Geoff Alexander describes the period from 1961 to 1985 as educational film's "golden era," in terms of the expansion of the industry as well as the improvement of the quality of the films themselves.[2] A series of federal-level policy shifts directing funds to educational institutions for the development of learning aids, instructional materials, and curricula and the purchasing of audiovisual material by schools provided a boost for a struggling industry.[3] The National Defense Education Act of 1958 and the Elementary and Secondary School Education Act of 1965 were instrumental in providing the funds for schools to purchase audiovisual equipment, establish libraries for films, and develop educational programming that grew the market for educational films in schools.[4] The passage of this legislation coincided with civil rights and post-1965 immigration, resulting in a growing market for classroom films for multiethnic education.

Evolving policies on immigration played a large role in the push toward reformulations of the curriculum to include diverse histories as part of American cultural knowledge. The 1965 Immigration and Nationality Act was a major turning point in the history of nonwhite immigration to the U.S. because it marked the abolition of racial quotas and national origin preferences that favored Europeans; instead, visas were made available on the basis of American labor needs and family relations. Where early periods of immigration were characterized by immigration from Europe, post-1965 immigration was ostensibly marked by a majority of new immigrants coming from Asia, Latin America, and the Caribbean. The 1975 Indochina Migration and Refugee Assistance Act further initiated a new wave of immigration from Southeast Asia and designated Vietnamese, Cambodian, and, later, Lao and Hmong peoples as refugees to be resettled in the U.S.[5] Post-1965 immigration dramatically altered the racial and ethnic diversity of the country.[6]

Meanwhile, the government supported educational reforms that endorsed multiculturalism and racial harmony. It was politically expedient to disseminate positive stories about race and U.S. democracy to combat Soviet Cold War accusations about racist practices in America.[7] Early moves toward ethnic-conscious programming in the curriculum had emerged after the 1954 *Brown v. Board of Education* decision led to school desegregation.[8] Title VI of the Civil Rights Act of 1964 further prohibited "discrimination on the basis of race, color, and national origin in programs and activities receiving federal financial assistance," thus putting pressure on school districts to demonstrate that desegregation measures were being undertaken.[9] The emergence of the field of multiethnic education in the 1960s and the anti-assimilationist ethnic studies movement led to calls for educational material that included minority histories to be part of the school curriculum. Early advocates railed against the absent or stereotypical representations of racial minorities in textbooks and called for more accurate and positive portrayals of racial minorities.[10] Eventually, multiethnic education broadened to encompass ethnic groups that were not racial minorities, such as Appalachian Americans, as well as immigrants and groups of different national origin, social class, gender, and sexuality—thereafter becoming known as "multicultural education."[11]

Studies emerged on how film and media could enhance a multicultural education. Researchers found that PBS's *Sesame Street* had a positive effect on the racial attitudes of children who watched it for long periods.[12] Educators believed that film enabled viewers to "experience intercultural contact with [their] eyes and ears," thus helping students develop empathy and understanding across racial lines and for characters with whom they would otherwise have little in common.[13] Teachers were also in need of classroom aids to address topics on discrimination, racism, and segregation that many felt unequipped or uncomfortable talking about.[14] Instructors unaccustomed to teaching in a multiethnic classroom were encouraged to learn from and teach with films and audiovisual material on diverse ethnic groups.[15] As educators from K–12 schools, universities, and other educational institutions turned to film as an ideal medium for multicultural education, a new market for educational films that featured ethnic minorities flourished in the 1970s.

Whereas in the 1950s, films that confronted issues of race and prejudice were implicitly addressed to a white audience, later decades also saw a new market emerge for films intended for nonwhite or mixed-group audiences.[16] This was particularly the case for new cohorts of first-generation immigrant youths who would have attended schools in mixed-race and multilanguage neighborhoods. For example, the LCA catalog marketed *Overture: Linh from Vietnam* (1981), a story about the intercultural conflict between a new Vietnamese immigrant family and a Mexican American community, as "especially useful in schools with multi-racial students, and of interest to church and community groups sponsoring immigrants or working with resettlement programs."[17] *Overture* and *Welcome to Miami, Cubanos* (1981) reflected the need for teaching materials that addressed racism and interracial tension between and within immigrant, nonwhite communities. The Bilingual Education Act of 1968, which enabled school districts to fund bilingual education programs with federal funds, allowed students to study in native languages such as Spanish or Chinese, thus calling for films that featured nonnative English speakers.

Federal support for films on multicultural education alongside these emerging markets had a significant effect on an industry that had traditionally been rather conservative.[18] Elementary and Secondary School Education Act funding, in particular, enabled educational film production companies to have bigger budgets that allowed for greater artistic creativity, professional actors, better sets, and multiple cameras.[19] Joining this new rush to create film content, in 1969 Columbia Pictures started the Learning Corporation of America as a subsidiary company. Under the direction of President William F. Deneen and Senior Vice President Linda Gottlieb, the LCA produced and distributed films that seized upon the cultural shifts that were gripping the field of education.

The culturally diversifying landscape of America became a major theme for many of the LCA's works.[20] Films from the LCA's *Learning to be Human* and *Searching for Values* series addressed aspects of ethnic and socioeconomic diversity. In the *Many Americans* series, the constellation of nonwhite characters brought the sensitive subject of racism and immigration to the screen. *Siu Mei Wong: Who Shall I Be?*, *Felipa: North of the Border* (1971), *Miguel: Up from Puerto Rico* (1970), *Overture: Linh from Vietnam*, and *Welcome to Miami, Cubanos* (1981) explicitly addressed the topic of immigration from Asia and Latin America. Synopses of the films in the LCA's catalogs emphasized how the *Many Americans* series aspired to help the viewer understand the emotional conflicts that young people from minority or immigrant families face. The catalog description for *Geronimo Jones* (1970), for instance, asks viewers to think about "How . . . an Indian boy feel[s] when he sees himself stereotyped by white America."[21] The LCA eventually became known as one of the most reputable producers of educational sociodramas.[22]

The LCA made its films and services easily available to schools and institutions through film libraries and from its nationwide regional offices. The broader audience for the *Many Americans* series were school-going youths of all ethnicities and socioeconomic groups from elementary school to junior high. Reviews in multiple town newspapers indicate that LCA films also traveled across the country, screening at school events, media fairs, and church gatherings.[23] Meanwhile, U.S. television sought to tell a story of "moderate racial progress" and "color-blind equality."[24] Alongside this move was the rise of public expectation that children's programming on network television had a cultural responsibility to represent America's racially diverse society. Nickelodeon, for example, was criticized by the *New York Times* for not featuring a show "with an ethnic focus."[25] The LCA's ability to produce multicultural and socially responsible content for television added to the company's reputation as "probably the most respected producer of young people's programs in the nation."[26]

The LCA also attempted to cultivate a culture of engagement around thorny issues of race and immigration. Study guides included in film cans helped teachers generate classroom discussions on race. Containing a summary of the film, stating lesson objectives, suggesting questions for discussion, and outlining postscreening activities such as role-plays and research projects, these guides positioned the films as avenues to discussion about race and American identity. For example, postscreening activities for *Angel and Big Joe* (1975)—which tells the story of a fifteen-year-old son of migrant laborers of Mexican and Puerto Rican descent—encouraged students to imagine themselves as migrant workers whose parents lose their jobs, or to consider how privileges such as unemployment benefits are denied to segments of the labor population. Rather than didactic talking heads, the films sought to bring perspectives of what it means to be American up for debate by capturing a day in the life of America's ethnic minorities "with sensitive photography, and with a minimum of dialogue in whatever language would naturally be used."[27]

Throughout the twentieth century, American citizens were defined against Asian immigrants.[28] As Lisa Lowe points out, the figure of the Asian immigrant "has served as a 'screen,' a phantasmatic site, on which the nation projects a series of condensed, complicated anxieties" that have to do with perceived threats to the symbolic whole of the nation.[29] Until the 1965 act, Asian immigration policies were shaped by beliefs that Asians were unable to assimilate and that the U.S. should limit the entry of Asians into the country.[30] Historical constructions of Asian Americans as "perpetual foreigners within"—linguistically, culturally, and racially outside of the national polity and yet ever present within America's workplaces—indicate the fundamental contradiction of nonwhite immigrants in the national imaginary, of being both "foreign" and "within."[31] The Asian American figure thus functions as a critical site where new ideas of American multiculturalism that celebrated racial, ethnic, and cultural diversity competed with long-held notions of assimilation as an inevitable (and desirable) outcome of immigration.

The racial formation of Asian Americans in the *Many Americans* series illustrates how educational films aestheticized and narrated state discourses of assimilation and alien citizenship amid turbulent ideas of what multiculturalism ought to look like in an era of widespread nonwhite immigration. *Siu Mei Wong: Who Shall I Be?* addresses the new wave of Asian immigration that followed the 1965 Immigration and Nationality Act. In the film, young Siu Mei Wong dreams of becoming a ballet dancer but is held back from pursuing her dream by her father, who insists that she attend Chinese language classes instead. Through a particular aesthetics of assimilation, the film delineates Chinese spaces as distinct from American ones and parses out Chinese values against American ideals through the use of repeated visual and stylistic binarisms that cast assimilation as the only way to become American.

Shot on location in Los Angeles, the film's opening is an ode to the American Chinatown, introducing the viewer to what is marked as a clearly ethnicized space. The first shot is of a rotating sign for the 76 gas station on Union Street: on one side of the spherical lantern, the words "seventy-six" are printed in Chinese characters; on the other, "76 Union" is written in English. This opening shot introduces the thematic binarisms that continue through the film—the supposedly incompatible existence of Siu Mei's immigrant Chinese heritage and her American identity, Cantonese and English, Chinese school and dance, the old ways and the new.

FIGURES 16.1–16.2. A rotating spherical lantern features English and Chinese characters on opposite faces. *Siu Mei Wong: Who Shall I Be?* (Michael Ahnemann, Learning Corporation of America, 1970). Frame enlargements courtesy of USC Hugh M. Hefner Moving Image Archive.

FIGURE 16.3. A shot of a desolate alley in Chinatown captures the austerity of immigrant life. *Siu Mei Wong: Who Shall I Be?* (Michael Ahnemann, Learning Corporation of America, 1970). Frame enlargement courtesy of usc Hugh M. Hefner Moving Image Archive.

From the very outset, Siu Mei's inevitable assimilation into Americanness is aestheticized through Michael Ahnemann's eye for documentary realism in his depiction of a declining Chinatown. Ahnemann had established himself as a documentary film producer with the United States Information Agency in the 1960s, directing the Academy Award–nominated short documentary *Cowboys* (1966). Los Angeles's Chinatown is pictured through scenes of industrial decay peppered with kitschy signifiers of Orientalism. Static shots of graphic shapes cast by deserted storefronts, a smoggy skyline, and littered alleys are juxtaposed with ornamented friezes and pagoda-styled rooftops against a stripped-down ambient soundtrack of birds chirping and dogs barking. The filmmaker's almost fetishistic preoccupation with Oriental architecture emphasizes the cultural and linguistic liminality of Chinatowns as alien spaces at the heart of American cities—a reference to the trope of the outsider within. In the contemporary public imaginary, they symbolized a space of lapsed assimilation and ethnic segregation that failed to accommodate Cold War ideas of acculturation.[32]

Along a littered and run-down alleyway, the camera pans up toward a window on the second floor, and Siu Mei Wong comes into view, her face caged inside the dilapidated building in which she lives. Like other films in the *Many Americans* series, *Siu Mei Wong* was shot on location, using streets and homes of people from the community. The use of real locations and a narrative motivated by the everyday struggles of new Asian immigrants in the United States reflects the film's desire to capture an authentic account of the challenges faced by new Americans.

In Siu Mei's bedroom, pinups of Chinese models sit beside a *New Standard English-Chinese Dictionary* alongside images of a Caucasian and a Chinese ballerina—a montage that represents the competing elements in Siu Mei's life. Her cramped breakfast table is not shared by a prototypical nuclear family, but rather by an extended family that reflects the familial dynamics that arose from the 1965 Immigration and Nationality Act, which was also referred to as the Brothers and Sisters Act since immigrants and naturalized Americans could petition for relatives to enter the United States. Siu Mei's living room has been converted into the workspace, and the relentless and dull mechanical clatter of her father's sewing machine recurs to remind the viewer of the realities of their crowded home and low-income labor. The home space of Siu Mei's world is unadorned but cluttered by the everyday exigencies of immigrant life.

The film's dramatic tension is predicated on the notion that Chinese tradition clashes with the American pursuit of individual identity. Scholars in Asian American studies have observed the "essential separation of Asians from 'Americans,' a distinction buttressed by a belief system deeply ingrained in an American imaginary which insists on the fundamental difference of racialized peoples."[33] This incompatibility between Chineseness and Americanness is embodied through the primary source of conflict in the plot—when Siu Mei's father insists that she attend extracurricular Chinese language classes instead of ballet so that she learns to "be proud to be Chinese." Failing to understand her father's attachment to the world they left behind, Siu Mei protests, "We live in America now!"

Aesthetically, this tension is expressed through the film's juxtaposition of a primarily realist mode with surrealist fantasy whenever Siu Mei dreams about ballet. Approximately midway through the film is a one-and-a-half-minute scene where Siu Mei dances in a field (figure 16.4). Shot in slow motion with long dissolves between shots, the camera takes on an almost painterly quality in its meditative gaze on Siu Mei's dancing form. The scene interrupts the narrative of the film, presenting a moment of elevating, evanescent beauty. Emblematic of America as the land of opportunity, this scene expresses how dance transports Siu Mei from cultural obligation into a world of individual freedom. At Siu Mei's English-language school, in a classroom

FIGURE 16.4. Long dissolves and slow-motion shots of Siu-Mei's solo dance in a small field amid the industrial setting of Chinatown. *Siu Mei Wong: Who Shall I Be?* (Michael Ahnemann, Learning Corporation of America, 1970). Frame enlargement courtesy of USC Hugh M. Hefner Moving Image Archive.

with other Asian children, she is taught how to spell the words "government," "disregard," "society," and "humanity" as the visuals crosscut with a poster of a Chinese ballerina (figure 16.5). The scene reveals Siu Mei's inner desires to disregard her social obligations (and previous ethnic-national identities) to pursue the supposedly American values of individualism and opportunity. The juxtaposition of the American fantasy space in contrast with the realist immigrant domain is embedded in the social and cultural politics of ethnic exclusion—signifying the dualism between beauty/individualism/modern American values and reality/social obligation/traditional Chinese values that has historically defined discourse about Asian Americans.

The film suggests that Siu Mei's desire to take ballet instead of attending Chinese school does not mean that she disavows being Chinese. Siu Mei says proudly to her class that her dream is not to simply be a ballet dancer, but to be a "Chinese ballet dancer." Siu Mei's ballet class is attended primarily by young Asian girls, reinforcing that being Chinese and a ballet dancer are not mutually exclusive.

FIGURE 16.5. Poster of the Chinese ballerina that inspires Siu Mei. *Siu Mei Wong: Who Shall I Be?* (Michael Ahnemann, Learning Corporation of America, 1970). Frame enlargement courtesy of USC Hugh M. Hefner Moving Image Archive.

What the figure of the Chinese ballet dancer lays bare is not multiculturalism, but a politically expedient logic of assimilation that erases diverse ethnic or cultural practices but leaves behind biological racial difference as a marker of U.S. progressive inclusion. Nicholas De Genova describes assimilation "as that horizon at which 'the ethnic' ceases to be 'ethnic.'"[34] Attending Chinese school is too ethnic, not only a marker of racialization but one that suggests a willfulness to be distinct from Anglo Americans by continuing to embrace a language largely inaccessible to non-Chinese Americans. The space of the Chinese-language school—a space that Siu Mei's father associates with having pride in one's Chinese heritage—is depicted as exclusionary and impossible to assimilate into mainstream America. The racial homogeneity of the language class held at the Confucius temple is juxtaposed with an earlier scene from a racially diverse ballet studio. As Siu Mei recites her lines in Cantonese, she dreams of dark- and light-skinned legs in ballet shoes. The temple's gated fence and obscured windows contrast with the welcoming space of the ballet studio, where the African American teacher invites Siu Mei to join the class. In contrast to the foreign, unassimilable, and racially homogenous space of the Chinese school, the ballet school is depicted as appropriately American—marked by biological racial diversity yet permeated by white middle-class sensibility. Not only is ballet typically perceived as a Western genre of dance and thus racially neutralized by the invisibility of whiteness, Siu Mei's picture of the Chinese ballet dancer (figure 16.5) is legible as a ballerina first and as Asian second. Edmond, Siu Mei's classmate, misidentifies the image as "a picture of a ballet dancer," to which Siu Mei protests, "No! It is a picture of a *Chinese* ballet dancer." The significance of this moment lies precisely in Edmond's failure to recognize the dancer's Asianness. Edmond sees the cultural whiteness of the image while Siu Mei inscribes it with Chineseness—but one that is merely skin deep. Siu Mei's aspirations toward being an Asian ballet dancer indicates what the film presents as just the right kind of upwardly mobile, yet neutered, racial pride.

Siu Mei's experience speaks to what is and what is not considered within the limits of acceptable ethnic behavior in Cold War assimilationist logics. Stereotypes of the poorly assimilated Asian stoked fears of "bad Asians" loyal to communist regimes, as was particularly the case with Chinese Americans.[35] Cindy Cheng describes assimilation as "a discursive sign that operated in conjunction with Cold War civil rights to develop a narrative of progress"— modernity in Asian America was about the exhibition of happy assimilation and cultural naturalization.[36] While Mr. Wong initially resists his daughter's desire to give up Chinese class for ballet, he grudgingly relents by the end of the film. Read in this light, the film presents *Siu Mei Wong* as an assimilation story, wherein some aspect of the immigrant's original cultural practices or values are given up in exchange for a mainstream identity.

The film's treatment of assimilation, however, is not without criticism of its inevitability. Just after Siu Mei's father relents and gives her the go-ahead to study ballet, he pauses. A close-up of Mr. Wong's face lingers on silent and suppressed emotions that shadow his features. This shot registers the weight of Mr. Wong's decision, suggesting deep sadness and sacrifice. Though he remains inarticulate, this powerful moment of *photogénie* touches the surface of an interiority whose depths the audience cannot comprehend but whose weight is distinctly felt.[37] We have a sense that something has been lost, both across the father-daughter generation and in Siu Mei's abandonment of her ties to her Chinese heritage.

At the end of the film, we return to the shot of the lonely alleyway, the camerawork mirroring the same shot at the beginning of the film. This time, however, Siu Mei is missing from her bedroom. One might read this as her successful assimilation into the American mainstream, a literal freeing from

FIGURE 16.6. A close-up of Mr. Wong as he contemplates questions of assimilation and cultural identity. *Siu Mei Wong: Who Shall I Be?* (Michael Ahnemann, Learning Corporation of America, 1970). Frame enlargement courtesy of USC Hugh M. Hefner Moving Image Archive.

the racially marked space of her Chinatown home. However, Ahnemann's decision to mirror the camerawork that opens the film suggests emptiness rather than liberation. Rather than music, it is the sound of Mr. Wong's sewing machine that breaks the stillness. The closing shot of the film is not of Siu Mei but of Mr. Wong working away at his machine, his back to the camera, alone in his work: an elderly Chinese gentleman, sequestered in a dark apartment, excluded from mainstream America. Rather than triumphalism, the film ends on a note of quiet lament.

While assimilation is presented in the film as the inevitable trajectory of becoming American, the film's ambiguous ending troubles such a straightforward reading, pointing toward deeper cultural instabilities and discursive tensions about assimilation versus cultural diversity, and about ethnic plurality. Extrafilmic materials reveal that the LCA was engaged in a deliberate effort to generate classroom discussion around thorny questions of what it meant to be American in the 1970s. In the extension activities suggested in the accompanying study guide for *Siu Mei Wong*, students are asked to pretend to be Mr. Wong and to write Siu Mei a letter asking her to keep her Chinese heritage alive. Discussing the concept of assimilation, students are encouraged to think about how Siu Mei "want[ed] to be very American and forget her Chinese past" and why it is important to be proud of one's background.[38] Encouraging every student to see his or her own history as a history of immigration, viewers were also invited to think about why their own ancestors immigrated to the U.S. *Siu Mei Wong* and its study guide thus seek to present a troubled view of the idea of assimilation.

The politics in the film reflect the fraught transition from earlier twentieth-century models of assimilation toward ideas of multiculturalism in the 1970s and 1980s, when ethnoracial groups supported the idea that the U.S. ought to enable rather than erode the diversity of distinctive cultures. In the era's new multiculturalist model, the preservation of diverse cultures by their practitioners and their safe consumption by the rest of society (students were encouraged to visit a Chinese restaurant in Chinatown on Chinese New Year after watching *Siu Mei Wong*) presented modern American citizenship as a celebration of ethnocultural diversity.

While old-fashioned ideas of assimilation were supposedly being displaced by contemporary ideals of multiculturalism post-1965, immigrants were still configured in the public imaginary as undergoing Americanization, a process that involved shedding particular markers of ethnic and cultural identity while performing certain others. The LCA catalog's description for *Felipa: North of the Border*, for example, states that "the 'Americanization' of the Mexican immigrant is a daily struggle to master both a new culture and a new language."[39] Even as a new era of multiculturalism ushered in an appreciation of cultural diversity, the inescapable inscription of alienness upon nonwhite immigrant bodies contained them in a precarious state of inside/outsideness.

The conditions of American multiculturalism are then predicated on the synthetic hypervisibility of racial difference whitewashed of troubling notions of imperialism, structural inequality, and equal-opportunity activism. Erasing histories of continued U.S. colonialism, for instance, *Lee Suzuki: Home in Hawaii* (1973) features Hawai'i as a microcosm of an idealized multicultural America. Against shots of Honolulu's multiracial residents, young Lee introduces himself by describing his mixed-race heritage: "Just like a lot of people who live in Hawai'i, I'm only part Hawai'ian. I am also part Japanese, part Irish, part Filipino, and somewhere way back, part Swedish." Hawai'i's story of ethnic diversity, racial harmony, and successful Asian American integration was exemplary of Cold War American democracy, multiculturalism, and racial inclusion.[40] Just like Siu Mei, who is proud to be a Chinese ballet dancer but who gives up Chinese school and the language, one wonders if these articulations of American multiculturalism are, in Susan Koshy's words, "loose and free floating signifier[s] of Asian Americanness that lack any cultural density."[41]

The LCA's 1971 catalog asks the question, "What does a child have to give up to be 'American'?"[42] In the *Many Americans* series, Americanness is an elusive concept. Defining who is American enough and who falls short is an endeavor circumscribed by finely tuned cultural logics of labor, language, race, and national values that inscribe minorities within the precarious task of living up to ever-shifting ideas of cultural legitimacy. The fundamental contradiction of nonwhite immigrants in the Cold War national imaginary as both desirably different and yet in need of assimilation troubles the projection of American multiculturalism. Even as the educational film industry thrived on the push for the visual representation of a diverse American citizenry in the classroom, rendering what such a vision of multiculturalism would look like on film resulted in an aesthetic that was caught between the celebration of ethnic difference and its erasure.

FILMOGRAPHY

All available films discussed in this chapter can be streamed through the book's web page at https://www.dukeupress.edu/Features/Screening-Race.

*Felipa: North of the Border* (1970), 17 min., 16mm
DIRECTOR/WRITER: Bert Salzman. PRODUCTION: Bert Salzman Production. PRESENTED BY: Learning Corporation of America. EDITOR: John Schmerling, Dick Cadenas, Lebowitz Films. PHOTOGRAPHY: Paul Glickman. SOUND: Wes Scott. CAST: Phyllis Valencia, David Herrera, Francisco Soto, Dolores Jaurique. CONSULTANT: Howard Storm. ACCESS: University of Southern California (USC) Hugh M. Hefner Moving Image Archive.

*Geronimo Jones* (1970), 21 min., 16mm
DIRECTOR/WRITER: Bert Salzman. PRODUCTION: Robert J. Kaplan. EDITOR: John Schmerling. PRESENTED BY: Learning Corporation of America. MUSIC: Michael Shapiro. CAST: Martin Soto, Chief Feronimo Kuth-Li, Mel Todd. CONSULTANT: Howard Storm. ACCESS: USC Hugh M. Hefner Moving Image Archive.

*Lee Suzuki: Home in Hawaii* (1973), 19 min., 16mm
DIRECTOR/WRITER: Bert Salzman. PRODUCERS: Peter Funk, Lou Girolami. PRODUCTION: Oberon Communications, Inc. PRESENTED BY: Learning Corporation of America. EDITOR: Lebowitz Films. PHOTOGRAPHY: Peter Eco. SOUND: Philip Wilson. CAST: Francs Keb, Elaine Keb, Ted Fukushima, Willard Gray,

William Mitchell, Giboney Whyte. ACCESS: USC Hugh M. Hefner Moving Image Archive.

*Matthew Aliuk: Eskimo in Two Worlds* (1973), 18 min., 16mm
DIRECTOR/WRITER: Bert Salzman. PRODUCERS: Peter Funk, Lou Girolami. PRESENTED BY: Learning Corporation of America. PHOTOGRAPHY: William Hartigan. EDITOR: Lebowitz Films. MUSIC: Arlon Ober, Mel Zelniker. SOUND: Steven Glover. CAST: Tony Pushruk, Simon Pushruk, Thomas Pushruk, Helen Pushruk. ACCESS: USC Hugh M. Hefner Moving Image Archive.

*Miguel: Up from Puerto Rico* (1970), 15 min., 16mm
DIRECTOR/WRITER: Bert Salzman. PRODUCER: Lynne Littman. PRODUCTION: Bert Salzman Production. PRESENTED BY: Learning Corporation of America. EDITOR: Barry Prince. PHOTOGRAPHY: Paul Glickman. CAST: Kelvin Malave, Ramona Torres, Allen Garfield, Jose Torres, Richard S. Diaz. CONSULTANT: Ramón Arbona. ACCESS: USC Hugh M. Hefner Moving Image Archive.

*Overture: Linh from Vietnam* (1981), 26 min., 16mm
DIRECTOR/WRITER: Seth Pinsker. PRODUCER: Elaine Sperber. EXECUTIVE PRODUCER: Ronald MacDonald. CAST: Kim Ngan Ly, Panchito Gomez. PRESENTED BY: Learning Corporation of America. ACCESS: USC Hugh M. Hefner Moving Image Archive.

*Siu Mei Wong: Who Shall I Be?* (1970), 17 min., 16mm
DIRECTOR: Michael Ahnemann. ASSISTANT DIRECTOR: Sarah Sappington Kuhn. PRODUCTION: Michael Ahnemann Motion Pictures. PRESENTED BY: Learning Corporation of America. PHOTOGRAPHY: Caleb Deschanel. ASSISTANT CAMERA: Frank Lisciandro. SOUND: Eric Stacey. CONSULTANT: Herbert Leong. ACCESS: USC Hugh M. Hefner Moving Image Archive.

*Todd: Up from Appalachia* (1970), 12 min., 16mm
DIRECTOR/WRITER: Herman J. Engel. PRESENTED BY: Learning Corporation of America. PRODUCTION: Herman J. Engel Film Productions. PHOTOGRAPHER: William P. Steele. COLLABORATOR: Jon Henrikson. ACCESS: USC Hugh M. Hefner Moving Image Archive.

*Welcome to Miami, Cubanos* (1981), 28 min., 16mm
DIRECTOR: Peter Mark Schifter. PRODUCER: Elaine Halpert Sperber. WRITERS: Luis Santeiro, Michael Bonadies, Franklin Getchell. EDITING: Pamela S. Arnold. PHOTOGRAPHY: Marty Pitts. MUSIC: Jose Raul Bernado. CAST: Manny Rodriguez, Frank Perez, Teresa Rojas. PRESENTED BY: Learning Corporation of America. ACCESS: USC Hugh M. Hefner Moving Image Archive.

*William: From Georgia to Harlem* (1971), 17 min., 16mm
DIRECTOR AND WRITER: Hank Nadler. PRODUCTION: Hank Nadler Perspectives Films. ASSOCIATE PRODUCER: Annetta Nadler. CAMERA: William Montgonery. ASSISTANT CAMERA: Daniel Lerner. MUSIC: Arlon Ober. PRESENTED BY: Learning Corporation of America. CAST: Shelly King, Steven Isler, Cornel Berry Jr., Maurice

Williams. CONSULTANT: Beverley Griggsby. ACCESS: USC Hugh M. Hefner Moving Image Archive.

NOTES

Dino Everett, archivist for the USC Hugh M. Hefner Moving Image Archive, made titles in the *Many Americans* series available online. Geoff Alexander, director of the Academic Film Archive of North America, generously extended his knowledge and time. Cheryl Naruse provided feedback on an earlier draft.

1   Anna McCarthy, "Screen Culture and Group Discussion in Postwar Race Rela-tions," in *Learning with the Lights Off: Educational Films in the United States*, ed. Devin Orgeron, Marsha Orgeron, and Dan Streible (New York: Oxford University Press, 2012), 397–423; Marsha Orgeron, "'A Decent and Orderly Society': Race Relations in Riot-Era Educational Films, 1966–1970," in Orgeron, Orgeron, and Streible, *Learning with the Lights Off*, 424–41.
2   Geoff Alexander, *Academic Films for the Classroom* (Jefferson, NC: McFarland, 2010), 9.
3   Devin Orgeron, Marsha Orgeron, and Dan Streible, "A History of Learning with the Lights Off," in Orgeron, Orgeron, and Streible, *Learning with the Lights Off*, 48.
4   Alexander, *Academic Films for the Classroom*, 38–47; Anthony G. Picciano and Joel Spring, *The Great American Education-Industrial Complex: Ideology, Technology, and Profit* (New York: Routledge, 2013), 144–46.
5   By the end of 1975, 130,000 Southeast Asians, the vast majority of whom were Vietnamese, were given refuge in the U.S. From 1975 to 1980, an additional 433,000 refugees from Vietnam, Cambodia, and Laos arrived in the U.S. Erika Lee, *The Making of Asian America: A History* (New York: Simon and Schuster, 2015), 323–25.
6   In 1965, whites of European descent accounted for 84 percent of the U.S. popula-tion, with Hispanics accounting for 4 percent and Asians accounting for less than 1 percent. Fifty years later, 62 percent of the U.S. population was white, 18 percent was Hispanic, and 6 percent was Asian. Muzaffar Chishti, Faye Hipsman, and Isabel Ball, "Fifty Years On, the 1965 Immigration and Nationality Act Continues to Reshape the United States," in *Migration Information Source*, Migration Policy Institute, October 15, 2015, http://www.migrationpolicy.org/article/fifty-years-1965 -immigration-and-nationality-act-continues-reshape-united-states.
7   Cindy I-Fen Cheng, *Citizens of Asian America: Democracy and Race during the Cold War* (New York: New York University Press, 2013); Mary L. Dudziak, *Cold War Civil Rights: Race and the Image of American Democracy* (Princeton, NJ: Princeton University Press, 2000); Brenda Gayle Plummer, *Rising Wind: Black Americans and U.S. Foreign Affairs, 1935–1960* (Chapel Hill: University of North Carolina Press, 1996).
8   Widely broadcast staged discussions about racial integration helped parents and teachers handle desegregation in schools. McCarthy, "Screen Culture and Group Discussion."

9   Civil Rights Act of 1964, § 7, 42 U.S.C. § 2000e et seq (1964).

10  For a history of multicultural education, see Geneva Gay, "Promoting Equality through Multicultural Education," *Journal of Curriculum and Supervision* 19, no. 3 (spring 2004): 193–216.

11  "As an idea or concept, multicultural education maintains that all students should have equal opportunities to learn regardless of the racial, ethnic, social-class, or gender group to which they belong. Additionally, multicultural education describes ways in which some students are denied equal educational opportunities because of their racial, ethnic, social-class, or gender characteristics." James A. Banks, "Multicultural Education and Curriculum Transformation," *Journal of Negro Education* 64, no. 4 (autumn 1995): 391. For a brief study of the history of "multicultural education," see James A. Banks, "Multicultural Education: Historical Development, Dimensions, and Practice," *Review of Research in Education* 19 (1993): 3–49.

12  Samuel Ball and Gerry Ann Bogatz, *Summative Research of Sesame Street: Implications for the Study of Preschool-Aged Children* (Princeton, NJ: Educational Testing Service, 1971), 1–27.

13  Ellen Summerfield, *Crossing Cultures through Film* (Yarmouth, ME: Intercultural Press, 1993), 1.

14  Workshops that sought to get teachers to admit their own participation in a racist system were unpopular among white teachers. Christine E. Sleeter, *Multicultural Education as Social Activism* (Albany: State University of New York Press, 1996), 12.

15  Willie J. Barnes, "How to Improve Teacher Behavior in Multiethnic Classrooms," *Educational Leadership* 34 (April 1977): 515, Association for Supervision and Curriculum Development, http://www.ascd.org/ASCD/pdf/journals/ed_lead/el _197704_barnes.pdf.

16  Orgeron, "'A Decent and Orderly Society,'" 425.

17  "Building Relationships," in *Film Video: Stimulating the Mind's Eye* (New York: Learning Corporation of America, n.d. [ca. 1980]), 55.

18  Alexander, *Academic Films for the Classroom*, 44, 64.

19  For a history of the federal programs advancing the educational film industry, see Alexander, *Academic Films for the Classroom*, 38–46. See also Orgeron, "'A Decent and Orderly Society,'" 424.

20  Alexander, *Academic Films for the Classroom*, 46.

21  "The Many Americans," in *Films: A Catalog of Films for Schools, Colleges and Libraries* (New York: Learning Corporation of America, 1975), 89.

22  Geoffrey Alexander, *Films You Saw in School: A Critical Review of 1,153 Educational Films* (Jefferson, NC: McFarland, 2013), 224.

23  "First Part of Unique Film Series at Ogunquit," *Lewiston Evening Journal*, July 15, 1974, 3; "North Heights Set Media Fair," *Rome New Tribune*, October 10, 1971, 2E; "Beth Abraham Men Prepare First Program," *Lewiston Maine Daily Sun*, October 12, 1973, 8.

24  Aniko Bodroghkozy, *Equal Time: Television and the Civil Rights Movement* (Urbana: University of Illinois Press, 2012), 11–12.

25  Alexis Greene, "What Cable Offers Children," *New York Times*, April 25, 1982, 28.

26  "New Cable Services," *Southeast Missourian*, January 11, 1980, 2.

27  "The Many Americans," in *Films: 1971/72 Catalog of Films, Film Loops and Filmstrips for Schools, Colleges and Libraries* (New York: Learning Corporation of America, 1971), 25.

28  For more on Asian racial exclusion in American citizenship, see Lisa Lowe, *Immigrant Acts* (Durham, NC: Duke University Press, 1996).

29  Lowe, *Immigrant Acts*, 18.

30  These include the Naturalization Act of 1790, the Page Act of 1875, the Chinese Exclusion Act of 1882, the Gentleman's Agreement of 1907, the Immigration Act of 1917, the Emergency Immigration Act of 1921, the Immigration Act of 1924 (Asian Exclusion Act), the War Brides Act of 1945, and the Immigration and Nationality Act of 1952.

31  Lowe, *Immigrant Acts*, 8–10; see also Cheng, *Citizens of Asian America*, 13.

32  Cheng, *Citizens of Asian America*, 69.

33  David Palumbo-Liu, *Asian/American: Historical Crossings of a Racial Frontier* (Stanford, CA: Stanford University Press, 1999), 3.

34  Nicholas De Genova, *Race, Space, and "Illegality" in Mexican Chicago* (Durham, NC: Duke University Press, 2005), 84.

35  Lee, *The Making of Asian America*, 275–76.

36  Cheng, *Citizens of Asian America*, 12.

37  Jean Epstein, "On Certain Characteristics of *Photogénie*," reprinted in Richard Abel, *French Film Theory and Criticism, 1907–1939: A History/Anthology*, vol. 1, *1907–1929* (Princeton, NJ: Princeton University Press, 1988), 314–18.

38  "Siu Mei Wong: Who Shall I Be?," study guide (New York: Learning Corporation of America, 1970). Academic Film Archive of North America.

39  "The Many Americans" (1975), 89.

40  Angela Krattiger, "Hawai'i's Cold War: American Empire and the 50th State" (PhD diss., University of Hawai'i at Mānoa, 2013), 2–15.

41  Susan Koshy, "Fiction of Asian American Literature," in *Asian American Studies: A Reader*, ed. Jean Yu-Wen Shen Wu and Min Song (New Brunswick, NJ: Rutgers University Press, 2007), 481.

42  "The Many Americans" (1971), 25.

# 17

## "The Right Kind of Family"

Memories to Light and the Home Movie
as Racialized Technology

CRYSTAL MUN-HYE BAIK

In March 2013, the Center for Asian American Media (CAAM), a nonprofit organization based in the San Francisco Bay Area, launched Memories to Light, a project committed to the preservation and digitization of 8mm, 16mm, and Super 8mm films shot by Asian Americans between 1930 and 1980.[1] Through this project, CAAM makes available, for the first time, privately owned home movies to a virtual audience in and beyond the United States. Since its inception, Memories to Light has collected over two hundred reels of film from participants throughout California. While these accumulated home films are stored in the Internet Archive, a digital library open to the public, a selection of digitized home film collections are showcased on the Memories to Light website.[2]

An expansive project undertaken by CAAM, Memories to Light holds significant implications for scholars in film studies, visual culture studies, and ethnic studies. Specifically, the online presence of these digitized home films provides an accessible means to imagine the textured lives of Asian Americans during a period characterized by racial violence, exclusion, and loss. Between 1800 and the 1960s, Asian Americans were precluded from U.S. citizenship through policies and practices such as immigration exclusion acts, state surveillance, and internment.[3] Unsurprisingly, popular print media and commercial film produced throughout the twentieth century portrayed Asian Americans as foreign "Orientals" affiliated with disease, vice, and ill intent.[4] Epitomized by the silver screen's racialized caricatures of Fu

Manchu and the Dragon Lady—the former an archetype of criminal genius and the latter a hypersexualized villain most commonly associated with the indomitable Chinese American actress Anna May Wong—Asian Americans existed beyond the boundaries of normative American life, coded as white, male, and heterosexual. Memories to Light challenges these virulent depictions by offering "polyvocalities" in which "contradictions and disjunctures abound."[5] A project that, at the moment, includes an edited assemblage of home movies donated by thirty families (this number continues to grow), Memories to Light suggests the different ways in which Asian Americans survived precarious conditions and generated their own networks of social viability. For Stephen Gong, the executive director of CAAM, these early home films attest to "how we [Asians] became American, and how this process [of becoming American] happened."[6]

While Memories to Light's potential contributions to Asian American film scholarship are exciting to consider, it is also necessary to contemplate the curatorial decisions and remediation practices that inform the making of any public archive. Remediation, as defined by Jay David Bolter and Richard Grusin, refers to the different ways in which newer media (for instance, digital technologies) incorporate older media (such as analog footage) to produce a distinct media object (the digitized home film, in this particular case).[7] While commonly affiliated with processes such as preservation, remediation generates new inscriptions, particularly as source materials are edited, remixed, and contextualized through narrative tools such as captions and voice-overs. For example, the majority of films that currently constitute Memories to Light engage a scope of experiences historically associated with Chinese, Japanese, and Filipino/a communities in the United States. As evident through narrations provided by family members and CAAM's captions that accompany the edited compilations of home movies featured on the Memories to Light website, many film donors link their family genealogies to agricultural laborers who arrived in the United States or Hawai'i during the late nineteenth and early twentieth centuries before the implementation of more restrictive immigration policies.[8] The collection of films also suggests a particular rendering of Asian American life affixed to the suburban, heterosexual, and middle-class family. These signposts construct a recognizable narrative of the American Dream, in which immigrants, through sheer will, sacrifice, and hard work, are folded into a multicultural populace. Missing from the home movie archive, then, are portrayals of other lives that unsettle the paradigm of the intact nuclear family, including the experiences of queer diasporic subjects and Southeast Asian war refugees—most of whom arrived in the United States after 1975 and were preoccupied with a host of pressing matters, including daily survival. These patterns, of course, are not unique to Memories to Light, but, as I argue here, underlie the genre of the home film.

Informed by these insights, this chapter examines how Memories to Light, as a curated endeavor, remediates experiences coded as Asian American to a general audience.[9] Focusing on the home films selectively featured on the Memories to Light website, I articulate how this project reproduces and challenges a core set of conditions pivotal to the home movie's development as a racialized technology, or a "carefully crafted, historically inflected system of tools, mediation, or enframing that builds history and identity."[10] By mobilizing a range of curatorial tactics, including editing techniques, voice-over narrations, and the discourse of national belonging, Memories to Light accentuates the significance of shared racialized experiences. While these diegetic cues gesture to a singular understanding of normative American life, they also generate contradictions and meaningful opportunities to contend with long-standing assumptions that haunt the home movie, as genre and practice.

By foregrounding race as the central analytic, this chapter builds upon and departs from existing literature that attends to the home film in relation to identity formation.[11] In the past twenty years, a steadily growing body of scholarship has focused on the home film and amateur filmmaking (in which home film is a subcategory). Key texts include Patricia Zimmerman's social history of amateur filmmaking in the United States, Michelle Citron's study of the home film as a fictional practice, James Moran's scholarship addressing the specificity of the home video, an anthology of essays edited by Zimmerman and Karen L. Ishizuka, Haidee Wasson's work that explores film practices beyond the movie theater, and, more recently, cultural histories of amateur filmmaking by Charles Tepperman and Laura Rascaroli, Gwenda Young, and Barry Monahan.[12] Others, including Veena Hariharan, Julia Noordegraaf, and Elvira Louw, scrutinize home movies shot by European colonial administrators and white settlers to trace the striking similarities between these films and ethnographic depictions of the colonized other.[13] In Asian American studies, Ishizuka addresses the importance of amateur films shot by Japanese Americans in internment camps during World War II by describing such works as oppositional practices and acts of resistance, while the Chinese Trinidadian Canadian filmmaker Richard Fung draws on his family's film archive to tease out his parents' desire for normative domestic life in Trinidad.[14]

While this literature carefully attends to the home movie in relation to the messy vectors of identity formation, race is largely approached as a problematic or an additive concern that conditions the home movie, rather than as a fundamental and constitutive element. Even as postcolonial scholars such as Hariharan explore the engendering of the colonial film archive, it is the blurring of genres and "dominant bourgeois ideology"—or class—that emerge as key discursive frameworks.[15] Class, as a primary category of analysis, dominates much of the existing literature on the home film, especially as the home movie is commonly portrayed as an affordable alternative to professional filmmaking. With the invention of 16mm film in 1923, 8mm in 1935, and Super 8mm in 1965, film hobbyists were able to pursue amateur filmmaking. According to Zimmerman, the emergence of a do-it-yourself culture in the post–World War II moment, as well as the invention of graduated camera lines for a range of consumers, led to an increase in leisure-based activities, including home filmmaking.[16] Zimmerman links the emergence of home film practice throughout the 1950s and 1960s to the extension of credit to middle-class families, the coalescing of an American middle class, and the suburbanization of the domestic population.[17] Yet companies such as Bell and Howell and Kodak explicitly developed the home film apparatus for a specific audience in mind: white middle-class families.

Throughout much of the Cold War period, Ciné-Kodak endorsements that circulated in middlebrow magazines, such as the *American Home* and *Life*, depicted the white nuclear family as the primary consumer of home film technology. In these advertisements, white parents are portrayed as avid documentarians recording familiar moments associated with the home movie: family vacations, children's birthday parties, weddings, and casual gatherings that unfold within the soothing confines of the suburban home.[18] The fantasy of middle-class suburban life is inextricably linked to white heteronormativity, as most middle-class luxuries—including home ownership, automobiles, and access to amateur film equipment—remained beyond the means of, or were foreclosed to, communities of color.[19] For instance, in Los Angeles, San Francisco, Sacramento, Chicago, and Boston, redlining practices and racially restrictive covenants established by the Federal Housing Administration and the Home Owners' Loan Corporation precluded most families of color, including Asian Americans, from living in or purchasing homes in white suburbanized zones well into the 1970s.[20] The interlocking dynamisms of race and class undergird the "right [kind of] family" commonly evoked by the genre of the home film.[21]

In the remainder of this chapter, I explore three home movie collections included in the Memories to Light website to trace the home film archive's logics of racial identity formation and sentiments of (filial, community, and national) belonging: the films of the Gee, Tachibana, and Bohulano Mabalon families. Each home film collection, to differing degrees, demonstrates how racial asymmetries are reproduced, rather than wholly rejected or erased, by celebratory discourses of immigration and settlement. Simultaneously, while these narrative strategies point to the obtainment of the American Dream by families, the website's curatorial cues also hint at an accrual of costs that undermine the idealization of white middle-class status as a normative standard. In this way, this essay diverges from more recent home film scholarship, including Ishizuka's work, by tackling the maintenance of social hierarchies and racialized norms through liberal discourses of national citizenship, multiculturalism, and social mobility, rather than through explicit modes of racial violence, such as systems of colonial surveillance and wartime incarceration.[22]

Though I situate the home movie as a racialized technology, I do not subscribe to an oppositional schematic of power; that is, the home film is not merely a practice that solely conveys subaltern histories, nor does it only generate fictional accounts that stray far from the embodied experiences of the filmmaker and their filmed subjects. Rather, as differentiated sources that encompass multiple contradictions, home films and their remediated versions attune viewers to the complexity of everyday life—and the yearning for visibility and survival expressed by historical subjects deemed disposable to the formal project of national citizenship. In this way, Memories to Light is a significant initiative; as a scholar of Asian transnational visual cultures, I draw on these films to track the discursive tensions that emerge as we rely on source footage to piece together varied narratives of the past in the contemporary moment. If anything, a robust reading of Memories to Light emphasizes its ability to generate lively discussions that propel curators, scholars, and the public to reconsider the different interpretations produced by the home movie. My hope, therefore, is to generate new analytical frames that expand upon the ways we understand the home movie.

## Encountering Memories to Light

As acknowledged on its website, Memories to Light does not present an uncurated, unedited, or complete home movie record of CAAM's collection. Instead, CAAM partners with the Internet Archive to collect and restore select film reels.[23] It is important to note, however, that the digitized films stored in the Internet Archive are not unaltered. Rather, CAAM provides family members with the option of excising footage they do not want to share with the public, though such modifications are not indicated on the Memories to Light website or the Internet Archive. Consequently, the films featured in Memories to Light are always already filtered to the extent that both CAAM and family members determine what footage is available to the viewing public. These curatorial decisions suggest that online access to home movies is not necessarily indicative of film preservation.

On the Memories to Light website, the Home Movies section showcases several compiled films that feature edited footage donated by six families, including the Tachibana, Chin, Bohulano/Mabalon, Jung, Udo, and Gee families. In each of these compilations, edited segments of home footage are interlaced with voice-over narrations provided by the children and/or grandchildren of the presumed filmmaker(s), still images and family photographs, and originally composed music. For Davin Agatep, the project coordinator of Memories to Light, these diegetic markers are necessary for developing understandable story lines for the public, especially since home films often encompass hours of fuzzy footage that are comprehensible to only a handful of family members, or long shots of domestic interiors that are inscrutable to nonfamilial viewers.[24]

A five-minute compilation of home movies on the Memories to Light website featuring the Gee family nicely expounds upon the project's intentions. Narrated by Brian Gee, the son of Malcolm and Rufina Gee of Sacramento, the source footage from the 1970s is accompanied by the following caption: "The Gee family of Sacramento was your typical nuclear family living in Suburbia. Mom. Dad. Son. Daughter. Occasionally a pet fish. Dad worked for the government . . . Mom worked as a nurse at UC Davis. Son and Daughter studied hard, took piano lessons, enjoyed summer break playing in the back yard."[25] Brian's description of his family as a "typical nuclear family living in Suburbia" is reaffirmed by his description of home footage excerpts included in the promotional film. At the beginning of the film, an adolescent Brian is riding his bicycle. Flashing a toothy grin as he waves at the camera, Brian meanders through a spacious neighborhood lined with cars and trees. The footage is overlaid with the following commentary: "Growing up in Sacramento was just like watching the Brady Bunch." The string of "Brady Bunch-esque" moments invoked by the film include images of Brian with his younger sister in a wading pool, the rambunctious Gee siblings in Halloween costumes, and family vaca-

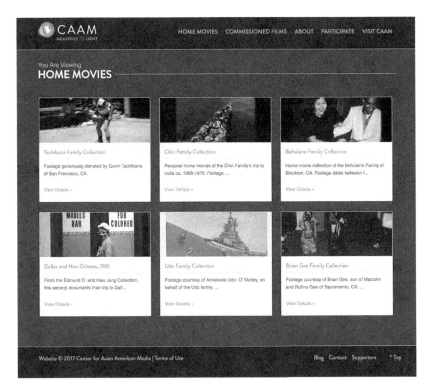

FIGURE 17.1. Memories to Light website Home Movies page. Courtesy of Center for Asian American Media.

tions taken at notable destinations such as Mount Rushmore and Yellowstone Park.

Through descriptions of his maternal grandfather's participation in the U.S. military and his parents' efforts to build a stable life for their children from meager resources, Brian's narration conveys a pull-yourself-up-by-the-bootstraps frame of mind. Such sentiments are best captured by an observation offered by Brian toward the conclusion of the film: "I think my family was living the American dream. . . . To me, the American dream is the equal opportunity to achieve a great life. No matter what social class you're born in, as long as you work hard, you'll be able to have a good life for yourself and a better life for your children."

While this narration seems to reproduce an oversimplified discourse of racial assimilation, juxtaposing these descriptions with more complicated insights offered by Brian destabilizes the Brady Bunch façade. In the beginning of the film, Brian provides the following observation of his childhood

FIGURE 17.2. Frame enlargement from Gee family home film depicting a family vacation at Mount Rushmore. Courtesy of Brian Gee and Center for Asian American Media.

neighborhood during the 1970s: "All of the stereotypes that you expect of suburbia was what we had, except . . . at least our neighborhood in Sacramento was one of the more diverse ones. Probably a third of the neighborhood was also Asian, so we didn't feel completely isolated." Brian's descriptions of his family's isolation and the racialized dynamics of his neighborhood allude to Sacramento's history of racial segregation, which continues to influence the city's housing market. According to sociologist Jesus Hernandez, entrenched practices endemic to all major metropolitan centers in the United States for much of the twentieth century, such as the valuation of property based on perceived race and mortgage redlining, produced cityscapes organized through the intersecting indices of race, ethnicity, and class.[26] In Sacramento, these practices generated concentrated pockets of low-income, predominantly Latino/a, African American, and Asian American neighborhoods in areas such as Del Paso Heights and North Franklin.[27] By 1970, zoning and housing policies produced a distinct racialized geography with

FIGURE 17.3. Frame enlargement from Gee family home film depicting a family vacation in Jackson Hole, Wyoming. Courtesy of Brian Gee and Center for Asian American Media.

wealthier white households occupying the eastern, midtown, and southwestern sections of Sacramento, while residents of color, including Gee's family, lived in the northern and western zones of the city.[28]

In another segment of the Gee family footage, Brian recounts a family road trip to the white settlement turned resort town of Jackson Hole, Wyoming. While Brian chronicles his mother's constant hankering for Chinese food during road trips to the main streets and rural towns across the United States, Brian and his toddler sister are shown sitting on top of an old buggy in Jackson Hole's well-preserved town square. Just adjacent to the buggy is a mannequin of a Chinese laborer, complete with a conical hat, seated at the wagon base with hands folded in a docile manner. Brian continues to describe his family's uneasy visit to what was then the only Chinese restaurant in the area for nearly a hundred miles: "Our server ended up being a white woman wearing a black wig and a Japanese kimono, and that should've given us a clue that something was awry." Brian's description of this racialized encounter, in which "Chinese" becomes interchangeable with "Japanese," emulates the ways in which the critical differences constitutive of Asian American communities are amalgamated, then erased, under the spectral figure of the Chinese indentured servant, or the "Oriental coolie."

What, then, do Brian's descriptions of his family footage tell us? In both of these excerpts, Brian's narration accentuates an array of racialized conditions and antagonistic experiences that underlie the historical making of Asian Americans as a political category. That is, if this archive of family footage, at first glance, produces impressions of suburban bliss and vertical movement across a social ladder, Brian's narration unhinges these assumptions by foregrounding the racialized vectors that condition inclusionary life in the United States. In that sense, the individuated image of the Gee's suburban home situated in a segregated neighborhood transforms into a metonym for the historical formation of a U.S. nation-home: the crucial role played by Asian immigrants and other sources of racialized labor in the consolidation of a hierarchical social order in the United States. This paradox points to what Lisa Lowe and Wendy Cheng describe as the motivating dynamics of racial capital, as certain populations in the United States, including Asian immigrants, are essential to the making of a national labor force but are simultaneously constructed as alien and other to an imagined community of national citizens.[29]

While the Gee family footage registers a disjuncture between surface imagery and the disconcerting conditions linked to the American suburban home, the Tachibana family films provide opportunities to sit with the entwined processes of remembering and forgetting that sustain racialized meanings of the identity categories Asian American and Japanese American. Narrated by Gavin, the son of Florence and Mason Tachibana, the three compilation films associated with the Tachibana family center on Gavin's upbringing in Southern California's South Bay and his childhood visits to his maternal grandparents' home in Hawai'i throughout the 1970s. From shots of Gavin roller-skating along the streets of his Torrance neighborhood to tender footage featuring a chubby Gavin with his grandfather, Masao Torigoe, the Tachibana family footage captures moments that Gavin is able to recall only through the rescreening of home footage: "I just don't have any memory of that . . . and to see it is just really striking. It's an incredible memory that's not even in my head."[30]

While home movies certainly function as mnemonic devices that bring forgotten experiences to the surface, the home film also intimates the excesses of memory—or the thick matrix of unspoken vestiges and present absences that dwell in the contemporary moment but resist visual representation. In some ways, these social residues are, as Eve Oishi suggests,

FIGURE 17.4. Frame enlargement from Tachibana family home film depicting Gavin Tachibana with Masao Torigoe. Courtesy of Gavin Tachibana and Center for Asian American Media.

indicative of the "guarded silence within families, as one generation holds on to its knowledge and secrets about the past."[31] But in a more pressing manner, we might theorize the home film as a cultural formation that facilitates the construction of oppositional memories. Subsequently, the home film produces a discursive gap insofar as certain memories are privileged over others. The home film, therefore, is not a repository of fixed memory, but actively recomposes layered memories as multiple audiences, situated in different times and cultural locales, struggle to make meaning of competing narratives. As Marita Sturken conceives of it, remembering inevitably entails a process of forgetting and the evacuation of other memories and interpretive renderings.[32]

This is a particularly important consideration for the Tachibana home films, as Gavin points to his family's history of dispossession and internment during World War II. On the Memories to Light website, Gavin provides the following caption of his family's source footage: "My dad, Mason, was born in Los Angeles to parents from Japan. In 1942, at the age of 7, he and his parents and five sisters were forced to relocate to Manzanar, the first of the ten concentration camps that incarcerated Japanese Americans during World

War II . . . Mason put himself through college at Cal State Northridge, then got his master's in social work at the University of Hawai'i in Mānoa."

While Gavin's decision to highlight this experience references the traumatic rupture produced by internment ("*forced* to relocate . . . to the first of the ten *concentration camps* that incarcerated Japanese Americans"), the compilation film and Gavin's voice-over do not depict this tumultuous period and its lingering aftereffects. In fact, a disjuncture emerges as the edited assemblage of home movies provides a different picture of daily life. In the voice-over, Gavin describes himself as an only child with an affinity for basketball, raised in a relatively comfortable home. While the digitized footage depicts an adolescent Gavin zipping down an asphalt court with a basketball in tow, Gavin half-jokingly describes his father's ambitions for his son as a potential basketball star and his parents' decision to name their son after Gavin Smith, a popular white UCLA basketball player.

What is most striking about Gavin's divergent narrations of the remediated footage, via his caption and voice-over, is how they index the irreconcilable social positions occupied by Japanese Americans before and immediately after World War II. In fact, while Gavin's descriptions vacillate between his father's terrifying war experiences and the pleasantries of suburban family life in Torrance, several questions come to mind: How did this radical shift happen and at what costs? As Japanese Americans were racialized from enemy residents to model minorities in the post–World War II era, which memories needed to be obscured in order for this transition to occur? These questions signify a greater discursive slippage that characterizes the postwar construction of everyday life and internment memories among Japanese Americans.

For Asian American film and media studies scholar Glen M. Mimura and filmmaker Rea Tajiri, the ramifications of wartime incarceration seep across temporal boundaries, as memories of war and detainment infiltrate the everyday lives of Japanese Americans born decades after the war.[33] Though a substantial number of Japanese American internees withheld their experiences of confinement from their children and grandchildren, such tortuous memories percolate through other means, including uncomfortable silences and unarticulated pain. As narrated by Tajiri in her film *History and Memory: For Akiko and Takashige*, these "secondhand" memories coagulate into a spectral presence that is sensed by younger Japanese Americans: "I remember having this feeling growing up—that I was haunted by something, that I was living in a family full of ghosts. There was this place they knew about. I had never been there, yet I had a memory for it."[34] Such anxieties do not merely indicate the limitations of formal redress. They also point to the ways in which intergenerational memories of family internment among Japanese Americans take unnamable forms, or a "sometimes dull, sometimes visceral feeling of *unknowing*—a psychical lack."[35] By taking stock of these observations, the Tachibana family films register the fragile boundary between memory and forgetting, as obscured memories of internment and survival are, nevertheless, linked to the visual and seemingly idyllic portrayals of Japanese Americans in postwar suburban America.

Finally, in the Bohulano Mabalon family footage, the home film emerges as a diasporic, rather than as a national and familial, formation. Skillfully narrated by Dawn Mabalon Bohulano, the eight-minute compilation film centered on the Bohulano Mabalon family provides a more nuanced contextualization than those offered in previously mentioned films; throughout the film, Dawn discusses the emergence of Stockton's burgeoning Filipino/a community from the early twentieth century to the 1970s.[36] Featuring an extensive archive of moving and still imagery, the Bohulano Mabalon film shifts between intimate family portrayals, such as domestic scenes of birthday parties, and public outings, including Stockton's annual Filipino/a American festival, the Barrio Fiesta. Arriving in Stockton, California, from the Philippines in 1929, both sides of Dawn's family worked in the fields along the West Coast and became pivotal figures within the city's Filipino/a diasporic community. With the formation of a Little Manila—replete with family-owned businesses, restaurants, post office, and community-based organizations—Filipino/as created a vibrant network of resources attentive to the particular needs of the emergent community. For instance, Dawn's paternal grandfather, Pablo Mabalon, opened a restaurant in Little Manila, which became a prominent institution frequented by Filipino/a labor organizers, such as Carlos Bulosan.

While these discrete segments from Dawn's family home movies depict the different ways Filipino/as cultivated cultural spaces rooted in camaraderie, Dawn does not characterize everyday life through rose-tinted glasses. Instead, she underscores the institutionalized practices that produced a racially segregated Stockton—a realization that only became obvious once she began to participate in a school busing program. Near the beginning of the compilation film, Dawn offers the following commentary: "It [Stockton] was a very, very segregated city. And that was something I didn't realize until I was six years old . . . and I realized, 'Oh, this is where all the white people are! And this is where all of the nice houses are, and the malls, the shopping areas.'"[37] She also describes the ramifications of such racialized practices:

FIGURE 17.5. Frame enlargement from Bohulano family home film depicting Filipino Town in Stockton, California. Courtesy of Dawn Bohulano Mabalon and Center for Asian American Media.

"Filipinos are still segregated to the South Side of Stockton. The high schools and the public schools I went to were still some of the worst-funded schools in the city." While Dawn discusses Stockton's racialized geography, a succession of images fills the screen, including footage of Filipino/a and African American teenagers playfully waving at the camera, an archival photograph of a public building posted with a sign, "Positively No Filipinos Allowed," and an excerpt depicting a gathering of Filipino/a military veterans, children, and young adults in what appears to be a community center. The Bohulano Mabalon compilation film thus alludes to a third way of addressing dominant social structures—practices that cannot be defined as absolute integration or radical opposition. While Dawn's own family did not wholly break from normative ideologies, their exclusion from white middle-class spaces compelled members to appropriate and refashion existing resources for their own purposes. In that sense, the Bohulano Mabalon family films offer a graduated narrative of survival informed by continuing policies of racialized exclusion and improvised modes of resistance forged by Filipino/a immigrants.

In another series of film excerpts, Dawn discusses Stockton's Filipino/a immigrant community beyond the insular logics of biological family ties.

While footage of a community-organized beauty pageant appears across the screen, Dawn describes how migration generates social affiliations that often exceed the confines of the nuclear family: "You really have to start over in America and create a new family. And the people who might not have been so close to you . . . somebody who lived down the block in the Philippines are suddenly as close as your blood." Fatima El-Tayeb's theorization of queer diaspora is especially useful in parsing out the different meanings of "family" potentially encompassed in the Bohulano Mabalon home films. According to El-Tayeb, diaspora does not signify the unidirectional scattering of a homogenous people from a single place of origin. Rather, as a point of departure that labors toward the future, diaspora underscores the production of a horizontal network that claims space "within the nation by moving beyond its containing structures."[38]

To that extent, audiences might imagine the pluralistic ways in which the Bohulano Mabalon film archive, filled with countless images of cross-racial relationships and intergenerational gatherings, encompasses a vast range of possible affinities and social orientations. That is, rather than solely privileging biological essence and blood relations that define the intact nuclear family, the Bohulano Mabalon archive visualizes a diasporic web contingent upon a shared set of structural conditions and histories of migration. Such renderings provide an imaginative reconceptualization of social kinship that accentuates the transnational dimensions of Asian American home film archives.

## Conclusion

In this chapter, I have considered the creative forging of CAAM's Memories to Light and the divergent meanings of belonging generated by the home film archive. Specifically, Memories to Light evokes popular tropes commonly associated with white middle-class life, even as it disrupts these racialized assumptions. As scholars of amateur film have long articulated, the home film is not a raw or objective source, but is always already mediated by a host of factors, including the filmmaker's subjective positioning, archival practices, and curatorial directives that frame what viewers see.[39]

By calling attention to the importance of curatorship and remediation, I do not mean to undermine the significance of the source footage itself. Indeed, as Richard Fung observes, working with home movies is an invaluable process because it reveals "much about the time and the society in which [the films] were made."[40] However, because of the "conventions of the technology" and "all that [is] associated with it," Fung finds it necessary to "manipulate their context and their surface" for counterhegemonic purposes.[41] In a similar fashion, the remediation of home footage can provide viewers with meaningful opportunities to grasp social textures that are not immediately apparent without additional context. In particular, projects such as Memories to Light encourage viewers to flesh out the strategic decisions that make the home movie recognizable to different audiences, ranging from family members featured in the films, to archivists and scholars, to a more general audience who know little to nothing about the imagery. Producing new analytical pathways, these interpretive moves attend to if not trouble the linkages that bind the moving image to racial formation in the United States. Given the historical moment we find ourselves in, these critical lines of inquiry—which contend with curatorial tactics, access to filmmaking, and screen representations of race in and beyond the theatrical film—are more pressing than ever.

## FILMOGRAPHY

All available films discussed in this chapter can be streamed through the book's web page at https://www.dukeupress.edu/Features/Screening-Race and the Memories to Light website.

Brian Gee Family Collection (1978–83), 30 short films, Super 8mm
ACCESS: Center for Asian American Media.

Tachibana Family Collection (1976–83), Super 8mm
ACCESS: Center for Asian American Media.

Bohulano Family Collection (c. 1950s–1970s), 15 short films, Super 8mm
ACCESS: Center for Asian American Media.

## NOTES

My gratitude goes to Davin Agatep and CAAM for speaking with me about this important project.

1   Center for Asian American Media (CAAM), Memories to Light, accessed January 14, 2019, http://caamedia.org/memoriestolight/.
2   Though most of the home films featured in Memories to Light portray Asian Americans in California, CAAM, since 2015, has raised funds to collect films shot by Asian Americans across the United States. Davin Agatep, phone interview with author, May 17, 2016.
3   Throughout this essay, I draw on "Asian American" as a politicized racial category that binds different constituencies vis-à-vis a shared set of historical experiences, social oppressions, and structural dynamics. The term first emerged as a racial

category during the 1960s student protests organized at San Francisco State University. See Glenn Omatsu, "The 'Four Prisons' and the Movements of Liberation: Asian American Activism from the 1960s to the 1990s," in *Asian American Studies Now: A Critical Reader*, ed. Jean Yu-wen Shen Wu and Thomas C. Chen (New Brunswick, NJ: Rutgers University Press, 2010), 496–514. For a general overview of racially exclusionary immigration policies targeting Asian Americans and popular media portrayals of Asian Americans from the early to mid-twentieth century, see Lisa Lowe, *Immigrant Acts: On Asian American Cultural Politics* (Durham, NC: Duke University Press, 1996); and Erika Lee, *The Making of Asian America: A History* (New York: Simon and Schuster, 2015).

4  This is not to say that racialized, gendered, and sexualized caricatures of Asians no longer exist in U.S. popular culture. As emphasized by Jane Chi Hyun Park, Orientalist depictions of Asians and Hollywood "white-washing" continue to shape portrayals of Asian Americans in mainstream films. Jane Chi Hyun Park, *Yellow Future: Oriental Style in Hollywood Cinema* (Minneapolis: University of Minnesota Press, 2010).

5  Patricia R. Zimmerman, "Introduction," in *Mining the Home Movie: Excavations in Histories and Memories*, ed. Karen Ishizuka and Patricia Zimmerman (Berkeley: University of California Press, 2008), 9.

6  Stephen Gong, executive director of CAAM, "MTL: An Inside Look," https://caamedia.org/memoriestolight/project/memories-to-light-an-inside-look/. See the 00:01:00 mark of the video titled "Memories to Light: An Inside Look," March 5, 2013.

7  Jay David Bolter and Richard Grusin, *Remediation: Understanding New Media* (Cambridge, MA: MIT Press, 1999).

8  Lee, *The Making of Asian America*.

9  As emphasized by Agatep, Memories to Light is conceptualized for a general audience rather than for an Asian American viewership. Agatep, phone interview.

10  Wendy Hui Kyong Chun, "Introduction: Race and/as Technology; or, How to Do Things to Race," *Camera Obscura* 24, no. 1 (2002): 6–35.

11  Although Peter Feng, Glen Mimura, Jun Okada, Darrell Hamamoto, Sandra Liu, and David Eng, among others, have addressed the home movie in their scholarship, their analyses focus more on experimental documentaries and films that make use of home footage than on the home movie as a cultural formation.

12  While there is a growing body of scholarship addressing filmmaking via digital technologies, this essay primarily focuses on the digital remediation of home footage (8mm, 16mm, and Super 8mm). For complete titles of cited works, please refer to the selected bibliography.

13  Veena Hariharan, "At Home in the Empire: Reading Colonial Home Movies—the Hyde Collection (1928–1937)," *BioScope* 5, no. 1 (2014): 49–61; Julia Noordegraaf and Elvira Louw, "Extended Family Films: Home Movies in the State-Sponsored Archive," *The Moving Image* 9, no. 1 (2009): 83–103.

14  Karen Ishizuka, *Lost and Found: Reclaiming the Japanese American Incarceration* (Champaign: University of Illinois Press, 2006); Karen Ishizuka, "The Moving

Image Archive of the Japanese American National Museum," in Ishizuka and Zimmerman, *Mining the Home Movie*, 122–25; and Richard Fung, "Remaking Home Movies," in Ishizuka and Zimmerman, *Mining the Home Movie*, 29–40.

15  Hariharan, "At Home in the Empire," 50.

16  Patricia Zimmerman, *Reel Families: A Social History of Amateur Film* (Bloomington: Indiana University Press, 1995), 112–42.

17  Zimmerman, *Reel Families*, 112–14.

18  Haidee Wasson, "Electric Homes! Automatic Movies! Efficient Entertainment! 16mm and Cinema's Domestication in the 1920s," *Cinema Journal* 48, no. 4 (2009): 1–21; Roger Odin, "Reflections on the Family Home Movie as Document: A Semio-Pragmatic Approach," in Ishizuka and Zimmerman, *Mining the Home Movie*, 255–71.

19  Even with the popularization of the 8mm film gauge, the average prices of home movie cameras were still high. In 1950, lower-end cameras, such as the Brownie 8mm and Revere 50, were approximately $50 (equivalent to a contemporary price tag of $435), while high-end semiprofessional cameras sold for as much as $365 (equivalent to today's $3,290). See Zimmerman, *Reel Families*, 115–17.

20  Zimmerman, *Reel Families*, 114.

21  Fung, "Remaking Home Movies," 35.

22  As argued by Jodi Melamed, Roderick Ferguson, and Chandan Reddy, racial liberalism first emerged in the post–World War II moment as the United States emerged as a Cold War superpower. By limiting racial justice to state-sanctioned processes of assimilation, positive cultural pluralism, and (now) global humanism, U.S. governmentality forged what Melamed describes as "official anti-racism" to foreclose radical critiques of the U.S. state and its systemic practices of racial violence. See Jodi Melamed, *Represent and Destroy: Rationalizing Violence in the New Racial Capitalism* (Minneapolis: University of Minnesota Press, 2011); Roderick Ferguson, *The Reorder of Things: The University and Its Pedagogies of Minority Difference* (Minneapolis: University of Minnesota Press, 2012); Chandan Reddy, *Freedom with Violence: Race, Sexuality, and the US State* (Durham, NC: Duke University Press, 2011).

23  To view this site, see the Memories to Light collection stored on the Internet Archive: https://archive.org/details/memoriestolight.

24  Agatep, phone interview.

25  The Brian Gee Family Collection in the Home Movies section of Memories to Light, https://caamedia.org/memoriestolight/project/brian-gee-family-collection/.

26  Jesus Hernandez, "Redlining Revisited: Mortgage Lending Patterns in Sacramento 1930–2004," *International Journal of Urban and Regional Research* 33 (2009): 291–313.

27  Hernandez, "Redlining Revisited." As observed by Hernandez, segregation continues in contemporary Sacramento. While realtors and local government agencies no longer enforce these particular discriminatory policies, other administrative practices, including urban renewal projects and the dense concentration

of the subprime loan market in neighborhoods of color, continually reproduce an uneven urban geography tethered to racial segregation and disenfranchisement.

28  Jesus Hernandez, "The Racial Impact of History: Connecting Residential Segregation, Mortgage Redlining and the Housing Crisis," report for Kirwan Institute for the Study of Race and Ethnicity, December 2009, 14.

29  Lowe, *Immigrant Acts*; and Wendy Cheng, "Strategic Orientalism: Racial Capitalism and the Problem of 'Asianness,'" *African Identities* 11, no. 2 (2013): 148–58.

30  Center for Asian American Media (CAAM), "The Tachibana Family: Masao Torigoe," YouTube, September 24, 2014, https://www.youtube.com/watch?v=t9xF79ed-Ug.

31  Eve Oishi, "Screen Memories: Fakeness in Asian American Media Practice," in *F Is for Phony: Fake Documentary and Truth's Undoing*, ed. Alexandra Juhasz and Jesse Lerner (Minneapolis: University of Minnesota Press, 2006), 197.

32  Marita Sturken, *Tangled Memories: The Vietnam War, the AIDS Epidemic, and the Politics of Remembering* (Berkeley: University of California Press, 1997).

33  Glen M. Mimura, "Uncanny Memories: Post-Redress Media in Japanese American History," in *Ghostlife of Third Cinema* (Minneapolis: University of Minnesota Press, 2009); and Rea Tajiri, *History and Memory: For Akiko and Takashige* (New York: Women Make Movies, 1991).

34  Tajiri, *History and Memory.*

35  Mimura, *Ghostlife of Third Cinema*, 98. Mimura's articulations of transgenerational transmission of memories allude to Marianne Hirsh's conceptualization of postmemory, or an afterlife of memories produced through family photographs. See Marianne Hirsh, *Family Frames: Photography, Narrative, and Postmemory* (Cambridge, MA: Harvard University Press, 1997).

36  Dawn Bohulano Mabalon, *Little Manila Is in the Heart: The Making of the Filipina/o American Community in Stockton, California* (Durham, NC: Duke University Press, 2013).

37  Center for Asian American Media (CAAM), "Memories to Light 2.0: The Bohulano Family," YouTube, March 26, 2014, https://www.youtube.com/watch?v=qjMTAh-gsmI.

38  Fatima El-Tayeb, *European Others: Queering Ethnicity in Postnational Europe* (Minneapolis: University of Minnesota Press, 2011), xxxiv.

39  Zimmerman, *Reel Families*; Fung, "Remaking Home Movies"; Laura Rascaroli, Barry Monahan, and Gwenda Young, *Amateur Filmmaking: The Home Movie, the Archive, the Web* (New York: Bloomsbury Academic, 2014).

40  Fung, "Remaking Home Movies," 39.

41  Fung, "Remaking Home Movies," 39.

# 18

## Black Home Movies

### Time to Represent

JASMYN R. CASTRO

Given the antipathy the film industry showed African Americans through-out the twentieth century, it is unsurprising that much of the scholarship concerned with African Americans and motion pictures has focused on the various ways in which black people have been negatively characterized and disproportionately relegated to racially exploitative roles. The ongo-ing struggles African Americans have faced in the quest for more authentic representation in mainstream cinema and concurrently for increased black self-representation have been dominant themes in African American cin-ema scholarship and in films directed and produced by black filmmakers. While important, this scholarship has focused primarily on movies intended for public exhibition, including fictional Hollywood films, sponsored non-fiction productions (government films, educational films, religious films), and on television.[1] Although these genres and modes of media production differ in important ways, they represent the African American experience for an audience that includes, implicitly or explicitly, whites and African American audiences who approach these representations through the prism of their respective experiences and entrenched perspectives.

In contrast to media produced for public exhibition, African American home movies capture black families and communities engaged in everyday activities that they themselves recorded and intended for private viewing. Because these films were not made with public exhibition in mind, they op-erate outside of the representational norms of mainstream theatrical media and are thereby arguably able to transcend its limitations. African American home movies work to redefine mis- and underrepresented black communities; they provide an intimate moving image record that complements and counters the often negative imagery in the media. They also respond to the burden of racial representation carried by race films, expanding on the ambitions of early black filmmakers by capturing the diversity of the black community through self-authorship. These films present multifaceted aspects of black life in the United States and provide a valuable historical resource for reexamining and understanding the African American experience.

This chapter takes African American home movies outside of the intimacy of the personal context of their filming and exhibition and considers their significance as moving images and as historical artifacts. African American home movies operate at the juncture of self-representation, individual and community engagements with moving picture technologies, and the broader representational mediascape in which portrayals of African Americans and black life circulate. Further, this chapter posits African American home movies as significant underutilized resources for research in a range of fields engaged with African American history and culture. One of the main themes emerging from recent home movie scholarship is that amateur filmmaking, including home movies, provides microhistories that challenge the parameters of broader histories and film canons.[2] Through archives and special collections dedicated to their preservation and access, African American home movies allow for a previously inaccessible glimpse into the diverse cultures of black communities in the United States. The ability of home movies to depict events throughout their subjects' lives affords a unique opportunity to trace these communities through multiple individualized perspectives. African American home movies allow us to revise the history of black representation in cinema to account for its most intimate self-representations. In so doing, they also provide a privileged view of the private lives of African Americans, one that serves as an important counterimage to theatrical screen representations of the black community.

## Black Self-Representation and Authorship

During the early 1900s, a number of African American filmmakers and organizations used the influence and popularity of cinema to produce films that depicted African American communities in a positive light. In the 1910s, early African American entrepreneurs sponsored and produced films that were defiantly self-representational and contrary to the racial narrative that was so prevalent in both mainstream popular entertainment and the emerging film industry. Some of these early attempts at capturing the African American experience were through actuality filmmaking, the production of nonfiction films by educators, entrepreneurs, and ministers, to name a few, who created short films that featured real events, places, and everyday people. These films were used as documentation, for community cohesion, and as marketing tools to raise funds for programs and various initiatives to promote the social and economic uplift of African Americans.[3] While the majority of these films are no longer extant, they were the earliest films created by black filmmakers specifically for the black community.

Other attempts at capturing and promoting positive African American images on film were through commercial race films, productions with all-black casts made for black audiences. Oscar Micheaux and Spencer Williams were two prolific filmmakers who recognized the need for black self-representation, even when the characters they created were more complex than idealized. From the 1920s through the 1940s they, along with other various race film enterprises, produced and directed films that projected images of race pride for black audiences. While these films were a much-needed counter to the black buffoonery that was prevalent in mainstream feature films, their fictional depictions of black life often participated in the stereotypical casting practices that were perpetuated in the mainstream media. As Anna Everett notes, both white- and black-owned motion picture companies of the time "constructed fictional black worlds characterized by fair-skinned protagonists and dark-skinned miscreants" and promoted "middle-class bourgeois norms over the more folk and working-class realities of the black masses who made up their target audience."[4] While these films mark pivotal moments in the emergence and development of self-representational black cinema, they were rooted in economic structures (e.g., Hollywood, educational institutions, religious organizations) that nonetheless (re)produced biased images of African Americans.

In *Uplift Cinema*, Allyson Nadia Field argues that "film history is a history of survivors, and scholarly writing is consequently disproportionately weighed towards extant films."[5] She argues for cinema scholarship to incorporate larger bodies of work that can contribute to discussions surrounding the various manifestations of racial uplift and black self-representation in early films. This imperative is addressed in no small way by African American home movies, which constitute some of the earliest surviving examples of black self-representation on film. Though the distinction between professional and amateur filmmaking was not so clearly delineated in early cinema, this is nonetheless a key point. Because most home movies were not shot with the expectation of remuneration or public exhibition, they are necessarily freer from the constraints of commercial and institutional productions. A number of home movies from the 1920s through the 1940s share many of the characteristics of uplift that were a central part of the actuality films of the 1910s, while still preserving their individualized perspectives.

Some examples of this investment in filming uplift can be seen in the J. Max Bond Sr. home movie collection acquired in 2016 by the Smithsonian Institution's National Museum of African American History and Culture (NMAAHC). Bond was an American educator who served in various college administrations at universities across the United States, as well as in Haiti and Liberia. From 1954 to 1967, Bond was an official of the United States Agency for International Development, with tours of duty in Afghanistan, Tunisia, Sierra Leone, and Malawi. Bond was an avid home movie filmmaker who made it a point to film the various communities in which he lived and worked, instead of shooting traditional home movie scenes of his family and friends. In *Tuskegee*, Bond provides a look inside the historic Tuskegee Institute in the early 1940s, at farmers, and inside a rural middle school. Through close-ups and shots staged for the camera, Bond documents handmade pottery in the Tuskegee Institute pottery studio and a man sculpting a bust of Booker T. Washington. In another scene, Bond films a class of girls learning to cook and weave cloth on a loom and, later, preparing meals with a chef. This film in particular highlights the accomplishments of the various educational programs at Tuskegee. Unlike the early uplift films shot at Tuskegee in the 1910s that Field discusses in *Uplift Cinema*, or the actuality films of the institute produced by white-owned companies in the 1920s, Bond's lens on Tuskegee is a personal record of the institute rather than primarily promotional, persuasive, or commercial. This insider perspective is echoed in a film titled *Good Good Good*, in which Bond films a rural family engaging in everyday tasks on the farm. The film includes shots of a young boy walking a mule toward the camera, an older man feeding a group of pigs, and the family gathering on the porch and waving at the camera before entering their home. These shots are followed by a number of scenes of the family working on the farm. *Good Good Good* also includes footage of a black rural middle school, in which children are shown walking in single file and being taught in the classroom. These two films convey the pride Bond felt in the institutions he worked for and the communities he visited; he concentrated on capturing everyday accomplishments and highlighting the progress he witnessed from a privileged, insider position as an educator in the African American community.

FIGURE 18.1. *Good Good Good* (J. Max Bond Sr., 1940s). Film held by the Smithsonian Institution, National Museum of American History.

## Doin' It for Themselves

The increasingly affordable home movie camera allowed for amateur access to filmmaking and resulted in the ability of individuals from underrepresented and marginalized groups to record their own lives, experiences, and stories. As archives increasingly are expanding their collections to include amateur film, the overall diversity of moving image material allows for a more comprehensive picture of the myriad uses of film. This is significant for an understanding of filmmaking in the United States in general, but it is crucial for African American film history, which is founded from a place of absence and whose surviving artifacts are complex in their racial figurings.[6]

To date, the earliest known 16mm African American home movie collection is the amateur footage shot by Reverend Solomon Sir Jones (1869–1936) of Oklahoma. This film collection is currently split between two archival institutions, with twenty-nine reels held by the Beinecke Rare Book and Manuscript Library at Yale University and nine reels archived at NMAAHC. These rare films take the viewer on a journey with Reverend Jones, a financially well-off minister and businessman who traveled extensively throughout his life. Jones was born in 1869 in Tennessee into a family of former slaves and went on to become a Baptist minister, successful businessman, amateur filmmaker, and avid traveler. He was also the head of the Boyd Faction of Negro Baptists in America and built and pastored fifteen churches. His surviving films capture African American communities between 1924 and 1928 throughout the Southern and Midwestern United States including schools, churches, social gatherings, and black-owned businesses. In the case of Tulsa, Oklahoma, Jones's films represent the last surviving moving image record of the thriving black business district. Homemade title cards, complete with dates, were meticulously placed in between each scene to identify the people and places he was filming. Each carefully constructed slate demonstrates the effort and care Jones put into producing his films and documenting the African American community.

In one reel, archived at the NMAAHC, Jones films an African American–owned oil field with people supervising the active oil wells, followed by an extraordinary wide shot revealing acres of land with five oil wells. Intertitles describe the footage: "Their first oil well, 2,000 barrels daily" and "Their second oil well, 3,000 barrels daily."[7] Rhea Combs, curator of film and photography at the museum, explains the importance of Rev. S. S. Jones's films and what he captured in these terms:

> It flies in the face of what I think some people consider part of African American history and culture. And I think that was one of the things that Oklahoma and S.S. Jones is really showing. That African American history and culture is not a monolith, and in a way it became a kind of marketing tool to encourage individuals to migrate, to move there.... There were still palpable racial tensions. There are lynchings, there is Jim Crow, segregation ... and you still have an African American community, or many communities, that really speak to the fortitude and resilience of black people in this country.[8]

In these ways, Jones's footage provides a lens on an aspect of American life for which little documentation survives. In doing so, it enhances our understanding of African American migration and the resilience of communities facing tremendous challenges.

In both their status as consumer product and their ability to record personal and community consumption, African American home movies also serve as vectors for tracing black purchasing power. In the 1930s, Montgomery Ward and Co., Lever Brothers, and Anheuser-Busch commissioned the National Negro Business League to conduct the first study of African

FIGURE 18.2. *Rev. Solomon Sir Jones, Film 5* (Solomon Sir Jones, 1924–28). Film held by the Smithsonian Institution, National Museum of African American History and Culture.

American consumers, and "based on the data gathered, the researchers estimated the disposable income of black consumers at the time to be approximately $1.65 billion."[9] While economic and social conditions in the United States played an important role in who and what was documented, it is important to remember that not all African Americans were poor, as evidenced by this study, nor were they uninformed consumers of media. As demonstrated by archival collections of African American home movies, wealthy and middle-class black professionals engaged with new recording technologies to self-document and to participate in new forms of leisure activity.

The Harold M. Anderson Black Wall Street home movies at the National Museum of American History are unique in their representation of a thriving black business district in the Greenwood neighborhood of Tulsa, Oklahoma, from 1948 to 1952. As curator of the Smithsonian Archives Center Wendy Shay notes, "At a time when segregation limited African American housing options and prevented black customers from patronizing businesses that catered to white customers only, it had one of the largest concentrations of

FIGURE 18.3. "All that was left of his home after Tulsa Race Riot—6-1-1921" (un-known, 1921). Central University Libraries, Southern Methodist University.

black-owned businesses in the country."[10] During the 1921 Tulsa race riot, Black Wall Street was burned down by angry white Oklahomans, and hundreds of African American residents were killed. The black community rebuilt the Greenwood neighborhood, and by 1940 black-owned businesses flourished once again.

Shay credits Anderson with playing a "major role" in Greenwood's resur-gence: "A successful businessman, Anderson managed and then owned two neighborhood movie theaters, a skating rink, a bowling alley, and a shop-ping strip, among other enterprises. He also brought the Golden Gloves box-ing tournament to the area, making it accessible to African American fans. Anderson was committed to the belief that, like in other majority African American communities during the Jim Crow era, it was critical that Black Wall Street sustain independent African American businesses to ensure resi-dent dollars would stay in the community and guarantee its future."[11] People and businesses highlighted in Anderson's films include a barber cutting a man's hair inside T. C.'s Scientific Barber Shop, a woman and a man making custom-ordered hats inside Manhattan Hatters, a Golden Gloves boxing match between two young men, and the exterior of a movie theater where teens can be seen socializing and exiting after a film. Brent D. Glass, for-mer director of the National Museum of American History, comments on the value of this collection: "This footage is especially important because it

FIGURE 18.4. *Black Wall Street* (Harold M. Anderson, 1948–52). Film held by the Smithsonian Institution, National Museum of American History.

looks at the Black Wall Street community through a personal lens. . . . It is rare because so few African American home movies from that time period exist, and it provides viewers with less-mediated footage."[12] Anderson's footage captures this revitalized community through his extensive coverage of Greenwood residents and black professionals, offering a rich illustration of black entrepreneurial spirit in the first half of the twentieth century.

In 1932, at the height of the Great Depression, Eastman Kodak Co. introduced regular 8mm film and began producing cameras and projectors for beginners and enthusiastic amateurs alike. For those who could still afford to shoot home movies, the new film gauge was smaller and more affordable. The definition of amateur film began expanding to include family films, in addition to the traditional artistic and documentary-style films that were shot on 16mm. One exemplary representation of this time period exists in the Sandra Bean Home Movie Collection at the African American Museum and Library at Oakland in California, which consists of nine 16mm and regular 8mm films shot during the 1930s and 1940s by a Bay Area resident named Ernest Bean.[13] The collection exhibits home movie footage of a middle-class family attending church, playing with their children, and engaging in extracurricular activities with family and friends. Most notably, the films are exceptional historical documentation of Ernest Bean at work as a sleeping-car porter for the Pullman Company.

During the late 1800s, the Pullman Company revolutionized train travel by providing stately sleeping and dining cars staffed with highly disciplined, orderly, and hospitable porters to tend to travelers. The first porters were recently freed slaves who would work long hours for little pay. Over a short time, the Pullman Company employed more African American men than any other company in the United States. The job of Pullman porter was coveted in the African American community, where reliable income and the opportunity to travel around the United States were not common. Still, the work of a porter was grueling, and they were expected to work eleven thousand miles or four hundred hours a month, whichever came first.[14] Bean's films offer a rare firsthand view into the lives of Pullman porters.

In addition to making this collection available for online viewing, the archivists at the African American Museum and Library at Oakland have created detailed guides, complete with both physical and time-stamped descriptions of the digital surrogates for each reel in the collection. Some scenes offer a glimpse into the personal life of a sleeping-car porter, including footage of family and friends socializing in the garden, men playing catch with a football outside of their home, and an interracial couple posing for the camera with their children on the front steps of their home. The footage also shows a sleeping-car porter standing by as passengers board a train, fellow Pullman porters on the job and socializing between shifts, and scenic mountain views captured from the window of a moving train. Similar to the Solomon Sir Jones films, these films have homemade title cards placed between many of the scenes. They are handwritten on a chalkboard and are often humorous attempts to describe as well as narrate. For example, one title reads, "Ducking the camera at 60 mi. per. hour" before a scene of a man running quickly in and out of the frame to grab something. During another scene, a sleeping-car Pullman porter, identified by his white buttoned-up jacket, walks toward the camera with upright posture on a train platform. Today, Ernest Bean's home movies exist as a surviving moving image record of an upwardly mobile African American family. They also provide a first-hand account of a profession with deep roots in the emergence of the black middle class. Home movies, like those made by Bean, present an enhanced

FIGURES 18.5–18.6. *Reel 2*, circa late 1940s–1950s (Ernest Bean). Film held by the African American Museum and Library at Oakland.

picture of the professional lives of African Americans in roles that were, at best, caricatured or degraded in mainstream films of the period, when they were shown at all. In the case of Bean's Pullman porter footage, they also provide a corrective recentering of black labor, a counterimage to Hollywood's filmic representation of Pullman porters as background to white lives and stories.

Between 1945 and 1955, the median income of black Americans increased more than 350 percent, while amateur filmmaking was simultaneously experiencing a major shift from a "relatively niche-market hobby to a mass cultural phenomenon."[15] With an estimated $16 billion in buying power, African Americans made up the second-largest and fastest-growing market segment in the United States. The black community was becoming larger and more concentrated, with increasing economic and social stability, more buying power, and sophisticated consumption patterns. At the same time, the Eastman Kodak Company catered to the growing home movie–making market and changing consumer demographics by introducing Super 8mm film in June 1965 and adopting a new ethnic marketing strategy that specifically targeted African Americans.[16] Even though Eastman began producing and selling motion picture film in 1889, the first home movie camera advertisement featuring African Americans was a 1964 print ad for the 8mm Brownie Fun Saver Movie Camera and Kodak Automatic B Projector.[17]

In 1972, Eastman's advertising agency, J. Walter Thompson Company, produced an advertisement for the Kodak Instamatic camera depicting a black Santa Claus in *Ebony* magazine.[18] For the first time, African Americans were targeted as a viable market for home movies. And, while they were underrepresented in commercials and print media, black families took part in chronicling their families as well.

The Spiller-Doughty home movies, a private film collection digitized and included on the African American Home Movie Archive website, is one film collection that features a middle-class family during the politically and socially transformational time of the 1960s and '70s. The Spiller-Doughty home movie collection features husband and wife Curtis and Emile Spiller of Gary, Indiana, and their three children, Curt, Meredith, and Noreen. Their family films record day trips to the beach, road trips to Kentucky and Tennessee, family reunions, Chicago Cubs games, trips to the zoo, the family before and after church, and other aspects of family life. Noreen is now the keeper of her family's home movies and is able to provide some contextual information about the films.[19] Her mother, Emile Spiller, graduated from Indiana University in 1948 and worked as a substitute and full-time teacher, while her father, Curtis Spiller, was a World War II veteran who worked for United States Steel until his retirement in 1982. In part of the footage, her father can be seen in attendance at the United Steelworkers of America Constitutional Convention in Atlantic City, New Jersey, where he served as a delegate. During the 1960s, black steelworkers were protesting job discrimination within the union. Many black steelworkers claimed they were shut out of opportunities to move up in the company, and consigned to the more dangerous and physically demanding positions. As Herbert Hill and James Jones note, "Delegates to the 1968 convention of the United Steelworkers of America were handed a series of leaflets each day by members of the Ad Hoc Committee, a nationwide caucus of black steelworkers which had placed picket lines at the entrance of the convention auditorium. In a widely distributed statement . . . the caucus stated . . . 'The time has come for black workers to speak and act for ourselves.'"[20] Protest within the United Steelworkers union was instrumental in creating equal working conditions, as well as access to equal advancement opportunities, for both black and white steelworkers. Through these home movies, the subjects share their story on a personal level, and we learn their history and culture within the familiar framework of an unfolding life.

While ostensibly training their lenses on subjects personal to the camera operator, home movies capture the incidental, yet not insignificant, traces of a given moment's history and culture. This record is especially powerful as a document of daily life under segregation. For example, footage from the Hayes Family Movies at the Lynn and Louis Wolfson II Florida Moving Image Archives at Miami Dade College shows an African American family enjoying a picnic at a segregated Virginia Key Beach.[21] Children wade in the water and wave at the camera, and family and friends dance and joke around with each other as they all enjoy a meal under the beach palm trees. This is a fascinating view of an African American leisure spot in its heyday. Virginia Key Beach, a Dade County Park, was established in 1945 as a vacation place for people of color. It was the first "colored only" beach in Miami-Dade County and "the only place where African-Americans and Bahamians, who made up one-third of Miami's population and helped build the city, could swim and enjoy beach activities."[22] In a case typifying environmental racism, the beach went downhill when a city sewage plant began discharging waste and dumping garbage in one of the Virginia Key Beach outlets. Despite these conditions, the beach remained open and was given park status before it was closed in 1982 due to a lack of city funding. In 2002, Virginia Key Beach was given historical status in Florida and placed on the

FIGURE 18.7. *Untitled* (Hayes family, 1956–62), WC05880. Film held by the Wolfson Archives at Miami Dade College.

National Register of Historic Places, reopening to the public in 2008. The Hayes Family Movies offer a glimpse of the experience of African American families enjoying a segregated beach in Florida, an important testament to life under segregation as well as the self-documentation of a particular family's leisure activities.

## Hiding in Plain Sight

Current home movie and amateur film scholarship has concluded that home movies counterbalance broader film canons and histories, so why have African American home movies been noticeably absent from the recurring conversation in cinema scholarship surrounding black self-representation? Their neglect, to date, is in large part due to roadblocks created by orphaned material, a lack of funding for preservation and digitization of existing collections, and the seemingly inevitable obscurity cast upon the majority of home movie collections overall. Of the twenty-nine African American home movie collections that have been located and identified as a result of my research, only twelve are available to be streamed online by researchers and other interested parties. This is a truly significant obstacle to access by researchers and amateur enthusiasts since today almost all research begins on the internet. When institutions lack a contemporary online presence that can enable researchers to review moving image collections, they inadvertently relegate access to a small, privileged group of people. Copyright is widely invoked as a justification for the lack of online presence. This barrier can be twofold in that institutions have not cleared the material they physically own, or they are uncomfortable with the terms and conditions of free online web streaming services that can easily be utilized. Consequently, the visual narrative of African American history and culture for much of the twentieth century has become unintentionally expressed by a fraction of the films that exist. Access and promotion are necessary for African American home movies to contribute effectively to a broader understanding of black communities during the first half of the twentieth century.

Many of the African American home movies held by various institutions do not have donor agreements as a result of their orphan status. This can happen a number of ways, but the most common reason is because the films are donated or purchased from someone who is not the original owner. Consequently, widespread access to these materials can be hindered by the parent institution's fear that they could face legal consequences for copyright infringement. What starts out as good intentions on the part of the repository, which is to take on the responsibility of preserving these materials and adding them to the pool of resources made available to their visitors for the purpose of researching and learning, instead ends up serving as a prison for the films. Although most archivists would agree that it is good practice to be wary of copyright, they would also acknowledge, as Albert Steg does with regard to another type of orphaned media, that most of these films "simply languish in their vaults, occupying a dreary 'someday when we get the time and resources' level of priority."[23]

Still, popularity is the main factor that has the most influence on the level of access these materials receive; if the demand is great, a film quickly becomes a high preservation priority purely based on its marketability. Toni Treadway, founder of the International Center for 8mm Film, argues for the importance of preserving home movies in these terms: "All records of the culture, be they amateur or professional, naively or purposefully constructed, could one day have value to the maker's descendants or to artists, historians and cultural anthropologists of the future. It is not for us today to guess which films will be important, rather let's save as many documents as possible for the future to examine."[24] If more collecting institutions adopted this approach and truly advocated and worked toward modern online access, African American home movie collections could finally start serving as a crucial tool in the understanding of American history and culture. Without this approach, these films fall back into general obscurity and become understudied simply because they're unavailable.

In light of the recent surge of interest in public digitization initiatives and exhibition-based projects, it is clear that there is a strong interest in home movies. The public, especially the African American community, is hungry for broader representation in history and in the mainstream media. African American home movies offer a candid depiction of the black community. While mainstream motion picture film and television has historically lacked diverse representation, black history was being preserved in these films. Through them, we may discover aspects of the black experience in ways that do not exist in any other moving images. Where popular media failed, personal documentation filled in the gaps.

As more collecting institutions make preservation and digitization a priority, it is imperative that these institutions make overall access to home movie collections a major focal point of their preservation philosophies. Archivists, preservationists, librarians, and scholars should see themselves as modern-day archeologists, studying and analyzing human history through the excavation of moving image collections thought otherwise to be lost or nonexistent. This ends not with analog preservation and digitization efforts, but with unencumbered access to all moving image collections. The understudied nature of home movies, copyright, and access are all intertwined, and when they are not addressed, the result is an incomplete picture of American history. This must change, and collecting institutions must prioritize conquering these obstacles and finding new and innovative ways of collecting with access as the main purpose, not merely the aspiration.

## Initiatives and Access

Home movies are powerful tools for digital storytelling and pedagogy initiatives. A number of organizations are looking to fill the moving image gap by promoting home movies as a means for learning about African American history and culture and contributing to a more inclusive and comprehensive American narrative. The following organizations are adopting and experimenting with this new way of learning about and exploring history.

## THE DIGITAL DIASPORA FAMILY REUNION

This traveling program is a transmedia community engagement project focused on outreach. It was started by Thomas Allen Harris and has adopted a digital storytelling model as part of a photographic archival outreach drive. Since 2009, the Digital Diaspora Family Reunion has traveled to different communities across the United States, with special appearances in Addis Ababa, Toronto, and Rio de Janeiro. According to the project's website, "Modeled on the Emmy-nominated PBS program 'Antiques Roadshow,' which examines family heirlooms and uncovers the stories behind them, the DDFR Roadshow is a community photo-sharing session, a veritable show-and-tell of fascinating family stories."[25] A typical program resembles a community gathering and consists of projected photographs that participants bring to the event. Other audience members react with their own insights and observations. Their overall goal is to "create a global movement that celebrates our shared values and experiences as Human Beings."[26]

## THE SOUTH SIDE HOME MOVIE PROJECT

This exhibition-based project is the brainchild of Jacqueline Stewart, professor of cinema and media studies at the University of Chicago. It began in 2004 and is dedicated to circulating the stories told in home movies shot by Chicago's diverse South Side residents. The project also collects original films and videos and has partnered with the NMAAHC to digitize a large number of these films as part of their Great Migration digitization initiative. The South Side Home Movie Project operates under the belief that these films not only document the various ethnic communities within Chicago's South Side, but that the films also "contain a wealth of information about the ways in which people have represented themselves and their views of the world."[27] Their website (http://southsidehomemovies.uchicago .edu/) provides information about the project, opportunities to view films from the collection at different neighborhood screenings, and stills from select home movies.

## THE AFRICAN AMERICAN HOME MOVIE ARCHIVE

In mid-2014, I created the African American Home Movie Archive (http:// www.aahma.org) to serve as an online resource for researchers, educators, students, archive and library professionals, amateur film aficionados, and other interested parties. The main feature of the website is the Black Home Movie Index, an aggregate of African American home movies from the early 1920s through the early 1980s. Complete with collection names, scope and content, dates, links to online finding aids, video streaming links (if provided by the institution), and contact information for each participating institution, the virtual archive aims to serve as a liaison for African American home movie research by streamlining access to this information. The website has been live since 2016 and has already aided a number of archival film researchers, museum curators, and graduate students conducting research. By encouraging access, research, and reuse of these films, the main goal is to open a gateway to a broader, more diversified understanding of the African American community. In addition to pointing to other collecting institutions, I actively collect, digitize, and provide access to acquired films via the website's AAHMA Film and Video Collection page (http://www.aahma.org/privatecollections).

SMITHSONIAN INSTITUTION, NATIONAL MUSEUM OF AFRICAN AMERICAN HISTORY AND CULTURE

Since its opening on September 24, 2016, NMAAHC has debuted a ground-breaking initiative focused on home movie preservation and access. In 2014, NMAAHC media archivist Walter Forsberg began laying the groundwork for a revolutionary public digitization program called The Great Migration: "The Great Migration is a unique digitization service program that partners the National Museum of African American History and Culture with individuals and organizations across the United States to preserve their valued analog audiovisual media."[28] In addition to partnering with other institutions to preserve and digitize audiovisual material related to African American history and culture, this initiative allows members of the public to schedule an appointment with the museum's audiovisual conservation team and have their media digitized in the Robert F. Smith Explore Your Family History Center on the second floor of the museum. Preservation and access are at the heart of this project, with a major component being online access to view these home movies on the museum's website. Families who opt in will enable people around the world to watch and experience African American history and culture through home movies. In addition to The Great Migration, NMAAHC has acquired, collected, and preserved a number of African American home movies. Notable home movie collections include the Cab Calloway Home Movies, the Maurice Sorrell Home Movies, the J. Max Bond Sr. Home Movies, the Michael Holman Home Movies, and the Rev. Solomon Sir Jones Home Movies.

All available films discussed in this chapter can be streamed through the book's web page at https://www.dukeupress.edu/Features/Screening-Race.

*Rev. Solomon Sir Jones Films* (1924–28)
ACCESS: Beinecke Rare Book and Manuscript Library, Yale University, Smithsonian Institution National Museum of African American History and Culture.

*Sandra Bean Home Movie Collection* (c. 1930s–1940s)
ACCESS: African American Museum and Library at Oakland, California.

*J. Max Bond Sr. Home Movies* (1940–46)
ACCESS: Smithsonian Institution National Museum of African American History and Culture.

*Harold M. Anderson Black Wall Street Home Movies* (1948–52)
ACCESS: Smithsonian Institution National Museum of American History.

*Spiller-Doughty Home Movies* (1950–85)
ACCESS: African American Home Movie Archive.

*Hayes Family Movies* (1956–62)
ACCESS: The Wolfson Archives at Miami Dade College.

RELATED FILMS
*The Michael Cook, Jr. Collection* (1960s)
ACCESS: Texas Archive of the Moving Image.

NOTES

1   See Donald Bogle, *Toms, Coons, Mulattoes, Mammies, and Bucks: An Interpretive History of Blacks in American Films* (New York: Bloomsbury, 1994); Allyson Nadia Field, *Uplift Cinema: The Emergence of African American Film and the Possibility of Black Modernity* (Durham, NC: Duke University Press, 2015); Michael Boyce Gillespie, *Film Blackness: American Cinema and the Idea of Black Film* (Durham, NC: Duke University Press, 2016); Ed Guerrero, *Framing Blackness: The African American Image in Film* (Philadelphia: Temple University Press, 2012).

2   For example, see Charles Tepperman, *Amateur Cinema: The Rise of North American Moviemaking, 1923–1960* (Berkeley: University of California Press, 2014); and Karen L. Ishizuka and Patricia R. Zimmermann, eds., *Mining the Home Movie: Excavations in Histories and Memories* (Berkeley: University of California Press, 2008).

3   See Field, *Uplift Cinema.*

4   Anna Everett, *Returning the Gaze: A Genealogy of Black Film Criticism, 1909–1949* (Durham, NC: Duke University Press, 2001), 120.

5   Field, *Uplift Cinema*, 23.

6   For a discussion of the significance of absence in African American film history, see Field, *Uplift Cinema*.

7   Rev. S. S. Jones, *Reel 5*, 1924–28, 16mm film, NMAAHC, Washington, DC.

8   James Burch interview with Rhea Combs, "National Geographic Interview with Rhea Combs, Curator of Film and Photography at the Smithsonian National Museum of African American History and Culture," *National Geographic*, October 23, 2016, https://youtu.be/1_dKmtCWWao.

9   "African-Americans: Representations in Advertising," *Ad Age*, September 15, 2003, http://adage.com/article/adage-encyclopedia/african-americans-representations-advertising/98304.

10  Wendy Shay with Patricia Sanders, "Black Wall Street on Film: A Story of Revival and Renewal," *O Say Can You See?* (blog), National Museum of American History, February 24, 2017, http://americanhistory.si.edu/blog/black-wall-street.

11  Shay with Sanders, "Black Wall Street on Film."

12  "Smithsonian Acquires Rare 'Black Wall Street' Film," Smithsonian National Museum of American History, October 17, 2010, http://americanhistory.si.edu/press/releases/smithsonian-acquires-rare-"black-wall-street"-film.

13  Ernest Bean, untitled film, c. 1930–50, 8mm, African American Museum and Library at Oakland, California.

14  Larry Tye, *Rising from the Rails: Pullman Porters and the Making of the Black Middle Class* (Clermont, FL: Paw Prints, 2010).

15  Laura Rascaroli, Barry Monahan, and Gwenda Young, eds., *Amateur Filmmaking: The Home Movie, the Archive, the Web* (New York: Bloomsbury Academic, 2014).

16  Roland Zavada, "The Standardization of the Super 8," *Journal of the University Film Association* 22, no. 2 (1970): 39–42.

17  Kodak, "Kodak gifts say 'Open me first' and save your Christmas in pictures!" (advertisement), *Ebony*, December 1964, 49.

18  Kodak, "Give the Pocket. Kodak pocket Instamatic camera" (advertisement), *Ebony*, December 1972, 139.

19  Noreen Doughty, "Spiller-Doughty Family Biography Discussion," email interview with author, July 3, 2015.

20  Herbert Hill and James E. Jones, *Race in America: The Struggle for Equality* (Madison: University of Wisconsin Press, 1993), 310.

21  Hayes Family, untitled film, 1956–62, 8mm, Wolfson Archives at Miami Dade College, Miami, Florida.

22  Caitlin Granfield, "Virginia Key, First 'Colored Only' Beach in Miami during Jim Crow Era, Celebrates 70 Years," *Miami Herald*, August 4, 2015, https://www.miamiherald.com/news/local/community/miami-dade/key-biscayne/article29945307.html.

23  Albert Steg, "The Itinerant Films of Arthur J. Higgins," *The Moving Image* 10, no. 1 (2010): 115–25.

24  Toni Treadway, "Home Movies: A Basic Primer on Care, Handling, and Storage," Little Film, 2001, http://www.littlefilm.org/Primer.20010717210308.html.

25 "Digital Diaspora Roadshows," 1World1Family.me, accessed January 15, 2019, http://1world1family.me/ddfr-roadshows/.

26 "Digital Diaspora Roadshows."

27 Jacqueline Stewart, "South Side Home Movie Project," University of Chicago Research Projects, 2004, http://blackfilm.uchicago.edu/research_projects/south _side_project.shtml.

28 "The Great Migration Home Movie Project," NMAAHC, accessed January 15, 2019, https://nmaahc.si.edu/explore/initiatives/great-migration-home-movie-project.

*Note:* This bibliography compiles secondary as well as select primary readings relevant to the study of race and nontheatrical film. Topic-specific sources are contained in the notes within each chapter.

Aaron, Michele, ed. *New Queer Cinema: A Critical Reader.* New Brunswick, NJ: Rutgers University Press, 2004.

Abu-Lughod, Janet L. *Race, Space, and Riots in Chicago, New York, and Los Angeles.* New York: Oxford University Press, 2007.

Acham, Christine. *Revolution Televised: Prime Time and the Struggle for Black Power.* Minneapolis: University of Minnesota Press, 2005.

Acland, Charles R., and Haidee Wasson, eds. *Useful Cinema.* Durham, NC: Duke University Press, 2011.

Alexander, Geoff. *Academic Films for the Classroom: A History.* Jefferson, NC: McFarland, 2010.

Alexander, Geoff. *Films You Saw in School: A Critical Review of 1,153 Educational Films (1958–1985) in 74 Subject Categories.* Jefferson, NC: McFarland, 2013.

Anderson, Nancy, and Michael R. Dietrich, eds. *The Educated Eye: Visual Culture and Pedagogy in the Life Sciences.* Hanover, NH: Dartmouth College Press, 2012.

Balides, Constance. "Sociological Film, Reform Publicity, and the Secular Spectator: Social Problems in the Transitional Era." *Feminist Media Histories* 3, no. 4 (2017): 10–45.

Bodroghkozy, Aniko. *Equal Time: Television and the Civil Rights Movement.* Urbana: University of Illinois Press, 2012.

Bogle, Donald. *Primetime Blues: African Americans on Network Television.* New York: Farrar, Straus and Giroux, 2015.

Bogle, Donald. *Toms, Coons, Mulattoes, Mammies, and Bucks: An Interpretive History of Blacks in American Films.* New York: Viking, 1973.

Bowser, Pearl, Jane Gaines, and Charles Musser. *Oscar Micheaux and His Circle: African-American Filmmaking and Race Cinema of the Silent Era.* Bloomington: Indiana University Press, 2001.

Braun, Marta, Charles Keil, Rob King, Paul Moore, and Louis Pelletier, eds. *Beyond the Screen: Institutions, Networks and Publics of Early Cinema.* London: John Libbey, 2012.

Bunn-Marcuse, Kathryn. "The Kwakwa̱ka'wakw on Film." In *Walking a Tightrope: Aboriginal People and Their Representations*, edited by Ute Lischke and David T. McNab, 305–33. Ontario: Wilfrid Laurier University Press, 2005.

Caddoo, Cara. *Envisioning Freedom: Cinema and the Building of Modern Black Life.* Cambridge, MA: Harvard University Press, 2014.

Cahan, Susan E. *Mounting Frustration: The Art Museum in the Age of Black Power.* Durham, NC: Duke University Press, 2016.

Campbell, Russell. *Cinema Strikes Back: Radical Filmmaking in the United States 1930–1942.* Ann Arbor, MI: UMI Research Press, 1982.

Charbonneau, Stephen. *Projecting Race: Postwar America, Civil Rights and Documentary Film.* New York: Wallflower, 2016.

Cheng, Cindy I-Fen. *Citizens of Asian America: Democracy and Race during the Cold War.* New York: New York University Press, 2013.

Chun, Wendy Hui Kyong. "Introduction: Race and/as Technology; or, How to Do Things to Race." *Camera Obscura* 24, no. 1 (2009): 7–34.

Citron, Michelle. *Home Movies and Other Necessary Fictions.* Minneapolis: University of Minnesota Press, 1998.

Cutler, Janet K., and Phyllis R. Klotman. *Struggles for Representation: African American Documentary Film and Video.* Bloomington: Indiana University Press, 1999.

De Genova, Nicholas. *Race, Space, and "Illegality" in Mexican Chicago.* Durham, NC: Duke University Press, 2005.

Distelberg, Brian J. "Visibility Matters: The Pursuit of American Belonging in the Age of Moving Images." PhD diss., Yale University, 2015.

Dudziak, Mary L. *Cold War Civil Rights: Race and the Image of American Democracy.* Princeton, NJ: Princeton University Press, 2000.

Evans, Brad, and Aaron Glass, eds. *Return to the Land of the Head Hunters: Edward S. Curtis, the Kwakwa̱ka'wakw, and the Making of Modern Cinema.* Seattle: University of Washington Press, 2014.

Everett, Anna. *Returning the Gaze: A Genealogy of Black Film Criticism, 1909–1949.* Durham, NC: Duke University Press, 2001.

Farmer, Herbert E. "USC Cinema in Perspective." *Journal of the University Film Producers Association* 11, no. 2 (winter 1959): 9–12.

Feng, Peter X. *Identities in Motion: Asian American Film and Video.* Durham, NC: Duke University Press, 2002.

Feng, Peter X, ed. *Screening Asian Americans.* New Brunswick, NJ: Rutgers University Press, 2002.

Field, Allyson Nadia. *Uplift Cinema: The Emergence of African American Film and the Possibility of Black Modernity.* Durham, NC: Duke University Press, 2015.

Field, Allyson Nadia, Jan-Christopher Horak, and Jacqueline Stewart, eds. *L.A. Rebellion: Creating a New Black Cinema.* Berkeley: University of California Press, 2015.

Fregoso, Rosa Linda. *The Bronze Screen: Chicana and Chicano Film Culture.* Minneapolis: University of Minnesota Press, 1993.

Friedman, Lester D., ed. *Unspeakable Images: Ethnicity and the American Cinema.* Urbana: University of Illinois Press, 1991.

Gay, Geneva. "Beyond Brown: Promoting Equality through Multicultural Education." *Journal of Curriculum and Supervision* 19, no. 3 (spring 2004): 193–216.

Gaycken, Oliver. *Devices of Curiosity: Early Cinema and Popular Science.* New York: Oxford University Press, 2015.

Gever, Martha, Pratibha Parmar, and John Greyson, eds. *Queer Looks: Perspectives on Lesbian and Gay Film and Video.* New York: Routledge, 1993.

Gillespie, Michael Boyce. *Film Blackness: American Cinema and the Idea of Black Film.* Durham, NC: Duke University Press, 2016.

Gordon, Marsha, and Allyson Nadia Field. "The Other Side of the Tracks: Nontheatrical Film History, Pre-Rebellion Watts, and *Felicia.*" *Cinema Journal* 55, no. 2 (winter 2016): 1–24.

Griffis, Noelle. "'This Film Is a Rebellion!' Filmmaker, Actor, *Black Journal* Producer, and Political Activist William Greaves (1924–2014)." *Black Camera* 6, no. 2 (spring 2015): 7–16.

Griffiths, Alison. *Wondrous Difference: Cinema, Anthropology, and Turn-of-the-Century Visual Culture.* New York: Columbia University Press, 2002.

Guerrero, Edward. *Framing Blackness: The African American Image in Film.* Philadelphia: Temple University Press, 1993.

Hall, Donald E., and Annamarie Jagose, eds. *The Routledge Queer Studies Reader.* New York: Routledge, 2013.

Hallam, Julia. "Film, Space and Place: Researching a City in Film." *New Review of Film and Television Studies* 8, no. 3 (2010): 277–96.

Halleck, DeeDee. "Making Movies with Kids on the Lower East Side." In *Captured: A Film/Video History of the Lower East Side,* edited by Clayton Patterson, 1–4. New York: Seven Stories, 2005.

Hamamoto, Darrell Y., and Sandra Liu, eds. *Countervisions: Asian American Film Criticism.* Philadelphia: Temple University Press, 2000.

Hariharan, Veena. "At Home in the Empire: Reading Colonial Home Movies—the Hyde Collection (1928–1937)." *BioScope: South Asian Screen Studies* 5, no. 1 (2014): 49–61.

Heitner, Devorah. *Black Power TV.* Durham, NC: Duke University Press, 2013.

Holm, Bill, and George Quimby. *In the Land of the War Canoes: A Pioneer Cinematographer in the Pacific Northwest.* Seattle: University of Washington Press, 1980.

Horne, Gerald. *Fire This Time: The Watts Uprising and the 1960s.* New York: Da Capo, 1995.

Ishizuka, Karen L. *Lost and Found: Reclaiming the Japanese American Incarceration.* Urbana: University of Illinois Press, 2006.

Ishizuka, Karen L., and Patricia Zimmermann, eds. *Mining the Home Movie: Excavations in Histories and Memories.* Berkeley: University of California Press, 2007.

Jacknis, Ira. "Visualizing Kwakwaka'wakw Tradition: The Films of William Heick, 1951–63." *BC Studies,* nos. 125/126 (spring/summer 2000): 99–146.

Jaikumar, Priya. *Cinema at the End of Empire: A Politics of Transition in Britain and India.* Durham, NC: Duke University Press, 2006.

Jiménez, Lillian. "From the Margin to the Center: Puerto Rican Cinema in New York." *Centro de Estudios Puertorriqueños Bulletin* 2, no. 8 (spring 1990): 28–43.

Johnson, Martin. *Main Street Movies: The History of Local Films in the United States.* Bloomington: Indiana University Press, 2018.

Kilpatrick, Jacquelyn. *Celluloid Indians: Native Americans and Film.* Lincoln: University of Nebraska Press, 1999.

Knee, Adam, and Charles Musser. "William Greaves, Documentary Film-Making, and the African-American Experience." *Film Quarterly* 45, no. 3 (spring 1992): 13–25.

Koenig, Gloria. *Charles and Ray Eames, 1907–1978, 1912–1988: Pioneers of Mid-century Modernism.* Los Angeles: Taschen, 2005.

Kunkel, Sonke. *Empire of Pictures: Global Media and the 1960s Remaking of American Foreign Policy.* Oxford: Berghahn, 2016.

Larson, Rodger. *A Guide for Film Teachers to Filmmaking by Teenagers.* New York: Cultural Affairs Foundation, 1968.

Larson, Rodger, Lynne Hofer, and Jaime Barrios. *Young Animators and Their Discoveries.* New York: Praeger, 1974.

Larson, Rodger, and Ellen Meade. *Young Filmmakers.* New York: E. P. Dutton, 1969.

Lee, Erika. *The Making of Asian America: A History.* New York: Simon and Schuster, 2015.

Lee, Robert. *Orientals: Asian Americans in Popular Culture.* Philadelphia: Temple University Press, 1999.

Leong, Russell, ed. *Moving the Image: Independent Asian Pacific American Media Arts.* Los Angeles: UCLA Asian American Studies Center, 1991.

Lott, Tommy Lee. "Documenting Society Issues: *Black Journal*, 1968–1970." In *Struggles for Representation: African American Documentary Film and Video*, edited by Phyllis R. Klotman and Janet K. Cutler, 71–98. Bloomington: Indiana University Press, 1999.

Lowe, Lisa. *Immigrant Acts.* Durham, NC: Duke University Press, 1996.

MacDonald, Scott. *American Ethnographic Film and Personal Documentary: The Cambridge Turn.* Berkeley: University of California Press, 2013.

Marchetti, Gina. *Romance and the "Yellow Peril": Race, Sex, and Discursive Strategies in Hollywood Fiction.* Berkeley: University of California Press, 1993.

Margulies, Ivone, ed. *Rites of Realism: Essays on Corporeal Cinema.* Durham, NC: Duke University Press, 2003.

Massood, Paula J. *Black City Cinema: African American Urban Experiences in Film.* Philadelphia: Temple University Press, 2003.

Mercer, John. *The Informational Film.* Champaign, IL: Stipes, 1981.

Mimura, Glen. *Ghostlife of Third Cinema.* Minneapolis: University of Minnesota Press, 2009.

Mogilevich, Mariana. "Arts as Public Policy." In *Summer in the City: John Lindsay, New York, and the American Dream*, edited by Joseph P. Viteritti, 195–224. Baltimore, MD: Johns Hopkins University Press, 2014.

Monticone, Paul. "'Useful Cinema,' of What Use? Assessing the Role of Motion Pictures in the Largest Public Relations Campaign of the 1920s." *Cinema Journal* 54, no. 4 (summer 2015): 74–99.

Moon, Spencer. *Reel Black Talk: A Sourcebook of 50 American Filmmakers.* London: Greenwood, 1997.

Moran, James. *There's No Place Like Home Video.* Minneapolis: University of Minnesota Press, 2002.

Morris, Rosalind. *New Worlds from Fragments: Film, Ethnography, and the Representation of Northwest Coast Cultures.* Boulder, CO: Westview, 1994.

Musser, Charles. "Carl Marzani and Union Films: Making Left-Wing Documentaries during the Cold War, 1946–53." *The Moving Image* 9, no. 1 (spring 2009): 104–60.

Nichols, Bill. *Representing Reality: Issues and Concepts in Documentary.* Bloomington: Indiana University Press, 1991.

Noble, Gil. *Black Is the Color of My TV Tube.* Seacaucus, NJ: Lyle Stuart, 1981.

Noordegraaf, Julia, and Elvira Pouw. "Extended Family Films: Home Movies in the State-Sponsored Archive." *The Moving Image* 9, no. 1 (spring 2009): 83–103.

Noriega, Chon. *Shot in America: Television, the State, and the Rise of Chicano Cinema.* Minneapolis: University of Minnesota Press, 2000.

Odin, Roger. "Reflections on the Family Home Movie as Document: A Semio-pragmatic Approach." In *Mining the Home Movie: Excavations in Histories and Memories,* edited by Karen L. Ishuzuka and Patricia R. Zimmermann, 255–71. Berkeley: University of California Press, 2008.

Oishi, Eve. "Screen Memories: Fakeness in Asian American Media Practice." In *F Is for Phony: Fake Documentary and Truth's Undoing,* edited by Alexandra Juhasz and Jesse Lerner, 196–222. Minneapolis: University of Minnesota Press, 2006.

Okada, Jun. *Making Asian American Film and Video: History, Institutions, Movements.* New Brunswick, NJ: Rutgers University Press, 2015.

Ongiri, Amy A. *Spectacular Blackness: The Cultural Politics of the Black Power Movement and the Search for a Black Aesthetic.* Charlottesville: University of Virginia Press, 2010.

Ontiveros, Randy. "No Golden Age: Television News and the Chicano Civil Rights Movement." *American Quarterly* 62, no. 4 (December 2010): 897–923.

Orgeron, Devin, Marsha Orgeron, and Dan Streible, eds. *Learning with the Lights Off: Educational Film in the United States.* New York: Oxford University Press, 2012.

Ostherr, Kirsten. *Cinematic Prophylaxis: Globalization and Contagion in the Discourse of World Health.* Durham, NC: Duke University Press, 2005.

Ostherr, Kirsten. *Medical Visions: Producing the Patient through Film, Television, and Imaging Technologies.* New York: Oxford University Press, 2013.

Park, Jane Chi Hyun. *Yellow Future: Oriental Style in Hollywood Cinema.* Minneapolis: University of Minnesota Press, 2010.

Perlman, Allison. *Public Interests: Media Advocacy and Struggles over U.S. Television.* New Brunswick, NJ: Rutgers University Press, 2016.

Peterson, Jennifer. *Education in the School of Dreams: Travelogues and Early Nonfiction Film.* Durham, NC: Duke University Press, 2013.

Peterson, Sidney. *Dark of the Screen.* New York: Anthology Film Archives and New York University Press, 1980.

Polan, Dana. *Scenes of Instruction: The Beginnings of the U.S. Study of Film.* Berkeley: University of California Press, 2007.

Prelinger, Rick. *The Field Guide to Sponsored Films.* San Francisco: National Film Preservation Foundation, 2006.

Rascaroli, Laura, Barry Monahan, and Gwenda Young, eds. *Amateur Filmmaking: The Home Movie, the Archive, the Web*. New York: Bloomsbury Academic, 2014.

Reed, Touré F. *Not Alms but Opportunity: The Urban League and the Politics of Racial Uplift, 1910–1950*. Chapel Hill: University of North Carolina Press, 2008.

Reid, Mark A. *Redefining Black Film*. Berkeley: University of California Press, 1993.

Rhines, Jesse Algeron. *Black Film/White Money*. New Brunswick, NJ: Rutgers University Press, 1996.

Rhodes, Jane. "The 'Electronic Stimulus for a Black Revolution': *Black Journal* and the 1960s Public Television." *Black Renaissance* 14, no. 2 (fall 2014): 136–51.

Rony, Fatimah Tobing. *The Third Eye: Race, Cinema, and Ethnographic Spectacle*. Durham, NC: Duke University Press, 1996.

Russell, Catherine. *Experimental Ethnography: The Work of Film in the Age of Video*. Durham, NC: Duke University Press, 1999.

San Filippo, Maria. "What a Long, Strange Trip It's Been: William Greaves' *Symbiopsychotaxiplasm: Take One*." *Film History* 13, no. 2 (2001): 216–25.

Savage, Barbara Dianne. *Broadcasting Freedom: Radio, War, and the Politics of Race, 1938–1948*. Chapel Hill: University of North Carolina Press, 1999.

Shimizu, Celine Parreñas. *The Hypersexuality of Race: Performing Asian/American Women on Screen and Scene*. Durham, NC: Duke University Press, 2007.

Singer, Beverly R. *Wiping the War Paint Off the Lens: Native American Film and Video*. Minneapolis: University of Minnesota Press, 2001.

Slide, Anthony. *Before Video: A History of the Non-theatrical Film*. Westport, CT: Greenwood, 1992.

Sloan, William. "The Documentary Film and the Negro: The Evolution of the Integration Film." *Journal of the Society of Cinematologists* 5 (1965): 66–69.

Solbrig, Heide. "The Personal Is Political: Voice and Citizenship in Affirmative-Action Videos in the Bell System, 1970–1984." In *Films That Work: Industrial Film and the Productivity of Media*, edited by Patrick Vonderau and Vinzenz Hediger, 259–82. Amsterdam: University of Amsterdam Press, 2009.

Steg, Albert. "The Itinerant Films of Arthur J. Higgins." *The Moving Image* 10, no. 1 (spring 2010): 115–25.

Stewart, Jacqueline Najuma. *Migrating to the Movies: Cinema and Black Urban Modernity*. Berkeley: University of California Press, 2005.

Streible, Dan. "Saving, Studying, and Screening: A History of the Orphan Film Symposium." In *Film Festival Yearbook 5: Archival Film Festivals*, edited by Alex Marlow-Mann, 163–76. St. Andrews, UK: St. Andrews Film Studies, 2013.

Summerfield, Ellen. *Crossing Cultures through Film*. Yarmouth, ME: Intercultural Press, 1993.

Tepperman, Charles. *Amateur Cinema: The Rise of North American Moviemaking, 1923–1960*. Berkeley: University of California Press, 2015.

Tilton, Lauren C. "In Local Hands: Participatory Media in the 1960s." PhD diss., Yale University, 2016.

Torres, Sasha. *Black, White, and in Color: Television and Black Civil Rights*. Princeton, NJ: Princeton University Press, 2003.

U.S. Department of Health, Education, and Welfare. *Selected Films on Child Life*. Washington, DC: Author, 1959; rev. ed. 1962, 1969.

Veeder, Gerry K. "The Red Cross Bureau of Pictures, 1917–1921: World War I, the Russian Revolution and the Sultan of Turkey's Harem." *Historical Journal of Film, Radio and Television* 10, no. 1 (March 1990): 47–70.

Vonderau, Patrick, and Vinzenz Hediger, eds. *Films That Work: Industrial Film and the Productivity of Media*. Amsterdam: Amsterdam University Press, 2009.

Wagner, Paul A. "What's Past Is Prologue." In *Sixty Years of 16mm Film 1923–1983*, edited by the Film Council of America, 9–18. Evanston, IL: Film Council of America, 1954.

Wallace, Michele, and Gina Dent, ed. *Black Popular Culture*. Seattle: Bay Press, 1992.

Waller, Greg. "Locating Early Non-theatrical Audiences." In *Audiences: Defining and Researching Screen Entertainment Reception*, edited by Ian Christie, 81–95. Amsterdam: University of Amsterdam Press, 2012.

Wasson, Haidee. "Electric Homes! Automatic Movies! Efficient Entertainment! 16mm and Cinema's Domestication in the 1920s." *Cinema Journal* 48, no. 4 (summer 2009): 1–21.

Wasson, Haidee. *Museum Movies: The Museum of Modern Art and the Birth of Art Cinema*. Berkeley: University of California Press, 2005.

Weisenfeld, Judith. *Hollywood Be Thy Name: African American Religion in American Film, 1929–1949*. Berkeley: University of California Press, 2007.

Widener, Daniel. *Black Arts West: Culture and Struggle in Postwar Los Angeles*. Durham, NC: Duke University Press, 2010.

Willis, Jack. "TV and the Social Documentary." *Film Library Quarterly* 1, no. 1 (winter 1967–68): 50–54.

Wray, Wendell. "Hey Mister, When's the Movies?" *Film Library Quarterly* 1, no. 1 (winter 1967–68): 9–14.

Zimmermann, Patricia. *Reel Families: A Social History of Amateur Film*. Bloomington: Indiana University Press, 1995.

Zwarich, Jennifer. "The Bureaucratic Activist: Federal Filmmakers and Social Change in the U.S. Department of Agriculture's Tick Eradication Campaign." *The Moving Image* 9, no. 1 (spring 2009): 19–53.

CRYSTAL MUN-HYE BAIK is assistant professor in the Department of Gender and Sexuality Studies at the University of California, Riverside.

JASMYN R. CASTRO founded the African American Home Movie Archive collection and index while she was an MA student in New York University's MIAP program, and served as media conservation and preservation associate for the Smithsonian Institution's National Museum of African American History and Culture from 2015 to 2018.

NADINE CHAN is assistant professor of cultural studies at Claremont Graduate University.

MARK GARRETT COOPER is professor of film and media studies at the University of South Carolina.

DINO EVERETT is the film archivist at the Hugh M. Hefner Moving Image Archive at the University of Southern California.

ALLYSON NADIA FIELD is associate professor of cinema and media studies at the University of Chicago.

WALTER FORSBERG is a media conservator with WET Labs in Mexico City and was the founding media archivist at the National Museum of African American History and Culture from 2014 to 2018.

JOSHUA GLICK is assistant professor of English and film and media studies at Hendrix College.

TANYA GOLDMAN is a PhD candidate in cinema studies at New York University.

MARSHA GORDON is professor of film studies at North Carolina State University.

NOELLE GRIFFIS is assistant professor of communication and media arts at Marymount Manhattan College.

COLIN GUNCKEL is associate professor of film, television, and media, American culture, and Latina/o studies at the University of Michigan.

MARTIN L. JOHNSON is assistant professor in the Department of English and Comparative Literature at the University of North Carolina, Chapel Hill.

MICHELLE KELLEY is a writer and educator based in St. Louis, Missouri, and holds a PhD in cinema studies from New York University.

TODD KUSHIGEMACHI is a PhD candidate in cinema and media studies at the University of California, Los Angeles.

CAITLIN MCGRATH is executive director of the Old Greenbelt Theatre, Greenbelt, Maryland.

ELENA ROSSI-SNOOK is the collection manager for the Reserve Film and Video Collection of the New York Public Library.

LAURA ISABEL SERNA is associate professor of cinema and media studies at the University of Southern California's School of Cinematic Arts.

JACQUELINE NAJUMA STEWART is professor of cinema and media studies at the University of Chicago and director of the South Side Home Movie Project.

DAN STREIBLE is associate professor of cinema studies at New York University.

LAUREN TILTON is assistant professor of digital humanities at the University of Richmond.

NOAH TSIKA is associate professor of media studies at Queens College, City University of New York.

TRAVIS L. WAGNER is a PhD candidate in the School of Library and Information Sciences at the University of South Carolina.

COLIN WILLIAMSON is assistant professor of American studies and cinema studies at Rutgers University, New Brunswick, New Jersey.

Note: An "*f*" after the page number indicates a figure.

New York Film Festival, 276, 283

*New York Herald*, on Dixon's advocacy for Native Americans, 44

New York Public Library (NYPL), films at, 253–70; civil rights movement, interactions with, 253–54; Film Club/Young Filmaker's Foundation works, 287n2; Film Library, 253–58, 260, 263–64, 265, 267n2; film prints, circulation of, 255; films as educational tools, 254–55; films at, debates over, 255, 268n9; introduction to, 253–54; marginalized voices, circulation of, 255–58; Young Filmaker's Foundation and, 254, 258–60, 261–66

New York State Council of the Arts, 273

*New York Times*: Gatch photograph in, 293; Greaves editorial in, 323; Nickelodeon, critiques of, 338; Petersen article in, 192n25

Nichols, Bill, 320

Nichols, Mike, 11

Nickelodeon, critiques of, 338

*A Night at Halsted's* (Halsted), 202, 214

92nd Street Y, 259, 272, 284

Nisei (second-generation Japanese Americans), 185

Nisei Week (cultural festival), 184

Nixon, Richard, 316

Nkrumah, Kwame, 115

NMAAHC (National Museum of African American History and Culture), 87, 112–13, 119, 388, 389

Noble, Gil, 118

. . . *No Lies* (Block), 202, 214

nonsynchronous sound, 205–6

nontheatrical films: afterlives of, 95, 107; American nontheatrical film history, 2–6; audience interactions with, xix, xxii; binaried presumed history of, 194; definitions of, 142; diversity of, 3; documentation on, lack of, 7–8; film on art, 143; importance of, 25; marginalization of, 106; as mode of cultural production, 142; numbers of, 3; otherness of, 212; queerness in, 198; research approaches to, xii–xiii; as revenue stream for USC film school, 178; scholarly attention to, challenges of, 4–5; social movements' impacts on, 149; techniques used in, xv; theatrical films, relationship to,

xiii, xiv; as urban films, 20; venues for, xiii. *See also* educational films; home movies; *titles of individual films*

Noordegraaf, Julia, 355

*No Way Out* (Mankiewicz), xv

NPR (National Public Radio), 29

NUL (National Urban League), 5, 157–61, 163, 169–70, 173n5

nurses. *See* Henry Street Settlement Visiting Nurse Service (VNS)

NYPD, blacks in, 236, 244, 248

NYPL. *See* New York Public Library (NYPL), films at

objective urban ethnography, 204

Office of Indian Affairs, 41

Office of the Coordinator of Inter-American Affairs, 138

official anti-racism, 370n22

*ofrendas* (offerings, home altars), 138, 141*f*

Oishi, Eve, 362–63

Okada, Jun, 177, 178, 369n9

Oklahoma, African Americans in, 73

Oladele, Francis, 128

Olin, Chuck, 94

Omura, Jimmie, 187

Ongiri, Amy Abugo, 245

*On Location with "The Owl and the Pussycat"* (Geisinger and Saland), 132

Ontiveros, Randy, 327

opacity, importance of, 212–13

Orange Mound, Memphis, 78, 89n20

Orbit Films, 92, 94, 95, 101–2, 103, 106

Orgeron, Marsha. *See* Gordon, Marsha

"Oriental coolie," 362

orphan films, xii, 386

Orphan Film Symposium, 3–4, 110n31, 290

Ostherr, Kirsten, 67n4, 295–96

Otero, Ismael, 278

*Othello* (White), 270n43

the other (otherness): American avant-garde cinema as, 104; Asians as, 181; in *The Challenge*, 181; of nontheatrical films, 212

"The Other Side of the Tracks" (Gordon and Field), 8

outhouses, 300, 302

*Overture: Linh from Vietnam* (Pinsker), 337–38, 349